A HISTORY OF THE CHURCH OF IRELAND 1691–2001

*For George, Alex and Barney*

Alan Acheson

# A History of the Church of Ireland
# 1691–2001

THE COLUMBA PRESS • APCK

First published in 1997 by
**THE COLUMBA PRESS**
55a Spruce Avenue, Stillorgan Industrial Estate, Blackrock, Co Dublin
and
**APCK**
St Ann's, Dawson Street, Dublin 2

Second, revised edition 2002

Cover by Bill Bolger
Origination by The Columba Press
Printed in Ireland by Colour Books Ltd, Dublin

ISBN 1 85607 388 2

# Contents

# *Preface to the Second Edition*

I can readily identify with the comment made by the Right Hon J.T. Ball when the Second Edition Revised of his *The Reformed Church of Ireland (1527-1889)* was published in 1890, four years after the first edition. Ball wrote:

> In the new edition now issued I have endeavoured to correct the errors, and to supply some at least of the defects, which were either pointed out in criticisms of the former edition, or perceived by myself upon re-examination.

I have taken the opportunity also to update much of the material relating to the final phase of the 20th century, to include an additional section 'At the turn of the century', and to provide in an appendix the sequence of episcopal elections in the Church of Ireland for the 130 years since disestablishment (1871-2001). Episcopal Succession Lists, in varying styles and content, were included in the histories by Mant (1840), Ball, and Phillips (1933). In this edition I have simply given for each of the 147 elections since 1871, the name of the bishop, the year of his election and the diocese to which he was elected, the body which elected him, the name of the bishop whom he succeeded, and the reason for the vacancy.

I acknowledge the generous help given me in preparing this edition. Philip Acheson compiled the appendix for publication; John Acheson and Sybil Fuller helped materially. Mrs Lesley McAdoo graciously gave permission for me to quote the late Archbishop H.R. McAdoo's letter of 21st October 1997. The Diocesan Council of Connor agreed that I might quote its 2000-01 report. I am indebted also to Bishop Michael Jackson for sharing with me his thoughts on cathedrals, and for his invitation to me, when he was Dean of Cork, to preach the Webster Memorial Sermon in St Fin Barre's Cathedral on Advent Sunday 2000: the occasion afforded opportunity to develop some of the thoughts which inform the final section of the book. Finally I thank the then editors of diocesan magazines, whose distribution of the publisher's flyer in 1997 led to strong pre-publication sales of the book and ensured its warm reception throughout the Church of Ireland.

*Alan R. Acheson*
*May 2002*

# *Preface*

Early in 1991, soon after my return to Ireland, I was encouraged by two friends, the late George Simms and the late James Hartin, to resume my interest in the history of the Church of Ireland. That encouragement was greatly extended when another old friend, the late Hugh Alexander Boyd, not only allowed me unlimited access to his voluminous private library and his well-stored mind, but also presented me with the *Journals of the General Convention* and most of the *Journals of the General Synod* from 1871-1945. I have been supported on the long road to publication by generous help from, among others, C.D.C. Armstrong, the Revd Peter Barrett (honorary secretary of APCK's publishing sub-committee), the Revd Canons John Barry, Dr Michael Kennedy and Edgar Turner, and Dr Jennifer Moreton. Sheila McCormick, Betty McLaughlin, Heather Smith and Dr Raymond Refaussé have all been most generous with assistance. My daughter Rachel and my son Philip did much word processing, while Ann McCafferty and Peter Moreton gave much needed help with technical problems in the earlier and later stages of preparation respectively. My son-in-law Mark Sherrington came from London to help with illustration, and more than a dozen photographs in the book are his work.

I acknowledge with gratitude the permission of the National Gallery of Ireland to publish the portrait of Bishop Robert and Mrs Clayton, of the Warden of St Columba's for use of the College's portrait of Dr J.H. Todd, and of the Dublin Diocesan Council for that of a portrait of Archbishop William King in Christ Church Cathedral. I thank also the Very Revd Jack Shearer, Dean of Belfast, for the photograph of the Black Santa and for permission to use the painting of the old parish church of St Anne, Mr J.G. Lefroy of Carrig-glass, Longford, for use of the portrait of the young Tom Lefroy, Mr Desmond McCarthy for his line drawing of St John's Sandymount, and Dr Hugh Weir for his line drawing of Foxford church (previously published in the *Church of Ireland Gazette*). I thank, too, Mrs Diana McFarlan for permission to make extensive use of her *Lift Thy Banner*, Patrick Comerford for letting me use his paper, 'Church of Ireland missionaries in Southern Africa', and Dr Peter B. Nockles for permssion to draw on his invaluable work on the High Church tradition of the Church of Ireland. (A revised version of Dr

Nockles's privately circulated paper will be published in the *Historical Journal* early next year.)

I am grateful to the Rt Revd Harold Miller, Bishop of Down and Dromore, for his thoughtful Foreword and for permission to photograph the portraits at the See House of two of his predecessors. Seán O Boyle of The Columba Press has been a tower of strength: I owe much to his wise counsel, unruffled patience and good-humoured friendship.

I acknowledge also generous financial support in respect of publishing costs from the Rt Revd James Moore, Bishop of Connor, the Diocesan Council of Down and Dromore, the Literature Committee of the General Synod, and – above all – the Select Vestry of Ramoan parish, which had been prepared to underwrite the entire cost. The Ramoan vestry has also kindly permitted me to use the portrait of Hugh McNeile in Holy Trinity church.

After an interval of thirty years, it is gratifying to be able to set my earlier research more fully in the context of the history of the Church of Ireland. The archives which I consulted in the early 1960s were not yet catalogued – letters in the CMS Archives (then in Salisbury Square in London) were in shoeboxes, identified only by year. In respect of both the CMS and PRONI records which I consulted at that time, I have continued to use the identification which I employed then, and not their current classification.

It is evident that the distinctive history of the Church of Ireland deserves a new deal. Too much the exclusive preserve of professional historians, it is distorted by a tendency to political correctness on commemorative occasions. It is largely ignored by the Church's reviving Evangelical tradition, in perverse disregard of those biblical emphases which Bishop Miller identifies in his Foreword. Nonetheless, as Archbishop King once said, 'The people will have it.' The point was brought home to me several years ago when the rector of Coleraine – my lifelong friend Canon Fanta Clarke – asked me to give a series of lectures on our Church's history. Given that there were alternative choices, he expected an attendance of five or six: instead, 50 or 60 St Patrick's parishioners attended the first lecture, and kept on attending. Inspired by that experience, my purpose now is to make our Church's history accessible to a much wider audience.

*Alan R. Acheson*
*September 1997*

# Foreword

Leon Uris' novel *Trinity* ends with the chilling and hopeless words:

... in Ireland there is no future,

only the past happening over and over.

This is a view of history with which every Irish-born person can identify — history as a cycle which simply keeps re-inventing itself. In this way of thinking, our lives become 'repeat performances', tied in fatalistically to acting out what has been before and will continue to be, world without end.

There are times when we fear that even the Hebrew scriptures might espouse this view of history. The lives of the people of Israel often seemed to be cyclical performances. A good leader would arise, the people would repent, the judgement of the Lord is averted, peace and security come, and off they go again on a cycle of self-reliance, sin, and lack of interest in the things of God. Yet, in truth, the history we read in the Hebrew scriptures, fulfilled in the Gospels, is much more than cyclical — it is actually our *heilsgeschichte* (salvation history). As we read through the Bible in its full sweep, we see the God of history who is guiding his people and his world in a clear forward-moving direction.

Dr Alan Acheson, in writing what he calls 'an accessible, one-volume history of the Church of Ireland during the past 300 years', leaves us with a sense of the full sweep of our recent story, and a hope and trust in the direction of our 'pre-venting' God. We see this same God at times correcting the church. But through thick and thin, and even when the cycles seem to repeat, his guiding hand is always there, and his church is moving forward.

All of this makes me, and I believe will make many others, truly appreciative of what it means to be 'catholic'; not just in the one-directional sense of 'world wide' but in the other-directional sense of being part of the church of Christ stretching back through history to our Lord himself.

*A History of the Church of Ireland 1691–1996* is both informative and well written. It is a joy to read not only because of the overview of history which it gives, but also, and perhaps particularly, because of the windows and vignettes it offers into specific situations, and specific people's experiences. These bring the book to life. What is particularly engaging about them is that you, like me, will probably recognise some of the 'scenes'. For example, in eight years as rector of Carrigrohane Union of Parishes in county Cork, I had never heard of the unfortunate Wm Cogan who, having been married clandestinely, was brought to his senses by being required 'to stand with a white wand in his hand and a paper on his breast declaring his fault, all ye time of divine service and sermon'!

History is never purely objective. The researcher and writer always brings to it his own particular interests, angles and experiences. Alan Acheson is no exception, nor would he claim to be. He brings a width of experience, not only in this country but also in Australia; and he brings a great love for the evangelical tradition within his church. Rather than narrowing down the book, these things give it its particular flavour and vitality. Alan also brings a great memory for detail, and the mind of a thorough-going historian, and I for one am grateful that he has used these skills in the service of the church of Christ.

I am glad to commend this book warmly, in gratitude to the God of history whom we praise for all that is past, and whom we trust for all that's to come.

@ *Harold Down and Dromore*
*August 1997*

# Abbreviations

| | |
|---|---|
| AAPB | *An Australian Prayer Book 1978* |
| ACC | Anglican Consultative Council |
| *ADB* | *Australian Dictionary of Biography* |
| APB | *Alternative Prayer Book 1984* |
| APCK | Association for Promoting Christian Knowledge |
| ARCIC | Anglican-Roman Catholic International Commission |
| ASB | *The Alternative Service Book 1980* [Church of England] |
| BCMS | Bible Churchmen's Missionary Society |
| BCP | *The Book of Common Prayer* |
| *CE* | *The Christian Examiner and Church of Ireland Magazine* |
| CMJ | Church Missions to Jews |
| CMS | Church Missionary Society |
| CMSI | Church Missionary Society Ireland (formerly HCMS) |
| *DNB* | *Dictionary of National Biography* |
| DUM | Dublin University Missions |
| FÁS | Foras Áisnéis Saothair |
| FTCD | Fellow of Trinity College Dublin |
| *Gazette* | *Irish Ecclesiastical Gazette / The Church of Ireland Gazette* |
| HCMS | Hibernian Auxiliary to the Church Missionary Society |
| ICM | Society for Irish Church Missions |
| *IHS* | *Irish Historical Studies* |
| IRA | Irish Republican Army |
| LAC | Liturgical Advisory Committee |
| NSM | Non-Stipendiary Minister |
| PRONI | Public Record Office of Northern Ireland |
| RCB | Representative Church Body |
| RDS | Royal Dublin Society |
| RUC | Royal Ulster Constabulary |
| SAMS | South American Missionary Society |
| SPCK | Society for the Promotion of Christian Knowledge |
| SPG | Society for the Propagation of the Gospel |
| TCD | Trinity College Dublin |
| UDR | Ulster Defence Regiment |
| UMCA | Universities' Mission to Central Africa |
| USPG | United Society for the Propagation of the Gospel |
| UVF | Ulster Volunteer Force (1911-14) |

# PART ONE

# Introduction

The Church of Ireland needs to recover a strong sense of its history, spirituality and ecclesiastical roots; only a Church with strong self-confidence can make a contribution to Ireland. We must find hope, fresh vision and inspiration from our past.
— *Bishop James Mehaffey, at a Centenary Eucharist in St Catherine and St James's Church Dublin in 1996* [1]

As we unfold the list of the Primates of All Ireland for 160 years between the Irishman, James Ussher, and the Irishman, Lord John George Beresford, we find a long succession of English Archbishops. You did not always send us a Bramhall or a Trench.
— *William Alexander, at Church Congress in Norwich in 1866* [2]

## I TOWARDS A HISTORY

The widespread thirst for knowledge of Ireland's past is being assuaged as research draws deeply from the wells of Irish cultural, religious, political and economic history, and as imaginative communication ensures that its draughts are widely shared. A new generation of historians, fresh approaches to the teaching of Irish history, and revived interest in local history, are agents in this advance. In common with other Irish churches, the Church of Ireland is athirst for information both about her own history and her involvement in Irish history in general. That thirst is satisfied in part through a spate of parish histories and a trickle of episcopal and decanal memoirs, in anniversary histories of schools, hospitals, charities and missions, in specialist studies of cathedrals and their musical traditions, hymnology and campanology, and in the growing number of commemorative occasions in province, diocese and parish. Out of this modern passion an older paradox is perceived. For a church which long boasted a proud heritage had, until very recently, been strangely negligent of her history and of the records from which it is derived. The corrective to that neglect is seen, for example, in the recent appointments of Dr Raymond Refaussé as archivist, and of Dr Kenneth Milne as historiographer, of the Church of Ireland; in the launch in 1994 of

the Church of Ireland Historical Society; and in the republication and continuation of the work of Canon J. B. Leslie and Dean H. B. Swanzy with
*Clergy of Connor* (1993) and *Clergy of Down and Dromore* (1996).

Against this amorphous background a twofold need is apparent. Given
what one historian has called 'the sheer importance of churchmen and
church-related issues in Irish public life',[3] the first need is a definitive history
of the Church of Ireland, critical and dispassionate in approach, based on the
latest research, and free from the constraints imposed upon the contributors
to the three-volume History edited by W. A. Phillips over 60 years ago. As
Kenneth Milne has put it, in allusion to the character of that work, 'any new
general history of the Church of Ireland must depend on the work of historians
from many religious traditions and from none, employing a broader range of
historical skills.'[4] The 1995 publication, *As by Law Established*, which comprises many of the papers read at the Dublin conference of 1993 – 'Towards
a History of the Church of Ireland' – indicates the range of scholarship which
might inform such a work.[5] Of its nature, however, that publication is, as
Thomas Stoney observes, 'directed towards a highly specialized, and therefore
limited, readership; in other words, to professional historians'.[6] The second
clear need, then, is an accessible, one-volume history of the Church of
Ireland during the past 300 years. It is that need which the present work seeks
to supply. It is intended primarily for Church of Ireland people, at home and
overseas, and those outside the church, who wish to know more of her recent
history, not so much in its institutional aspects, as in point of how the church
lived, moved and had her being. It seeks to be, in Fergus O'Ferrall's words, a
'sympathetic treatment of the internal and religious life of the church.'[7] It
therefore dwells on the expression of her reformed faith and catholic heritage
in spirituality, worship and pastoral care, in philanthropy and mission, in
relations with other Irish churches, and in her contribution to the worldwide
development of Anglicanism. If the present volume helps to reinforce the
Church of Ireland's burgeoning awareness of her history, and of its relevance
to her mission on the eve of the third Christian millennium, it will have
achieved its primary purpose.

Among earlier histories, Bishop Richard Mant's two-volume *History of the
Church of Ireland* (1840) – from the Reformation to the Union – remains an
invaluable work of reference, particularly for statutes and episcopal succession. General histories were published later by clerics, Thomas Olden in
1892, and in 1953 T. J. Johnston, J. L. Robinson and R. W. Jackson, hailed
by Stoney as 'that familiar, if not greatly loved trio'. A former Lord
Chancellor of Ireland, the Right Hon J. T. Ball, published in 1886 *The
Reformed Church of Ireland, 1537-1886*, with a second edition in 1890. Its
hallmark is his layman's, if not his lawyer's, instinct for reducing complex

issues to readable form. The church's experience in the century after dises-
tablishment was appraised both by a team of non-Anglican scholars in *Irish
Anglicanism, 1869-1969*, edited by Michael Hurley, and in R. B. Mc Dowell's
*The Church of Ireland, 1869-1969*, written at the suggestion of Archbishop
George Simms. The best known short history is Milne's, which issued its third
edition in 1994: Henry Patton's of 1907 was written for use in schools, while
Robert MacCarthy's *Ancient and Modern* appeared in 1995. Thematic studies of theology, ecclesiology, or the church's intellectual life are sparse, with
the notable exceptions of H. R. McAdoo's work on the Carolines and F. R.
Bolton's *The Caroline Tradition* (1958), while the only substantial diocesan
history is C. A. Webster's *The Diocese of Cork* (1920), which drew largely on
material in the Public Record Office of Ireland so soon before its destruction
in the Civil War. If, however, in the words of Ralph Waldo Emerson, 'there
is properly no history; only biography', then the Church of Ireland, in the
pedagogic cliché, could do better. Her outstanding sons of the 18th century,
King, Berkeley and Swift – the last a veritable national institution, but an
underrated churchman – have had their biographers, as have Primates Day,
Gregg and Simms, Archbishop Bernard of Dublin, and Provost Mahaffy of
TCD, in the 20th century. But although Lord John George Beresford and
three 19th century Archbishops of Dublin – Whately, Trench and Plunket –
have been the subjects of modern biographies, Archbishop Magee of Dublin,
Primate Alexander and Provost Salmon have been curiously neglected. The
same holds true for leading members of the laity, with the exceptions of Mrs
C. F. Alexander, W. E. H. Lecky and the Guinness family.

Again, while the final phase of the Establishment has attracted several
North American scholars, their very negatives need to be addressed in assessing the church's inner life. Thus D. H. Akenson, in defining his magisterial
work as 'the biography of an Irish organization', expressly states that it has
'everything to do with men and nothing to do with God'.[8] Edward Brynn
focuses on the impact of nationalism on the church as an 'erastian system',
rather than 'the revitalization of [her] spiritual life';[9] and Desmond Bowen,
though recognizing the influence of the 'new evangelical spirit' in the recovery
of her spiritual vitality, yet channels that spirit into the narrow confines of his
'Protestant crusade'.[10] God, the renewal of spiritual life, and the character of
the evangelical revival are, on the contrary, germane to the purposes of the
present volume, together with as much of ecclesiology and biography as
space will allow.

The arrangement of the book in five disparate parts needs explanation.
This introduction began as a preparatory note on technicalities and anachron-
isms, particularly from the era of the Established Church, but has evolved
into a narrative presentation. With scope in this way for illustration, what

follows may prove more interesting than the original plan. The second section (1691-1729) spans the episcopate of William King, the central figure of the period, whose reputation as 'a great Archbishop of Dublin' is at some risk from revisionism. The third section (1730-1822) is the longest. It represents a new twist in the current debate on the delimits of the 18th century, but is justified by the church's experience. For a protracted period of, first, decline and then recovery – the latter brought about after 1800 by (shades of Trollope) new men, new measures and new movements – culminated in 1822 in three distinct developments: the appointment of the Irishmen, Beresford and Magee, to the primatial sees of Armagh and Dublin respectively, the completion of a massive programme of state-financed church building, and the coming of age of the Evangelical movement, arguably the church's defining tradition in the 19th century. This 'long century' was succeeded by a pulsating half century (1823-70) marked, on the one hand, by recurrent crisis – popular agitation, tithe war, famine and reform of the church; and on the other, by theological vigour, spiritual revival, and outreach at home and overseas: until in 1869 the church was stopped dead in her tracks by the Irish Church Act, and forced to regroup in the General Convention of 1870. Finally, the story of the independent Church of Ireland over a century and a quarter comprises the fifth section (1871-1995). It began with the exacting process of reconstruction to which disestablishment necessarily gave rise, and which was completed by 1878. It continued in more subdued vein throughout the 60 years to 1938 that were so dominated by external events – the land revolution, the Great War, the Easter Rising, the Anglo-Irish and Civil Wars, and the creation and early development of the two Irish states – that the church's experience throughout has been largely ignored. And it ended, first in assured stability under the patrician rule of Primate Gregg (1939-59), and then in engagement with ecumenism, internal change and sectarian conflict in the unsettled environment of the late 20th century.

## II OF TITLES AND DEFINITIONS

Under the Act of Union of 1800, the Church of Ireland became part of the United Church of England and Ireland. Until 1800, she had been the Church of Ireland formally, and popularly 'the church', over against dissent. Between 1801 and 1870, she was designated the Irish Church or the Establishment, while her people generally identified themselves as 'Church of England' – as Anglicans in Canada did until 1955, and in Australia until 1981. The Irish Church was regulated by statute and ruled by the executive until 1870 – it required an Act of Parliament to build a new church, for example, or to obtain a divorce. The bishops, appointed by the Crown usually on the recommendation of the Viceroy, all sat in the Irish Parliament until 1800, and by rotation at Westminster thereafter, while the clergy were variously appointed to incumbencies by the Crown, lay patrons, or the bishops. This scheme of things ended with disestablishment. With the temporalities remaining after disendowment vested by the Irish Church Act in the Representative Church Body (RCB), the General Convention of 1870 provided for the annual meeting of a General Synod, with a House of Bishops, and representatives of clergy and laity elected triennially. Its first session, in 1871, was the first representative assembly of the Irish Church since 1711. In addition to its ordinary sessions, the General Synod may be convened in special session at any time: the first such session took place in 1886, the most recent in 1971.

From the first, the President of the General Synod has been the Archbishop of Armagh, Primate of All Ireland. Although the Archbishop of Dublin enjoys the style, Primate of Ireland, for centuries the occupant of the see of Armagh has been known to his church as 'The Primate'. This usage contrasts with that in England, where the Primate of All England is invariably referred to as the Archbishop of Canterbury, but corresponds with that in Scotland, where the presiding bishop of the Episcopal Church, whatever his see, is known as the Primus. Strictly speaking, the titles 'Lord Archbishop' and 'Lord Bishop' have been redundant in Ireland (as in Wales) since disestablishment, but have, incongruously, survived both in official usage and common parlance. Again, the number (12), but not the arrangement, of dioceses remains the same as in 1870. Until 1833 there had normally been 22 dioceses, organized in four provinces. The Church Temporalities Act of 1833-4 suppressed 10 dioceses, and reduced the metropolitan sees from four to two, Tuam and Cashel becoming suffragan sees within the provinces of Armagh and Dublin respectively. The independent church separated Clogher from Armagh in 1886, and Connor from Down and Dromore in 1945, to give a maximum of 14 dioceses since 1870. This number was again reduced to 12 when in the 1970s Cashel was united with Ossory, and Killaloe with Limerick. No further reduction ensued from General Synod's appointment in 1995 of a commission to examine the Church's episcopal needs 'in a time of change'. Externally, the Church of Ireland is a constituent branch of the Anglican Communion. Her bishops attend the decadal Lambeth Conference – the next is due in 2008 – and she appoints two representatives (of whom one has always been a lay person) to the Anglican Consultative Council, which has met triennially since 1971. She belongs also to the World Council of Churches, the Council of Churches for Britain and Ireland, and the Irish Council of Churches.

Where constitutional practices and technical terms peculiar to the Established Church are necessarily introduced in the text, definitions or explanations are first given here. Thus the rich terminology pertaining to the pre-disestablishment clergy and parishes, most of it redundant since 1870, is teased out in the next section. Some miscellaneous terms are taken up now, like that of vicar-general. Usually a cleric but sometimes a layman, the vicar-general of each diocese was appointed by the bishop as his deputy in matters of jurisdiction and administration. He presided, for example, at the consistorial court of the diocese, and was involved with episcopal visitations. His office was the more important in that before 1833 archdeacons in Ireland did not exercise the powers of their English counterparts. Two peculiars, the exempt jurisdictions of Newry and Mourne, and the wardenship of Galway, survived until the 1860s. The term erastianism (after the German layman Erastus) meant, in the context of the state's government of the church, the subordination of spiritual to secular considerations. Though by definition redundant since disestablishment, Archbishop Walton Empey in effect discerned its influence as living on when he deplored the want of a chapel in Church of Ireland House in Dublin.[11] Again, a clergyman was formally 'inhibited' when a bishop refused to allow him to preach in the churches of his diocese: the device was sometimes used against early evangelical clergy. A bishop, by contrast, was inhibited during metropolitical visitations of his diocese. For the archbishops visited each diocese in their provinces every third year, the jurisdiction of the diocesan being formally suspended for the duration. In the Caroline era the period of inhibition began six months before, and ended three months after this triennial visitation, thus encompassing virtually an entire year, but by the early 19th century was limited to a few weeks. There was also an annual visitation of each diocese by its own bishop, and it became the custom either for the newest incumbent to preach at the outset to the assembled clergy, or for the bishop to deliver a formal charge to them. These sermons and charges were often published. The Canadian historian Philip Carrington gave a useful summary of this custom:

> The 'Visitation' was the ancestor of the modern Synod; it enabled the Bishop to obtain statistics and information; there was discussion and clarification of problems; he issued 'Injunctions' or directives on various points; there were services, sermons and devotions; personal relationships were established.

At national level, convocation, when summoned by the Crown, met at the same time as parliament, and like it consisted in two Houses, with the archbishops and bishops (who also sat in parliament) forming the Upper House, and the deans, archdeacons, and elected representatives of cathedral chapters and diocesan clergy, the Lower House. But writs for its meeting were issued only during Anne's reign (and previously on only four occasions from 1615 to 1661); and after 1711 convocation was never again summoned.[12]

Although the Church of Ireland is part of 'the Holy Catholick Church', that catholic word 'Catholic' is, ironically, often employed in an exclusive religious sense. While the text adopts the accepted usage of Irish Catholics and Protestants, it refers properly to the church of the majority as the Roman Catholic Church. This dichotomy should at once avoid misunderstanding and offence.

Defining the Church of Ireland in terms of size, whether actual membership or relative to other Irish churches, is virtually impossible before the 19th century. The census of 1861 was the first to include an analysis of the population by religious denomination, and before 1861 the only official estimate was that of the commissioners of public instruction in 1834. Determining the size of the Irish population is difficult also. In 1670, Sir William Petty had computed it at 1.1 million, including 300,000 Protestants, and an estimate based on hearth-money returns in the 1730s gave Protestants as 30 per cent – 60 per cent in Ulster, less than 10 per cent in Connacht – of a larger population. (It was estimated by Professor Connell at 2.8 million in 1712 and 3.5 million in 1767.) Presbyterians outnumbered members of the Established Church in Ulster and may have done so in all Ireland – historians are divided – before the considerable Presbyterian emigration of the early Georgian period. In 1834, the commissioners' figures were to show 853,160 members of the Established Church and 643,058 Presbyterians, or just under 1.5 million in aggregate – there were additionally 21,822 other Protestants – in the total Irish population of just under 8.0 million. Socially, adherents of the Church of Ireland included most of the landowning class, many tenant farmers among the gentry, especially in Ulster, and their higher servants, most members of the professions and the public service, many of those involved in commerce, many skilled urban workers, especially in Dublin, and some of the labouring class. The movement up the social scale of both families and individuals strengthened what J. C. Beckett called 'the natural coherence of the Protestant community'.[13]

## III WITH CURE OF SOULS?

A wide range of definitions relates – to use modern terminology – to the parish and parochial clergy. Under the Established Church, a cleric was nominated to a living by its patron. This right of presentation, technically the advowson, belonged in some cases to the Crown, in others to institutions or lay patrons, and in most (in Ireland, as distinct from England) to the bishops. A clergyman who obtained preferment was legally the incumbent of a benefice. In popular parlance he was the parson, his living the parsonage. Incumbents were known collectively as the beneficed clergy. A benefice consisted either of a single parish, or more often of a group (or union) of two or more parishes. Possession of a benefice entailed both rights and duties. It came 'with cure of souls', for pastoral oversight of the people was the incumbent's primary responsibility. His rights consisted in the parson's freehold (as it was known in England), and he enjoyed, during his lifetime, the freehold 'of the parsonage – house, glebe, tythes and other dues'.[14] The glebe was the land belonging to the benefice, and a house built thereon for the incumbent's residence was therefore the glebe house, or parsonage house or manse house. The land might yield the parson an income from rent, while the extent of his entitlement to tithes depended on his status as rector or vicar. In law a tax on property, tithes were the spiritual profits of the parish. On the debit side, an incumbent was liable for first fruits: an amount equivalent to his first year's revenue, and payable to the Crown.

The ideal was, in practice, distorted by exploitation and abuse. Patrons saw livings as being in their gift (as, indeed, they were legally), and usually preferred close relatives – the practice of nepotism – or those who had favour with them through wider family or social connections. The ultimate abuse was to sell the living – the sin of simony. The advowson, too, might be sold, normally for a 'turn' or two, after which the right of presentation reverted to the original patron. The confusion arising from such usages was, however, worse confounded by developments which predated the Reformation, and which were continued in, or adapted to, the different circumstances of the post-Reformation church. Thus where patrons had gifted parishes to monasteries, or where parishes had been set aside in each diocese for the support of the bishop and members of the chapter, they were said to be 'appropriate'. After the dissolution of the monasteries, their appropriate parishes came to the Crown, were mostly made over to the nobility, and were now said to be 'impropriate'. A further twist in the tale is that some parishes were assigned to town corporations and colleges. Thus in the Plantation of Ulster, Trinity College Dublin acquired a number of parishes in the dioceses of Armagh, Clogher, Derry and Raphoe – the College livings. The parishes appropriate to diocesan dignitaries, however, remained as such after the Reformation. Those set aside for the bishop were known as mensal parishes, that is they supplied the episcopal table: an example is the Dromore parish of Kilbroney (Rostrevor). Those set aside for the chapter were known as prebendal parishes, that is they provided for the support of those who held the prebends in the cathedral. The corps of the archdeaconry, for example, would normally be made up of several appropriate parishes: in Dromore these were Donaghcloney (until 1832) at the head of the corps, Seagoe and Magherally.[15]

The attraction of these arrangements for patrons and dignitaries is obvious, for the parishes and inferior clergy less so. Only where a rectory was neither appropriate nor impropriate – numbers varied greatly from one diocese to another – might a cleric be preferred to both rectory and vicarage, and enjoy both categories of tithe. The monasteries, as rectors of the parishes appropriate to them, had supplied the cures either by deputing a monk to do the duty, or by appointing a vicar as deputy. The rectorial (or great) tithes were retained by the monastery, while its vicar was either allocated the vicarial (or small) tithes, or paid a stipend instead. (Some parishes were 'entire rectories' and had no provision for a vicar.) With typically light touch, Anthony Trollope explained the complexities here in *Framley Parsonage:*

> That a rector, being a big sort of a parson, owned the tithes of his parish in full ... and that a vicar was somebody's deputy, and therefore entitled only to little tithes, as being a little body: of so much we that are simple in such matters have a general idea.[16]

The vicar could be removed at will. The bishops tended to press for them to be made perpetual, that is unable to be removed at will by rectors, and with some provision for endowment of their vicarages. After the Reformation, the lay rectors of the now impropriate parishes had the inherited duty of appointing vicars as incumbents (or in some cases curates – Leslie uses the title Impropriate Curate).

A lay rector, though a contradiction in terms to modern ears, was a familiar being before disestablishment. When in 1824 the vicar of Dundalk, Elias Thackeray, upbraided the Earl of Roden for contributing to an Independent (Congregational) chapel in his town, he did so on the ground that Roden was not only 'a pillar of the Established Church', but also rector and patron of the parish.[17] (The right of presentation, in fact, alternated between the Primate and Lord Roden.) Again, as late as 1870 the senior clergyman in Belfast was styled Vicar of Belfast, the rector of the parish being Lord Donegall. The lay rectors, of course, retained the rectorial tithes. But their self-interest did not always end there. They often seized the glebe lands, leaving to the incumbent only the legal minimum – the churchyard – and denying him land on which to build a parsonage house. So paltry was the provision for many vicars, indeed, that it became necessary to amalgamate parishes so that their combined vicarial tithes might provide a viable income: often as many as 10 parishes, particularly in the south and west. The consequences were sometimes dire. Where a church existed, but no services were performed, the church was technically 'in ruins'. Where benefices provided neither a church nor a parson's residence they were popularly deemed non-cures. Mant saw the practice as an 'anomaly unknown to the law', and observed that their parishioners had to rely on the voluntary services of neighbouring clergy.[18]

The incidence of non-residence generally was high until reforms were instigated in the 1820s. One obvious reason for it was pluralism – the holding of two (or more) benefices by the same incumbent. It was authorized by a faculty granted either by the bishop or the metropolitan. A pluralist who resided in one benefice was clearly not resident in the other(s), so that pluralists were non-residents by definition. But non-residence might also be enforced by circumstances, as previously noted, or might be elective: through the age or infirmity of the incumbent, for example, or by combining an incumbency with a non-parochial ecclesiastical office. As to the former, since incumbencies lasted for life, old clergy never retired; they only faded away. Men of advanced years or plagued by illness simply withdrew from the parochial scene. Thus one of the best known of the Georgian clergy, Philip Skelton, after years of devoted service to several Clogher parishes, spent his winters in old age in Dundalk or Dublin, sensibly leaving his parish in the care of his curate.[19] The other category included Fellows of TCD and the Masters (Headmasters) of endowed schools such as the Royal Schools of Ulster. Most Fellows were incumbents of College livings, and could serve these in person only during vacations, if at all. The same held for the Masters. The career of Dr Robert Burrowes, Master of the Royal School Enniskillen (or Portora, as it became known), well illustrates contemporary practice. A former Fellow of TCD, and a doctor of divinity of Dublin University, he became Archdeacon of Ferns in 1796, resigned the archdeaconry on appointment to Portora in 1798, and relinquished the headship on being appointed Dean of Cork in 1819. Throughout his entire period as archdeacon, headmaster and dean, however, he held a College living in the diocese of Derry: he was rector of Cappagh 1796-1807, and of Drumragh (Omagh) 1807-41. He died in 1841 at the age of 84.[20]

It is against this complex background that the noble army of martyrs, alias curates, has to be considered, in their evident ubiquity, apparent poverty, and actual indispensibility. Strictly speaking, all clergy were curates, responsible that is for the cure of souls – the Prayer for the Church Militant craves grace for 'all Bishops and Curates'. But gradually a peculiar office of curate evolved. The monks had first served the cures themselves as temporary curates, and then either by vicars or stipendiary curates. After the Reformation such curacies became perpetual – capable of endowment, and also affording security of tenure in that the curate was removable only on the bishop's revocation of his licence to officiate, and not at the pleasure of the impropriator. As the population of England grew during the 18th century, the title Perpetual Curate came to be given to the incumbent of an ecclesiastical district, with its own chapel, which formed part of an ancient parish. A similar development took place in Ireland under Primate Richard Robinson (1765-94) – he was created Baron Rokeby of Armagh in 1777 – when Acts of Parliament provided for chapels of ease to be erected, and perpetual curacies created, in those parochial districts which had neither an endowed vicarage nor a perpetual curacy, and which were served rather by stipendiary curates. But there were also, less laudably, perpetual curates of a non-technical variety – men who were denied promotion and remained curates throughout their ministry. Such men had no 'claim' upon a patron, whether bishop or nobleman. Leslie found this cryptic notice in the *Gentleman's Magazine* for February 1851: 'Died 5 Dec 1850, at Dromore, aged 85, the Rev Benjamin Marshall, for 57 years a Curate, 55 of which he lived at Dromore'.[21] John Jebb's brother warned him, 'you will live and die a curate', a prospect which, happily, did not deter the future bishop from seeking ordination.[22] William Alexander recalled that, despite many admirable qualities, one of his father's curates remained a curate all his days, and once heard another old curate cry out,

> the hire of the labourers who have reaped down your fields, which is of you kept back by fraud, crieth: and the cries of them which have reaped are entered into the ear of the Lord of Sabaoth.[23]

These perpetual stand-ins for pluralists apart, however, the role of curate developed from that of the man who did the work in a parish held by a professional non-resident, to include the deputy of a 'retired' incumbent, and finally to denote – its modern meaning – the assistant to a resident incumbent of a large parish. Such curate assistant was nominated by the incumbent, who paid his stipend, and was licensed by the bishop for duty in the latter's parish. His titled lapsed when there was a change of incumbent.

The situation, then, which obtained three centuries ago and survived until the high Victorian period, may perhaps have come more clearly into focus. It is well delineated in the early Georgian period. In 1721 Archbishop King estimated that there were about 600 clergy, 'and one-half of these curates, at about £30 per annum'.[24] The going rate in fact varied, as there was something of a market in curates. As Bishop of Derry, King had observed in 1692 that 'my absentees and pluralists care not whom they employ, and therefore take Scotch curates, as gentlemen used to take Irish servants merely because cheaper than others'.[25] In Dublin he complained that he had 40 curates, worthy men and of long service in some cases, for whom he could not procure even a vicarage, as so many inferior clergy were arriving in the train of dignitaries from England. But were the vicarages worth obtaining in any case? Jonathan Swift thought not. In a spirited defence of the Irish clergy he denied that non-residence was their 'crying sin'. Pluralities apart, absences were 'pardonably few', although many parishes had 'not an inch of glebe'. Through, as he put it, 'the confusion of the times, by violence, fraud, oppression and other unlawful means', most glebes were in the hands of the laity, leaving the clergy at the mercy of the landlords 'for a small piece of ground in their parishes, at a most exorbitant rent', and usually on short lease, on which to build a house for their residence. He yet bore witness that the Irish clergy were 'more constant residents' than the clergy in England, 'where the meanest vicar has a convenient dwelling, with a barn, a garden, and a field or two for his cattle, beside the certainty of his little income from honest farmers'. But if many vicars had to fend for themselves, the burdens of some curates seem to have been self-inflicted. In an interesting insight into the settled situation then prevalent in parts of Ulster, Bishop Rundle of Derry wrote in 1740 that he had 35 beneficed clergy under his care – 'all regular, decent and neighbourly'; not a scholar among them, but all of good 'general learning'.

> And I have rather more curates, who are allowed by their rectors such a stipend, as hath alas! tempted most of them to marry; and it is not uncommon to have curates that are fathers of eight or ten children, without anything but an allowance of £40 a year to support them.

Some 85 years later, when government in London had assumed responsibility for the Irish Church, all Acts relating to curates' salaries were repealed and their provisions embodied in a new statute. By then the maximum salary had risen to £75 (Irish) per annum, and where the incumbent was non-resident for at least four months of the year, the curate was also entitled either to the use of the glebe house with its gardens and stables – things had improved since Swift's day – or to an annual allowance of £15 in lieu. The Act did not empower the bishops to regulate the salaries of curates (appointed after 3 February 1824) of resident incumbents, but expressly obliged them to allocate increased salaries to the curates of non-resident incumbents. That hardy annual of the Church of Ireland, the minimum stipend, has a long pedigree.

# PART TWO

# The era of Archbishop King, 1691-1729

I am more sensible of the ill aspect that the generality of men cast upon the Church and churchmen; the faith of religion is very weak amongst all, and the sense of it almost lost; and the matter is laid deeper than most men are aware of.
– *William King to Nathaniel Foy, 1697* [1]

Here is all that generous piety which is so remarkable in our Church. Here is religion in its native beauty and most charming dress, as it bears the greatest resemblance to its Divine Founder, and has most of God, and Christ, and heaven in it ... This Church he honoured and loved, and her misfortunes he bewailed.
– *Edward Wetenhall, at James Bonnell's funeral, 1699* [2]

## I PRELUDE

On 27 January 1661, two archbishops and ten bishops were consecrated in St Patrick's Cathedral Dublin, by Primate John Bramhall, assisted by four of the other seven surviving Irish bishops. The preacher was Jeremy Taylor, the new Bishop of Down and Connor, 'the whole ceremony such as was calculated at once to impress and hearten'. Recalling this extraordinary occasion more than 250 years later, the Chancellor of St Fin Barre's Cathedral, Charles Webster, continued:

> The Lord had turned again the captivity of Zion; the Church's children were like unto them that dream; their mouth was filled with laughter and their tongue with joy. There must have been some present...[who] longed for the presence of Bedell and Ussher, as the Church, with her restored patrimony, once again set her face towards the future. But Bedell's body was lying beneath the shadow of his beloved Kilmore, and Ussher rested amongst the mighty dead in Westminster Abbey.[3]

The significance of the occasion was great. As the preface to the 1662 Prayer Book put it, 'his Majesty's happy restoration' to the throne had ended 'the late unhappy confusions' of the Civil Wars and Interregnum. The restoration of the monarchy was accompanied, in Ireland as in England, by the re-estab-

Raphoe  Derry  Connor

Down

ARMAGH  Dromore

Clogher

Killala  Kilmore

Achonry

Ardagh  Meath

Elphin

TUAM

(Tuam)  Kildare

Clonfert  DUBLIN

Kilmacduagh

Kilfenora  Leighlin

Killaloe  Ossory

Ferns

CASHEL

Limerick  Emly

Lismore

Ardfert
and  Cloyne
Aghadoe  Waterford

Cork

Ross
Ross

- - -  Provincial boundaries
......  Diocesan boundaries

Provinces and Dioceses of the Church of Ireland until 1833
*(Adapted from Revd Dr Beaufort's map of 1792)*

lishment of the Protestant Episcopal Church, and by the return to the Church of the lands which had been confiscated by the Commonwealth. The Crown nominated bishops to the vacant sees, and both the Irish convocation and parliament approved the Church of England's revised Prayer Book of 1662: it was brought into use by statute, assent to it being required of every beneficed clergyman. This liturgy (referred to today simply as 'BCP' or '1662') was to be used in the Church of Ireland without alternative, though with some later additions, for 300 years. It had adopted the Authorized Version of the Bible (except for the psalter and parts of the Communion service), introduced a General Thanksgiving and a prayer for use 'in the time of dearth and famine', and provided an office of baptism for 'such as are of riper years' – the preface noted that it would be 'useful for the baptizing of Natives in our plantations'. To the new anniversary services, which related to events (such as the execution of Charles I) in 'the late unhappy' period, the Irish parliament had added a service for 23 October, the anniversary of the outbreak of the 1641 rebellion.[4]

Under these arrangements, then, the Church of Ireland resumed her previous polity. She was singularly blessed in the scholarship, spirituality, and practical divinity which characterized the Caroline period, and which were epitomized in Jeremy Taylor's devotional manuals, *Holy Living* and *Holy Dying*. The strength of this Caroline spirit would preserve its vitality far into the next century, while its integrity and magnetism would ensure its lasting influence in the church.

A mere 25 years after her restoration in 1660, however, the church was again plunged into crisis. Her very existence was threatened by the crusading ardour of a Catholic monarch, James II, and his Irish Lord Lieutenant, the Earl of Tyrconnell. Vacant sees were left unfilled; two archbishops, seven bishops, and more than 80 clergy were attainted by the Jacobite Parliament of 1689; most bishops and many clergy driven to take refuge in England; and the leaders of the intrepid minority who remained at their posts imprisoned. The church had held to her allegiance to the Crown for as long as her survival was not imperilled, and embraced the principles of the Whig Revolution only out of necessity. But initially she had found no security in the accession of William III and Queen Mary. For one thing, the new king might not be victorious in battle; for another, he was a Dutch Calvinist who might favour a Presbyterian, rather than an Anglican, polity in the national church. (That bishops were abolished in Scotland underlines the validity of the fears entertained by church leaders in Ireland.) During this agonizing period of uncertainty, in short, the church found herself between a rock and a hard place. Plans to meet either contingency – Catholic victory or Presbyterian triumph – were prepared by the Dean of St Patrick's, William

King, who was himself held prisoner for four months in Dublin Castle. And when the crisis was over, and the church could relax in the certainty of her survival as the Irish religious establishment, and restore her returning exiles to their former stations, her exemplars gave way then to her prophets, as they denounced the national sins that had brought such a fiery trial down upon them, and preached repentance to a stiff-necked people. In this atmosphere her reforming bishops seized the initiative as they urged restitution of church property, restoration of the church's independence, and a reformation of the morals – the contemporary word was manners – of Irish society. Alas! for them, the leaders of the political nation, landowners all, had looked into the abyss during the late reign, felt the tremors caused by Tyrconnell's *revanche* policy, and discerned now that their future salvation lay in measures very different from those advocated by the reformers. As the latter were, in practice, forced to depend on the Protestant landowners, and work within the Irish parliament which they controlled, they could not – as the aged Primate, Michael Boyle, who had been through a war or two, bluntly advised the reformers – set the agenda. So was begun that close alliance of church and state that was to dominate the next, erastian, century. Idealism gave way to reality, principle to pragmatism, as compromises were fashioned. The church conceded a great deal, but also gained much. Only a stubborn minority chose to ask: what if she gained the whole (political) nation, and lost her own (religious) soul?

The generation between the Restoration and the Revolution had, however, seen a good deal of progress amid relative peace and prosperity. In Connacht, the former soldiers of Cromwell's armies became model farmers, dutiful husbands and conforming churchmen. In Ulster, English settlers arrived in appreciable numbers, many of them skilled weavers from Yorkshire, and fanned out along the line of the 'English road' – it ran from Carrickfergus through south Antrim and west Down to mid-Armagh. Their arrival strengthened the church numerically and helped to balance the strong Presbyterian community. So large, indeed, did its presence loom that Narcissus Marsh inaptly described the province as having 'many dissenters and but few papists'. The threat to the church consisted in more than numbers, however, for Presbyterians had developed an efficient organization, and enjoyed a cohesion which derived in part from their concentrated patterns of settlement, and in part from their rigorous discipline. Legal disability and deprivation of political power only served to purify their worship and clarify their ambition. Closely in touch with mutinous Scotland, their allegiance to the established order never absolutely assured, they appeared to some nervous churchmen as an established church in waiting.

## II THE CAROLINE LEGACY

Writing of the Irish church of the Restoration and Revolution, Canon R.H. Murray observed that the great prelates like Jeremy Taylor and William King 'did noble work in building up the life of the Church'; but 'without the unobtrusive piety and loyal devotion' of the leading laity, their work would have been in vain.[5] Laymen of saintly and scholarly distinction had graced the Caroline church. One such was John Stearne, a relative of Archbishop Ussher. Skilled in medicine, law and theology, he was both professor of law in TCD and founder of the Irish College of Physicians (incorporated in 1667). The greater genius of Hon Robert Boyle, son of the 1st Earl of Cork, shone as brilliantly as that of his fellow pioneer scientists, Halley and Newton. Renowned for 'Boyle's Law', a founder of the Royal Society, and a man of faith and vision, he was both a governor of the Corporation for the Spread of the Gospel in New England, and, nearer home, involved in efforts to make the Bible available in the Irish language. The personal piety of the highest layman in the land, James, Duke of Ormonde (who died in 1688) was exemplary: his prayers and meditations were highlighted by his early Georgian biographer.[6] Likewise Roger Boyle, Earl of Orrery, published a set of devotional poems which provide a good insight into the link between religion and politics so characteristic of the period.[7] A church influenced by such men bequeathed worthy successors to the Williamite church. Prominent among them were James Bonnell, the accountant general of Ireland, a man of renowned piety, and Sir Robert Southwell, the first secretary of state for Ireland, who furthered the church's interests with great wisdom. Again, when the Irish branch of SPG (founded in 1701) was formed in Dublin in 1714, three laymen joined the prelates of Ireland on its committee. One of these was Dr Marmaduke Coghill, who later became a judge of the prerogative court and a member of the privy council.[8] There was, too, an episcopal succession of pious and able men. Among the bishops appointed by Charles II, Edward Synge – one of five bishops in his family in the space of three generations – was a gifted preacher, who held the united sees of Cork, Cloyne and Ross from 1663 to 1678. The towering intellect and strong leadership of Jeremy Taylor left an indelible mark during his too brief episcopate – he died in 1667, after only six years in office. Of the Caroline bishops who survived the Revolution, Narcissus Marsh, Anthony Dopping, Richard Tenison and Edward Wetenhall were spiritual leaders and active reformers of vision and courage.

*1. The episcopal reformers*
Narcissus Marsh, intellectual and other-worldly, had arrived in Dublin in 1679 as Provost of Trinity College. He was a founder of the Royal Dublin

Society, and in co-operation with Robert Huntington and Robert Boyle, who financed the project, supervised the translation of the Old Testament into Irish. In Trinity, he built a chapel, and introduced both services and lectures in Irish. Marsh was appointed Bishop of Ferns in 1683, whereupon Huntington, an orientalist and friend of Marsh, agreed reluctantly to accept the provostship. The experience of these two gentle scholars illustrates the dangers which beset the Irish Church. Both fled to England in 1688-9, but returned after the battle of the Boyne, Marsh becoming Archbishop of Cashel in 1691 and, after his translation to Dublin three years later, the acknowledged leader of the reformers. Huntington, for his part, declined the see of Kilmore and resigned the provostship in 1692. But as a rector in rural Essex he pined for the books and society which he had left behind, and returned to Dublin a second time: he was consecrated Bishop of Raphoe on 20 July 1701, only to die six weeks later. He was buried near the door of Trinity chapel, leaving many manuscripts to the college (as well as the silver salver he had presented earlier). The perennial importance of TCD, not only to the Irish, but also to the wider church, is apparent in the Caroline era. Jonathan Swift entered Trinity while Marsh was provost, and had as his contemporaries the three future bishops, Peter Browne of Cork, Edward Chandler of Durham, and Thomas Wilson. The last, a native of Cheshire, had been educated at the King's School Chester, and turned from medicine to ordination under the influence of his friend Michael Hewetson. He was made deacon on St Peter's Day 1686 in Kildare Cathedral, on the occasion of the consecration of the rebuilt choir. To mark it, Hewetson and he presented a paten with the inscription, *Deo et Altari Ecclesia Cathedralis Stae. Brigidae Darensis Sacrum.* Hewetson was later Archdeacon of Armagh, while Wilson became Bishop of Sodor and Man in 1697 at the age of 33. With a zeal akin to that of Marsh himself, he built churches, established parochial libraries, enforced discipline, and published both the 'Manx Catechism' and St Matthew's gospel in Manx. He went one better than Marsh, who was a bachelor, when his son Thomas was born during his episcopate: he was to become rector of St Margaret's Westminster. Richard Tenison, educated at TCD and appointed to the see of Killala in 1682, was another bishop who had been driven into exile under Tyrconnell. He and his metropolitan, John Vesey of Tuam, had remained at their posts as long as they dared, Vesey fleeing when attainted in 1689. Tenison had found employment in London as lecturer at St Helen's Bishopsgate, and on returning to Ireland in 1691 was translated to Clogher, thence to Meath in 1697. (His vicar at St Helen's, the renowned preacher Henry Hesketh, was nominated to succeed him in Killala, but was not consecrated.) In the course of one visitation in Clogher, Tenison confirmed some 2500 persons and was noted 'for the constant exercise of preaching, by which he reduced many dissenters to the church'.[9] He also renovated the episcopal palace at Clogher, and left funds for the support of clergy widows and orphans. Vice Chancellor of Dublin University from 1698, Tenison died in 1705. On 12 October 1694, he had written to William King to recommend the rector of Enniskillen, Thomas Smith, for promotion. While the occasion of his appeal – 'Inniskilling does not agree with his wife and children being a cold moyst place' – was unlikely to have carried weight with King, he may have been gratified that another reformer was being pressed into episcopal service.[10] It is a clear indication early in King's own episcopate (he had been appointed Bishop of Derry in 1691) of the influence he was perceived to wield. Smith was appointed Bishop of Limerick in 1695, though it is likely that his promotion was due rather to the circumstance that Thomas Tenison, who was related to Bishop Tenison of Clogher, had just become Archbishop of Canterbury (1695-1715). William and Mary had first made him Archdeacon of London, and then Bishop of Lincoln. The problems of the Irish church are highlighted in his experience, for he was first offered the archbishopric of Dublin on Francis Marsh's death in 1693. Tenison thereupon requested the king to restore to the parish churches of the diocese the impropriations pertaining to the estates forfeited after the Revolution. These, however, had already been granted to William's Dutch favourites, and Tenison's request could not be granted. He therefore declined to come to Dublin.

Anthony Dopping had been Richard Tenison's predecessor in both Killala and Meath. A Fellow of TCD, and a doctor of divinity before he was 30, he had been chaplain to the Duke of Ormonde. He was appointed to Killala in 1679, when only 35, and on his translation to Meath in 1682, to the Privy Council. With Edward Wetenhall of Cork (and two other bishops), he had sat in the 1689 Parliament, and shown courage in opposing the confiscatory measures carried by the government. It was Dopping who proposed a national fast to William III in 1690. On his early death in 1697, William King described him as 'a most useful and eminent pillar of our church before his recent impairment by sickness'.[11] In December 1693 Dopping and King had been appointed by royal authority to investigate the diocese of Down and Connor. (The third member of this episcopal commission, Wiseman of Dromore, was ill and unable to act.) The two bishops purged the diocese. In March 1694 they deposed the bishop, Thomas Hacket, an habitual absentee since 1672, for simony and other abuses. They deprived also Archdeacon Matthews of Down of five of his nine parishes, and of his archdeaconry for neglect of duty; and Dean Ward of Connor of his deanery for adultery. They censured and suspended other clergy also, in a thorough exercise of their power to 'reform all errors, abuses, offences, contempts, and enormities, committed or permitted by the said Bishop Hacket, or any of the clergy in the said diocese'. This state of affairs in Down highlights the difficulties faced by the reformers. Primate Boyle had apparently proposed to Tenison's predecessor in Canterbury that a coadjutor be appointed in Down. Archbishop Tillotson (1691-94) had given that short shrift: 'I think it much fitter to have the bishoprick made void, for the bishop's scandalous neglect of his charge'.[12] But Boyle took no action, and the commissioners were appointed on the state's initiative more than two years later.

The reformers, moreover, had little else to show for their efforts. There was not much that Dopping could do about the situation in his own diocese, where 42 of the 59 rectories were impropriate, 24 of them to one man.[13] Their sole informal success in a decade was the appointment of Samuel Foley to Down in 1694 in place of the deposed Hacket. But that had been by a circuitous route – through Sir Robert Southwell to Tillotson and so to Queen Mary. Foley, a former Fellow of TCD, and chancellor of St Patrick's from 1689, was described by King as 'very meritorious, very useful and laborious in the church'. But his episcopal promise was not fulfilled, for he died in 1695 at the age of 40. His successor, Edward Walkington – formerly Senior Fellow of TCD – had been chaplain to the Irish House of Commons, and uniquely recommended by that body for a bishopric. He, too, was of the reformers; he, too, died early, after just four years as a bishop.[14] The heroic group which had remained in Ireland throughout the crisis of 1688-90, however, had earlier provided another episcopal reformer. After Hugh Gore, Bishop of Waterford from 1666, had died in 1690 'in consequence of some inhuman treatment inflicted on him by Irish ruffians', Nathaniel Foy succeeded him in 1691. Another former Fellow of TCD, Foy had been incumbent of St Bride's since 1678, and imprisoned by the Jacobite government for his sermons there. His neighbour in Dublin, William King, paid tribute in 1697 to his prudence in governing his parish 'in very difficult times with the greatest love and highest approbation of his parishioners'. Universally respected and loved, his name lived on after his death in 1707 in Bishop Foy's School, which he founded in Waterford. Writing to Archbishop Tenison in 1699, King lamented that there had been 'a very great mortality of bishops since the Revolution ... and most of them have died young men, that is under fifty'.[15] By contrast, the archbishops were the great survivors. Six of them shared 168 archiepiscopal years (and 215 episcopal years in all). Michael Boyle, sometime Lord Chancellor of Ireland, served a total of 39 years in Dublin (1663-78) and Armagh (1678-1702); John Vesey, biographer of Bramhall, 38 in Tuam (1678-1716); and William Palliser 32 in Cashel (1694-1726). The two Marshes – they were apparently not related – spanned 37 years between them: Francis eleven in Dublin (1682-93), and Narcissus three in Cashel, nine in Dublin (1694-1703) and a decade in Armagh (1703-13). King himself had 26 years in Dublin (1703-29) after he succeeded Narcissus Marsh. The latter had in effect been Primate for some time before his translation to Armagh, for Boyle, who was well over 90 when he died, had been deaf and blind for years. Active though he was in Armagh diocese, Marsh in turn was often incapacitated by illness and lack of strength, while King in Dublin was asserting strong leadership. Precluded from promotion to the primacy during the High Tory ascendancy at the end of Anne's reign because he was a Whig, King came into his own when the Whigs regained power with the accession of the Hanoverian, George I. For the same reason, Primate Thomas Lindsay (1714-24), who had been promoted to Armagh for his Tory soundness, was something of a nonentity in the new reign. The *DNB*, although it alludes to such in the course of its long article on King, in fact has no entry for Lindsay. But his name is not utterly cast away, for St Thomas's Church on Rathlin Island was dedicated in his honour during his primacy.

Not all bishops were reformers, as the reformers themselves well knew. When William Fitzgerald, a protégé of Richard Boyle, 2nd Earl of Cork, was appointed to the see of Clonfert in 1691, Narcissus Marsh, then in Cashel, noted: 'in which consecration I had no hand, the Lord's name be praised for it', while King commented curtly that he was 'the weakest of the order, having no qualification to recommend him'.[16] Mortality, that bane of so many reforming bishops, did not overtake Fitzgerald until 1721, nor Simon Digby of Elphin, another of the 1691 appointees, until 1720. On the latter's death, King wrote to Archbishop Wake that he had left his diocese 'in a miserable condition: churches greatly wanting, and those that are, ill supplied ... only about thirteen clergymen in it'. Of Thomas Milles, Regius professor of Greek at Oxford, appointed by Queen Anne in 1708, King wrote in 1725 to the Rt Hon Edward Southwell: 'The bishop of Waterford has not only given all livings of value in his gift to his brothers and relations, but likewise his vicar-generalship and registry, though none of them reside in the kingdom'. Killaloe, which Thomas Lindsay had served for 15 years before he became Primate (he was briefly Bishop of Raphoe), was described by King in 1714 as being 'in a miserable condition, both as to the churches, the cures, and discipline. It abounds with Papists.' Lack of continuity was a drawback for some dioceses, as with Raphoe. When William Smith, a native of Lisburn, had become bishop in 1682, he appointed as his chancellor Dr Benjamin Spanne, who, in King's words, 'got the churches generally repaired and the cures generally settled and attended'. When Spanne went off to Kilmore with Smith, Alexander Cairncross, who had been Archbishop of Glasgow, carried on this constructive work: King, his neighbour in Derry, preached at his funeral in

1701. The diocese then suffered Robert Huntington's early death, Robert Pooley's 12 years of mostly non-residence ('discipline has been much neglected', King observed in 1714), and Thomas Lindsay's one year, and Edward Synge's two year, tenures, before it could settle under Nicholas Forster's episcopate of almost 30 years. During his time the transepts of St Eunan's Raphoe were built, and a tower added to the cathedral at the bishop's own expense, while he also repaired churches, built chapels of ease in large parishes, and endowed a residence for clergy widows.[17] But where consistency was lacking at episcopal level, it might be provided by inferiors. Alexander Hamilton was Archdeacon of Raphoe for 64 years (1690-1754), and served under 10 bishops – there were three further appointments within a decade of Forster's death in 1744.

A viable discipline in moral and parochial matters was the limit of the church's power. 'We have but a shadow of discipline left,' Foy lamented, 'which can be exercised without the concurrence of the state.' Convocation was not summoned by William III. When it met in Anne's reign, it achieved very little. It had been summoned only because in the face of a united demand by the church – a formal protest by the bishops in the Lords' Journal in 1699, and a petition to the Crown in 1703 – the government had deemed it prudent to give way. It was a pyhrric victory, for its meeting only served to expose the church's disunity, and her consequent inability to take decisive action. The demise of convocation left the church dependent on the secular power, and therefore on the landed interest. Beckett saw the close alliance of bishops and landlords as 'the basis of the church's political influence during the 18th century', its forming as a compromise after the clash of the rival claims of church and state. The reformers had lost out in this rivalry. In 1692, Foy had been keen to institute a fund for the purchase of impropriations, but by 1697 he was in despair over 'our sinking church', which faced the prospect of ruin and needed 'a persecution [to] preserve us'.[18] The landlords were prepared to defend the church against the dissenters, but they were not willing to support reform either at their own expense, as impropriators, or at the expense of their clerical relations, as pluralists. Primate Boyle warned the reformers of these realities. Dopping was dismissed from the Privy Council, and in general their efforts were thwarted. Worse, they were obliged to act at the behest of the administration against the church's interests. In 1702 Bishop Smith of Limerick was directed to institute a Dr Richards into two parishes in his diocese, so taking his total of livings to 14. The bishop remonstrated in vain: 'the poison breath of the Castle,' he wrote, was blighting the work of 'the better sort of clergy'.[19] After 1714, Whig bishops were unable to influence a mostly Tory clergy, even where they were inclined to try. 'The slugs of seven or eight hundred pounds a year,' as Foy had called them, might live as they pleased, beyond the reach of discipline. Beckett summarized:

The reformers of the post-revolution period were the remnants of a past age, not the heralds of a new one. The strength of the church lay not in its influence over the people, but in its alliance with the landlords; its interest was political and economic, not spiritual. And this interest bound it ever more closely to England and to a whig ministry whose ecclesiastical policy was latitudinarian. At the same time the disappearance of convocation, by depriving the lower clergy of any voice in the affairs of the church, increased the influence of the episcopate, where the English interest was steadily growing.[20]

## 2. The diocese of Cork

With the diocese of Cork, it need hardly be said, things were different. In the 125 years from Edward Synge's appointment in 1663 to Isaac Mann's death in 1788, it had only seven bishops. Synge's three successors in Cork and Ross – Cloyne became a separate diocese at his death – were Caroline scholars. Edward Wetenhall, a former Fellow of Trinity College, Cambridge, had come to Dublin in 1672 as Master of the Free School (popularly the Bluecoat School; later King's Hospital) founded by Dublin Corporation in 1669; Dive Downes had been Senior Fellow of TCD and Archdeacon of Dublin from 1690; and Peter Browne – the subject of a modern biography – had been Fellow, and from 1699 Provost, of TCD, and prior to taking up the provostship, the first incumbent of St Mary's Dublin. All three were resident and hard-working, committed to their clergy and people, and zealous for the well-being of the diocese. Wetenhall shepherded it through the devastation of civil war, Downes carried on the recovery which he had begun, and Browne laid the foundations of the strength that distinguished the diocese from most others in the Georgian era.[21]

Edward Wetenhall (1679-99) was an heroic leader during the crisis of 1689-91, a time of fear and privation, when many fled to England. Prior to the siege of Cork, he travelled the diocese exhorting the people 'to stand fast in the faith'. He also raised and distributed 'large sums (our conditions considered) to the relief of plundered and famishing families throughout my diocese'. During the siege, when the churches of Holy Trinity and St Anne Shandon were destroyed, he was a prisoner in the city along with his clergy and some 1300 of their people. The crisis over, Wetenhall went to London, published *The Case of the Irish Protestants*, and preached before Queen Mary. He held an ordination in 1692, and worked to fill his many vacant benefices. A report of 1693 showed 25 churches in good repair, evidence probably of the care he had bestowed on them early in his episcopate. Bonnell, who was related to his wife, visited him in 1694 and found that 'he preaches constantly at Cork and has very good clergy about him'. In his visitations, he urged on the clergy their duty to catechize, and expected it to be discharged in church. In the 1696 edition of his *The Catechism of the Church of England*, he directed that it was not just an exercise for Lent, but for the entire year 'except the dead quarter of winter'. This work had been published in 1678, and was revised in 1698 as *A Tried Method of Catechizing*. Wetenhall also urged the unity of Protestants, stressing in *The Protestant Peace-Maker* (1682) love, peace and union as 'the only Means (now left us) of Safety and Reformation of the Public Manners'. But there were limits to his ecumenism, for when William Penn visited him in 1698, and presented him with a statement of the Quaker position on sacraments, the bishop confuted this in print. Bonnell summed him up as 'a vigorous, good man, and very useful to the Church', and although 'not thorough in his prints', as having an excellency in his preaching. Wetenhall was translated to Kilmore, but although he lived until 1715 was incapacitated by illness for many years. He died in London and was buried in Westminster Abbey.

Dive Downes (1699-1709) had won from William King the accolade that he was 'not only considerable for his gravity and prudence, but likewise for his learning, both in divinity, ecclesiastical laws, and other sciences'. He, too, excelled in his personal oversight of the diocese. He visited and confirmed regularly, directed that parochial registers be kept, catechized children, and distributed bibles, prayer books – both 'Common Prayer Books and small Prayer Books' – and copies of Tillotson's sermons and Asheton's devotions. He found that Holy Communion was celebrated three or four times a year in rural churches. At Schull, service was held in a private house on three Sundays in the month, and on the fourth at Kilmoe: although the church at Schull was roofless, he gathered the people within the walls, and confirmed 40 of them from the two parishes. Neither possessed bible, prayer book, glebe or register. Downes may have been in ill-health from 1706, when his diary entries cease. He died at the early age of 56.

Peter Browne (1710-35) was noted for the quality of his devotional life, and for both the gracefulness of his manner and his fine elocution as a preacher. He insisted that his clergy live on or near their benefices, strove to provide more residences for them, gave precise directions for the conduct of worship, and clear guidance on confirmation: notice was to be given in each church on the first Sunday in Lent, and the rite administered after Easter. He also directed the clergy as to how they were to instruct their schoolmasters to teach the catechism to children, and 'to make them get select Psalms and other Scriptures by heart'. He recommended that the clergy catechize in the homes of their people, and did so himself in the poorer households of St Fin Barre's. He showed practical concern for clergy widows and their children, for poor housekeepers and the poor in general, and for the charity schools at

Kinsale and Bandon. Like King in Dublin, he made the building and repair of churches a priority. From 1720, in Cork city, the churches of St Paul, St Anne Shandon with its famous carillon, Holy Trinity and St Nicholas were built or rebuilt, and plans drawn up for rebuilding St Fin Barre's Cathedral, a project completed in 1735 just after the bishop's death. A new church was also built at Passage West. Webster, an authority on the subject, saw in the presentations of church plate to churches all over the diocese evidence of the reawakening of its spiritual life in Browne's time. From sources in the ill-fated Public Record Office in Dublin, Webster found evidence that public penance was a feature of the discipline applied in Cork under each of these three bishops. On 2 September 1694, for his sin in marrying clandestinely, without licence or consent, one William Cogan was bidden to repair to the parish church of Carrigrohane, and there to stand with a white wand in his hand and a paper on his breast declaring his fault, 'all ye time of divine service and sermon', and then to have his penance certified by the churchwardens. Again, a Certificate of Performance dated 11 February 1733 shows that Cuthbert Waddington of Christ Church was ordered to confess publicly and to repeat, at the place of offence and in the presence of parishioners, the abusive language which he had used towards another man's wife: and to bring his certificate signed to the registrar's office.[22] Two successive Sundays in December 1708 had seen a more severe penance imposed for adultery. A parishioner of Holy Trinity was made

> to stand on a stool in the middle alley over against the reading desk, in a white sheet, with a white wand in his hand and a paper telling of his sin on his breast, and after the Nicene Creed, to confess his sin.

He had to do this not only in Christ Church, but also in the Cathedral. A similar discipline was enforced by another Caroline. On the Isle of Man, Thomas Wilson went overboard on the matter of penance: his Manx miscreants were taken out to sea and ducked from boats.

### 3. The Caroline tradition

The Carolines boasted a distinctive church architecture in the auditory style. Although it emphasized preaching – William King often referred to worshippers as 'auditors' – it was designed to assist seeing also, and so draw congregations more intimately into worship. Inigo Jones had been the first Caroline architect to depart from the medieval plan, and the new style was popularized by Sir Christopher Wren. He set out to build 'auditories' in which everyone could see as well as hear the minister, and so built London churches which were smaller than traditional churches. Auditory churches were also known as 'room' churches, built that is as a single room, typically an aisled rectangle with galleries on three sides. The Dublin church of St Mary, built in 1697, epitomized the style, with its galleries and nave which curved inwards to a shallow chancel, but was smaller again than Wren's London churches, John Wesley in 1747 finding it 'mean' by comparison. The very width of these churches enhanced intimacy. They had no arches, screens, or structural chancels, and the nave came up to 'the Communion part', from which it was separated by a single step. There was often enough space for communicants to assemble in the wide outer chancel before the Prayer of Humble Access, as in James Bonnell's Dublin, or St Michan's in 1724, (or Hillsborough church, county Down, in 1774). King's *Offices to be Used for the Consecration of a Church* of 1719 reflects these trends in its rubrics, the 'Chancel doors' of 1666 having, for example, become 'the Doors of the Rails enclosing the Communion Table'. A shallow recess or inner chancel, 'the Place of the Altar' was 'decently' set off from the outer chancel by these communion rails, and was often given structural distinction. In town churches, the corinthian altarpiece of the late 17th century might obscure the east window, like that in the chapel of the Royal Hospital Kilmainham (1686-7). The typical auditory church had three liturgical centres: font, altar, and three-decker pulpit. This last was arranged with the clerk's pew at the lowest level, the reading desk in the middle, and the pulpit on top. The narthex was revived in the form of an entrance hall, the vestries were spacious, and the windows, of plain glass, were 'lightsome'.[23] St George's in Belfast, built in 1816, is a late example of the style, its sanctuary and screen being later additions.

The taking of the liturgy to the people was achieved not only through architecture but in the ordering of worship. Baptism was administered during public worship, catechizing in association with it. Services began at 11 o'clock, or more often at 12 noon – 'the usual hour in Ireland', John Wesley would note – and on Communion Sundays might continue until 3 o'clock. Narcissus Marsh in 1706 enjoined the clergy in Armagh province to have a short break after this service, 'and then assemble the congregation again, and read the evening service and catechize their children before they depart'. Wetenhall in Cork had claimed earlier, 'we can get people to church twice in the day, and keep them there too, and have full congregations, if we so often preach diligently to them'. While he also held that it was a Christian duty 'to receive the Lord's Supper, every Lord's Day', in practice weekly celebration was unknown, even in city churches. James Bonnell was able to communicate every Sunday in Dublin only by 'going from church to church', a practice which King commended in 1694 for cities and large towns, while commenting: 'universally the Lord's Supper is celebrated thrice every year; and where either our persuasions, arguments or entreaties can prevail with our people, we have Monthly Communions'. Dr Bolton tabulated the arrangements devised by Dublin and Cork parishes to ensure that weekly Communion, after Bonnell's practice, was available in the same district; and found that in 1728 these included early celebrations at 6 am in seven Dublin churches in rotation, and at 7 am (twice monthly) in St Ann's. The gifts of the laity enhanced eucharistic worship. The communion plate in use in All Saints Antrim dates from 1701, and was 'The gift of Madame Abigail Parnell to ye Parish of Antrim'.[24] Bolton established that there was no Caroline precedent for altar cross, metal book-stand, or flower vases, that the Communion table was furnished with dignity and simplicity, and that the northward position of the celebrant was traditional Anglican usage, common to Carolines and early Tractarians alike. He observed, too, that although the traditional vestments prescribed in the 1549 Prayer Book (and not those of 1552) had legal validity in Ireland, 'in practice the Church of Ireland has generally from Caroline times adopted the minimum Anglican usage in ministerial vesture'. It was also Irish Caroline custom for the people to stand for the psalms, lessons and epistles, as well as the gospel, and to face east at the *Gloria Patri* and the creeds. There is evidence that prayers were read daily in city churches – in Waterford workmen attended early worship with their tools under their arms – that services on Holy Days were well attended, and that fasting was observed on Wednesdays and Fridays. King had insisted on daily prayers in town churches in Derry diocese and (as Commissary for Primate Boyle) in towns of the province of Armagh.[25]

The metrical psalms, sung usually before and after the sermon, were either from the Old Version of 1560 by Sternhold and Hopkins, or the New Version compiled in 1696 by two Irishmen: Nicholas Brady, who had been Wetenhall's chaplain in Cork, and Nahum Tate, the poet laureate. This latter version, 'allowed' by the Crown and 'permitted to be used' in all churches, gained a hymn supplement in 1698 which Queen Anne authorized for use in 1703. Mant found 'Four Hymns' from it printed 'to be used in the Parish Church of Coleraine' during her reign, including 'While shepherds watched' (attributed to Tate). A modern liturgiologist has pointed out that the Church of Ireland also showed imagination in providing supplementary services and printing these as appendices to the Book of Common Prayer. They included the Caroline form for consecration of churches, printed from 1666; *The Form for Receiving Lapsed Protestants, and Reconciling Converted Papists to our Church*, added in 1700; and a *Form of Prayer for the Visitation of Prisoners*, adopted by convocation in 1711 and printed from 1721 until 1926.[26]

The tradition of providing libraries in cathedral cities was begun by the Caroline bishop, Thomas Otway of Ossory (1680-93). He gave his 'books – folios, quartos, octavos and £200 in money – or more, if need should be – for the beginning of a Library for the Cathedral of St Canice and for the use of the Clergy about it'; and also £5 a year for the keeper, and £5 for a weekly fire to preserve the books. It was carried on by Narcissus Marsh, whose famous Library in Dublin was, despite opposition from four of his episcopal colleagues, made a public institution by Act of Parliament (6 Queen Anne, c.19). Marsh bought Bishop Stillingfleet's library, appointed the Huguenot Dr Bouhereau as librarian, and was encouraged by the support of the English divine, Dr Thomas Smith, who told him that London had 'no library in it which deserves to be called by that name'.[27] The tradition persisted, and during the 18th century diocesan libraries were founded in Cashel, Cork, Derry, Raphoe, and Waterford; and in the 19th century in Belfast, Lismore, Ross, and Tuam. Primate Robinson's library in Armagh, as a public institution founded by statute, emulated Marsh's Library. Those heirs of the Carolines, John Stearne and Theophilus Bolton, founded the libraries in Clogher and Cashel respectively, but the tradition was perpetuated also by bishops of latitudinarian outlook: William Nicholson, translated from Carlisle to Derry in 1718, founded the fine diocesan library there. These collections of theology, history and literature were (as with Otway's) intended originally to educate the clergy: John Jebb was able to pursue his patristic studies at Cashel, where Bolton had provided a complete set of the Greek and Latin Fathers. During the 20th century they were to be neglected, other than by academics and antiquaries, or even sold and dismembered. Recent refurbishment of both buildings and collections has, however, honoured a worthy tradition. The most notable transformation has been that in Cashel, where the late Dean Woodworth restored the decrepit Georgian foundation, and developed an exhibition centre for its distinctive collection of manuscripts (including a 13th century psalter), early printed books, and church plate. In the same diocese, the library in Waterford is being refurbished as part of Conservation 2000, a project to conserve and develop Christ Church Cathedral which An Taoiseach, John Bruton, launched in June 1995.[28]

Like the Irish economy, the church gained much from European immigration. Whereas, in the aftermath of defeat in 1691, the 'Wild Geese' left Ireland by agreement, and formed Irish brigades in the armies of Catholic Europe, the immigrants were refugees from religious persecution under Louis XIV of France. There were two such groups, Huguenots and Palatines.[29] The latter were German Protestants from the Palatinate in the Rhine valley which France had conquered. Reminded by their plight of 'how lately we were turned out of our dwellings by violence and oppression and forced to seek shelter in England', the Council of Ireland in 1709 proposed that Queen Anne send the Palatines to Ireland, and Primate Marsh ordered a collection in all churches for their support. More arrived, however, than chose to stay, and by 1720 there were but 185 Palatine families in Ireland, most of them on the Southwell estates near Rathkeale in Limerick, and a few in Dublin, Gorey, New Ross, and county Cork.[30] The Huguenots had arrived earlier in greater numbers. Although only a minority fled France, they dispersed widely: to Prussia and the Netherlands, Virginia and South Carolina. Some 7000 settled in England and Ireland. French colonies were established in Irish cities during Charles II's reign and Huguenot regiments fought at the Boyne in 1690. After the war, the Huguenot general, the Marquis de Ruvigny, was granted an estate at Portarlington, where he settled former soldiers who lived on their pensions and cultivated the fruit trees, flowers, and vegetables for which the colony was famed. Another was established at Lisburn by Louis Crommelin, whom William III had invited from Holland and made 'Overseer of the Linen Manufactory of Ireland', so ensuring the success of the Ulster linen industry. Other Huguenots, through their entrepreneurial skills, mobility, and family links with Britain and France, contributed to the commercial life of the expanding cities, with silk-weaving in Dublin, woollen cloth manufacture in Cork, and branches of the linen industry in Kilkenny (under William Crommelin) and Waterford.[31] As the Georgian century progressed, many Huguenots became prominent in public life. They served in parliament, army and church, and made their mark in banking, law and literature. The names of La Touche, Le Fanu, Maturin, Lefroy and Perrin became nationally known. Dean Le Tablère of Tuam, who came of one of the most illustrious families of Lower Poitou, compiled a list of Huguenot descendants in his day: it included two generals and 35 officers of the rank of captain and above, and a bishop, three deans – the two others were Brocas and Champagne – and 33 clergy.[32] The bishop was Richard Chenevix of Waterford (1746-79), to which see Power Le Poer Trench was also appointed in 1802. The Trench (formerly La Tranche) family joined the Irish aristocracy in both its Ashtown and Clancarty branches, while Richard Chenevix Trench, Archbishop of Dublin at disestablishment, was of double Huguenot descent.

An Act of 1692 had granted these 'Protestant strangers' entire freedom of worship. While some Huguenots formed independent congregations with Reformed pastors, others conformed, the bishops licensing their pastors and authorizing their services in French. The Dublin Huguenots, who were initially concentrated in the Liberties, had three congregations, two of which were nonconformist. The third worshipped from 1662 until 1816 in St Mary's chapel in St Patrick's Cathedral, set aside for their use by the dean and chapter. The main Huguenot cemetery in the city adjoined St Stephen's Green. One of the earliest Huguenot dignitaries was Jacques Abbadie, who had been minister of the French church in Berlin. His lack of fluency in English inhibited William III from appointing him Dean of St Patrick's, but in 1699 he was made Dean of Killaloe. In Waterford the choir of the old Franciscan monastery was, with the bishop's assent, assigned to the Huguenots, and a stipend provided by the corporation for its French pastor. A solitary portrait today graces the boardrooms in Church of Ireland House, that by James Latham of Gasper Caillard, the first Anglican pastor of Portarlington. The church built by the colony was consecrated by Bishop Moreton of Kildare in 1702, after the form of 1666 which he had translated into French. Its services were conducted, and its register kept in French until 1817. Its last French-speaking pastor was Charles Vignoles, later Dean of Ossory, whose father, John Vignoles, previously a major in the 39th Foot, was also one of five Anglican pastors between 1702 and 1817. A French translation of the Book of Common Prayer was published in various editions in Dublin from 1715 to 1817.[33]

There were in the experience of the post-Revolution church elements of what a later age would discern as a renewal movement. Its course in England has been, and in Ireland is being, well researched.[34] Its voluntary religious societies, given to prayer and personal piety, and attracting among others Dublin apprentices, were preached up by reforming bishops and patronized by men such as Bonnell and Benedict Scroggs, professor of Hebrew in TCD. Other societies promoted reform of manners, and pressure for improvement in public morality influenced legislation in 1695 against swearing and sabbath breaking. Prophetic preaching at once denounced social evils and materialism, and extolled family values and devotions. Church discipline, involving public penance, and attacks on heterodox beliefs such as early deism, were also prominent. Parochial poor relief and other philanthropic schemes were legion, many of them figuring women. Again, parochial schools were revived, charity schools founded – almost 200 have been identified by David Hayton – and a society formed in Dublin in 1717 to promote them. Landowners provided schools: Lords Weymouth in Monaghan, Lanesborough in Leitrim and Longford, Digby in King's County; Lady Lanesborough and Sir Richard Cox in Cork, and Sir John Rawdon in Down. So did such leading clerics as Edward Nicholson in Sligo, and Henry Maule, founder of the Green Coat School in Cork. The charity schools were primarily aimed at inculcating true religion, industry and economic benefits among poor Protestants, both in the country and in response to rapid growth in Dublin, but were seen also as a means of influencing Roman Catholics. (Such evangelism, and the tensions surrounding it, are discussed later.)

In the end this reformation ran into the sand. It was vitiated by party politics, particularly during Anne's reign, Whig anticlericalism, high church idealism, and unrealistic attempts either to enforce morality by statute (allied to the intrusions of informers) or to curb the growth of Roman Catholicism.

It was also weakened by sectarian jealousies – Presbyterians dominated many Dublin societies – by its being largely confined (charity schools apart) to the capital, by the strength of political, as distinct from evangelical Protestantism, and by outright opposition or indifference on the part of the establishment, including many bishops. But above all, despite early promise it failed to become a popular reformation; and a long century was to elapse before that phenomenon evolved in the Evangelical revival. There were nonetheless vital links between the two eras. The Dublin rector, Henry Echlin of St Catherine's (1716-52), held from 1744, except on the third Sunday, a weekly celebration. In 1746, *A Friendly Letter to All Young Men who are Desirous to live Godly Lives* was printed, together with the *Rules and Orders Observed by the Religious Society of St Catherine's.* Its members were committed both 'to reinforce upon one another the principles of Christianity [and] to live up to the doctrines of our Church', and also 'to frequent the Holy Sacrament every Lord's Day, and the public prayers every day'. Thus the spirit of Narcissus Marsh lived on in a society which his successor had founded.[35]

## III A GREAT ARCHBISHOP OF DUBLIN

William King has had a bad press of late in the learned journals. There is a note of irritation that much of the knowledge of the church of his day should derive from his voluminous correspondence: but that is hardly his fault. And there is a touch of *ad hominem* comment in descriptions of him as self-righteous, short-tempered, and confrontational. King was, indeed, a strong personality. He expressed himself with forceful candour. He was not inclined to suffer fools gladly. Like his avowed exemplar St Paul, he catalogued his achievements; but he exhibited, too, the apostle's humility, fearless leadership, and single-minded devotion to his calling. To Englishmen in high places he offered recommendations, sought or unsought; to his episcopal colleagues throughout Ireland – he was no respecter of provincial boundaries – encouragement or rebuke, as he judged appropriate.

King opposed the policy of appointing more Englishmen to Irish sees in 'the English interest' as injurious to the church's interest, in that its rationale, and the priority of men so appointed, was the service of the state. He was not opposed to the appointment of Englishmen as such, and in one case expressly recommended it. His stance was not inconsistent with his own public services or political loyalties. He was a Whig, and had held Dublin steady for the house of Hanover in 1714. He was appointed a lord justice on four occasions during George I's reign. His responsibilities as archbishop embraced, inescapably, both kingdom and church. But he never lost sight of his priority:

*Detail from a portrait of Archbishop King
in Christ Church Cathedral, Dublin*

he was first the servant of the church. There is an essential distinction between King's holding office intermittently as a lord justice because he was Archbishop of Dublin, and Hugh Boulter's being appointed Primate in order that he might become, as the first among the lord justices, the effective head of the Irish government.[36] King, moreover, was a prolific writer. While his first serious publication had been *The State of the Protestants under the late King James's Government* (1691), his theological scholarship in *De origine mali* (1702 ) was widely acclaimed, and his *Discourse on Predestination* was to be edited by Whately two centuries later.

*1. King's men*

King's standing in England was high. The diarist, John Evelyn, dined in his company at Lambeth Palace in 1705, and described him as 'a sharp ready man in politics, as well as very learned'. In October 1716, when King was the guest of the new Archbishop of Canterbury, William Wake (1716-37), the new Archbishop of Tuam, Edward Synge, wrote to his host that no man was better able to brief him on the Irish clergy, laity and university. Six months earlier, Robert Howard had written to King from London: 'I find they don't think of sending us another bishop; from your side they expect recommendations'. They got them; for within six weeks King had written to Wake recommending Drs John Bolton and Ralph Lambert, the respective Deans of Derry and Down, for promotion. Lambert was duly appointed to Dromore in 1717, to fill the vacancy created by Dr Stearne's translation to Clogher after King had pressed to have him 'closer'. These were not the first episcopal appointments which King had influenced, nor were they the last. Of the 17 appointments (exclusive of translations) made between 1714 and his death in 1729, seven were of men whom he had recommended.[37] With the other 10, mostly of men from England, his influence is not apparent – he had in some cases proposed alternative names. They included Hugh Boulter. When the vacancy arose at Armagh in 1724, King urged only that the choice of Primate be made in the church's best interest. He was then in his 75th year, and his correspondence suggests that he neither sought, nor expected, the primacy for himself.[38]

King's record here was remarkable, given that he was not Primate. At George I's accession in 1714, he had recommended to Archbishop Tenison eight names for consideration for the three dioceses then vacant, explaining that they all had been 'persons candidate' under the Tories, when the Duke of Shrewsbury ('the favourite of the nation', in Swift's phrase) was Lord Lieutenant. Of these, Timothy Goodwin had been appointed to Kilmore, Edward Synge to Raphoe, and Nicholas Forster to Killaloe, before the year was out. (On Synge's translation to Tuam in 1716, Forster – 'a very deserving, learned and pious man' – succeeded him in Raphoe.) King's integrity is apparent here. He gave his approbation to the men nominated by a Tory administration which had passed him over for the primacy on account of his Whig predilections; and he recommended the Englishman Goodwin – Archdeacon of Oxford and previously chaplain to Shrewsbury – as a 'grave, sober, good man, and well affected to His Majesty's government'. Of King's other five nominees in 1714, one was Dr John Bolton, whom he was to nominate again in 1716: 'a good, sober, learned man, and fit for a Bishop'. Also in 1716, he first drew Wake's attention to Dr Theophilus Bolton, Chancellor of St Patrick's, 'a man in all respects qualified for a Bishop, if his age, which is about 36 or 37 years, be not an Exception. He is now my Vicar General and truly of his age I know not his fellow'.

The archbishop pressed Theophilus Bolton's claims again – he appears to have abandoned those of John Bolton – in 1721, and could finally write to Wake in 1722 that he was 'glad on many accounts' that the government had procured Clonfert for him.[39] In 1722, too, he first recommended Henry Maule, Dean of Cloyne, and again when a vacancy arose at Cloyne itself in 1726, this time directly to the Lord Lieutenant, and with success. A year later, Robert Howard, his confidant over many years, was appointed to Killala. These last two appointments, notably, were made after Boulter's arrival. Maule was the new Primate's second choice for Cloyne; but he was King's first choice on account of his reputation in the diocese for 'charity, piety, and zeal for religion and His Majesty's interest'. Lord Carteret, the Viceroy, had not wanted him at all. In exercising his privilege of recommending for the episcopate – 'Your Excellency hath indulged me to use great freedom', he wrote to Carteret[40] – King invariably sought out men of good character, scholarship and ability, who took their vocation seriously. At his death, two of his protégés were archbishops, Synge in Tuam and Goodwin in Cashel, while Bolton was to succeed to Cashel later. Synge, conscientious and caring, consecrated his eldest son, Edward, as Bishop of Clonfert in 1730. Henry Maule served as bishop for 32 years, in Cloyne, Dromore, and Meath, and was an early promoter of the Charter schools. Robert Howard – son of Ralph, professor of physics at TCD, and father of Ralph, 1st Viscount Wicklow – had for 20 years been Fellow of TCD, and the first Archbishop King's lecturer in divinity, the post endowed by the archbishop in 1718. Translated to Elphin in 1729, he died at the age of 56 in 1740.

Just as the Caroline bishops and other bishops nurtured in the Caroline church had influenced the post-Revolution period, so King's men perpetuated his influence well into the Georgian era. He kept up with them until his death, giving them counsel, sharing his thoughts with them. To Howard, he confided on 6 August 1728 that he was very weak 'by the gout' – it had plagued him for years – and awaiting death, no longer able to discharge his duties in person. He expressed his hope that 'the state of religion' in Connacht was much mended, for it had been 'most wretched' when he was a young cleric there, and his pleasure in hearing that Howard had increased his clergy. He believed that his brethren of Tuam and Clonfert would 'heartily concur with you and assist you', and hoped that they would provoke one another, and their neighbouring bishops, 'in the reformation of your dioceses'. On the same day he counselled Henry Maule that 'there is no stopping in this course until God calls us from it by death'. He urged him to take St Paul as his example, and added this epitaph:

> I am ashamed, every time that I think of the course he ran, when I compare it with my own. I was consecrated on the day we celebrate for his conversion, and proposed him to myself for a pattern. But God knows how short the copy comes of the original.[41]

As metropolitan of the province of Dublin, King grieved over the state of the diocese of Ferns. On 3 June 1712, during his triennial visitation, he wrote to Francis Annesley that the clergy were very regular and diligent, but miserably maintained: 'some have eight, nine, nay ten parishes and not forty pounds per annum out of them.' Writing from 'Gory' four days later he elaborated on 'the miserable state of the diocese'. It had no bishop, dean, or archdeacon residing in it. Of its 131 parishes, 71 were impropriate in lay hands, 28 appropriate to the bishop, dignitaries and prebendaries of the cathedral, and only 32 'in the hands of the clergy that serve the cures, and generally these are the worst, for the monks seldom troubled themselves but with the best'. Hence there were but 13 beneficed clergy, few of whom had £100 ('I cannot reckon five'), and nine 'very poorly provided curates' on about £30 per annum. King added that he did not blame the bishop – Bartholomew Vigors, appointed in 1691 – who was resident in his other diocese of Leighlin, for in view of the interest of the Crown, the lay patrons, and the appropriators, he did not see how he 'could order the cures better than he has done'. Ten years later he took exception to the nomination of Josiah Hort as Vigors' successor, informing the Duke of Grafton that although Hort had neither doctorate nor degree, he had on legal advice issued a commission for his consecration, and adding: 'this gentleman is the first I ever heard of, that pretended to a bishoprick without any degree at all.' Hort, a friend of Isaac Watts, had been educated in a dissenting academy in England.[42] Proper though his concern for academic or 'personal qualifications' was, King saw these as immaterial once a bishop had been consecrated, whereas 'his presence and dwelling amongst the people has generally a good effect'.

King's criticisms of the northern bishops arose mainly from their failings in this regard. Only two (and formerly only one) of the seven were in regular residence, he observed in 1714, expressly denying the title of resident to any bishop who went to his diocese only 'to settle his rents or make a visitation.' He disapproved of his successor in Derry, Charles Hickman, an habitual absentee who on one of his visits had uprooted for private gain a wood which King had planted for the future benefit of the diocese. He was not much enamoured either of Hickman's successor, William Nicholson, nor yet of Henry Downes in whose interest the latter chose to vacate the see (Nicholson was translated to Cashel, but died before he could leave Derry). The antipathy was mutual, and King got as good as he gave in the correspondence between these two: 'we foreigners, and our foreign friends, are railed at by the natives of one, two, or more descents', Downes wrote. [43] Nicholson, whose chief interests were scholarly – he was an author and antiquarian, and did much for the diocesan archives in Derry – epitomized the new culture that characterized the bench in the Georgian era. At its best intellectual, and of high literary attainment, in style liberal and easy going, and at worst inclined to heterodoxy, it was anathema to King. His rejection of it cannot be understood in simplistic terms as the friction of native and foreigner. The friction was there: but it represented essentially the clash between the heirs of the Caroline tradition and the heralds of the new latitudinarian age.

The archbishop was, in any case, no respecter of background where he perceived that the interests of the people were being sacrificed on the altar of private advantage. On 17 August 1704 he wrote a long letter of remonstrance to the Bishop of Clogher. This was St George Ashe, former Fellow of TCD, Provost from 1692 until he became Bishop of Cloyne, and a man highly esteemed by the literary world. On his death in 1718, Joseph Addison was to express his condolences to Swift – Ashe had been his tutor – on the loss of an excellent man of 'humanity, agreeable conversation, and all kinds of learning'. King saw him rather as a negligent diocesan. His letter reproached him for presenting his brother Dr Dillon Ashe to three parishes in Clogher when he had no intention of residing there, but had elected to remain in Dublin 'to hold Finglass', and to place curates in his Clogher parishes instead. The reasons which King listed in deploring this arrangement are a telling critique of unreformed practices. Aside from the provocative comment that it was 'a breach of my own method', he observed pertinently that if three parishes could yet support curates, while sending their rectorial tithes to Dublin, there was no justification for the church's levying these great tithes. A resident rector spent his income 'on the place', but a non-resident's tithes might as well belong to the landlords, who spent them in London and Dublin. Again, deserving as Dr Ashe no doubt was, if all such clergy were to enjoy four livings, 'there will be nothing but curates in the north'. The fatal effects of that situation had been seen in the past, and in any case northern people had a peculiar aversion to curates in charge, and called them 'hirelings'. The archbishop's final point was that a humour which preferred 'the clergyman's ease to the salvation of the people' should not be indulged. Bishop Ashe was upbraided later for his personal style. In seeming to make his bishopric 'only a pompous sinecure' by his long absences from Clogher, King alleged, he had justified the reproach of a leading Presbyterian critic of the church, James Boyse of Dublin.[44]

While King's interventions were resented by those who suffered them, the silence of one contemporary speaks volumes. For no word of censure came from the pen of Jonathan Swift. The great dean's contempt and venom spared none who deserved them: they were never vented on the archbishop. This is more remarkable given the contrast in their personalities, the awkwardness of their early relationship, and the discontinuance of their correspondence between 1711 and 1716. As Bishop of Derry, King had set his face against Swift's becoming Dean of Derry in 1700: he preferred 'a grave and resident Divine' to a man of 32 who would be 'eternally flying backwards and forwards to London'. And when in 1713 Swift became Dean of St Patrick's, he deplored the removal of Dr Stearne, his vicar general in Dublin, who was promoted Bishop of Dromore 'to make room for Dr Swift', but acquiesced in the move because he 'thought a dean could do less mischief than a bishop'. It was, as it were, his mark of protest. And yet Swift's letters to King show, without a trace of sycophancy, a deep respect for him. If the key to an understanding of Swift as priest is, as Beckett argued, his vigilance in defending the dignity of his order, then it also explains his attitude to King. For Swift recognized in the austere figure at St Sepulchure's one who strove incessantly for the well-being of the clergy. The archbishop, on his side, played to the strength of 'the priest in politics'. In the Irish church's bid of 1710 to recover the first fruits and twentieths – the Queen had already rebated them to the English church – King kept in close touch with Swift, the advocate in London of the Irish case. Swift wrote to him that he was 'caressed by both parties': but he succeeded through his influence with the Tory statesman Harley.[45] His 'flying to London' could be approved after all.

## 2. The diocese of Dublin
King inherited a diocese at once well administered and well disposed to meet the needs of an expanding population. Dublin, the second city of the Empire, grew at an unprecedented rate after the Revolution. Its population stood at 47,000 in 1695: by the time King completed his survey in c.1715 of men capable of bearing arms, it had risen to 89,000. Of that number, some 60,000 (or two-thirds) were Protestants, a figure which was to rise to 75,000 by 1733, out of a total Dublin population of 123,000.[46] To provide for their spiritual needs, King carried on Marsh's work of creating new city parishes and providing churches for them. He also built, rebuilt, or repaired many churches in the country. He improved the lot of his clergy by endowing their vicarages with glebe, and enhancing their incomes. Without detriment to the interests of his successors, he was able to reorganize the see lands in ways that assisted materially in this design. He coveted, coaxed, and cajoled help from wealthy laity in these tasks. He took on vested interests also, not least the chapter of Christ Church Cathedral, which had neglected the cures appropriate to it. He adopted sensible policies in relation to the selection, promotion, and professional development of his clergy. Like Marsh before him, he was regularly on the move in his diocese. His letter from Gorey in 1712 had informed Annesley of his intention to visit those parts of it that lay between Ferns and Dublin, to hold confirmations in 10 or more places, and to consecrate a new church. And in 1720 he told Bishop Stearne that he had gone through the diocese, confirming in 20 country churches and giving a 'discourse' in each.

In 1695 the city of Dublin was divided into 12 civil parishes. About 78 per cent of the population lived south of the Liffey, with St Michan's as the only parish north of the river. In 1697 it was divided into three, and new churches – both of them galleried – were built for the new St Mary's and St Paul's parishes. King continued this development. In 1707 the ancient parish of St James was separated from St Catherine's, St Luke's formed out of that of St Nicholas Without, and St Ann's parish created. Churches were built in the three new parishes. St James's acquired 'a long, low and narrow building' – it was to collapse in 1761; St Luke's galleried church, designed by Thomas Burgh, was built in 1714, and St Ann's in 1720. Meanwhile, as King had told Southwell in 1707,

> St Nicholas within the Walls is pulled down, and in a pretty forward way of reparation. We have a bill gone over to finish it. If I live to see the three churches erected in the city, and four or five more in the country, I shall think I have done pretty well for my time.

He had already provided rural churches at Arklow, Stillorgan, Kilgobban, Ringsend, and Glasnevin, and in the event went one better in the city when in 1715 Burgh – who built the library in TCD and Dr Steevens' Hospital also – designed a new church for St Werburgh's parish, its elegant classical facade alone surviving the major restoration of 1759. Surveying progress to 1725, King gave an interesting insight into church attendance in early Georgian Dublin. He recalled that after it had been filled by 'a good minister' (replacing one who was 'not agreeable'), the capacity of the small church in the parish of St Nicholas Without had been doubled by the provision of galleries. As it still 'wanted room … service was opened in the cathedral of St Patrick's which was not officiated before regularly; that was likewise filled' – with 'usually a thousand people every Lord's-day'. It was against this background that St Luke's church had been built in the Coombe, and it, too, was 'frequented every Lord's-day with about a thousand hearers, and yet there wants room; so that we are about enlarging the old church'. As to the north side, he estimated a population of 30,000 and noted simply, 'Dublin greatly wants churches'. He identified Grangegorman as ripe for erection into 'a parish or chapelry', as its people had been turned out of the 'small' St Paul's church (it held about 1,000) which was inadequate for its own parishioners. He also intimated that St Mary's parish was about to be divided, as it had 'thriven so prodigiously'. (He had earlier described its then incumbent, Dr Francis, as 'very agreeable to his parish, a constant Resident and one that is much followed for his preaching, especially by the fair Sex'.) In 1728 King was to tell Lady Carteret that although he would not live to see them, it was 'absolutely necessary' that the city should have four more churches (and the country two). In the event, four new city churches were built in mid-century, and with the creation also of the parishes of St Thomas and St George on the north side, Georgian Dublin had expanded to 19 parishes and two deaneries, the position in 1798, when Whitelaw's survey of Dublin was undertaken.[47]

King kept raising his sights in the country also. He told Thomas Wentworth in 1713 that in his first ten years as archbishop he had got 17 churches built or rebuilt, nine of them 'where there has been no service or church, that I can find, since the Reformation', and as many more repaired. He wanted 12 more to have the diocese 'tolerably served'. He got them: in 1715 he boasted 'near 40 churches', and four years later 50 in all consecrated or restored. He claimed 28 new churches in 1725, and 31 in 1727, pointing out that although there was no fund for building or rebuilding churches, they had been provided both by the Crown and by individual patrons. He went for quantity rather than quality, telling Lord Palmerston that he agreed with him that 'we ought rather to multiply the number of churches than to make them magnificent'.[48] (There was a price for false economy. St Brigid's Stillorgan, constructed 1706-12, was of poor quality and needed heavy restoration in 1760.)[49] The going rate for a new church was then £800. But if there was no fund as such, there were yet funds. In 1719 he calculated that during his episcopate £70,000 ('besides what is private') had been laid out on visible charities 'such as building churches, poor-houses, schools and hospitals'. He thought this effort 'a great deal in so poor a country', and claimed more charity schools in Dublin than 'in most of the kingdom besides'.[50]

But the provision of churches was only half the battle. In 1704 King confided to Bishop Moore of Norwich his initial impulse to decline the see of Dublin (as Tenison had done in 1693). For with his 30 years' knowledge of it, he was aware that its many appropriations and impropriations made 'the due service of the cures and right order almost impracticable.' In thanking Wentworth in 1713 for relinquishing £40 of impropriate tithes in the parish of Newcastle, he commented on the 'miserable condition' of the diocese – that favourite phrase was evidently not reserved for the sees of negligent bishops – in respect of churches, and provision for the cures: 'we have not half the maintenance for the ministers we have, nor half the ministers enough to serve the people'. Although in 1721 he could report 48 rural churches in repair, with incumbents who officiated, in 1714 he had counted 48 that 'wanted glebe or maintenance, or both'. By 1719 several of these had been endowed with tithes or glebes, and had newly built 'manse-houses', while he had himself 'laid out land to endow four more'. In 1727 he noted 11 manse houses built, and £300 in recovered impropriations. It was modest enough progress. As he had observed earlier to Dr Maule, among the landowners there were 'very few willing to sell either glebes or impropriations'. Hence most benefices consisted of eight or more parishes. To Wentworth again he had cited Wicklow and Arklow as typical, the one requiring 10, the other 11 parishes 'to make a competency', each minister having two churches to serve, at some distance apart. He acknowledged that the clergy in his province were in no better condition as to glebes, with some unable to find even a local lodging, and having to ride many miles to do their duty, and others who had procured a lodging or small farm, finding their entire income taken up in rent.[51]

In encouraging landowners to invest more in their parishes, King indicated the dividends that they might expect. He suggested that a resident incumbent attracted Protestant tenants, so that a settled, well disposed community developed around the church. He instanced the improvement at Ringsend since he had provided it with a church, a good clergyman, and regular service. Previously 'one of the lewdest irreligious places near Dublin', its large congregation was now a model of decency and devotion. Glasnevin, too, was much improved: 'good houses are built in it, and the place civilized'. He urged Lord Palmerston and Sir John Stanley, as the landed proprietors, to do something similar for Grangegorman, with the added enticement that Sir John Rogerson, who had built the church at Glasnevin, had 'doubled or trebled his rent'. He also pointed them to Mr Joseph Dawson's experience. For very little he had purchased 'a piece of ground' near St Stephen's Green, had begun its development by building St Ann's Church, had been able then to set his ground for above £500 per annum, 'and now has Dawson-street, one of the best in Dublin, built upon it'. So had begun the Georgian expansion that was to take the city to the banks of the Grand Canal. Finally, King claimed that such church extension was the most effectual means 'to break both dissenters' and Papists' meetings.' As usual he gave an example:

> The county of Wicklow was full of Quakers and dissenters; but having got seven new churches in it, and filled them with good men, there is hardly a meeting left in that part that is in the diocese of Dublin.[52]

While much of the information here is, of its nature, anecdotal and piecemeal, Mant's summary of all that King achieved for his clergy remains apposite. He first supplied the new churches with pastors by dividing contiguous benefices as they became vacant, and settling a clergyman in each. He then set about providing them with glebe. Where this was feasible, he apportioned a glebe of 20 acres out of the see land, availing of a recent statute (2 Queen Anne c.10) for this purpose. Where the see had no estate, however, he either procured from the trustees of the first fruits a grant to purchase, or failing that purchased, at his own expense, a similar acreage. He also annexed the prebends of St Patrick's as they fell vacant to their separated vicarages. By these various means most of the Dublin vicarages were supplied with glebe. King also purchased impropriate tithes to augment the small cures, and executed new leases to the vicars as the leases of appropriate tithes expired, thereby doubling the incomes of many of them. At the same time he protected the interests of his successors by purchasing new lands for the see. His exertions on behalf of his clergy were extolled by Swift after his death, and the failure of other diocesans to follow his example deplored.[53]

In managing his clergy, King promoted them as extensively as his limited opportunities allowed, and their record of service deserved. His hands were tied by the fact that so much patronage was vested in the Crown and lay impropriators, but he was the patron of some – mostly less wealthy – benefices, and made the most of the vacancies in these by bringing about several 'removes' at the same time. He regarded this policy as giving recognition to deserving men, providing incentive to conscientious clergy in inferior posts, and discouraging idlers from applying for vacancies. Interestingly, he also saw it as affording the clergy a chance to recycle their sermons on the mysteries of the faith, and to devote the time thereby saved to pursuing their studies more widely. When it came to selecting men for orders, he made it a rule that he ordained only those whom he had personally known for some time, and admitted candidates from other dioceses only at the request of their bishop. He examined his candidates privately, and when they had satisfied him as to their 'life, title and learning', summoned four or five of his clergy, as required by the canons, to assist him in a public examination over four days. He would not ordain candidates who had been divorced, and therefore refused Francis Annesley's request to ordain his eldest son, 'lately freed from an unhappy marriage by Act of Parliament'. By these methods, he claimed, he 'avoided all importunity and surprise about conferring orders'.[54]

### 3. 'Mighty high churchmen'

In the battle for improved standards, King's chief foes were those of his own household. They involved him in litigation for over two decades, and his letters to Archbishop Wake often alluded to it. Thus in 1717 he expressed himself obliged to the Bishops of Lincoln and Gloucester, to the Lord Chief Justice, Lord Macclesfield, and to Lord Coningsby, Lord President of the Council, for speaking in his cause in parliament – 'and in truth it was the cause of Episcopacy against obstinate Usurpers'; and again in 1722 wrote of the inconvenience and expense of soliciting 'a Cause by which I am not to gain a Farthing but only to do justice to my jurisdiction'. His opponents were none other than the Dean and Chapter of Christ Church. (The Dean was the Bishop of Kildare for the time being: William Moreton until 1705, and Welbore Ellis thereafter.) Their opposition had begun in 1703, and it was not until the spring of 1724 that King was able to express his 'gratitude to your Grace, and to the whole House of Lords', for giving judgment in his favour, with costs, in the two causes (there had been two earlier ones also). These concerned his archdeacon's right to a seat and voice in the chapter, and his own general right of visitation and jurisdiction. Their successful conclusion ended a prolonged saga which had seen three judgments given for him in the Irish Court of Common Pleas, and four in the King's Bench; and four in all in the House of Lords, in England.

Impasse had begun when King held a visitation, and in their absence pronounced a sentence of contumacy against the dean and chapter. As Primate
Marsh noted, they had responded by petitioning the queen that as Christ
Church was the chapel royal ('where the State goes to church'), it must therefore be exempt from the archbishop's jurisdiction. They had also taken their
cause to the English courts and obtained an inhibition against him. But two
could play the same game. Replying to Swift from London, King noted that
his adversaries had been assiduous in misrepresenting his cause, and astute in
taking theirs to England in the hope that it would not be understood: it was
the misfortune of the Irish, he averred, 'to have our causes judged here by
persons that neither understand nor regard our affairs'. King's persistence
bore down the advantage initially enjoyed by his opponents. His understanding was that the visitations held by his predecessors had been ineffectual,
as they had not known the extent of their powers and feared involvement 'in
an expensive contention'. By implication, he knew all and feared nothing –
the very reason for the chapter's determined resistance to him. He took on
this vested interest because it was corrupt. He denied any intention 'to invade
their rights and privileges, but think myself obliged to take care that they
should do their duty'. To this end he entreated Wake not to resent the trouble he was causing him, and to send as many bishops as he could influence
to fight his cause in the Lords, if he could not be there in person.

> You see how I am pushed in my jurisdiction. If this were by dissenters or
> Papists, I should bear it more easily; but it is by the members of my
> cathedral, who pretend to be mighty high churchmen, and whose church
> was built and endowed by my predecessors out of the bishoprick, who
> now will not own me, though constantly visited by all my predecessors,
> till I came in.

King's motive was not so much to defend the high ground of principle as to
redress the practical consequences of its violation. The chapter had appropriated 27 parishes, and either supplied the cures not at all, or very poorly. They
would not agree to rebuild ruined churches 'for fear they should be obliged
to supply them with curates', and were greatly put out at his getting several
churches built in parishes belonging to Christ Church which they had
neglected. But he had much more against them. For, as he told Francis
Annesley, they had 'turned their chapter-house into a toy-shop [and] their
vaults into wine cellars' and had let their cathedral lapse into 'a pitiful condition', whereas St Patrick's, with not half the establishment of Christ
Church, was 'much better beautified', and had great sums of money laid out
on it. Again, as he reported to Wake, the members of the chapter were held
in general contempt 'as persons of no conscience or prudence': the clergy had
withdrawn from preaching for them, and the nobility and gentry from

attending worship 'because they did not see that decency in the service of God and edification in the preaching which they used to have'. These considerations, too, he claimed, had made him zealous to settle his jurisdiction over them, and them zealous to resist it. After the Lords had given judgment, he told Annesley, he visited Christ Church, was received with submission and the contempt purged. And a year later he informed Lord Palmerston that the dean and chapter were not only submitting to him, but also joining him in making some provision for the cures dependent on them.[55]

## IV PAPISTS AND DISSENTERS

To describe, with candour and compassion, the Church of Ireland's historic relations with other Christian communions is no easy task. Three centuries from now, when historians note that the Irish churches began talking together in the late 20th century only when Irishmen were killing one another in the name of religion, it may seem to them that ecumenical progress was limited. That thought should induce caution about earlier periods in the church's history, and the realization that these can be understood, much less judged, only in their own context. Until 1870 the Church of Ireland not only maintained a polity at once reformed and episcopal, but also constituted a national religious establishment. Many of her people, Primate Alexander was to recall in 1905, 'pronounced the words "Church and State" not only as men shout them in their cups, but as they breathe them in their prayers'.[56] It is certain, however, that Roman Catholics and Presbyterians neither shouted nor prayed with the same enthusiasm.

The Revolution had re-established the Protestant Ascendancy, 'Protestant' connoting adherents of the Established Church. Nonconformists were either 'papists' or 'dissenters', the latter mostly Presbyterians. While the church would have denied religious toleration to all nonconformists, the state permitted their worship in law, or at least in practice: hence mass houses and meeting houses, as well as churches. Ireland was not unique. Throughout Europe the state established its religion, restricted power to those who conformed, and denied full civil rights to those who dissented. This philosophical stance was reinforced in Ireland by the realities of Catholic numerical preponderance and Presbyterian expansion; and in its privileged, yet precarious, position from 1691, the church favoured now coercion, now persuasion.

### 1. The Presbyterian question
Presbyterian fortunes had fluctuated during the 17th century. The influx of Scots settlers into Ulster in its early years had produced the experiment of 'prescopalianism', when out of weakness the church had accommodated both

episcopalian and presbyterian traditions. As Finlay Holmes acknowledges, this 'represented a compromise which was bound to come to an end when either party was in a position to enforce the principles of their church polity'.[57] It was so ended by the rigorous discipline imposed by the Laudian bishops, the episcopal triumph being confirmed (after the temporary, if total, reverse under the Interregnum) in the post-Restoration settlement, as a result of which almost 70 Presbyterian ministers were ejected from their church livings. The events of 1688-90, however, evoked the spectre of Presbyterian victory, and William King, then Dean of St Patrick's, devised a plan of again accommodating the two traditions within the one national church, as the only means of salvaging episcopacy in the event of a Presbyterian ascendancy. How viable his strategy might have been was never put to the test of reality, and far from Presbyterians in Ireland achieving the ascendancy they achieved in Scotland, they were even denied the freedom of worship allowed to dissenters in England under the Toleration Act of 1689. Presbyterian worship was, however, permitted *de facto* until the Toleration Act of 1719 was passed by the Irish parliament. In view of their loyalty and service to the state during the Revolution, it seemed to Presbyterians that they had been bleakly rewarded.

In his position paper, *The present state of the Church*, King proposed changes intended to make the church's liturgy and government acceptable to Presbyterians, and where that design failed, offered in effect the alternative of internal dissent. Thus he proposed that toleration be extended to those who found the 'publick and established worship unlawful'. To those, however, who were willing to use 'a form of prayer', he offered a programme of moderate reform. It involved a revision of the prayer book and psalter; less use of surplices and organs; prohibiting readings from the Apocrypha; and a 'better edition of the singing psalms (since the people will have them)'. In regard to other contentious matters, he proposed both that the sign of the cross be optional, and the direct responsibility of godparents be removed, in baptism; freedom either to stand or kneel when receiving communion; and optional use of the prayer book burial service.[58] These proposals represented not so much an ecumenical agenda, as a plan for emergency action. When the crisis passed, nothing came of them. Ironically, some would be adopted later, not with regard to Presbyterian sensibilities, but rather to accommodate diverse opinions within the Victorian Church as the liturgy came under attack from nonconformists, and as internal moves for prayer book revision were initiated.

With respect to orders, King first proposed a formal declaration to any Presbyterian minister willing to submit to reordination that this was intended not 'to invalidate … the power he had before but only to make it more unexceptional to the church'. But for any minister not so willing, King made the radical proposal 'that he be connived at to officiate in his own congregation and owned as a brother by the other clergy'. Andrew Carpenter points out that King seemed here to 'admit the legality of presbyterian orders *per se*', and suggests that in this he ran counter to the official position of the post-Restoration church.[59] While it is true that Jeremy Taylor and the Caroline divines in general held an exclusive view of episcopacy, however, King was reverting to the earlier Anglican position – espoused by the Reformers and expounded by Hooker – that the continental churches had valid, though non-episcopal, orders. The exclusive view of episcopacy was taken up at the time by the Non-Jurors (replacing the 'godly prince' with the bishop), and later by the Tractarians. There were few of either in Ireland, and King's position was maintained by the generality of Irish churchmen. All in all, though of academic interest only in the event, his paper is of importance in revealing the thinking on essential points of one of the greatest sons of the Caroline church.

The 'Presbyterian question' was settled for the time being, not on theological, but on political grounds. Like Charles II before him, William III was inclined to be more tolerant than his parliaments, but increasingly it was parliament which called the shots. The king granted *regium donum* to Presbyterian ministers, and this financial support (withdrawn at the end of Anne's reign but restored by George I) not only lasted until disestablishment, but was increased and extended in later reigns. But William could grant little else. The Irish parliament thwarted his plans to extend legal toleration to Presbyterian worship in both 1692 and 1695, and the delayed Toleration Act was passed only narrowly in 1719, and in the teeth of opposition from the leading bishops. But if the worship of Presbyterians was now legal, their civil disabilities lasted until 1780. The sacramental test introduced in 1704 restricted public office – in the militia, local government, the university, or parliament – to those who received communion according to the Anglican rite. (Service in the militia was indemnified in 1719.) The Presbyterians were thus effectively barred from office, and lost their control of the town corporations of Belfast and Londonderry. Most of the bishops supported the test: Wetenhall alone voted against it as a profanation of the sacrament. They also resisted London's attempts to have it repealed in 1707-09, and again in 1719. The harsh logic in this regime was voiced by the Lord Chancellor, Sir Richard Cox: 'I was content every man should have liberty of going to heaven, but I desired nobody might have liberty of coming into government but those who would conform to it.'[60] Modern research has established that the large scale Presbyterian emigration to the American colonies during the 18th century was precipitated more by economic pressures in Ulster than by religious discrimination. Even so it is no coincidence that these emigrants influenced the founding American tradition that all denominations should be equal, and none established, and that civil rights should not depend on religious affiliation.

William King's part in all this is perhaps the least happy aspect of his leadership in the church. His years as Bishop of Derry (1691-1702) brought him into contact with the Presbyterian community in the north-west at a time when it was being reinforced by immigration from Scotland. In his visitation sermons King sought to convince Presbyterians of the merits of episcopacy, and, in his *Inventions of Men in the Worship of God,* of the biblical basis of Anglican worship. This publication drew a riposte from Joseph Boyse, minister of the Wood Street congregation in Dublin, who had sparred with King in Dublin in 1688, but had also urged the mutual respect and co-operation of Anglican and Presbyterian in the face of resurgent Catholicism. Although conceding some points to the bishop now, Boyse exposed inaccuracies in his survey of the Presbyterian experience, and dismissed his claim that dissent involved disloyalty to the state: it was, he insisted, true neither of Scottish Episcopalians nor Irish Presbyterians. And he added, gratuitously, that (as King was well aware) the Church of Ireland lacked an effective ecclesiastical discipline.[61] King seems seriously to have misjudged the Presbyterians. He saw them as misguided and open to persuasion, whereas they were a proudly independent people, tenacious of their Reformed traditions. They also had friends at court, for the ruling Whigs favoured their cause. When King, unable to win them by persuasion, tried to enforce the full rigour of the law against them, the Presbyterians invoked the government's help and defied his authority.

In fairness to King, not all Presbyterians were as 'the great Mr Boyse' in his eirenic outlook, any more than, in the 19th century, they would be with the great Dr Cooke when he proclaimed their 'banns of marriage' with the Anglicans. Holmes's comment (on the intolerant 1630s) that 'episcopalians would have been similarly treated had the positions been reversed',[62] exactly states the recurrent nightmare of King and his contemporaries, none more so than Dean Swift, whose attitude was coloured by his early experiences in Kilroot. His fear of a Presbyterian takeover persisted all his life, and found expression in his will. In 1732, soon after King's death, he took issue with the Irish parliament over both 'the sacred tenth' and the sacramental test. Swift was incensed by the form of address – 'Brother Protestants and Fellow Christians' – used by those who sought to remove the test. One of his biographers suggests that 'the tribune of the people sinks into an advocate of the tithe proctor and the Anglican bigot'. It was true that legislative independence and commercial freedom for Ireland – aims espoused by Swift – were achieved only after Anglicans and Presbyterians joined forces after 1780 in a situation of civil equality. But Beckett contends that national advantage was never Swift's guiding principle; rather it was the interest of the church, which he held to be an apostolic model – 'the most perfect of all others in discipline and doctrine'. Hence his conviction, reinforced by Presbyterian expansionism, that parliament must be kept in the hands of those who supported the church, lest the establishment be transferred to another polity.[63]

Power, then, was the critical issue in the religious history of the 18th century. Otherwise its course is a sobering reminder that the church's avowed better governance by bishops did not save her from a near-terminal decline, and that their boasted purity of worship and government did not save the Presbyterians from a near-total descent into the abyss of heresy.

### 2. 'His Majesty's Catholick subjects'

If Presbyterians suffered civil discrimination because they were non-Anglicans, Roman Catholics suffered because they were Catholics. Having been persecuted under James II, Protestants were determined to avoid future persecution. Mant was to point to 'their sense of the dangers from which they had escaped, and to which they were still exposed, from the unrestricted spirit of Popery'.[64] In that sense the Protestant nation devised the Penal Laws. Their inspiration was fear, their aim security, their method total control. They conferred on Protestants a monopoly of civil and military offices, and on Catholics a political, economic, and social inferiority, while yet tolerating – within strict limits – the practice of their religion. Ireland, however, was not unique. In face of the Jacobite claim to the throne, anti-Catholic legislation was found throughout the king's dominions. In Ireland a resolute parliament carried all before it. In the face of its implacable attitude, William III had to abandon his more conciliatory policy, and to compromise the guarantees given to the Catholic nation in the Treaty of Limerick. Its supporters were also swept aside, Sir Richard Cox being forced to resign from the Privy Council. For her part, the church identified at once with the fear and the policy of the Protestant nation. Her preachers kept alive the sense of danger and deliverance in the annual sermons commemorative of 23 October 1641.[65] Her parliamentarians, including the bishops, voted for the penal legislation. William King insisted that its purpose was, not to oppress the papists, but to keep them in subjection. The Catholic nation would, however, find that nice distinction a difficult one to make emotionally.

The land settlement of the 1690s resumed the process of land transfer which the Jacobite Parliament had reversed, and buttressed it with laws which both denied Catholics access to land through long leases or marriage, and required them to divide their estates at death. The alternative was to convert to the Established Church. By these means the Catholic gentry virtually disappeared. The percentage of land in Catholic hands fell from 22 in 1688 to 14 in 1703, and to only 5 per cent by 1779. By 1789 there had been some 5500 conversions, mostly for the purpose of protecting land and social position: modern research is establishing that many converts privately kept the faith which they had formally renounced.[66] Otherwise the Penal Laws removed from Catholics the capacity to bear arms, influence public affairs, provide education, or practice law – there was, for example, an 'Act to prevent Papists being Solicitors'. As to the practice of the Roman Catholic religion, it was not intended to ban worship, but rather to prevent that church from functioning as an independent and self-perpetuating society. Thus bishops and regulars were banished, secular priests required to register (one was allowed in each parish), and education abroad prohibited. This regulatory zeal reached its zenith early in Anne's reign, with Acts to prevent 'Popish priests from coming into the kingdom' and 'further growth of Popery' – the clause imposing the sacramental test was, ironically for Presbyterians, written into the latter statute. These measures were not vigorously enforced – the consensus among historians is that they were never intended to be – and they were relaxed when the Jacobite threat receded after 1745. (Until then it had been taken seriously, with even Presbyterian ministers having to abjure the Pretender as well as the Pope.)[67] The Roman Catholic Church was therefore able in practice to introduce bishops into the country, ordain priests, train them in the seminaries of Europe, build mass houses, maintain 'popish schools', and keep alive the Gaelic culture which the Catholic gentry had previously patronized.

The tension between formal rigour and practical leniency was highlighted in 1715 when Archbishop King, who was in good standing with the Hanoverian regime, sought assurances from the Viceroy, the Earl of Sunderland. He pointed out that the design that there would be no succession in the Roman priesthood, as registered priests died and could not legally be replaced, had been thwarted during the late reign through government's non-enforcement of the law and indifference as to the consequences. Hence illegal immigrants had arrived from abroad: 'and there are in the country Popish bishops concealed, that ordain many'. If the law were now to be strictly enforced, he urged, strict inquiry should first be made into the actual situation, and intruders driven out of the kingdom. But if 'the same mild hand' were to be shown, then it would be better to make 'no noise' about them as ineffectual inquiry only made them 'more secure and daring'. Experience, in short, had shown that empty proclamations 'do a great deal of hurt, discourage the Protestants, and animate the Papists'. As King appeared to anticipate, no decisive action was taken, and shortly before his death in 1729 he lamented that in 60 years he could 'never remember Popery so much encouraged' except under James II. His point had been underlined in one particular: in

1727, when John Richardson's *The Great Folly, Superstition and Idolatry of Pilgrimages in Ireland* showed that pilgrimages were thriving, especially that at Lough Derg, despite their being banned under an Act of 1702. Primate Boulter claimed that same year, soon after his arrival in Ireland, that there were but 800 incumbents and curates as against 3,000 'Popish priests of all sorts here', and opined that there was no hope 'of getting ground of the Papists' without more churches and chapels, and more resident clergymen.[68]

Essential attitudes remained constant. A century after King's death the Protestant nation looked on the granting of Catholic Emancipation under George IV with the same unease as he had government policy under George I. The fear which spanned that century, and which sustained its intolerant spirit, had roots as much in religious, as in material, exclusiveness. Viewed as beyond the pale of the one Holy Catholic Church reformed, the 'Popish' religion and people merited only derogatory notice. Early Victorian churchmen spoke in the same terms as the early Georgians. Regret at the state's failure both to enforce the laws against 'Popish ecclesiastics', and to support the church in weaning 'the deluded victims of a fond superstition from their blind attachment to a foreign religious dictator', was clearly King's attitude in 1720; but the language is that of Mant in 1840. Mant was comfortable with the sentiments of Georgian churchmen because he shared them so completely. By the same token he was incensed by the 'remarkable' phraseology adopted by government in its bill of 1792 to remove the civil disabilities of 'Romanists' (his marginal gloss). For the customary 'Papists' and 'Popery', he protested, there had been substituted, respectively, 'his Majesty's Roman Catholick subjects' and 'the Roman Catholick religion'. As if that were not injury enough, the Lord Lieutenant had, in his speech at the opening of the 1793 session of parliament, designated 'the sectarists of a foreign church' as 'his Majesty's Catholick subjects'.[69]

*3. Towards the conversion of Ireland?*
If the church sought to convince Presbyterians of the merits of episcopacy, she sought only to convert Roman Catholics. For the former were wrong in the head only, the latter in the heart. Put another way, whereas within the reformed tradition there was a better, episcopal, form of government, as between Rome and the Reformation a great gulf was fixed with respect to the gospel. But if the church was of one accord in seeking the conversion of Catholics, she was divided both as to the means of achieving it, and to what conversion entailed. When churchmen came to put in place a scheme for English Protestant schools – 'wherein the children of the Irish natives might be instructed in the English tongue' – they petitioned the Crown in revealing terms. The schools would attend to 'the converting and civilizing of these

poor deluded people', so as to present them 'good Christians and faithful subjects', rather than abandon them in their native condition of 'superstition, idolatry, and disaffection to your Majesty'. The Incorporated Society in Dublin was duly constituted by letters-patent dated 24 October 1733.[70] Its inception signalled the abandonment (until the 19th century) of the attempts, passionately pursued by some few individuals, but sustained at best half-heartedly by the establishment, to influence the native population through the medium of the Irish language. Bishop Berkeley was to ask in the *Querist* whether there was any instance of a people being converted in a Christian sense other than by preaching to them and instructing them in their own language. That perception had guided the noble spirits who had striven to make the Bible available in Irish – Bedell, Narcissus Marsh, Robert Boyle and others – and this Caroline legacy was taken up both locally and centrally in Anne's reign. In Kilmore diocese the flamboyant Philip Macbrady, vicar of Inishmagrath in county Leitrim, was fluent in Irish and famed both for his wit and his popularity among the native Irish. In Kilmore also the scholarly John Richardson had been rector of Annagh (Belturbet) since 1693. He translated John Lewis's *The Church catechism explain'd*, published sermons in Irish (including one by Archbishop Tillotson and three by Bishop Beveridge, translated respectively by Macbrady and John Mulchroni), and published also a short history of the efforts made for the conversion of 'the Popish Natives of Ireland'.[71] The evidence which he adduced, however, showed how limited these were. Two contemporary clergy stood out as exceptions. Nicholas Brown, rector of Dromore and Rossory in Clogher, and a fluent Irish speaker, was reputedly much loved by Roman Catholics for his humanity and charity, and from 1702 until his death in 1708 held services for them in Irish and instructed them in the Scriptures both in public and private. The other was Walter Atkins, vicar of Middleton and treasurer of Cloyne cathedral. He read the liturgy and preached in Irish with such acceptance among his Roman Catholic parishioners that they turned to him for baptism, marriage, visitation of the sick, and burial. Both men were encouraged by their bishops, Brown by St George Ashe, and Atkins by Charles Crow. In Armagh, Primate Marsh and his clergy raised a subscription to support two Irish missionaries in the diocese, as did their counterparts in Derry. Training in Irish was also provided for TCD students, first privately, at the expense of the vice provost, Dr Hall, and then publicly. In 1715 Archbishop King sent the Rt Hon William Conolly a list of 45 ordinands 'taught to read Irish by Mr Linegar in the College'. Alluding to the less than wholehearted support for this scheme, King claimed that, had it received proper encouragement, one-third of the Irish clergy could within a few years have been fluent in Irish, without expense to the public.[72]

When convocation met during Anne's reign, some attempt was made to extend such local initiatives. Thus in 1703 the Lower House claimed that preaching in the Irish tongue would be 'a great means of the conversion' of Catholics, and referred to the Upper House the questions of the numbers of Irish preachers needed in each diocese, and of the means of their support. Although the bishops pronounced such preaching 'useful where it is practicable', nothing was apparently done. In 1705, William King wrote from England urging Archbishop Vesey to dissuade the bishops from obstructing the proposals of the Lower House for the church's advantage, and in this unpromising situation there was again no apparent progress. In 1709, however, 'the bishops being at present so engaged by their constant attendance in parliament', invited the clergy to take the initiative. The Lower House responded with an ambitious set of proposals: to print the Bible and liturgy in Irish (but in the English character); to prepare an exposition of the catechism suitable for Roman Catholics, in both English and Irish; to second Irish-speaking incumbents, or employ converted Roman Catholic priests, for missionary work in each diocese; and, finally, to apply to parliament for funds, and to the queen for a 'corporation' to receive and disperse charitable contributions 'for promoting the conversion of Papists in this kingdom.' Under this encouragement Richardson went to work on his translation of Lewis's catechism (the bilingual text being published in 1712), and also brought forward his *Proposal for the Conversion of the Popish Natives of Ireland* (Dublin 1711), which recommended the provision of Irish-speaking ministers, the Bible, prayer book, and catechism in Irish, and charity schools. Also in 1711, on the recommendation of Francis Annesley, in terms influenced by Richardson, and in the name of his bishop, Edward Wetenhall, together with some of the nobility, gentry and clergy (unnamed), a memorial was presented to the Lord Lieutenant, the Duke of Ormonde, praying that 'our pure and holy religion' be propagated among the Irish people by 'evangelical and religious means'.

This memorial seems to have represented a compromise between those who favoured Irish and those who favoured English as the medium of such propagation. For the means comprised printing New Testament, prayer book, catechism, and 'select sermons upon the principle points of religion', in the Irish language and character – the only extant set of Irish types having already been bought in Britain; providing charity schools in every parish for the instruction of Irish children in the English tongue and 'the catechism and religion' of the Church of Ireland, 'that the whole nation may in time be made both Protestant and English'; 'suing out' a charter from the queen for an incorporated society to finance and manage these designs; and, in consultation with such bishops as Ormonde saw fit, drawing up and presenting a petition to the queen. Ormonde's response was encouraging. He referred the memorial to the Primate through the lords justices, and when the bishops intimated that it would require the advice of parliament and convocation, procured the queen's licence for the latter to consider it. Under the impetus of this development, and with King's patronage, Richardson was able to influence SPCK in London to print copies of the Bible, prayer book, and catechism in both Irish and English, and to publish his short history of the progress made to date.[73]

But all was not as it seemed. Bishop Lindsay's account of the discussion among the seven prelates who met in the Primate's house in Dublin to consider Ormonde's letter, shows that King was isolated. His colleagues concluded that the Irish types had been purchased at his expense, but were not inclined to follow his lead in general, so that King 'left us in anger, saying that what was proposed should be done whether we would or no'. But the realities determined otherwise. With the Archbishops of Dublin and Tuam involved in council, five bishops carried the adjournment of convocation during the parliamentary recess, so that six weeks were lost. After the recess, the lack of time, the Primate's indisposition, and the delaying tactics of opponents, combined to nullify both the positive support from the Commons and the activating resolutions sent up by the Lower House, including canons for regulating both the charity schools and 'the assistants in the conversion of the Irish'. These resolutions appear not to have been adopted by the Upper House, and with convocation never to meet again, the opportunity had been lost. King realized that, for all his zeal, Richardson would not be able to further a design that had been refused by those 'whose duty it is to do it'. If the bishops of Ireland, he wrote, 'had heartily and unanimously come into this work', then with the countenance of government, and 'due encouragement from the parliament', the conversion of the natives would have been effected, whereas a private man, denied encouragement and subject to open disapprobation, would achieve nothing. (Twenty years later, in recommending Richardson for preferment, Boulter was to refer to the financial losses which he had incurred, and to his having met 'with great opposition, not to say oppression here, instead of either thanks or assistance'.)[74]

It is clear that dissension both as to ends and means worked against the design of converting the native population. Opposition to use of the Irish language was trenchant. Swift himself, although he had both introduced Richardson to Ormonde, and supported him in London, out of his respect for King, was so opposed because their love of Irish prevented the natives from 'being tamed'. Many of the bishops, according to Lindsay, held to the Henrician statute which required the appointment only of English-speaking clergy, and Irish speakers to take an oath to learn English. To King, that

stance represented convenience rather than conscience, for the use of the ver-
nacular was 'the doctrine of our Church', as prescribed by the canons. As
Bishop of Derry, he had provided two Gaelic-speaking ministers for the
Highland Scots who settled in Inishowen, and been gratified by the results,
and he believed that the 'cause of the natives continuing Papists' at the
Reformation lay in the failure to preach, and to provide service, in Irish.[75]
King shared the general Protestant aim of seeing the Irish become 'English',
but his approach was first to win their hearts and minds 'by evangelical and
religious means', through the medium of Irish. That approach carried no logical conviction with his opponents, some of whom could not see that the
making of Protestants had anything to do with 'religion', nor others that the
making of 'English' subjects could be advanced by reliance on the Irish language. Historians are currently reappraising the Irish religious experience after
the Revolution, and in some cases reassessing King's assertions about the attitudes of his contemporaries. But he is still entitled to be heard, not least in
terms of the summary given in his letter to Swift of 28 July 1711, as he awaited
the ill-fated meeting of parliament and convocation:

> We shall, I believe, have some considerations of methods to convert the
> natives; but I do not find that it is desired by all that they should be con-
> verted. There is a party among us that have little sense of religion and
> heartily hate the Church; they would have the natives made Protestants,
> but such as themselves; are deadly afraid they should come into the
> Church, because, say they, this would strengthen the Church too much.
> Others would have them come in, but can't approve of the methods pro-
> posed, which are to preach to them in their own language, and have the
> service in Irish, as our own canons require. So that, between them, I am
> afraid that little will be done.[76]

# PART THREE

# *The Georgian Church, 1730-1822*

Their discourses from the pulpit are generally dry, methodical, and unaffecting; delivered with the most insipid calmness, in so much that should the peaceful preacher lift his head over the cushion, he might discover his audience, instead of being awakened to remorse, actually sleeping over his mechanical and laboured composition.
*– Oliver Goldsmith, Some Remarks on the Modern Manner of Preaching, 1760.*

You ask why don't I preach morality to you? God knows I have been preaching it to you these twenty years, until I have fairly preached it out of the Church, and knew nothing of it either in myself, or in anyone else. It is now time for me to try some other way, and to seek some better hope.
*– Edward Pidgeon, rector of St Mary's Kilkenny, c.1800, after his evangelical conversion.*[1]

## I THE LONG CENTURY

### 1. As others see us

Victorian churchmen had a poor opinion of their Georgian predecessors. Richard Mant saw the latter half of the 18th century as 'a season of supineness and inaction as to religion in these kingdoms: and the Irish clergy in general may be judged to have partaken of this character'. William Alexander, on reading Gibbon's 'degrading record' of Oxford, his *alma mater*, made the withering comment: 'those were the days of a silken prelacy, a slumbering priesthood, a silent laity; of a theology precise in form, but pale, pulseless and pedantic'.[2] Evangelicals, for their part, echoed William King. His late Victorian successor, Lord Plunket, wrote in 1884 of 'the dawning of religious life which ushered in' the 19th century, while the *Christian Examiner* 'rejoiced' that the historian of the Georgian church was an Englishman, in that Mant had adduced

> unanswerable evidence, that English worldly political mismanagement of the Irish Church made her what she was at the end of the century, and by

a just retribution has rendered this country a scourge and a thorn in the side of England. She sought, without regard to religion, to make the Church the means of forming an English interest, and by leaving the Irish without true religion, she effectually defeated her own object, and almost annihilated an English interest in the country.

The reviewer arraigned three successive Primates – Boulter, Hoadly and Stone – as the arch-villains, reserving his severest censure for Hugh Boulter. His regime represented 'the greatest injury that was ever done to the Irish Church', her 'miserable, low state' in 1800 being his legacy.

He was the very description of a man most qualified to do evil in his situation. A man without personal religion; as far as he had any opinions on the subject, heterodox in his views, and deeply steeped in political partisanship, which engrossed the full exercise of his talents.[3]

This harsh judgment of Boulter can be tempered on the evidence, while the Georgian Church at large presents both positive and negative faces. The negative has tended to be a dismissive stereotype, and merits a more trenchant analysis. The positive has, until recently, been ignored in its substantial aspects, the stereotype allowing only for some over-exposed individual exceptions. A balanced appraisal of a misunderstood era is called for.

The 'bad' picture is derived mainly from statistics, and from the denunciations of the 18th century moralists. The official statistics appear stark enough. A report of 1791 gave the number of parishes in Ireland as 2,436, but the number of benefices with cure of souls as only 1,120. Churches in repair numbered 1,001, parsonage houses only 355: Tuam had but 17, Cashel 61, and Dublin 64, the majority – 213 – being in the province of Armagh. The rectorial tithes of 562 parishes, almost a quarter of the total, were reportedly in lay hands.[4] To get these figures into some sort of perspective, however, in 1993 the number of benefices in the Church of Ireland was 484, with 949 churches between them. Only in the provision of clerical residences was the church of 1993 ahead of that of 1791.

The age, again, claimed to preach 'plain, practical morality'; it came close to destroying it. Bishop Berkeley noted in 1738 that morality had collapsed 'to a degree that has never been known in any Christian country', the prognosis being 'terrible', the symptoms worse from day to day. The great evils which threatened a general 'destruction of these realms', he blamed on 'the irreligion and bad example of those styled the better sort'.[5] From William King in 1697 to William Magee in 1796, indeed, there was a consensus among good men that 'the sense of religion was almost lost'. For Magee's analysis of society in the 1790s was as devastating as King's 100, and Berkeley's 60 years before. Born in Enniskillen in 1766 and educated at its

Royal School, the brilliant Magee became a Fellow of TCD in 1788, was ordained in 1790 and appointed professor of mathematics and Senior Fellow in 1800. His great energies were variously applied to theology, university reform, and the renewal of the church, and in an age of great orators, he was a preacher of considerable power. It was significant that the Association for Discountenancing Vice and Promoting the Knowledge and Practice of the Christian Religion (later APCK) had not been founded until 1792. Magee preached its Annual Sermon in 1796. He dwelt on the spirit of an age which had already seen revolution and war in Europe, and was about to see rebellion in Ireland, and hailed this 'age of reason' rather as

> an age which, infected with the vanities of reason, and intoxicated with the pride of philosophy, affects to deride the great truths of Christ's holy religion, and mock at the sublime mysteries of our redemption ... and [in which] the simplicity of God's sacred word is branded with the name of folly.

Applying his sombre analysis to the Irish scene, Magee – echoing Berkeley– concluded that the example of irreligion on the part of its highest names had shot the poison of their vices and crimes through every class, and that the 'fatal lesson' had now returned upon them in that 'those whom they have taught to disrespect their God, have learned to despise their governors'. The decline of Christianity and of morality, and 'the threatened ruin of our country', were in Magee's view evinced in the widespread desertion of churches, disregard of the Sabbath, and ridicule of Christian duties; and in what he discerned as the prevalent hedonism, extravagance, lawlessness and insurrection in the nation.[6]

But historians have perceived the Georgian era in a more favourable light. Despite (or because of) its secular spirit, G. R. Cragg saw it as a 'golden age of philanthropy' for the church, and the late Victorian professor of ecclesiastical history in TCD, G. T. Stokes, as a time when 'bishops and clergy alike strove with quietness to do their duty'. Fine cathedrals were built or restored, fine churches provided for Dublin and Cork, market towns and landed estates. Catechisms were widely used: Richardson's bilingual version printed 13 editions (in London) 1712-1825, Bishop Mann's nine Dublin editions 1769-1800, and editions in Limerick 1773, Newry 1786, and Cork 1798. [7] The Irish church was also attuned to developments in theology and mission; some clergy proved able apologists in the battle against heterodoxy, while others welcomed John Wesley as a partner in mission. Such considerations inform the revisionist view that there was light as well as darkness in the church's experience. It is clear that it varied from diocese to diocese, and from one generation to another. Serious decline late in the century is reflected in the neglect seen in Tuam, with its lapsed church population, and in North

Connor, with its churches in ruins. It was arrested by the combined influences of reforming bishops, evangelical revival, and (after 1800) Westminster's lavish church building programme. Much detailed research has yet to be undertaken, and conclusions now being tentatively drawn can be attested only on the basis of such research. But in order to understand the Georgian church as it was, rather than as perceived by high-minded Victorians, it is useful to set it in the context of its age, and to delineate those factors which influenced it: the national experience, government policy, episcopal preoccupations, theological fashions, and the spirit of the age itself. For a depressing national scene, pursuit of an 'English interest' in the church, a 'pulseless theology', and the supremacy of reason, were debilitating influences, and need to be taken into account in assessing both the church's capacity to fulfil, and her effectiveness in fulfilling, her spiritual mission.

## 2. Church and nation

The traditional picture of 18th century Ireland, after the rebellions, wars, and religious intensities of the 17th century, is one of peace, stability, and religious indifference. But it is now accepted that it blocked out the dark side: the poverty, famine, agrarian unrest, sporadic paramilitary activity, and rising sectarian tension. The period is essentially one of contrasts: between the decline in population during its first half, and the population explosion in the second half; between early poverty and later relative prosperity; between the magnificent lifestyle of the landowners and the subsistence living of the landless; and between the prosperous north-east and the less favoured southern provinces.

Epidemics kept the population of Britain static until 1740, as famine and emigration did that of Ireland; but the easing of these phenomena made for rapid growth in both islands between 1750 and 1800. Thus the population of England and Wales rose from 5½ to 9 million, and that of Ireland from 2 to over 4½ million. The capital cities grew correspondingly: by 1800 London had half a million inhabitants, and Dublin – the second city of the Empire – some 180,000. But pre-industrial England had few large towns, and the major Irish towns were as populous (and as prosperous) as these. The second and third towns of the kingdom, Cork (with 90,000 people by 1750) and Limerick, were supported by an extensive seaborne trade. Commercial expansion and the growing trade with North America also promoted the development of Belfast and Londonderry, while Waterford, too, had a sizeable mercantile fleet. Kilkenny was the most important of the inland towns, Newry of the Ulster towns. Linked by canal from 1741 with Lough Neagh and five Ulster counties, and to the sea from 1761, Newry was the chief supply port of the northern province. But if the emergence of an urban middle class had social and political significance, its affluence was in marked contrast with the grinding poverty of the lower classes during the early part of the century. The prevalent misery aroused the ire of one of Ireland's most spirited public figures. On a journey between Dublin and Dundalk in 1730, Swift noted that travellers were scantily dressed, up to a third of townspeople went barefoot, and houses were badly built and sparsely furnished: 'in short, I saw not one single house, in the best town I travelled through, which had not the manifest appearances of beggary and want'. In the previous year thousands had died during famine, and Swift had given vent to savage indignation in his *Modest Proposal*. Behind the biting irony was his conviction that Ireland's misery was due to London's misgovernment through its Irish administration. Public offices and pensions were given to Englishmen, many of whom were non-resident, the resident Irish gentry were ignored and discouraged, and parliamentary opposition was bought off with titles and places – the party of reform in Swift's day numbered under 30 in an Irish Commons of 300 members.[8]

The second half of the century brought greater prosperity. The decline in smuggling, the demand in industrial Britain for Irish grain and linen, the health of the old woollen industry in the south and of the new cotton manufacture in the north-east, and the revival of brewing, all contributed. Land values (and rents) rose, the population doubled, the peasantry were better fed and clothed, the landed proprietors more magnificently housed. Edward Willes, chief baron of the Exchequer (1757-68), wrote interesting letters as he travelled about on his official duties. He thought the cattle fair at Ballinasloe one of the largest in Europe, and in 1764 noted 'the general spirit of improvement' and the high regard for landowners who reclaimed and drained land, sowed flax or wheat, and planted trees. Willes observed that Ireland was 'very thinly inhabited … except in large trading towns', and opined that she could support three times the population.[9] The marked prosperity of the northern province rested on the linen industry. It extended through all nine counties, though Donegal and Fermanagh were less affected than the others. Its centre was the triangle, Belfast – Armagh – Dungannon; and with its linen-halls, markets – Lurgan had one of the largest – and general commerce, it raised the standard of living of the Ulster people. Organized as a cottage industry, it supplemented the income of the tenant farmers and allowed them to pay the rent of their farms out of the profits of their looms. Some 90 per cent of all linen products reached the English market, no import restrictions being imposed. In this Ulster enjoyed an advantage over the other provinces, as restrictions on their woollen, glass, and silver exports were imposed for protectionist reasons by Westminster.

Ireland's 'Big Houses' are monuments to this national prosperity. William

Conolly, speaker of the Irish Commons, had led the way with the Palladian splendour of Castletown in county Kildare, begun in 1722; but most of the classical Irish mansions are post-1750, as with Castle Coole in Fermanagh, built by 1st Earl of Belmore and designed by James Wyatt. Richard Cassels, of German Huguenot descent, was the leading architect in mid-century, and after him James Gandon (1743-1823), an Englishman who settled in Dublin in 1781. The city's Georgian elegance dates from the end of the century. Gandon designed the King's Inns and Four Courts, enhanced the Parliament House, and in 1791 completed his masterpiece, the Custom House. When, under Romantic influence, the classical style was replaced by Gothic, its early 19th century exponents were Sir Richard Morrison, a pupil of Gandon, and Francis Johnston, a native of Armagh. John Nash, the architect of Buckingham Palace and much of Regency London, also worked extensively in Ireland.

In the political sphere, Swift's ideals of free trade and legislative independence for Ireland were unattainable until in 1778 France sided with the American colonies in their war with Britain. Ireland's opportunity arose from England's difficulty. With a large part of the army withdrawn, the government relied on the landowners to raise Volunteer companies to guard against a French invasion. Once raised, they were (in Henry Grattan's phrase) 'the armed property of the nation', and a potent argument in negotiation with Westminster. The result was that constitutional independence was devolved upon 'Grattan's Parliament' in 1782. That long-desired development, however, coincided with events that were as complex, as dangerous, and as fast-moving as any in Irish history, and was terminated by the Act of Union of 1800. The down side of the population explosion had been pressure on land, and agrarian unrest from the 1760s had spawned secret societies which resorted to direct action. While the social structure of land ownership and the narrow political franchise were typical of Europe at large, the Irish Protestant nation faced other problems also. Some Ulster Presbyterians, shut out of a share in political power that their commercial strength warranted, became more radical in their pursuit of reform. The first society of United Irishmen was founded in Belfast in 1791, and its revolutionary tendency was a new element in a situation made more tense by Britain's involvement in war in Europe from 1793. The Volunteer movement, for its part, had increased the political confusion, with one section of it favouring political rights for Catholics. In the event, and on the eve of war, Pitt forced the Irish parliament into passing the 1793 Relief Act, which restored the right to vote to Catholics – not the last occasion that a reform, passed under duress, would be deemed too little and too late. Meanwhile sectarian strife disfigured county Armagh, whether in spite of, or because of, its densely populated and industrially developed character; and a French force attempted a landing in Cork.

The government resorted to draconian measures in its desperate attempts to stave off insurrection and invasion, but was unable to stop United Irishmen from rising in Antrim and Down, and in Wexford; or to prevent a French expedition from landing in the west – the Gallic version of too little and too late. These events convinced Pitt that Ireland should be brought under direct rule from Westminster, and the Irish parliament was cajoled or bribed into voting for its own demise. The Union of Great Britain and Ireland was symbolized by the addition of the cross of St Patrick to the Union flag of 1707, while Ireland sent 100 MPs and a number of representative peers, including bishops, to Westminster. Article 5 of the Act of Union created the United Church of England and Ireland, and declared it to be a 'fundamental part' of the Union. The Roman Catholic bishops, out of their dread of revolution, welcomed the Union; the Ulster Presbyterians for the most part opposed it. But the expectation that Catholic Emancipation would soon follow was not realized, and attitudes changed. Until 1815, as an integral part of the United Kingdom at war, Ireland duly celebrated a succession of national victories – Trafalgar, the Peninsular War and Waterloo – and honoured the victors with the Nelson Pillar in what was then Sackville Street in Dublin and the Wellington Monument in the Phoenix Park. As at the end of all Britain's wars, the return of peace brought home thousands of Irish soldiers. The normal post-war problems were exacerbated by the distress caused by famine in 1817 – an ominous pointer to disasters ahead.

## 3. 'English interest'

Constitutionally, the bishops of the Established Church were the lords spiritual of the realm, with seats in the House of Lords. This commitment was heavy. The bishops had to be resident in London or (until 1800) Dublin during parliamentary sessions. Dr Proudie, after all, had no sooner reached Barchester than he was on his way back to London in the 1850s; while in the 1990s the bishops of the Church of England devised a rotation scheme for attendance at Westminster. During the 18th century, when communication was difficult, the English and Welsh bishops saw little enough of their vast dioceses; most Irish dioceses were smaller, distances to the capital shorter. Problems were real, excuses ready to hand. There were conscientious bishops: scholars, spiritual leaders, and effective diocesans. There were many who were none of these things. The clerical profession as a whole was overcrowded. With preferment depending on patronage, there was intensive lobbying for bishoprics and benefices alike. Nepotism was normal, and given the gross disparities in clerical incomes, pluralism was common.

Hugh Boulter's pursuit of an 'English interest' in appointments did not exactly endear him to a church in which, at the outset of his primacy, King's influence and Swift's invective were paramount. But while Irish resentment had its xenophobic edge, the antagonism was more complex. During the long Whig supremacy, when most of the Irish clergy were stubbornly Tory, bishops were appointed for their political reliability. Swift's passion to prevent any extension of episcopal control led him to influence the Irish Commons in 1732 to block measures to dissolve unions, require the clergy to build glebe houses, and reform tithe – failure in this last was to cost the clergy dearly a century later. The bishops in any case enjoyed wealth, prestige, and the power of patronage. They were considerable landed proprietors: between them they controlled 5 per cent of all Irish land – as much as Irish Catholics by 1789. They kept townhouses in Dublin. Bishop Rundle of Derry, an Englishman, wrote in 1740:

> At Dublin, I enjoy the most delightful habitation, the finest landscape, and the mildest climate ... I have a house there, rather too elegant and magnificent, in the North an easy diocese, and a large revenue.[10]

Many of his fellow bishops, with more difficult dioceses and more modest incomes, were inclined to solicit an early move. Most dioceses in the south and west were 'climbing sees' for men aspiring to go north or east: not every Englishman wanted to see out his days in Clonfert or Killaloe.

The bishops were one thing, their chaplains and dependents another. The 'misfortune of having bishops perpetually from England', Swift told Lord Carteret in 1725, was discouraging for the Irish clergy in that 'those prelates usually draw after them colonies of sons, nephews, cousins, or old college companions, to whom they bestow the best preferments in their gift,' leaving clergy educated at TCD 'no better prospect than to be curates, or small country vicars, for life'. The viceroys were deemed the worst offenders here. Each brought with him up to three chaplains, and usually appointed the first chaplain to a bishopric and the others to rich benefices. As the tenure of the viceroyalty was short, the process recurred often. Swift told Carteret plainly that he hoped that, having gratified his dependents with a bishopric and the best deanery (Derry) in the kingdom, he would now spare some of his patronage for the Irish clergy, and so encourage those gentry with sons, 'who usually breed one of them to the Church'. He acknowledged, however, that this viceroy had let him name Irish clergy who were esteemed 'for their learning and piety', and not friends of his own. Of the five whom Swift recommended, Dr Patrick Delany – hailed by Boulter as 'one of our most celebrated preachers' – was to be appointed Dean of Down, Francis Corbet to the deanery of St Patrick's, and Edward Synge to the see of Clonfert.[11] The reality was not always as bleak as Irish critics of the regime made out.

Boulter's situation needs to be understood. During the early Hanoverian period the government depended on the votes of the Irish bishops, the dependence easing as more temporal peers were created after 1750. Its interest was therefore to appoint to the episcopate men on whose support it could implicitly rely, and its policy, which predated Boulter's arrival, was to select men of proven loyalty. Boulter implemented this policy with decision. He saw that the safest course was to appoint Englishmen, and not only to the episcopate. Uneasy on reaching Dublin over speculation that the attorney-general was to be made lord chancellor of Ireland, he advised the secretary of state that 'the English here' thought the only way to keep things quiet, 'and make them easy to the ministry, is by filling the great places with natives of England'. He took his own advice over church appointments. His aim was 'to form proper dependencies here, to break the present Dublin faction on the bench', his method 'to get as many Englishmen on the bench here as can decently be sent hither'. But not any Englishman: for an 'imprudent' bishop from England might be 'tempted by Irish flattery' to set himself at the head of the Archbishop of Dublin's party in opposition to him. He was, naturally, anxious about King's successor, urging on the Duke of Newcastle that 'whenever he drops the place be filled with an Englishman'.[12] It was: John Hoadly, appointed to Ferns in 1727, succeeded King in 1730 and Boulter himself in 1742. His brief primacy was followed by that of George Stone (1747-64), who continued to pursue the English interest.

Mant, having studied Boulter's correspondence, raised a polite eyebrow over his making little mention of the religious, moral, theological, and literary merits of his nominees for vacant sees, and of his dwelling mainly on political and secular considerations. Ball commented, more aptly, that in the nature of things the latter were bound to predominate, and that bishops so chosen must inevitably infect their clergy with 'a secularism of ideas and habits': for, unlike his own, it was that sort of age. Failure to take account of moral character could have yet more disastrous results. William Stuart, apprised soon after his arrival in Armagh in 1800 of government's intention to move George Beresford from Clonfert to Kilmore (not every Irishman fancied Clonfert either), exploded with the comment that he was 'reported to be one of the most profligate men in Europe'. The irony in the situation does not detract from the new Primate's blunt warning that 'profligate bishops never fail to produce a profligate clergy. They ordain the refuse of society and give the most important places to the most worthless individuals'. Stuart's anger was reinforced by his estimate of his other five northern bishops (for, despite his protestations, Beresford was translated to Kilmore): 'three are men of tolerable moral character, but are inactive and useless, and two are of acknowledged bad character.' It is perhaps not surprising that the office of confirmation had been given up in most Ulster dioceses, and that the church was collapsing in parts of county Antrim. As late as 1820, in the record of his triennial visitation of his province, Stuart made the cryptic entry: 'Glynn.

Vicar, the Rev John Dobbs, M.A., resides on his parish in the diocese of Derry. No Church; no Glebe; no Manse; no Clerk; no Schoolmaster.'[13]

As for the much maligned Boulter, a just appraisal needs to distinguish the man from the system. Inevitably, he saw little of his diocese – 'Ye Bishop of Drummore' deputized for him at the consecration of Drumbanagher church; and no doubt on other occasions also. But given his range of responsibilities he could no more be resident in Armagh in 1735 than the Secretary of State for Northern Ireland could be permanently resident in Hillsborough in 1995. The latter had duties in cabinet and parliament, and an English constituency to serve, in addition to his department; the former had an English government to serve and an Irish administration to direct, in addition to his diocese. The dismissive attitude of the *Christian Examiner* to Boulter was unjustified. If he ruled with his head, his heart was in the right place. The evangelist George Whitefield recorded in his diary that, having heard of him from a friend in Gibraltar, Boulter welcomed him in Dublin on Dr Delany's introduction, and invited him to dine. He accepted 'and was courteously received by him and his clergy', as he was by Bishop Rundle also. Tyerman in his biography of Whitefield dwelt on facets of Boulter's complex character that are seldom noted.

> He expended £30,000 – an enormous sum in those days – in the augmentation of small livings; erected and endowed hospitals, at Drogheda and Armagh, for the reception of clergymen's widows; supported the sons of many poor divines at the University; contributed greatly to the establishment of the Protestant charter schools; and, during a scarcity of food, in 1740, provided, at his own expense, two meals a day for upwards of two thousand five hundred distressed persons.

The journal might, with more reason, have directed a more trenchant criticism on Primates Hoadly and Stone. The former had in 1728 assisted the incapacitated King with 'the necessary office of confirmation', his metropolitan hoping that he could confirm at Arklow, Dunganstown, Wicklow, Delgany and Bray on his way from Ferns to Dublin. As King's successor, he managed the Lords for the government, built a palace at Tallaght, and improved agriculture 'by his skill, his purse, and his example'. Mant demurred at such claims to fame, and failed to find any benefit to the church from his primacy. Stone's longer primacy belongs to the political history of Ireland, Mant commenting acidly that his epithet, 'the beauty of holiness', had reference only to his handsome physique. In Stone's own words, he 'injured his constitution by sitting up late, and rising early, to do the business of government in Ireland.'[14] His successor, Richard Robinson, represented a different sort of English interest. With no stomach for politics, he brought his disordered diocese under control, built churches and glebe houses – the present church and rectory in Lisnadill parish, for example – and influenced the passing of statutes to the church's material benefit. He also repaired his cathedral and presented it with an organ, built the archiepiscopal palace which sufficed until the 1970s, and spent much of his wealth in improving the town of Armagh. He built houses, planted trees, provided a registry, music room and public library, encouraged the building of a barracks, a county gaol, and an infirmary, and in 1793 (when he was 85) founded and endowed the Armagh Observatory. William Newcome's brief primacy (1795-1800) separated Robinson's 30 years in Armagh from Stuart's 22 years.

As Stuart soon learned, the fundamentals did not change when the interests of the London government required the appointment of Irishmen to vacant sees. The weakness of his position after 1800 was that he had no control over the 'Union engagements' which Castlereagh had made with leading Anglo-Irish families in return for their voting the Irish parliament into extinction. These provided for the promotion of their younger sons to bishoprics as they fell vacant. A younger son himself of the Earl of Bute, the Prime Minister, and previously Bishop of St David's, Stuart had arrived with a reformer's zeal to raise standards in his province, but been obliged to look on helplessly as government honoured its pledges and the results worked through – in 1807 he received his second Beresford when Lord John George was translated to Raphoe. But Stuart's aggressive protests against this blatant erastianism were of belated avail. For with William Knox's translation from Killaloe to Derry in 1803, the standard began perceptibly to be raised. Of the aristocratic Northland family of Tyrone, and a former chaplain to the Irish House of Commons, Knox was a conscientious diocesan and renowned philanthropist. It was Lord John George Beresford who bridged the gap between two eras. Eventually a worthy successor to Stuart in Armagh, he had been an indifferent younger bishop, much given to family business and other secular concerns. 'Discipline has been unknown in this diocese for 20 years,' Magee wrote to Stuart on succeeding him at Raphoe in 1819. While allowing for Magee's prejudice here – 'the production and maintenance of Beresfords,' he said, 'is not the final cause of the Irish Church' – Lord John George seems to have experienced a conversion on the road (through Dublin) to Armagh.[15]

### 4. The age of reason – and revival

The Enlightenment dominated 18th century thought. The spirit of the age was at once secular and sceptical, with rationalism as its intellectual rage and nature as its inspiration. It found God in nature, but only (in Voltaire's phrase) as the prime mover. He had created the universe, and then abdicated in favour of that supremely rational being, man. His very religion was 'natural'. Traditional Christian beliefs were either denied outright, or perverted into one form or other of heterodoxy – 'Deism, Atheism, Pantheism and all manner of isms due to Enlightenment', as a Victorian writer was to put it. The deist heresy suited the mood of the age, for as Kenneth Hylson Smith has it, 'like gnosticism in the early church, deism was a tendency rather than a body of definable belief'.[16] Superstition was out, certainly, and with it witchcraft and magic; but so, too, were miracle, prophecy, and revelation, for the supernatural was totally rejected. Paradoxically, nature was revered as the sphere of remorseless scientific laws. But there was no place for awe and wonder in this reverence, or for mystery in religion. Christian apologetics might rationally combat heresy, and mysticism or piety complement its intellectual rigour. But the human spirit was to rebel against the spiritual austerity of the age both in the Romantic movement and in the evangelical revival. Latitudinarian (or liberal) in outlook, the national churches preached virtue and benevolence, with typical pragmatism stressing the reward motive. In Scotland, the Kirk was dominated by the intellectual fashion known as Moderatism. Its influence made Edinburgh one of the most brilliant cities of Europe, but its experience was as that of moonlight – clear and cold. Burns poured poetic scorn on 'the cauld harangues on practice and on morals' from the pulpit. The established churches failed to warm or thrill, much less convert, men's hearts; or to change their lives. Enthusiasm was anathema, personal experience not advised. The individualism of the Enlightenment made little impact on society. Immorality was rife at its highest levels, drunkenness – induced by cheap gin in England, by whiskey in Ireland – at its lowest. Dublin's Hell Fire Club bespoke the profanity of an age which not only reviled the passions of religion, but rejected its credal confessions as well. In his *Sentiments of a Church of England Man* (1708), Swift had stressed belief in 'God and His providence, together with revealed religion and the divinity of Christ'. It is a fair summary of the essentials which were discarded by many in the churches. Latitudinarianism, for all that it had contested deism, itself veered towards unitarianism. Its Arian and Socinian expressions found much acceptance, especially among Presbyterians. It infiltrated the Moderates in Scotland, while in Ulster, as Dr Thomas Witherow was to put it, 'Arianism was silently laying its cold and clammy hand over the congregations of the province.'[17]

The Church of Ireland boasted several prominent apologists in the war against heresy. While the best known defence of orthodoxy was *The Analogy*, published in 1736 by Bishop Joseph Butler of Durham, Bishop Berkeley's *Alciphron* (1732), a thoroughgoing answer to the popular case against revealed religion, had anticipated Butler. Later, the *Evidences of Christianity* (1794), by a Cambridge man, William Paley, 'provided a powerful defence against the corrosive influence' of Hume, Gibbon and Paine; but it, too, had been anticipated by more than a century by Dean Abbadie's three-volume apology for Christianity, which combated atheism, deism, and Socinianism, and was praised by William Pitt as the best book on the subject that he had read. (Its English translation, entitled *A Sovereign Antidote against Arian Poyson*, had appeared in London in 1719; and again, as *The Deity of Jesus Christ essential to the Christian Religion*, in 1777.) The most telling riposte to early rationalism was, however, provided by the philosopher, David Hume, whose scepticism – like that of Joseph Priestley's *History of Early Opinions concerning Jesus Christ* (1786) – posed a more insidious threat to the Christian faith than had the deists. Hume and Priestley were challenged by two counter-Enlightenment prophets, Bishop Samuel Horsley, who represented the Caroline tradition in the later Georgian church, and George Horne, President of Magdalen College Oxford, who became Bishop of Norwich in 1790. Horne, a disciple of Archbishop Thomas Secker, was a forerunner (he died in 1792) of the conservatism of the war years after 1793, the ideological reaction to all that had epitomized the high Georgian era, and which was best represented by Edmund Burke, 'the foundation of [whose] doctrine is a deep religious reverence'. Horne was also 'much entertained' and inspired by two volumes of Swift's prose published in 1762. He told his friend George Berkeley (a son of Bishop Berkeley) that Swift could have been 'the hammer of infidelity, but was turned aside by those "cursed politics" as he himself styled them'. But Swift had turned aside from politics also. His restraint was rather his perception that to defend the faith with the weapons of reason was ultimately self-defeating, much as William Pitt again found that Butler's *Analogy* raised more doubts in his mind than it answered.[18] In Dublin, Horne's contemporary, William Magee, preached in 1798-9 a series of sermons in TCD chapel in refutation of unitarianism: they were published as *Discourses on the Scriptural Doctrines of Atonement and Sacrifice* (1801).

Earlier, a Fellow of Emmanuel College, Cambridge, William Law, had proved to be an able apologist in his *Case of Reason*, published in reply to Tindal's *Christianity as Old as Creation* (1730), but as uneasy as Swift about over-reliance on reason, he had also responded to the formalism of the Latitudinarian church with his pietistic writings. His *Serious Call to a Devout and Holy Life* (1728) not only influenced John Wesley, but became the handbook of the early Evangelicals. The Irish church had its own William Law in the person of Philip Skelton (1707-87). His ministry was mostly spent in Clogher diocese, first as curate of Monaghan, and then as incumbent of, successively, Templecarne (Pettigo) on the Fermanagh-Donegal border, Devenish on Lough Erne, and Fintona in Tyrone. Skelton was a mystic, a devoted pastor and an able controversialist. As a young man he had published his *Proposal for the Revival of Christianity* (1736) and *Deism Revealed* (1748), and in 1770 he gave the profits from the sale of his collected works to the Magdalen Asylum. A visiting English preacher, Dr Peckwell, wrote that he was a man of great learning and universally liked, and that his system 'very nearly assimilates to that of Mr Law', while Wesley, after spending an hour with him, recorded that he was 'full as extraordinary a man' as Law. The greatest preacher at the turn of the century was Walter Blake Kirwan (1754-1805). Educated in the college of the English Jesuits at St Omer, and intended for the Roman Catholic priesthood, he had become professor of natural and moral philosophy at Louvain in 1777. On joining the Established Church, he first preached in Dublin in 1787 at St Peter's and thereafter in all the leading city pulpits. He was appointed incumbent of St Nicholas Without, and in 1800 Dean of Killala. As an orator, Kirwan was considered to rank next to Henry Grattan. His reputation rested also on his prophetic preaching, for like Magee he preached down the evils of society. Grattan himself said in 1792: 'He came to disturb the repose of the pulpit, and shakes one world with the thunder of another'.[19]

Meanwhile a religious movement which one writer has called 'the revival of the Reformation' had been influencing churches on both sides of the Atlantic. It began with the pietist movement in Germany, affected the Lutheran Church, and caught up the settlement of Moravian refugees on Count Zinzendorf's estates in Saxony. Its influence was felt in Britain from the 1720s and in America from the 1730s. In England it first touched the Independents, and produced leaders in Isaac Watts and Philip Doddridge. It was encouraged by the ubiquitous Moravians, who were instrumental in John Wesley's evangelical conversion in 1738, and advanced by the Methodists, John and Charles Wesley, George Whitefield – all three in Anglican orders – and Selina, Countess of Huntingdon. But the emergence of the Evangelicals, the earliest in Wales and Cornwall, predated the conversions of the Methodist leaders, and despite initial correspondence their movement was essentially distinct from Methodism. North of the Border, revival from 1739 by-passed both seceders and Moderates and targeted the congregations of the evangelical remnant in the Kirk. Whitefield first preached in Scotland in 1741, making an impact both in the highlands and in Edinburgh, while John Wesley visited from 1751 not as evangelist, but as teacher. He founded few Methodist societies, but he strengthened the orthodox faith of the Kirk in face of the Arian and Socinian tendencies of its Moderate majority. Whatever the diffuse origins, concepts of church order, and later organization of the several strands of the revival in Britain, the essentials of evangelical faith were held in common. Its preachers taught the corruption of human nature, the need for repentance, salvation by grace through faith in Christ, and – as the evidence of saving faith – 'a devout and holy life'. It was less easy for a sceptical age to scoff at the supernatural when converts were evident miracles of grace; less easy to ridicule enthusiasm when thousands of men and women met in barns, courthouses, and the open air, to hear the sermons and sing the hymns of the revival. Its epicentre was not an ism, but a Person. 'Had I a thousand tongues, I would employ them all to praise Him', said Peter Böhler, the Moravian leader, to Charles Wesley, thereby inspiring one of the latter's greatest hymns. Those hymns in turn – and those, too, of Watts and Doddridge, of Zinzendorf, and later of the Anglicans, John Newton and William Cowper – were the inspiration of the revival.[20]

Ireland attracted the great evangelists. The first to visit was the Moravian, John Cennick, who preached initially to large numbers in Dublin, and banded his followers in societies. The Moravians stood well with the Church of England – in 1749 parliament recognized them as 'an ancient and episcopal Church', in line with Archbishop Potter's approval in 1737 of their doctrine and order – and on moving north, initially to a hostile reception, Cennick received support from John Ryder, Bishop of Down and Connor (1743-52). He spent five years founding societies and chapels in Ulster. When some clergy complained that their churches were being deserted, Ryder retorted: 'Preach what Cennick preaches; preach Christ crucified, and then the people will have no need to go to Cennick to hear the gospel.'[21] Cennick died in 1755 at the age of 36: his memorial is the Moravian community which he founded at Gracehill. The first visit of 'the prince of preachers' was fortuitous, for in 1738 Whitefield was shipwrecked off county Clare. He was warmly received in Limerick by Bishop Burscough, invited to preach in St Mary's Cathedral, and offered hospitality for as long as he chose to stay. On his electing to go on to Dublin, he was farewelled with an episcopal kiss and blessing. In the capital he preached in St Andrew's and St Werburgh's and (as already noted) dined among church dignitaries. Whitefield returned to Ireland on three preaching tours, his perfunctory role as a visiting celebrity in contrast to his influence in Scotland and America, where his powerful preaching strengthened revivals begun under indigenous leadership. Lady Huntingdon, for her part, developed a surrogate interest in 'poor, wicked Ireland'. For years she had spread the gospel among the English upper classes: in her London drawing room, through her chapels – her aristocratic privilege – in Bath and other resorts of fashion, and by her sponsorship of preachers. Her cousin the Earl of Moira, a resident Ulster landowner, had married her daughter Elizabeth, and her purposes at last embraced Ireland. A former Presbyterian meeting house in Plunket Street became her Dublin chapel, and she provided chapels in Cork and Sligo also, supplying them with preachers. She also bade incumbents with Irish connections go and preach in the

Dublin churches. One who obeyed was Joseph Townsend, rector of Pewsey, whose father represented Lord Shelburne's borough of Calne, another Dr Peckwell, a Lincolnshire rector.[22] Of the Wesley brothers, John's extended ministry in Ireland is considered later. Charles Wesley made only two visits. And yet his influence persists in the church through his hymns: at ordinations ('O Thou who camest from above'), at weddings ('Love Divine all loves excelling'), and on Christmas morning ('Hark! the herald angels sing').

## 5. The Georgian episcopate

The Georgian bishops have suffered from the generalizations that their era is wont to attract. Until a serious study of the Irish episcopate is undertaken, however, they can be defended only with other generalizations. Their antecedents, functions, and reputation were quite different from those of the Victorian bishops, whose backgrounds were usually academic or, less often, pastoral, and who represented a high standard of spiritual leadership, allied to scholarly eminence and administrative ability. The Georgian bishops were, by definition, the lords spiritual of Ireland, with responsibilities and residences in the capital, generally men of culture and liberal education, often specialists of scholarly distinction. If Englishmen, they had usually been chaplains of viceroys or lords justices, and before that either university dons or church dignitaries; if Irishmen, often the younger sons of Anglo-Irish families, or well enough connected otherwise to enjoy patronage and advancement. The best known among them, with but few exceptions, made their mark in fields other than the theological or conventionally episcopal. They excelled in estate management, as men of letters or patrons of the arts, as classicists and linguists, as authors, travellers and collectors. Some of them knew Italy as well as they knew Ireland. While the influence of men raised in the Caroline tradition persisted until the 1740s and ensured the survival until then of its distinctive piety and conscientiousness, and while that of a new generation of episcopal reformers was to be exerted from the late 1790s, it seems clear that during the intervening half century most episcopal appointments were undistinguished in strictly ecclesiastical terms.[23] Primate Stuart, after all, found no bishop in Ulster in 1800 to whom he could refer in terms of unqualified approval. In a sense the impasse lay not so much in characteristics which he deplored (and was given to exaggerate), as in the very different expectations which the new Primate entertained of the episcopal office, and which, to his credit, were to become the norm in the course of the 19th century.

Within the Caroline succession, Archbishop Synge (Tuam 1716-41) worked to increase his churches and cures and to strengthen the allegiance to the church of the appreciable Protestant population in Connemara. In relinquishing the *quarta pars episcopalis* – the bishop's share of parish tithes – he showed, in Mant's opinion, an unusual sense of justice and liberality towards his clergy. He was apt to teach, and published scores of 'small tracts written in a sensible and easy manner'. John Stearne (Clogher 1717-45) was renowned for his hospitality and generosity, for the rigorous examination (in Latin) to which he subjected candidates for orders, and for his treatise on the Visitation of the Sick (an English translation was to be published in 1807). He rebuilt the episcopal residence, as in Dromore earlier, financed the completion of Clogher cathedral, and provided capital to the trustees of the First Fruits to purchase glebes and impropriations for resident incumbents. Vice-Chancellor of Dublin University, he financed both a printing-house and 10 annual exhibitions, and also bequeathed his manuscripts to the college library and his books to Marsh's library and his own clergy. He was, too, a benefactor of the Bluecoat School, and left £50,000 to St Werburgh's. George Berkeley (Cloyne 1735-53), honoured in the history of ideas as a philosopher, and for his *Querist* in which he anticipated the theories of Hume and Adam Smith, was also a visionary, saint, and devoted pastor. He founded a missionary college in Bermuda, but was naïve enough to think that the Prime Minister, Walpole, shared his vision for the evangelization of the new world: he received promises but no support from that cynical statesman, and the project failed. As a bishop he did not seek and would not accept promotion to a richer see. As a resident diocesan (he attended the House of Lords on one occasion only) he lived simply, urged the virtue of good works, and when famine and disease ravaged the diocese in 1740-41, acted as both physician and provider to its suffering people.

Many of the appointments to the episcopal bench in the second half of the century were of men known primarily for their secular achievements. Richard Pococke (Ossory 1756-65: he was translated to Meath three months before he died) epitomized this new genre of bishop. At the age of 21 he had been appointed precentor of Lismore by his uncle, Bishop Milles of Waterford. He was nominated to Ossory when Archdeacon of Dublin, and although he was wont to supervise from as early as 4.00am the workmen engaged in the restoration of St Canice's Cathedral, and established the Lintown factory at Kilkenny to teach the art of weaving to (mostly orphan) boys, he was best known as a traveller. He published descriptions of his tours in Europe (1733-6), the Orient (1737-40), and England, Ireland, and Scotland (where he held the first confirmations since 1660); and was the author also of *Irish Antiquities*. Thomas Percy (Dromore 1782-1811) was a member of Samuel Johnson's Literary Club, and immortalized for his editing the *Reliques of Ancient English Poetry*, which revived Romantic interest in older poetry. Whereas to Dr Johnson he was 'a man out of whose company

I never go without having learned something', to Primate Stuart he was 'inactive and useless' as a diocesan. Mant, however, pointed to Percy's reputation for piety, hospitality, and benevolence, and while this stock vocabulary of the Victorians tends to be applied uncritically, it is clear that Stuart's peremptory dismissal is too harsh, and that Percy both lived in and presided genially over his diocese (the most compact in Ireland). Another who enjoyed Dr Johnson's friendship – as he did that of Goldsmith, Burke, and Sir Joshua Reynolds – was Thomas Barnard, son of Bishop William Barnard of Derry; he was Archdeacon and then Dean of Derry before serving as Bishop of Killaloe (1780-94), and of Limerick until 1806.[24]

Two Ulster bishops achieved, for different reasons, a degree of notoriety. One was the Englishman, Frederick Augustus Hervey, who was Bishop of Derry for 35 years (1768-1803) – he had been Bishop of Cloyne briefly – and Earl of Bristol from 1779. His political opinions were advanced, for he advocated abolition of tithe, reform of parliament, and repeal of the Penal Laws. He was what Ulster people call 'a character', and very popular. He took part in flamboyant style in the Volunteer movement, spent some of his wealth on public works, and encouraged the building of churches in his diocese. But he also squandered a fortune on the palaces which he built at Downhill ('the Bishop's Folly') and Ballyscullion, despite having inherited the family seat of Ickworth in Suffolk, where he built a lavish Rotunda. He exhibited the malicious streak which has surfaced in most generations of his family, and Primate Stuart's exasperated dismissal of him as 'profligate' is elaborated in the comment of his peer, Lord Charlemont, that 'his ambition and his lust alone can get the better of his avarice'. He was seldom clear of either the burden of debt or the whiff of scandal, and – sensibly enough – lived mostly in Italy during his last years. Earlier, Robert Clayton's notoriety had arisen, ironically, from his theological writings. The son of Dr John Clayton, rector of St Michan's, he had been born in Dublin in 1695 and educated at Westminster and TCD, of which he was Fellow from 1714, and Senior Fellow 1724-28. He was successfully Bishop of Killala (1730-5), Cork (1735-45), and Clogher (1745-58). He was as cultured as any, Lord Orrery noting sarcastically in 1742 that Cork was 'not entirely devoid of elegance', as he detailed the works of art that Clayton had procured on the continent, and as benevolent also, for as a member of the Linen Board he secured employment for the poor of his diocese of Clogher. Clayton had become a friend of Dr Samuel Clarke, a prominent English Arian, and was influenced by his thinking. He became a leader in the movement for the abolition of subscription to the church's formularies, and developed this liberal stance in his more radical proposal in the House of Lords that both the Athanasian and Nicene Creeds be expunged from the prayer book. His *Essay on Spirit* (1751) denied the doctrine of the Trinity, and he rashly reiterated his views in the third part of his *Vindication of the Old and New Testament* (1757). In the controversy over the former publication he had been denied the archbishopric of Tuam, and on his publishing the latter, government took action to prosecute him. He was summoned to appear before the bishops at the Primate's house in Dublin. He faced censure, and probable deprivation. Before the hearing could begin, however, he was seized with a nervous fever, and died. [25]

The later Georgian bishops seem to have been preoccupied either with the perilous state of the nation, in the revolutionary unrest exacerbated by the French Revolution, or the parlous condition of the church as the episcopal reformers found it. The harsh realities in the last two decades of the century, particularly in the south-east and the north-west, required bishops of character and courage. They were not wanting. Richard Woodward (Cloyne 1781-94), a native of Gloucestershire, was appointed Dean of Clogher in 1764, holding this dignity first with St Werburgh's and then the rectory of Louth. He was an advocate of state provision for the poor on the English model, and procured a statutory House of Industry for Dublin. Like Hervey, he favoured removal of the Penal Laws. His promotion to the see of Cloyne coincided with the outbreak of Whiteboy agitation against tithes, and in his *The Present State of the Church of Ireland* (1787), which issued nine editions in a few months, he detailed the widespread desecration of churches and intimidation of clergy in Munster and parts of Leinster. A close friend of Skelton, and father-in-law of the Hon Charles Brodrick, Archbishop of Cashel (1801-22), Woodward was revered for his piety and charity, his preaching ('one of the most easy, natural preachers' to Wesley), and his fearlessness in championing the church's interests at a dangerous juncture. John Law, appointed Archdeacon of Carlisle when his father was bishop, was nominated to Clonfert in 1782 at the age of 37, translated to Killala in 1787, and finally to Elphin (1795-1810). He was known as the friend of the apologist, William Paley, for his tolerant approach to Roman Catholicism (so earning a reprimand from Mant), for his courageous leadership during the 1798 rebellion, when he fortified his palace and, by defying the insurgents and rallying the Roscommon gentry, saved the lives and property of many Protestants. Joseph Stock, Bishop of Killala (1798-1810), was engaged in his primary visitation when the French landed in Mayo, became General Humbert's prisoner, and published an impartial record of his experiences in his *Narrative of what passed at Killala in the Summer of 1798*. The son of a Dublin hosier, Stock was a Fellow of TCD, a fine classicist and linguist, an able Hebrew scholar and controversial theologian, and the first biographer of Berkeley. He was translated to Waterford in 1810. Stock had been appointed Master of Enniskillen Royal School in 1795. The stepping stone to a bishopric in his case, Portora had earlier been compensation for the poet, and friend of Swift, William Dunkin, (Headmaster 1746-65), who consoled himself with writing his verse by the Erne.

Meanwhile the episcopal reformers had begun to assert a new authority. They displayed energy, zeal for improvement, an intention to enforce the canons bearing on clerical duty, and intolerance of lax standards. One of them was Power Trench, Stock's predecessor in Waterford (1802-10), and Law's successor in Elphin (1810-19), before he became Archbishop of Tuam in 1819. Another was Thomas O'Beirne (Ossory 1795-8; Meath 1798-1823). He had been educated for the Roman Catholic priesthood at St Omer, chaplain of the fleet under Admiral Howe, and then chaplain to Lord Fitzwilliam who, during his brief period as Viceroy, raised him to the bench (as he did Newcome to the primacy). His successor in Ossory, Hugh Hamilton (1799-1805) was a prodigious scholar. He had become professor of natural philosophy in Dublin at the age of 30, and was Fellow of the Royal Society and member of the Royal Irish Academy. His long tenure as Dean of Armagh (1768-95) had ended with his nomination to the see of Clonfert. Apart from the reforms which he instigated in Ossory in the light of the Visitation Returns of 1799, Hamilton gave his patronage to the Clerical Association founded in 1800 by the young Evangelical clergy of the diocese, some of whom he had appointed. Matthew Young, a Senior Fellow of TCD, also professor of natural philosophy, and renowned as much for his humility and childlike spirit as for his courage in curbing the abuse of executive power in Trinity, succeeded Hamilton in Clonfert. The mortality which had plagued the bench of the 1690s, however, reasserted itself, and Young died of cancer in 1800, in his 50th year.[26]

## II CHURCH LIFE: POSITIVE ASPECTS

The negative characteristics of the Georgian church were real enough, but not the only reality. It was not in the interest of moralist or reformer, Methodist or Evangelical, to highlight the positive side of the church's experience, and it has been undervalued through over-reliance on their testimony. To attempt to redress the balance is to take into account the provision of churches and cathedrals, the pursuit of charity, the pastoral faithfulness of many clergy, the contribution of John Wesley, and the vibrant quality of church life in Cork.

### 1. The diocese of Cork
Cork maintained its distinctive record throughout the Georgian era. Most of its bishops served it well. Just as the episcopates of the three Carolines had

spanned 56 years, so those of the first three Georgian bishops spanned the 53 years from Peter Browne's death in 1735: Robert Clayton (1735-45), Jemmett Browne (1745-72), and Isaac Mann (1772-88). The fluidity at the turn of the century then overtook even Cork, so that it had five bishops during the 18 years from 1789 to 1807. William Bennet (1790-4) was translated to Cloyne after four years, though his successor, the scholarly and hospitable Hon Thomas Stopford, served for more than a decade (1794-1805); but Euseby Cleaver and William Foster (Mann's successors) and Lord John George Beresford (Stopford's successor) managed less than four years between them. Normal service was resumed under Hon Thomas St Lawrence (1807-31), who, like his two immediate predecessors, was the son of an Irish aristocrat, an example of the particular manipulation of episcopal appointments at the time of the Union.

The early Georgian bishops were as exemplary as their predecessors. Clayton's heterodoxy was not made public until after he had left the diocese, and he bade his Cork clergy keep alive the spirit of true faith among the people, urging them to visit all their parishioners, especially Roman Catholics. A man of private means, and liberal in his use of money, he made loans available to the chapter of St Fin Barre's to expedite the rebuilding of the cathedral. Jemmett Browne, a Corcagian himself, was related to Peter Browne, had been ordained by him in 1723, and been resident at Bishop Court or Bishopstown during the latter part of his episcopate. He was appointed to the see of Killaloe in 1743. In Cork he continued the tradition of intimate, caring relationships between bishop, clergy and people. At the confirmation held in St Fin Barre's on Whitsunday 1762, he laid his hands (crossed)

> on the heads of above 200 young persons, and said the prayer and benediction individually over each person. After this ceremony he administered the Communion to everyone of them all, but was assisted in this by his clergy, and the whole was not over until near three o'clock.

When Berkeley left for Oxford shortly before his death, Browne undertook to provide episcopal oversight in Cloyne, and to confirm there as soon as Dr Berkeley – rector of Midleton, the bishop's brother – had fixed the times and places. When some Huguenots settled at Innishannon to rear silkworms about 1760, Browne licensed their pastor Robert Cortez to conduct service in French, preach and administer the sacraments, in the parish church 'or wherever else may be appointed for the congregation to assemble'. Isaac Mann, born in Norwich, was educated at TCD and enjoyed the patronage of Robert Jocelyn, Lord Chancellor of Ireland (1739-56). Chaplain of St Matthew Ringsend, and then a rector in Meath diocese, he was vicar of St Andrew's, Archdeacon of Dublin, and chaplain to the Viceroy, Lord Townshend, on his nomination to the see of Cork. He was widely known for his *Exposition on the Church Catechism*, and also published *The Four Gospels and Acts, with Notes Explanatory and Practical, for the use of Families and Schools*. Until incapacitated by severe illness in his last years, he was a resident diocesan, hospitable, and exemplary in his care of others (he took into his bachelor home his brother's widow and five children). He was also an eminent preacher, gentle in manner, persuasive, and – in Mant's tribute – one who spoke to the heart rather than indulging the fashion of rhetorical declamation. His sermon before the Lord Lieutenant and the House of Lords on 27 February 1778, on the occasion of the general fast ordered when France declared war on the side of the American colonies, was informed by prophetic courage.

> If we have indeed the great end of national reformation and prosperity at heart ... we shall not only deplore the sins of the nation, but shall, everyone for himself, with true contrition of heart, cast off your [sic] own. So shall all our complaints cease that the former days were better than these. So shall we be a people whom the Lord will delight to bless.

Mann's Visitation Book of 1781 detailed the state of the diocese. Its arrangements under him provide a salutary reminder that statistics can be misleading. Drawing on mid-century histories of counties Cork, Waterford, and Kerry, Mant gave the number of churches in repair (and in ruins) thus: Cork and Ross 41 (67); Cloyne, notably, 47 (22); Waterford and Lismore 23 (71); Ardfert and Aghadoe 15 (54). In 1781, however, Bishop Mann recorded that 35 central churches were used for worship in Cork, and every ancient parish, however few its parishioners, came under the care of the clergy who officiated in these: there were 67 clergy in the diocese. (Except for Killaspugmullane and Kilmichael, all 35 churches were still in use in 1919.) The deanery of Kinalea *citia* illustrates this scheme of things. The rectories of Ballyfeard, Polyplecke, Clontead, Kinure, and Tracton were impropriate to Lord Shannon, and the entire rectories of Nohoval and Kilmonoge appropriate to the archdeacon. Only the churches of Tracton and Nohoval were returned as 'in repair', the other four impropriate rectories having been joined to Tracton in 1755. Each church had a parish clerk and two churchwardens, and Nohoval a schoolmaster also, and were jointly served by a curate. (The vicarage of Ballyfeard was held by a non-resident, the church being 'in ruins'.)

Most of the churches in Cork city dated from the building programme initiated by Peter Browne, and sufficed until well into the next century. Except that, in 1763, the corporation applied to parliament for a grant of £5000 to rebuild St Peter's, which stood within the walls of the old city and served its rapidly growing population. The rebuilding was not begun until 1783, however, and was completed in 1788, the year of Mann's death. In 1810 the chapel of the Foundling Hospital, maintained by the Poor Law Commissioners, was consecrated by St Lawrence. Intended primarily for the inmates, it was in practice much used by the parishioners of St Anne's, especially for baptisms and marriages. But even in Cork progress could be lopsided. Edward Willes, when Judge of Assize there, recounted his experience in Holy Trinity, when Jemmett Browne preached. It was not the sermon which he recalled so much as the leaning steeple, for when the western tower had reached a height of 136 feet, its foundation of piles had sunk, with the result that it gave way and was 32 inches out of the perpendicular – 'a terror to everybody that passed along the street'. The parish had taken no action until it was indicted for a nuisance, and had then reduced its height. Willes took up the story.

> At present, the remaining portion of the steeple is fourteen inches out of the perpendicular; and the judges sit in a gallery on Sundays directly under the steeple. I considered myself, while at church, like an officer placed upon a mine, where it was my duty to stay till relieved, and said my prayers more fervently than usual.

It was not until 1810 that 40 feet more had to be taken down, the remainder being removed when the church was renovated after 1824.[27]

### 2. Some Georgian clergy

The backgrounds of the clergy, their selection, training and motivation, and the place of Trinity College and its livings and fellowships in the church's polity await detailed investigation. It is not difficult to identify clergy of scholarly attainment, blameless life, and pastoral zeal; the problem lies in ascertaining how typical they were of their profession. John Wesley came upon resident clergy who were cultured, hospitable and conscientious. He described Dr Hort, rector of Longford, as 'a learned, sensible and pious man, and a pattern for both clergy and laity'. Dr Thomas Leland (1722-85), professor of oratory in Dublin, wrote his *History of Ireland* when he was vicar of Bray. In 1773, the year of its publication, he became vicar of St Ann's Dublin, retaining his TCD fellowship until he went to the college living of Ardstraw (Derry) in 1781. His successor there, Dr Wilson, was host to Wesley, who found him 'uncommonly learned', especially in oriental languages. Wesley's follower, Adam Averell, served his only curacy (1789-91) with the antiquary, Dr Edward Ledwich (1738-1823), vicar of Aghavoe (Ossory) from 1772 to 1797. He lived on friendly terms with his mostly Roman Catholic parishioners, built a limekiln for the tenants of his glebe, and wrote *A Statistical Account of the Parish of Aghaboe* (1796). Saumaurez Dourbourdieu, son of the minister of the Savoy Chapel in London, was minister for 45 years of the French Church in Lisburn, and after it closed, vicar of Glenavy from 1783 until his death (aged 95) in 1812. His son John became rector of Annahilt and author of statistical surveys of Down and Armagh.

If the Synges produced five bishops in three generations, the Digbys formed another clerical dynasty. They supplied the prebendary of Geashill (Kildare) in every generation, Lord Digby having the right of presentation. Essex Digby had gone on to be, successively, vicar of Belfast during the Commonwealth, Dean of Cashel and Bishop of Dromore, and his son Simon to be a bishop – of Limerick, then Elphin – for 40 years. During the Georgian era, Benjamin Digby's 25-year incumbency was followed by that of his nephew, William Digby (1769-1812), who was concurrently Dean of Clonfert. He married two cousins, first Marianne Birthles and then Mary Digby. Mary's sister Elizabeth had eloped with her soldier-lover, Henry Pilot of Portarlington, taught the faith to her black servants in Florida, and on return home became a founder in 1809 of the Irish auxiliary to the Church's Mission to the Jews (CMJ). She recalled that her father, Benjamin Digby, had 'considered his flock his children; and from the Great-house as it was called, relief was ever extended with a liberal hand', for he had been both squire and parson. William Digby, for his part, published *Twenty One Lectures on Divinity* (1787) and *Essays on Religious Education* (1788). His son, also William Digby, became Archdeacon of Elphin.[28] The idyllic picture painted by Mrs Pilot was not, however, universal in Ireland (and in England traditional village life was being eroded by the march of industrialization).

While conscientious clergy living in rural obscurity were legion, information about them is sparse. George Hamilton, the foremost Hebraist of his day, served a brief curacy (unrecorded by Leslie) in Killaloe diocese before he became rector of the Ossory parish of Killermogh in 1809. In a letter written from Portumna on 26 May 1808 to Sophia Kiernan, whom he was soon to marry, he related how he had dined the previous day 'with Mr Peacocke, my fellow curate'. (This was Robert Peacock, Chancellor of Kilfenora c.1764-1809, who lived at Lorrha).

He is an old and infirm Man – has a large family, living at 6 miles from here. We had a good deal of conversation, and indeed I was much affected and delighted with what he said – he told me that now when death was drawing nearer every day, his only comfort was, that he was invited to throw himself as a Sinner on the free mercy of God – to receive Salvation thro' the death and Righteousness of the Eternal Jehovah ... He is a simple minded man, unaquainted from his long seclusion from the world, with the ways of men – and very much what would be drawn as the character of one, who had once made a figure in college, and then retired with his books to an obscure retreat, where he lived forty eight years.

When Hamilton moved to Ossory in 1809, he found among the members of its Clerical Association another unsung hero, Edward Carr. For 30 years from 1772 he had been curate of the Rower at a salary of £40 until, under

Bishop Hamilton, it became £50 in 1799 and £75 in 1800, and he was appointed rector of Kilmacow in 1802. In 1792 his rector, George Lambert, a pluralist who resided at St Peter's Drogheda, wrote that there was no glebe or house in the parish, and added:

> when I got the parish I found a gentleman acting as Curate of a most irreproachable character, having a large family, the chief support of whom depended on his salary as Curate; he has been 23 years Curate of this parish and never a complaint against him; discharges his duty diligently.[29]

While some Irish-born clergy, usually from aristocratic families, were educated at Oxford or Cambridge, most were graduates of TCD. Swift claimed that Trinity students were 'trained with a much greater discipline than either in Oxford or Cambridge'. Chapel worship was part of it, with three daily statutory services. Andrew Sall, a convert to the Church of Ireland, had found in the 1670s 'more practice of sobriety, devotion and piety than I ever saw in a College of so many young men on the Romish side'. This Caroline tradition persisted, John Wesley recording in 1756 that he had never seen such decency in any chapel in Oxford as that at the Holy Communion in Trinity on 3 April: 'scarce any person stirred or coughed or spit from the beginning to the end of the Service'. A new chapel was consecrated on 8 July 1798. The collect for the Communion service in *An Office for Consecration of Churches according to the Use of the Province of Dublin* of 1760 was used. It contained the petition: 'Vouchsafe, we beseech thee, to make thyself spiritually present to us, both now and ever, when the holy Sacrament of thy blessed Body and Blood shall be prepared for us at this thy Table'. At the same period some control was asserted over the training of clergy: a special school was established in TCD for divinity students, and in 1790 the bishops met and resolved not to ordain any candidate without a BA degree and a certificate of attendance at divinity lectures for one academic year of four terms. An arrangement was also made between the College Board and the bishops that an examination be held prior to ordination in the set texts on which students had been prepared by the assistant to the Archbishop King's lecturer in divinity. For his part, Dr Joseph Stopford, the Evangelical who held that lectureship until 1810, gave informal lectures in his chambers on the duties of a clergyman. Later, Dr Richard Graves, Regius professor of divinity from 1814, who admired the training given at Maynooth to Catholic seminarians, instituted a voluntary annual examination for divinity students. There matters stood until reforms were instigated in 1833.[30]

Clergy trained in the divinity school in TCD were to serve the worldwide Anglican Church in the 19th and 20th centuries. But the way was pioneered by the Georgians. During the 55 years 1706-61, 26 Irish clergy served with SPG, all but four in the American colonies. William Smith was the first missionary to the Bahamas. The best known was Charles Inglis (1734 - 1816), the first colonial bishop. But in the 55 years 1766-1821, only 10 Irish clergy were sponsored overseas by SPG, of whom two were a son and nephew of Inglis, while a third became his son-in-law.

The experience of the clerical Inglis family encapsulated much 18th century church history. Charles's great-grandfather had been driven from his preferment in Glasgow in 1690, and given a living in Raphoe by another Scottish exile, Bishop Cairncross. His grandfather and his father Archibald had been Donegal incumbents also at a more settled time, the latter as vicar of Glencolumbkille. Charles taught in Pennsylvania before he was ordained by the Bishop of London in 1759 for the Delaware parish of Dover. Here he was influenced by George Whitefield's preaching, promoted work among the Mohawk Indians, and urged the need for a bishop for the colonies. In 1765 he settled in New York as assistant in Trinity church to Dr Auchmuty, the nephew of Dean Auchmuty of Armagh. Inglis succeeded Auchmuty as rector in 1777, early in the American rebellion, and suffered for his adherence to the loyalist side (he was attainted in 1779 and all his property confiscated). Trinity church was itself destroyed by insurgents. In 1783 Inglis and his family joined the emigration of over 30,000 loyalists to Nova Scotia. Many clergy were among them, and churches were quickly built. But there were no bishops on either side of the border. To meet the need for an American bishop, the Scottish bishops in 1784 consecrated George Seabury as Bishop of Connecticut. Then on 12 August 1787, Charles Inglis was consecrated in Lambeth Palace as Bishop of Nova Scotia. Two months later, in the first Anglican ordination in Canada, he ordained his nephew Archibald Inglis, and appointed him head of his academy at Windsor – in 1790 he laid the foundation stone for both academy and university, the first founded overseas after the loss of the American colonies.

Charles Inglis had jurisdiction over Quebec, Newfoundland and New Brunswick. He travelled extensively through this vast region in the course of his visitations. His son John (who in 1825 became the third Bishop of Nova Scotia) was his commissary in Nova Scotia, and his son-in-law, George Pidgeon from Kilkenny, in New Brunswick. The creation of the diocese of Quebec in 1793 eased Inglis's burden. He worked on until he was 82. A 20th century Archbishop of Quebec, Philip Carrington, hailed Charles Inglis as 'the founder of the Anglican Church in the Maritimes', and paid him this tribute: 'He was a man of learning and integrity and of great courage, an able administrator and a good missionary'.[31]

Meanwhile, Henry Fulton (1765-1840), probably a native of Lisburn, was a convict-priest in New South Wales. He had been vicar of Monsea in Killaloe when he was convicted of 'seditious practices' after the 1798 rebellion, and sentenced to transportation for life. His evangelical commitment to social reform appears to have been misconstrued by the authorities at a time of revolutionary tension. He arrived in Sydney on the *SS Minerva* out of Cork in 1800, his wife and child on board as free settlers. Ann Fulton was the daughter of James Walker, a Killaloe incumbent, and sister of John Walker, Fellow of TCD: her maternal grandfather was Dr Thomas Leland. Fulton was on arrival conditionally (and later, absolutely) pardoned, and able to resume his ministry. He worked for five years on Norfolk Island, then settled at Castlereagh in the Nepean region: he was incumbent of St Peter's Richmond, and founded St Stephen's Penrith. William Knox (now Bishop of Derry), who had ordained him in Killaloe, procured for him in 1811 a Crown chaplaincy and part of the principal chaplain's salary. The Fultons were ideal pioneers. Possessed of heroic strength, they also introduced a strain of Irish gentleness into the harshness of early Australian society.[32]

*3. Churches and cathedrals*

Before parliamentary grants (1777-1822) facilitated first a steady, and from 1808 a spectacular programme of mainly rural church building, new churches were provided by bishops, landowners, and affluent urban communities. Thus the church at Villierstown, county Waterford, was built by the Earl of Grandison for the colony of weavers which he brought there from Ulster, and St Olave's in Waterford town by Bishop Milles in 1733-4; while the mercantile community in Drogheda built St Peter's in 1752. In Down and Connor, 'the gracious church' in Ballycastle was built in 1756 by Colonel Hugh Boyd with stone quarried locally, and St Malachy's Hillsborough, noted for its Gothic revival interior, by Wills, Earl of Hillsborough (later 1st Marquis of Downshire), in 1773. In north-west Ulster, although Derry Cathedral and Clonfeacle church at Benburb – 'the most perfect Planters' church to survive', in Alastair Rowan's phrase – date from the early 17th century, no churches remain from the period 1660-1714. Georgian churches in the region designed in the classical style included St John's Ballymore, which Richard Pococke saw being built during his tour of 1752, Lisbellaw chapel of ease, built in 1764 by the Earl of Rosse, and St Augustine's in Londonderry, with its pedimented front, rebuilt by Bishop Barnard. His successor, the earl-bishop, added a spire to St Columb's Cathedral in 1776, and built several churches in the Gothic revival style, notably at Ballykelly and Banagher. Rowan sees Cappagh church, built at Mountjoy Forest in 1768, with its glorious site and elegant spire, as the finest early example of this style. Most mid-Georgian churches in the north-west, however, were later abandoned, and St Augustine's rebuilt in Victorian Gothic.[33] But in east Ulster, Ballycastle church, St John's Moira, built in 1724, and Knockbreda church, built in

1737 (probably by Richard Cassels), survive in their original style. Elsewhere, Cassels's churches at Sligo and Castlebar, both admired by Pococke, were rebuilt during the 19th century. Much local pride is taken today in Georgian churches which have survived, in some cases enhanced by furniture from those which have not. The church of St Iberius in Wexford was built c.1760 at the height of the classical revival. Its length – about half that of Dublin's Georgian churches – is said to have been restricted by the fact that the Slaney estuary was then much closer. The church was extensively renovated in 1990, when the bow-fronted Communion rails from St George's Dublin were incorporated. In 1784, Philip Homan, rector of the parish of Rathfarnham, laid the foundation stone of a new church on the village green to accommodate his growing congregation. The church was consecrated in 1795, transepts, tower and spire being added in the next century.

Richard Pococke wrote of Belfast town in 1752:

The church seems to be an old tower or castle to which they have built so as to make it a Greek cross, and it is a very mean fabric for such a fashionable place; indeed the congregation is but small, and most of them are of the lower rank, for of the 400 houses there are about sixty families that go to church. The richer people, with a number of others, are of the New Light Presbyterians, the rest of the Old Light and Papists. The New Light are looked on as Arians; and those two Lights have greater aversion to each other than they have to the Church.

The sole church was the corporation church in High Street. Dangerous as well as 'mean', it was taken down in 1774. An Order in Council (10 May 1776) then changed 'the parish church of Belfast, which is Shankill, to the town of Belfast', and a church, dedicated to St Anne, was erected in Donegall Street by the rector, the Earl (later 1st Marquis) of Donegall. St Anne's stood alone until in 1816 St George's chapel of ease was built on the site of the old corporation church. (Until 1860 St George's was the church of the perpetual curacy of Upper Falls).[34] John Bowden, an architect to the Board of First Fruits, began building St George's in 1811. Its striking feature was the magnificent portico from Bishop Hervey's unfinished Ballyscullion House at Bellaghy. Otherwise the new chapel was a plain, galleried hall. But then the appeal of the auditory style did not reside primarily in the ornate.

In the city of Dublin, Roman Catholics overtook Protestants during the 1750s as migration from the southern provinces and a higher fertility rate took effect. The Protestant population also fell from its peak of 75,000 in 1733 to 54,000 in 1798 – or from 67 to 30 per cent of the total – due both to the erosion of the Protestant working class and middle class movement outward to Drumcondra and the southern suburbs of Blackrock, Sandymount and Ranelagh. City churches were nonetheless built in mid-century. John Smith designed the new St Thomas's (1758-62), and St Catherine's (1760-9) in Thomas Street, its granite exterior acclaimed as the finest classical facade in Dublin. Parliamentary grants also enabled new churches to be built for the parishes of St Mark and St John (1766-9). St Werburgh's, the parish church of the Castle, was rebuilt after its destruction by fire, and reopened in 1759. The tower and spire added in 1768 were taken down in 1810 (ostensibly for safety, arguably for security reasons, after Emmet's rebellion in 1803). Then at the turn of the century Francis Johnston completed the new church for St Andrew's, the ancient parish of parliament, and built the fashionable St George's (1802-14) in Hardwicke Place – the parish was created in 1793 – with the most elegant spire in the city: Arthur Wellesley, later Duke of Wellington, and Kitty Pakenham were married there in 1806. Johnston also built the Chapel Royal in Dublin Castle (1807-14). Auditory churches continued to be built until the 1830s. They represented essentially the taking of the liturgy to the people. Their width and their galleries, and their location of choir and organ in a west gallery, ensured that no worshipper was far either from the minister or the 'Communion part', a result enhanced in elliptical (or round) churches, which were variations of the basic style. Two of Francis Johnston's churches were typical. That which he built for Primate Robinson at Ballymakenny, near Rokeby Hall in county Louth, was a good example of a small auditory church, and his rebuilt St Andrew's (it was to be burned down in 1860) of a city 'round church'. While most auditory churches in England had three liturgical centres, those in Dublin had one such centre. St Werburgh's had its three-storeyed pulpit and font in front of the altar; St George's had the altar in front of the pulpit, reading desk and clerk's seat, in a shallow apse with semi-circular rails, and its pews all directed to the main liturgical centre. St Andrew's again had pulpit and reading desk behind the altar, the rails following the lines of its oval plan. Contemporary authorities suggested that these churches were popular because the preacher's voice was not obstructed, while Holy Communion was more audible and the altar visible from every part of the building. Meanwhile a plan was adopted in rural parish churches to bring the people in sight of the altar. The congregation were placed in seats along the north and south walls, as in a cathedral choir or college chapel. Glenealy in county Wicklow, built in 1783, had this arrangement, with canopies over the seats in the back rows. Kilbixy in Westmeath, built in 1798 – 'a charming example of late 18th century Gothic' to Addleshaw and Etchells – had two rows of seats on each side of a central alley some 17 feet wide, while reading desk and pulpit, of equal height, stood on each side of the altar place. This last (unusual) feature makes the point that dismissive assumptions about Georgian ecclesiology are misplaced. George Herbert had prescribed reading desk and pulpit of the same size and height, 'that prayer and preaching' might have 'an equal honour and estimation'.[35]

Cathedrals built during the Georgian era included Cork (1735), Clogher (1745), Waterford (c.1773) with its delicate rococo interior, Cashel (1778) and Achonry (1823). They were usually single room buildings, with the stalls at the west end, the choir and organ in a west gallery, the bishop's throne – often a capacious pew for the episcopal family – in the middle of the north or south side, and the reading desk and pulpit near the altar. As in Spanish cathedrals, therefore, the people were between the chapter and the officiating minister, and not 'strained spectators in the nave'. The new cathedrals were also no larger than good-sized parish churches, and mostly served as such, after the pattern of Killala cathedral (rebuilt c.1670). Its seating arrangements suited the parish congregation, with eight returned stalls at the west end and the bishop's throne set among the people on the south side of the nave. The font stood in the aisle between the throne recess and the altar, the reading desk to the north, and the pulpit to the south, of the altar. In the early Georgian period Mary Granville – better known as Mrs Patrick Delany, the diarist – wrote facetiously after the service at Killala that there were 'no such popish things' as an organ and choir, but a 'good parish minister' and '*bawling* of psalms' in a building 'you would not dream was a cathedral.'[36] Intimacy and congregational participation were evidently the hallmarks of rural cathedral worship. By royal charter of 1662 the parish church of St Thomas in Lisburn had been created 'Christ Church Cathedral of Down and Connor', and during the 1720s a new cathedral was built, with spacious chancel and elegant spire, the seat being removed from the ancient church of Connor. But Down cathedral, although a ruin since the fire of 1538, was regarded by the Dean and Chapter of Down as their *de facto* cathedral, and three Georgian bishops were enthroned, and five deans installed, within the ruined walls. Then between 1790 and 1818, on the initiative of Dean Annesley and Lord Downshire, the medieval choir, with a nave of one bay, was rebuilt. The western bay, or ante-nave, was made to serve as a narthex and baptistry, and was divided from the nave by a pulpitum, or organ loft, with the returned chapter stalls on its eastern face. Meanwhile Dromore Cathedral, which Jeremy Taylor had rebuilt on its ancient site, and beneath the chancel of which he is buried, was repaired in 1808 and a new transept added – Bishop Percy's aisle.

Worship in the Georgian church, whether in cathedral, town church or country parish, had its distinctive features, and deserves to be recalled with respect. John Wesley appreciated the music in Armagh Cathedral in Primate Robinson's time, particularly an anthem sung in a way that 'would not have disgraced any of our English cathedrals'. St Olave's Waterford (1734) might segregate its congregation, the men on the north side, the women on the south; but it also provided 500 free seats for the poor and offered two daily services. Bolton saw it as 'perhaps the most unspoiled church in the whole of Ireland' in 1958, pointing to its handsome altarpiece, richly carved rails, black and white marble paving, and font of black marble in the centre of the western narthex. The church also had an 'exceptionally fine' three-storeyed pulpit, each level with a separate door and accessed by a staircase running up the side. Most 'three-deckers' were well equipped, each level having a seat and a desk wide enough to take a folio BCP and bible, cushions with tassels, an hour-glass for the pulpit, peg for the preacher's gown, and psalm board attached; often a music stand in the clerk's seat. The vicarage pew might be part of the pulpit. Other types of pulpit were movable. But if preaching was prominent in worship, so too was the eucharistic mystery, as the furnishing of many churches testified. 'The communion table is decently railed in; wainscotted about, and ceiled overhead with coloured boards' – so Bishop Nicholson had described a Carlisle church in 1703. The ceiling over the altar in St Mary's Dublin (1697) was painted with gold stars on a blue ground; so, too, that in Ballycastle church. Fine stucco work adorns all three walls of the altar place in St Peter's Drogheda (1752). Sometimes a dove, like the gilt one which projects from the top of the central panel in the reredos at St Werburgh's (refurnished 1759) symbolized – as for James Bonnell in his day – that the Holy Communion was an action done in the power of the Holy Spirit.[37]

## 4. 'One in charity'

Although the era of paternalistic landowners and parochial welfare schemes lay in the future, the Georgian era had its improving landlords, caring clergy, and public-spirited urban laity. Many of them were associated with the Dublin Society, founded in 1731 for the improvement of 'husbandary, manufactures and other useful arts', as with Sir Thomas Molyneux, Dr Samuel Madden, Dr Delany and Richard Pococke. The society provided information to its members, imported new ploughs and other implements, encouraged tree-planting, fish-curing and flax cultivation, and set up a model farm and botanic garden. Corporate activity aside, individuals sought to improve standards. Arthur Young praised enlightened clerical landlords in several localities. Some bishops led by example. Hoadly, whatever his spiritual failings, was a skilled agriculturist who drained bogs and improved husbandry. Berkeley set himself 'to feed the hungry and clothe the naked by promoting an honest industry': he founded a spinning school, and had the Dublin Society supply seeds and implements to the peasantry. Denison Cumberland of Clonfert (and later Kilmore), a governor of the Linen Board, introduced

Detail from a portrait of Bishop Jeremy Taylor (See House, Belfast)

*Bishop Robert Clayton and his wife, Katherine,*
by James Latham
(National Gallery of Ireland)

*Gaspar Caillard, Pastor of Portarlington,*
by James Latham
(Church of Ireland House, Rathmines)

St Ann's Dublin 1720

Holy Trinity Ballycastle 1756

St John's Moira 1724

St Peter's Drogheda 1752

Tullagh 1714-15                    Aberstrewry 1772

TCD Chapel, with W. E. H. Lecky looking on

The Parish Church of St Anne Belfast in 1865 (Built 1776, demolished 1904)

CFA: Mrs C. F. Alexander

James Henthorn Todd
(from a portrait in St Columba's College)

Power Le Poer Trench, the last Archbishop of Tuam

Hugh McNeile, Dean of Ripon (from a portrait in Holy Trinity Ballycastle)

Tom Lefroy, later Lord Chief Justice Thomas Lefroy

Trinity Church 1839, Lower Gardiner Street – now the Labour Exchange

St John's Sandymount 1850

English methods of husbandry among his tenantry: hay was made in stacks, potatoes laid in rows, and cabins provided with chimneys and thatched. An example of provincial benevolence was discovered by Pococke in 1752. He described the north coast town of Ballycastle as 'a strong instance of the assiduity and judgement of one person, Mr Boyd, to whom the place belongs, who holds it as a fee farm under Lord Antrim'. Among his creations Pococke listed a safe harbour of three good quays, an inn, a brewery, a tanyard, places for boiling soap and making candles, and a bleach yard; and also collieries which attracted much attention for their ingenious machinery and various shafts. In all, employment was provided for about 300 people. To the traveller's experienced eye, Boyd's achievement was 'a very uncommon and extraordinary instance, in a practical way, of human understanding and prudence'.

Although during the famine and fever in 1741 Berkeley provided food from his kitchen and acted as a doctor to his suffering people, the Church of Ireland's role during recurring famine awaits detailed research. In 1851 the Census of Ireland Commissioners listed 24 failures of the potato crop, from that of 1728 which provoked 'a great rising of the populace of Cork' (and the anger of Swift), through those of the 'entire failures' of 1739-40 (which had aroused Berkeley's pastoral concern) and the failure of 1770 owing to curl, to the 'general' failure of 1800 and the destruction of half the crop by frost in 1807. It is not, however, until the failures of 1821-2 in Connacht that accessible evidence of the church's involvement in famine relief is available - a story which is taken up later, and continued through the persistent privations of the 1830s to the ultimate catastrophe of the Great Famine itself. As for the cities, Primate Robinson's creative benevolence in Armagh was unique, though the vicar general of Limerick, Deane Hoare, who in 1752 renovated and beautified St Mary's Cathedral, was a noted philanthropist and a founder of the County Hospital. In Cork, a Musical Society was founded in 1744 and the proceeds from its performance given to support a Charitable Infirmary in the parish of St Ann Shandon. By an Act of Parliament of 1754 the house and grounds were vested in clerical and lay trustees, and in 1759 they appointed two salaried physicians, a surgeon, and an apothecary who was also the resident warden – services until then had been given voluntarily. A ward of six beds had expanded to 21 by 1771, and the infirmary also had a large complement of outpatients.[38]

Much of the philanthropy of the period was centred on the capital. Private enterprise provided an impressive range of hospitals in Georgian Dublin, some of which were pioneer institutions in their field. In 1684 the Caroline Royal Hospital at Kilmainham had been opened for military pensioners, and in 1711 a 'madhouse' attached to its infirmary. The Georgians were not slow to follow this lead. In 1718 six surgeons opened a house in

Cook Street for 'the maimed and wounded poor'; in 1728 it became the Charitable Infirmary, and later Jervis Street Hospital. Meanwhile Dr Richard Steevens (who was in deacon's orders), President of the Irish College of Physicians at his death in 1710, had left an ample estate out of which his sister, Grizel, founded the oldest general hospital in the British Isles. Built by Thomas Burgh, it was opened in 1733 as Dr Steevens' Hospital. Others followed: Mercer's Hospital in 1734, the Hospital for Incurables at Donnybrook in 1744, the Meath Hospital in 1753, and both the Rotunda Lying-in Hospital and Swift's Hospital in 1757. The Rotunda, with its uniquely elaborate baroque chapel, was designed by Richard Cassels. Its founder was Dr Bartholomew Mosse. In 1745 he had rented a house in George's Lane for poor lying-in women, and set about raising funds for a maternity hospital: Handel's *Judas Maccabaeus* had its first public performance in the Music Hall in Fishamble Street in this cause. After Mosse's death in 1759, the Rotunda Room was built in 1764, and the capacious Assembly Rooms added in 1787. Swift's Hospital, St Patrick's, was the first psychiatric hospital. The dean had worked on this project in his last years, and on his death in 1745 it was founded with funds which he had left for the purpose. Swift had also been associated with some earlier foundations, as a governor of the Bluecoat School, a trustee from 1734 of Mercer's, and (probably) with Dr Steevens' Hospital.

Another of the capital's noted philanthropists was Lady Arabella Denny, sister of the Earl of Shelburne and widow of Arthur Denny MP, of Tralee. In 1765 she was presented with the freedom of Dublin in recognition of 'her many great charities and constant care of the poor foundling children in the city workhouse'. She also founded the Magdalen Asylum in Leeson Street, which was opened in 1766. With the inmates discreetly screened out of sight, its chapel was one of the fashionable places of worship in Dublin, and unused to the evangelical preaching of Dr Peckwell whom the Countess of Moira had recommended to Lady Arabella. In the ensuing uproar the archbishop was petitioned to put a curb on 'methodism'. The intricate connection of religion and philanthropy is seen in the popular charity sermon; in the legal entitlement which charitable foundations had to their own chapels; and in the way forward which was thus afforded to the Church Evangelicals to establish their own identity and distance themselves from schismatic movements, which by the mid-1780s included both wings of Methodism. So it was that William Smyth, a Dublin merchant, founded the Bethesda Chapel in Dorset Street in 1784 in connection with a female orphanage (and from 1794 with the Lock penitentiary also). A sermon preached in 1794 by its co-chaplain, John Walker FTCD, merits quotation both for its rhetorical indications of 'liberal beneficence' to date and its indictment of complacency.

When have so many charitable institutions been founded? When such ample contributions raised for their support? When – Stop my friends! Yours may be great generosity for men; but to professing Christians it is a reproach. You will tell me of the thousands that are relieved in this populous city – of the asylums opened for the widow and the orphan, for the aged and the diseased. But I will tell you of the thousands, here and in all parts of the kingdom, that are left to pine in sickness and in want, desolate and unnoticed.[39]

Dublin parishes had a record of philanthropy, as the alms-houses for widows at the Coombe entrance to St Luke's testified, or the 'St Bride's Widows' Alms House', as it was described in a tablet over the entry from Great Ship Street. St Bride's alms-house had been founded in Bull Alley in 1683, in succession to an older widows' house in Bride Street, and in 1786 moved to the building (on the site of the ancient church of St Michael-le-Pole) in which in 1706 Dr John Jones had founded his famous Latin school: Henry Grattan was educated there. St Catherine's parish at the turn of the century had two notable philanthropists. One was its rector, James Whitelaw (1749-1813), the celebrated statistician. Presented by the Earl of Meath first to St James's, then to St Catherine's, Whitelaw did much for the poor of the Liberties. The Meath charitable loan which he formed in 1808 supported the weavers of the Combe during times of distress. He also procured £2000 from the trustees of the Erasmus Smith fund for a free school for the Combe. Whitelaw took a census of the city in 1798 (it was published in 1805), and was also co-author, with John Warburton, of *History of the City of Dublin* (1818), a work completed by Robert Walsh after their deaths. The good rector had died of fever contracted when visiting the poor of St Catherine's. Its other noted philanthropist was Arthur Guinness (1768-1855), second son and business successor of Arthur Guinness who founded the brewery at St James's Gate. The second Arthur was prominent in public life for half a century, president of the Dublin Chamber of Commerce, and involved in a plethora of civic and charitable causes, among them the Farming Society of Ireland, the Dublin Society and the Meath Hospital. His charity began at home, for he was the major provider of the prolific Guinness family – his elder brother, Dr Hosea Guinness, rector of St Werburgh's, had 13 children – whether impecunious nephews, black sheep, clergy in penury (as in the 1830s), or his five unmarried daughters. Guinness linked church and chapel, for although a lifelong parishioner of St Catherine's (where in 1786 he co-founded the Sunday school, the second oldest in Ireland), he was also an accustomed worshipper at the Bethesda, committed to its charities, and involved in the rescue operation mounted in 1805 when John Walker seceded from the church but tried to remain chaplain of the Dorset (as the Lock penitentiary was known).[40]

Guinness moved in a circle of Dublin philanthropists which, centred on the Bethesda, embraced Trinity College and the professional and business communities. It included his brother Benjamin – they had married two daughters of the Lee family of Merrion – the apothecary, George Kiernan of Blackhall, whose family founded, and whose daughters ran, the Retreat for the Industrious Poor at Drumcondra, Josiah Smyly, surgeon to the Meath Hospital and vice-president of the Royal College of Surgeons of Ireland, and Dr Robert Perceval (1756-1839), the most illustrious of them all. The first professor of chemistry in Dublin University, Perceval was a founder of the Royal Irish Academy, of which he became the secretary. He was physician-general to the Forces from 1819, and associated professionally with the Hospital for Incurables. He was a trustee, too, of the property left by Sir Patrick Dun, and the opening in 1808 of the hospital named for its bene-factor was largely his achievement, in the teeth of opposition. With H. J. Monck-Mason, librarian of the King's Inns, he was also a founder of the Prison Discipline Society, which merged later with the Howard Society. Like Surgeon Smyly, Perceval gave all fees earned on Sunday to charity. On his death, Dr R. J. Graves said to the Medico-Chirurgical Society of Dublin:

> It would be but feeble praise to say he was charitable; he was munificent … We may rest assured that no honorary distinction, no title conferred even by Royalty itself, no literary or scientific diploma, granted to our col-leagues by foreign institutions, ever dignified the profession so much, or raised its members so high in public estimation, as the unostentatious and Christian benevolence of Dr Perceval.

But all members of the Church of Ireland had regular opportunity for unob-trusive charitable giving. The weekly collection for the poor, sustained throughout the long century, was a custom peculiar to Ireland. It was taken up at Sunday services before the sermon, usually while a metrical psalm was being sung, and also at weekday celebrations of Holy Communion. This 'col-lection' was thus distinct from the offertory (or rubrical collection) taken up after the sermon. Jeremy Taylor in 1661, and Dr Delany in 1745, both com-mended the custom. In 1824 Bishop Jebb told the House of Lords that 'in all our churches, on the first day of the week, after the manner of primitive times, a collection is made for the relief of the poor': it was, he added, gen-erally applied 'in aid of the Roman Catholic poor'.[41]

## 5. John Wesley and the Church of Ireland

Between 1747 and 1789 John Wesley made 21 visits to an Ireland where few dissenters 'knew anything of the power of religion; and in the Established Church there was hardly anything but the form of religion remaining'. Mant, in quoting Dr Coke, did not dissent from his conclusion. Wesley himself confirmed it. He found a spiritual famine, and noted the hunger of the people for the word of life:

> They want only to hear it; and they will hear me, high and low, rich and poor. What a mystery of Providence is this! In England they may hear, but will not. In Ireland they fain would hear, but cannot.

Wesley's protean gifts were used in the three kingdoms as local situations warranted. In England he was an educator and social reformer, in Scotland a mentor, in Ireland an evangelist. He wrote to Charles Wesley : 'Your business as well as mine is to save souls. When we took priest's orders, we undertook to it make it our *one business*'.[42] So driven, the man who rose daily at 4 o'clock, rode annually 6,000 miles and 'preach'd, or someways taught, a thousand times a year', spent six years in aggregate in Ireland. He attended church on Sundays wherever he was, commenting positively on the sermon and commending ministerial zeal whenever he might, and preaching himself when invited. In the early years he preached for, among others, Jacques Ingram in Limerick, two rectors in Mayo, Horn of Westport and Ellison of Castlebar, and Richard Lloyd of Rathcormack in county Cork. As in England, he also preached as opportunity arose: in courthouses and market squares; in the Custom House at Kilkenny, a Seceder chapel in Armagh, and an orchard at Derryanvil near Portadown; and because he was received by 'high' as well as low, in the hall at Newport of Sir Charles Bingham MP (later Earl of Lucan), under a tree in the demesne of the Tighes of Rosanna, and in the parsonage house at Killyman of Hon Charles Caulfield, a scion of the house of Charlemont. On his penultimate visit in 1787, when he was in his 85th year and still – in Archbishop Secker's words – 'labouring to bring all the world to solid, inward, vital religion', he preached to a large crowd at Downpatrick, rode on to Rathfriland – the Presbyterian minister, Barber, 'offering me his new spacious preaching-house' – and thence to Tandragee where, as before, he was the guest of the rector, Dr Leslie. Here he preached 'from the step at Mr Godley's door' to a crowd which he estimated to be larger by a third than that at Downpatrick: 'I scarce remember to have seen a larger, unless in London, Yorkshire or Cornwall'. County Armagh in the late Georgian period could evidently hold its own with the heartlands of English Methodism.

Wesley never wasted an opportunity, failed in a courtesy, or missed a nuance in the course of his Irish travels. His first day set the pattern. He arrived at St George's Quay in Dublin on Sunday, 9 August 1747, to hear church bells ringing, found their source, attended morning service at St Mary's and preached there in the evening. His journal offers shrewd comment on Irish social and religious life. It was no wonder that Roman Catholics remained such, he wrote, when Protestants could find 'no better ways to convert them than Penal Laws and Acts of Parliament'. Finding dirty and ragged children in the charter school at Ballinrobe, but no sign of their master, he reported the situation to the Dublin Commissioners. His congregations inspired cryptic comment. His first, in St Mary's, was 'as gay and senseless a congregation as ever I saw', that in Ballymoney years later 'very civil, but very dull'. Dublin irreverence shocked him. He was 'much grieved at St Peter's church at such a sight as I never saw in England – communicants, as well as others, behaving in a manner that shocked common sense as well as religion'. Even in St Patrick's – Swift had died in 1745 – he found 'carelessness and indecency', but could only approve of Francis Corbet's initiative when, in 1775, 'the good old dean desired me to come within the rails, and assist him at the Lord's Supper'. He was at home among the landed proprietors: he stayed in Lord Moira's residence near Dublin, conversed with Lord Monteagle after service at Castlebar, and was protected from a mob by Sir John Alcock in Waterford. They, in turn, responded to him over many years. In 1756 in county Meath 'two coaches full of gentry' came to hear him in church, and when he preached to the Palatines in 1789 'all the neighbouring gentry' were present.[43]

Wesley ministered regularly among the Palatines. The Rathkeale vestry books, extant from 1741, show that they were the main support of that parish. In mid-century they spread into Tipperary and North Kerry, and within county Limerick to the locality of Kilfinnane, when the Rt Hon Silver Oliver settled 66 families on his estate. Its core was the village of Clonodfoy and the 1000-acre demesne of Castle Oliver. The Palatines maintained their German language and customs for over a century, and travellers commended their industry and habits – Arthur Young in 1776, and the French royalist, De Latocnaye, in 1796-7. But Wesley saw the most of them. He visited their settlements on 13 occasions – he had learned to speak German among the Moravians and had translated many of their hymns. Methodism was first taken to America by families from Ballingarane whom Wesley had influenced, and particularly by Philip Embury and Barbara Heck. Wesley loved to be among 'the plain, artless, serious Palatines', and on his visit to Kilfinnane in 1778 recorded that in the neighbourhood there was 'a considerable revival of the work of God'.[44]

Within the church Wesley attracted hostility and indifference as well as support. The early Georgian bishops disapproved of his irregularity. On his waiting on Archbishop Cobbe of Dublin in his new mansion at Newbridge during his first visit, they conversed for several hours, 'in which I answered an abundance of objections' – he did not specify these. Bishop Berkeley directed Richard Lloyd to confine his pulpit to preachers licensed in Cloyne (or in Cork), and although Lloyd protested that Wesley had preached before the University of Oxford, the order stood. Bishop Maule in Meath disapproved of the preaching invitations extended to Wesley by one of his clergy, Moore Booker. Although Booker did not identify with the Methodists, he yet valued their influence, and protested publicly: 'how these poor, simple, honest Christians have rendered themselves so formidable, is what I cannot account for … my church, or at least its Communion table, owes almost nine in ten of its company to their labours'. (Booker was later lost at sea with the Earl of Drogheda whom he had accompanied overseas as chaplain.) James Creighton, curate of Swanlinbar, did identify with Methodism, and itinerated in south-west Ulster. At the Bishop of Kilmore's visitation he was advised that, although his doctrine was in harmony with the church's teaching, his 'preaching out of his parish' was not approved. His dilemma was resolved when Wesley invited him to join him, and in 1783 he resigned his curacy to become a resident minister at the City Road chapel in London. John Abraham, curate of the chapel of ease in Londonderry, also resigned and became a Methodist itinerant. But the traffic was two-way. One of Wesley's Dublin preachers, John Haughton, was ordained, and became rector of Kilrea in Derry diocese. Wesley was his guest in 1778, but preached in the Presbyterian meeting house as the church was 'a heap of ruins'. Two successive Bishops of Derry associated with Wesley. William Barnard, Dean of Rochester before his appointment to Derry in 1747, ordained Thomas Maxfield in 1762 to be an associate evangelist with Wesley: 'Sir, I ordain you to assist that good man that he may not work himself to death.' Four years later Wesley spent some hours in conversation with the bishop in Bristol. (Barnard was also friendly with Lady Huntingdon, and attended her chapel in Bath.) In 1773, Wesley recorded that five Derry clergy had attended his service every evening, and wrote of 'the friendship of the clergy, joined with the goodwill of the bishop and the dean'. Hervey was now bishop. Two years later Wesley was invited to dine with him, and wrote approvingly of his hospitality, the 'admirable solemnity' with which he celebrated Holy Communion, and his 'judicious' sermon on the blasphemy of the Holy Ghost. The two Derry bishops apart, however, Wesley seems to have been ignored by the Irish episcopate. He was accorded nothing like the support he received from such later Georgian bishops in England as Lowth of London, Ross of Exeter, and Hallifax of Gloucester.

Although Wesley had boasted, 'I live and die a member of the Church of England', and counselled his societies never to separate from her communion, within 30 years of his death, in 1818, Irish Methodists seceded from the Church of Ireland: except, that is, for the Irish Primitive Wesleyan Methodists who, led by Adam Averell, separated instead from the Irish Conference and maintained their formal allegiance to the church until after disestablishment. Wesley had foreseen this schism. His directions, banning chapel services during 'Church hours', and barring his lay preachers from celebrating the Lord's Supper, were increasingly ignored. As early as 1760 the preachers had administered the sacrament in his absence, at Omagh in 1773 he had warned 'against this madness that is spreading among you – leaving the Church', and at the Dublin Conference in 1778 had again urged: 'it is our duty not to leave the Church wherein God has blessed us, and does bless us still'. The problem was that not all Methodists enjoyed such blessing. In England the point was brought home to him, poignantly, in the parish of Epworth. He accepted that he could not compel his people to attend a church where, as he said, the incumbent was 'not a pious man, but rather an enemy to piety, who frequently preaches against the truth'. Generally he was both unable to prevent absence from church services, and unwilling to insist on attendance, for 'the case of Epworth is the case of every church where the minister neither loves nor preaches the gospel'.[45] But there was more to it than that. For there was in the dynamic of the Wesleyan movement, in its very organization and tradition, that which made for completeness, and so weakened attachment to the Church. Wesley's rhetoric might postpone, but could not prevent, separation: his very genius for organization had made it inevitable. The point was understood by his Irish friend, Alexander Knox:

> How was he so competent to form a religious polity so compact, and permanent? I can only express my firm conviction that he was totally incapable of *preconceiving* such a scheme … That he had an uncommon acuteness in fitting expedients to conjunctives, is most certain: this, in fact, was his great talent.[46]

In the end, and in his consuming passion for evangelism, organization took him over. To Charles Wesley's dismay, and in disregard of Lord Mansfield's dictum, 'ordination is separation', he held his first ordinations in 1784. His Deed of Declaration, drawn up in the same year, gave Methodism a legal status as an independent corporate body (James Creighton being listed among his Hundred Preachers); and in 1787 he licensed his chapels under the Toleration Act. The consequences of his actions were delayed in Ireland, but could not be avoided. The twin pillars of the Methodist Church, a superb organization and a separate order of ministry, were in place when Wesley died in 1791.

But although, despite himself, Wesley ultimately launched a new denomination, he left a fuller legacy. Methodism was the catalyst of change. David Hempton and Myrtle Hill instance 'the stimulus it gave to a much wider evangelicalism', in point of its itinerant preaching, voluntary religious societies, and more flexible forms and structures.[47] But Wesley's inheritance is richer still. Before even Law's *Serious Call*, he had been steeped in the piety

of the Caroline divines, and first (from 1725) in Taylor's *Holy Living* and
*Holy Dying*. He represented to the Irish church of his day a spirituality which
she had almost quenched. It was for that reason, not least, that he won the
devotion of Alexander Knox. Mystic, theologian, public servant – he was secretary to Castlereagh before the Union – correspondent of John Jebb, and
forerunner with him of the Tractarians, Knox was also attracted by Wesley's
mind: 'he would have been an enthusiast if he could ... [but] there was a
firmness to his intellectual texture that would not bend to illusion'. Wesley's
biographer Henry Rack sees him as 'an empiricist disciple of Locke', as one
who combined radical religious values with a High Church piety, and who
strove to concentrate on the agreed truths of Christianity while tolerating differences on secondary matters. But he was not an ecumenist in the modern
sense. His anti-Catholicism was as strong as that of any Irish Protestant. John
Wolffe suggests that Wesley was as much a product of the Enlightenment –
which, in England as in Germany, 'throve within piety' – rather than a rebel
against it; and that his anti-Catholic animus may have been reinforced by
'Enlightened' thought.[48] Be that as it may, Wesley remains a man for all generations – and for all traditions – in the Church of Ireland: a scholar and
saint, who blended evangelical assurance with catholic piety and reformed
doctrine. General Synod's resolution of 1991 was, with good reason, passed
unanimously:

> In this decade of evangelism, the Church of Ireland places on record, in
> thanksgiving to Almighty God, her historical indebtedness to the service,
> preaching ministry, and influence of the Reverend John Wesley, priest and
> evangelist, who died on 2 March 1791.

## III DECLINE AND RECOVERY

### 1. 'Drove entirely out of the kingdom'

That the church experienced a serious decline in the late 18th century is well
attested. Among identifiable factors are the lack of material resources, indifference on the part of landowning lay-rectors, absence of effective episcopal
oversight, and clerical negligence. Another was insurrection. In Bishop
Woodward's account of Whiteboy militance in the south, the church's property was violated, and clergy and witnesses intimidated. During the 1798
rebellion, clergy were murdered, the bishop's palace at Ferns attacked,
churches desecrated or even destroyed – at Gorey, Enniscorthy, Blessington,
Hollywood and Fonstown. Although from 1777 a grant of £5000 was voted
annually by parliament for building churches and glebe houses, only a hand-
ful could be provided from this modest resource, and more churches fell into
ruin than were built. Again, pluralism persisted, even if notorious cases were

rare, and non-cures became more prevalent. Both Newcome and O'Beirne inveighed against this last abuse in 1795, the Primate at his primary visitation of the province of Ulster, O'Beirne in his primary charge to the Ossory clergy. As the non-cures were normally without glebe and parsonage house also, non-residence was the obvious response of clergy standing, as O'Beirne put it, 'on the mere privilege of an accommodating conscience', and ignoring every other consideration. The Primate pointed to the 'double inconvenience' for parishioners thus deprived of both minister and church, the bishop to their being left 'to pick up "the word by the wayside"; to beg even for baptism for their children from some charitable hand, often from ministers of another faith'. As O'Beirne saw it, indeed, the spiritual destitution of these parishes, and the inadequate ministrations offered in others, were the causes 'not only of persons not being added to the church, but of others falling away from and deserting her communion'. The Primate recommended that, as a temporary expedient, 'some other place may perhaps be obtained for the publick worship of a few pious parishioners'.[49] Ironically, when the rector of Killermogh, Edward Price, found such a place in Tentower, Adam Averell's home situated in his parish, O'Beirne forbade him to hold service there on the ground that he was establishing a conventicle, but he did permit him to hold service in the glebe house which he procured in the parish some time later.[50]

Another drawback was that many resident clergy were inclined to take their social opportunities, and in some cases their secular responsibilities, more seriously than their professional duties. On his translation to Meath in 1798, O'Beirne criticized in his primary charge those clergy who were 'mere men of the world', and whose passport into society was that they had 'nothing of the clergyman about them'. The laity could not respect such men or look to them for spiritual guidance, he suggested, and might even 'look on the revenue set apart for our support as a robbery on the public'.[51] Four years later a northern curate, Benjamin Mathias, spoke in similar vein to the new Dromore Clerical Society. In his sermon, 'The Watchman', he alluded to clergy whose hours were spent in 'the routine of the drawing room or assembly, at the receptions of the great, in political studies and parties, at the hunt or the racecourse', or devoted to the business of their farms or the pursuit of philosophy and *belles lettres*. Such clergy might be polite gentlemen, good jockeys and farmers, deep philosophers or elegant poets, he opined, but could not be watchmen.[52]

The bishops had only themselves to blame. They connived at irregularities: men were often ordained below the canonical age of 23, at the wrong seasons, and without letters dimissory. Even the well-ordered diocese of Cork was not immune. Bishop William Bennet was enthroned *in absentia* in 1790, after applying to his predecessor 'to name some respectable clergyman of my Diocese who will not think it too much trouble to be my proxy on the occasion'. Bennet held ordinations in Dublin, and ordained Power Trench there both as deacon (at the age of 21) and priest, but not for service in Cork, for within a week of his ordination to the priesthood Trench was on 30 June 1792 inducted into the union of Creagh, a benefice in the diocese of Clonfert. The third son of William Power Keating Trench, MP for county Galway from 1760, who was to be raised to the peerage in 1797 and created Earl of Clancarty in 1803, Trench had both the family seat of Garbally and the fair town of Ballinasloe in his union. In 1793 he was presented to the union of Rawdenstown in Meath diocese, and obtained a faculty to hold it with Creagh, where he continued to reside, acting as his father's business agent and serving as a captain of yeomanry, in addition to his clerical duties. An accomplished horseman, he was an early riser and a man of disciplined habit, with great stamina and a capacity for hard work, but the point is not so much his conscientious record as a priest as his very involvement in occupations which lesser men used to excuse their pastoral negligence. In 1802, at the age of 32, Trench was nominated to the see of Waterford by the Earl of Hardwicke, and was consecrated by the Archbishop of Tuam and the Bishops of Clonfert and Kilmore in Tuam Cathedral. His biographer would deem the nomination a divine appointment, and the circumstances of the consecration 'a very remarkable arrangement of Providence', given that he was to be the last Archbishop of Tuam, but this pious gloss does not disguise the reality that the one was in fulfilment of a 'Union engagement' to his family, and the other (albeit under licence of his metropolitan in Cashel) as unorthodox as his ordination had been 10 years earlier.[53]

There is much evidence, too, that the Established Church gave ground to Roman Catholicism around the turn of the century. Not only were there many more Roman Catholic priests, but they were untrammelled by responsibilies arising from Ascendancy roles, as with the militia, the magistracy, or the management of family estates. O'Beirne, in his second charge in Ossory of 1796, addressed the questions of 'the pertinacious prevalency' of the Roman Catholic religion, and of how amidst so many impediments it had maintained its influence over the great bulk of the Irish people. He had no doubt as to the answer.

> Their clergy are indefatigable. Their labours are unremitting. They live in a constant familiar intercourse with all who are subject to their pastoral inspection. They visit them from house to house. Their only care, their sole employment, is to attend to the administration of their sacraments, and to their multiplied observances and rites. They watch and surround the beds of the sick.

They reproved and exhorted with patience and doctrine ('such as it is') O'Beirne went on, quoting Archbishop Secker: 'they are wise in their generation, and if we hope to be a match for them, we must imitate them'. O'Beirne (himself a convert from Rome) called on his clergy to emulate the Roman Catholic priests in the faithful discharge of pastoral duty, and so secure 'the respect, the love, the attachment, and the confidence of our flocks'. Such exhortation was widely needed. When Archbishop Brodrick made his triennial visitation of Waterford diocese during the vacancy of 1802, he noted at Lismore the non-residence of clergy, the paucity of glebe houses, the neglected condition of churches, the perfunctory nature of much public worship, and the failure to catechize children. The attitude of the clergy was crucial. When Brodrick enquired of one incumbent, in whose parish there was both church and glebe house, the cause of the diminution of Protestants, he received the petulant reply 'that they had all *evaporated* in the rebellion.' His indignant retort was that 'there was not a Protestant from the Monevullagh mountains to the sea'.[54] Generally, then, the church's experience was a long way from the ideal postulated by John Wesley in 1771: 'if the parish ministers were zealous for God, the Protestants in Ireland would soon outnumber the Papists.'

Roman Catholicism had made notable progress in Connacht. Adam Averell observed in 1795 that while population and industry in Galway had increased during the previous 20 years, Protestantism was in retreat due both to the zeal of the 'popish clergy' and to 'that vile sloth' which characterized those of the Established Church. Dr Thomas Grace, on becoming incumbent of Aughaval (Westport) in 1799, found the 'scanty and scattered' Protestants of his extensive, mountainous union at risk of being drawn into the Roman Catholic Church, which he saw as both zealous and artful in its proselytizing schemes. Albert Blest, the Sligo based agent of the London Hibernian Society, recalled that in his youth in the province many Protestant families had been obliged to have recourse to the Roman Catholic priests for want of their own clergy. This fact was confirmed by James Daly, the Warden of Galway, when he first toured Connemara in 1813. As he was to recall almost 50 years later, he found that only English was spoken, and that the poor, who talked candidly to him, had 'lapsed for want of a minister of their own church to baptize their children, to marry their daughters, and to bury their dead'. Once they had got into the habit of applying to the Roman Catholic priest out of Christian necessity, he noted, 'the rest followed as a matter of course'. Daly contrasted the situation in 1813 with that obtaining half a century earlier, when records showed that half the population of Connemara had belonged to the Established Church. (But the decline had begun even earlier: Boulter, early in his primacy, had instanced among those

'gone off to popery' the descendants of 'many of Cromwell's officers and soldiers'.) In 1803 the members of the new Ossory Clerical Association identified a dozen reasons for the growth of Roman Catholicism. These can be
grouped under several heads. The first was ignorance: the want of education
among the lower classes, of knowledge among the masters and ushers of the
charter schools, and of knowledge of the Bible in general. The second was the
proselytizing zeal of Roman Catholics, and their intermarriage with
Protestants. The third cause was neglect: on the part of absentee landlords; of
the clergy, whose failure to visit and catechize their people was exacerbated
by non-residence and lack of churches; and of the pulpit, which preached
justification by works 'instead of the doctrine of scripture' – justification by
faith.[55]

That Ulster was not immune from the failings which beset the church in
the other provinces is also on record. The diocese of Connor boasted one of
the most notorious pluralists in Ireland. This was George Macartney, who
had begun, reasonably enough, as vicar of Glynn (1771-3), a non-cure in the
patronage of the Donegall family. From 1773, however, he was both vicar of
Antrim, with Muckamore (until his death in 1824), and also of Templepatrick
(until 1813). He added the vicarage of Duneane union (1791-1804) and the
rectory of Skerry and Rathcavan (1799-1824), and for a time recovered the
vicarage of Glynn. For good measure he acquired also the rectory of
O'Mullud and Kilsely in Killaloe diocese (1805-24). Macartney was also a
magistrate of county Antrim for 57 years, and with members of his family
was active in suppressing the 1798 rebellion there. A graphic picture of
neglect in North Connor was drawn in 1789 for the local landowner, Lord
Macartney, then in London, by his agent in Coleraine, Richard Jackson. He
reported that the vicarial tithes were not paid in Loughguile parish, so that
even if there were a parish minister at Lissanoure, he would receive no subsistence from the parish. He went on to say that the church was on the brink
of ruin, the timbers and roof rotten, the windows and seats broken, the
building too dangerous to enter, and service out of the question. He added
that the school houses in the district were 'all kept by Papists'. Most interesting of all are the general conclusions which Jackson drew from this local situation:

> It is really scandalous for the government to suffer these matters to go to
> such a length – for no individual can put them to rights – and if the bish-
> ops do not unite to form some effectual plan the ensuing session for
> securing the property and support of the Church, the established religion
> will in a few years be drove entirely out of this part of the kingdom. There
> is a large handsome mass house now roofing near Lissanoure and will be
> soon fit to receive a great congregation. Many of the Church people of the

parish now go to that worship – the remainder to Kilraughts and Clough Meeting Houses. And all the children are baptized by the priest for there is no other minister to do it. I am sorry to send you this state of your church but you are not single: it is the state of almost all the vicarages in the diocese of Connor.[56]

The Established Church, in summary, was in grave danger. Roman Catholics, for their part, were not impervious to the moral advantage which they enjoyed, nor unaware of their opportunity. In a revealing speech to the Catholic Board in 1813, Dr Dromgoole gave from their perspective an encouraging analysis of the church's condition. She was, he said, at war both within and without. For her 'articles of association' were widely despised by men who pretended to be governed by them, while 'Socinians and men of strange faith' were amongst those in command. From without, she was attacked by, among others, the Methodists, 'a sort of Cossack infantry ... who, possessing themselves of the fields and hedges, are carrying on a desultory but destructive warfare against her'. Meanwhile – and here the speaker reached his point – the columns of Catholicity were collecting, who 'challenged the possession of the Ark'.[57] The battle for the survival of the church establishment might be fought out in the political arena, but its initial impact came from the religious theatre. The paradox of the 19th century was that the church lost the political battle only after she had regained the commanding heights of spiritual and moral authority.

## 2. The reforming church

Overshadowed by the ensuing high profile period (1822-38), the first two decades under the Union receive less attention than they warrant. For they saw marked progress, arising both from the new constitutional situation and from influences coincidentally at work within the church. The government committed large resources to church building and education, and the episcopate, released from obligation to sit in the House of Lords – only one of the four archbishops and three of the 18 bishops attended Westminster each session – provided more effective leadership. More constantly resident in their dioceses, able to lead by example and with more time for enforcement, the bishops were also equipped with an Act of 1808 (48 Geo. III c.66) which required incumbents to reside in their benefices for nine months of the year. Standards of clerical residence were thus improved, albeit slowly; for, as Bowen points out, ecclesiastical law was so complex and the machinery for reform so inadequate, that it was rather 'a new evangelical spirit' among clergy and laity, than establishment pressure, which inspired 'the kind of reformation that was needed'. And yet most reforming bishops were suspicious of, or even hostile to, the early Evangelicals. The irony here is that both sought the reformation of the church, while the Evangelical clergy, by their preaching, pastoral diligence, and holiness of life, realized the very ideals that the episcopal reformers advocated. The resolution of this potentially destructive conflict is considered later.

Again, there was a post-Union bonus for the Irish church in the form of a substantial church building programme. Among the Beresford papers is a memorandum of c.1829, probably by Dr Edward Stopford, summarizing the building record of the First Fruits Commissioners before and after the Union. From 1777 until 1800 they had been able to draw on the annual parliamentary grant of £5000 for building or rebuilding churches in parishes where service had not been held for 20 years, and this grant was continued by the British parliament until 1807. The typical grant was £600, and small grants were also made for building glebe houses. By these means 102 churches were built wholly by gift between 1787 and 1805, while another 41 received gifts of £100 towards their building costs. Churches were also sometimes built by parish cesses, but as Bishop William Knox found, on being translated to Derry from Killaloe in 1804, northern parishes, although reportedly better, were actually worse off, in that Presbyterians (unlike Roman Catholics) had voting rights on vestries and could therefore block expenditure on church building where they were in a majority (as in North Antrim). The value of the parish, Knox pointed out, lay not in its size, but in the glebe: in other words, its capital was tied up in land. In this situation a substantial injection of state funds was vital if the church was to move forward at a time

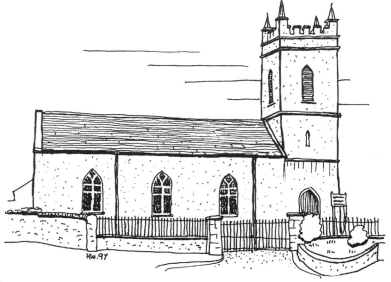

*Foxford, Co Mayo: This is a typical simple barn and tower 'First Fruits gothic' style church as found in many rural parishes throughout Ireland*

of rapid population growth. That injection was given. Stopford's summary shows that in the years 1808-16, £50,000 was provided in one, and £60,000 in each of the other eight years – a total of over £500,000 within a decade – with a further £30,000 in each of the years 1817-21, and a final allocation of £10,000 in both 1822 and 1823. (No grants were made in 1824-6.) Moreover, new legislation enabled the Commissioners to provide loans to incumbents with incomes over £400 per annum, and gifts from £100 to £450 to those under that figure. Loans were to be repaid initially at six per cent, and then at four per cent. The results achieved through this largesse were dramatic. In the period 1808-29, 633 churches and 550 glebe houses were built by gift, while 193 glebes were procured. The churches were mostly the simple tower-and-hall structures so familiar in the Irish countryside, their architecture the facetious 'First Fruits Gothic'. Stopford calculated, however, that a further 236 churches were needed, as many glebe houses again (he put it at 545), and 396 glebes, involving an estimated outlay of £1,034,200. But the Commissioners' funds were now exhausted, except for the estimated £20,000 per annum due from loan repayments.[58] If the church had still some distance to go, however, clearly it had come a long way under Westminster's munificent policy.

On the part of the episcopal reformers, progress could normally be made only by taking on the vested interests of both the clergy and their patrons among the landed proprietors. In the case of the diocese of Clogher, Brynn has shown that successive bishops reduced non-residence 'by the painfully slow process of suits of court, direct pressure, and exhortation', so that clerical residence improved from 50 to 80 per cent over a period of 30 years. Sometimes, however, otherwise conscientious lay patrons were ill-advised (or unlucky) in their choice of incumbents. Thus when the Marquis of Ely presented Thomas Brooke Clarke to the parish of Inishmacsaint, and he was instituted on 1 July 1797, as early as 6 August Ely met with refusal when he demanded that Clarke either reside in the parish himself, or raise the salary of his two curates. Bishop Porter (1797-1819) also failed to move him, and the problem of an absentee rector was not resolved until Hugh Hamilton, the youngest son of Bishop Hamilton and an Evangelical, was presented to Inishmacsaint in 1824. Porter, a Cumbrian, and former Regius professor of Hebrew at Cambridge, failed again, in rather different circumstances, when he supported his archdeacon, John Brinkley, in his bid of 1810 to restore the wealthy parish of Clones to the corps of his dignity. He instituted Brinkley on the day that the Hon Richard Roper died, after an incumbency of 56 years, only to be issued with a *Quare Impedit*, when Sir Thomas Lennard claimed his right as patron. The presentation was awarded to Sir Thomas after a trial at Bar, and in 1812 he presented Henry Roper, Dean of

Clonmacnoise, the eldest son of the previous incumbent. As Henry Roper lived to be 86, the incumbencies of father and son spanned over 90 years, while Henry's eldest son, William Lennard Roper, became rector of Monaghan. It helped if the bishop came from an aristocratic background, and was prepared to take on his own in the church's interest, as with Lord Ely's son, Lord Robert Ponsonby Tottenham (Loftus), who was translated from Killaloe to Clogher in 1822, after the brief episcopates of Lord John George Beresford and Hon Percy Jocelyn (who was deposed by a commission of bishops for his criminal sexual behaviour, soon after his translation from Ferns). Dismissed by Primate Stuart in 1800 as 'utterly unacquainted with his profession', Tottenham well understood his peers. He strove to restore church property in the more remote parishes, demanding that landowners renting church land adjacent to their estates resume payment of fines and increase rents due to the diocese. His exacting payment from defaulting members of his own family helped to ensure his success. He also made plans to rebuild the church in the village of Garrison, persuading reluctant landowners to co-operate and bringing one recalcitrant to the attention of both Irish administration and parliament. A new chapel of ease at Garrison, within the extensive parish of Devenish, was duly consecrated in 1827. In this Tottenham had better success than a Georgian (and English) predecessor, John Garnett, who in 1769 had had to abandon plans for a church at Garrison for want of landlord compliance, despite his procuring £100 from First Fruits and donating the same amount himself.

The extent to which the burgeoning Evangelical revival at once dovetailed with episcopal reforming activity and depended on aristocratic networking and patronage, is also seen in Clogher. In 1807 Bishop Tottenham had married Hon Alicia Maude, daughter of 1st Viscount Harwarden of county Tipperary, whose family had identified with the revival. Soon after Tottenham's translation to Clogher, two of his wife's brothers became members of the chapter – they had previously been incumbents in Killaloe under Tottenham. In 1825 Hon (John) Charles Maude, educated at Christ Church, Oxford, was presented by TCD to the precentorship, of which the corps was the rectory of Enniskillen. Next year his elder brother, Hon Robert Maude, educated at Trinity College, Cambridge, was presented by the Crown to the deanery. Also in 1826, John A. Russell, a graduate of TCD and, like the Maude brothers, an Evangelical, became archdeacon, the presentation having fallen to the Crown with Brinkley's promotion to the see of Cloyne. Dean Maude was 42, his brother and Archdeacon Russell both in their early 30s: all three served until the 1860s. The longest serving Evangelical in the chapter, however, was William Atthill, whom Bishop Porter had appointed prebendary of Donacavey (Fintona) in 1798 at the age of 24. A former Fellow of Caius, and a nephew of the bishop's wife, Atthill also remained in post until shortly before his death in 1847. William Lennard Roper (who was to die of cholera in 1849) was a leading Evangelical in the south of the diocese. The ranks of these eminent Evangelicals in Clogher might have been swollen in 1819 when, on Dr Burrowes's presentation to the deanery of Cork, the future Bishop of Winchester, Charles Sumner, was offered the Mastership of Enniskillen School on the recommendation of Charles Grant, the chief secretary. Sumner consulted widely among family and friends – he was advised that the post carried 'a clear salary of £1800' as against the £500 he could at best command in England – but in the end turned down the Viceroy's offer of Portora.[59]

By contrast with Clogher (and Armagh, to be considered later), neither social standing nor academic distinction could protect early Evangelical clergy in Dublin from episcopal hostility. In 1794 Archbishop Fowler inhibited three young clergy within weeks of their becoming trustees of the Bethesda foundation. Two of them, Henry Maturin and John Walker, were Fellows of TCD, while the third, Thomas Kelly, was the son of Chief Baron Kelly and the friend of Edmund Burke. Fowler had already denied patronage to both Walter Kirwan and Walter Shirley Jr, the son-in-law of Sir Edward Newenham, MP for Dublin County (1776-97). Later, Archbishop Brodrick of Cashel, who from 1809 acted in Dublin for the insane Euseby Cleaver, also opposed the Evangelicals. On the eve of the arrival in 1814 of the CMS deputation from London, a meeting of the Dublin clergy was convened by the archdeacon on his behalf, and a resolution hostile to the Society prevented only because one of the most respected clergy in the city spoke in defence of CMS: William Bushe, rector of St George's, a nephew of Henry Grattan and brother-in-law of Bishop Beresford of Kilmore, whom he attended as chaplain. Bushe's evangelical conversion was very recent and, given his active and fearless leadership, was one of the most important in a decade marked by such conversions. Brodrick had a powerful ally in Rt Hon Patrick Duigenan, chancellor of Dublin and vicar general of Armagh and several other dioceses, and MP after 1800 of Armagh city. But the Evangelicals had allies also. On Duigenan's arrival at Westminster some years earlier, the Prime Minister, Spencer Perceval, himself an Evangelical, sent for him and bade him desist from his attempts to debar Evangelical clergy from the Dublin pulpits. The first city incumbency acquired by an Evangelical in the ordinary way was that of St James, when in 1821 Hon Edward Wingfield – himself a convert when rector of the Ferns parish of Myshal – was presented by his uncle, the Earl of Meath. In a neglected parish with an almost deserted church, he established schools and built up a crowded congregation. His early death (he was 33) in 1825 deprived Dublin, 'in the prime of life and in the very meridian of his usefulness, of one of the brightest luminaries of our National Church.'[60] His brother, Hon William Wingfield – Thomas Kelly's son-in-law – succeeded him briefly in St James's before embarking on his long incumbency in Abbeyleix. The two parishes apart, however, Evangelical clergy in Dublin were restricted to the chapels of charitable institutions. By 1815, as well as Bethesda, they had acquired those of the Magdalen and the new Molyneux Asylum for the blind (which George Bernard Shaw was to attend in childhood).

The course of one episcopal reformer can be traced in some detail. Power Trench responded with characteristic energy to the neglect which Brodrick's visitation of Waterford and Lismore had highlighted, travelling his dioceses on horseback and supervising the implementation of the reforms which he instigated. He directed that parish registers of births, marriages and burials be maintained (this legal requirement had not been observed); that a poor collection-book, with the name of the preacher each Sunday, be kept; that children be catechized weekly; and that rural deans be appointed and report to the registrar's office prior to the annual visitation of the diocese. He revived the funds for the repair of churches and the support of clergy widows, and the economy fund for the maintenance of Lismore Cathedral. In Waterford, he re-roofed 'The Widows' Apartments', a residence for the widows of poor clergy, rescued the House of Industry, an asylum for reduced tradesmen and citizens, from abuses and inefficient management, resited – and in effect refounded – Bishop Foy's School, and renovated the episcopal residence. He was a frequent applicant to the Board of First Fruits for aid for churches and glebe houses. He joined forces with John Palliser, the proprietor who gave the land, to provide in 1809 a church at Kilrossinty, at the foot of the Monevullagh mountains. (His biographer noted in 1842 that it had a resident incumbent and sizeable congregation.) He enforced the lapsed order which required local incumbents to preach in Waterford Cathedral on holydays. Not least, he declined to ordain his brother, Hon Charles Le Poer Trench, on the ground that he was unsuited to the clerical profession. Trench received with equanimity the congratulations of his archdeacon, George Fleury (who in 1802 had been in post for half a century) on his recovery from 'scarlet fever', an allusion to his early fondness for military company; and with some panache a three-day visit in 1809 from the Viceroy, the Duke of Richmond. Promoted next year by Richmond to the see of Elphin, his style in a remote and poor district brought benefit to the entire community. He built a private schoolhouse in Elphin, and secured a new gaol for Roscommon, on one occasion procuring the admission of a Roman Catholic priest to a parish which had tried to resist his appointment, and on another, leading in person a detachment of Enniskillen Dragoons against rioting

Whiteboys. As the only dispensaries for supplying medicines to the poor were that attached to the Roscommon infirmary and one provided by Lord Lorton in Boyle, the bishop built a dispensary in Elphin at his own expense, provided it with medicine, engaged a medical practitioner, Dr Feeney, at £100 per annum, and through him ascertained and supplied the material needs of the poor (though he sometimes unobtrusively found out for himself). When Dr Feeney died of fever, he procured a pension for his widow. During the distress caused by famine and disease in 1817-18, Trench supplied the poor of the town with fuel, blankets, clothing and food. Dr Dillon of Elphin, a Roman Catholic, recalled him as 'a kind, tender-hearted, humane man', who in his philanthropic efforts 'made no distinction of sect or party'.

A vice-patron of the Hibernian Bible Society, in 1812 Trench convened a meeting in Elphin Cathedral and, supported by Viscount Lorton, formed a diocesan branch. It opened depositories for the sale of bibles and testaments in Elphin, Boyle, Strokestown, Roscommon, Sligo and Ahascragh. Trench thought well of Evangelicals in his dioceses. In Waterford, John Quarry, curate of Tallow, was one of three clergy whom he praised by name at his primary visitation, while in Elphin he applauded the self-denying charity of his archdeacon, William Digby, and found in Lord Lorton a tower of strength. He was convinced, however, that the doctrines of the Evangelicals were erroneous, and preached against them at his visitation in 1816, alluding to both Digby and Charles Seymour, curate of Ardcarne, as wrong-headed. The sequel to that sermon (to be noticed later) was to have far-reaching consequences.[61]

### 3. The diocese of Armagh

Although the 'epidemic fever by which this city was most awfully visited' in 1817 claimed the life of Thomas Carpendale, Headmaster of Armagh Royal School (1786-1817), generally the experience of county Armagh, the most densely populated in Ireland, was very different from that of poverty-stricken Roscommon. The Church of Ireland's healthy condition in the post-Union period reflected at once the solidity of the Protestant population, the achievements of both Primate Robinson and committed clergy and landowners, and early Evangelical influence. In 1804, when Sir Charles Coote completed his statistical survey of Armagh, 15 of the 17 parishes wholly within the county were in the primatial diocese, and two – Seagoe and Shankill (Lurgan) – in Dromore. Four others branched into the county: two from Tyrone, Clonfeacle (a College living) and Killyman; and two from Down, Magheralin and Newry. The 17 were wealthy parishes. Only four were under £400 in value, most were between £450 and £900, and the four wealthiest above £1100: Armagh parish was worth £1400. All except Shankill had glebes, ranging from extensive (Mullabrack had some 1200 acres) to small, and all – except Shankill again and Killeavy – had parsonages, some rather older (Derrynoose was 'old but neat') and some recently built, as with Loughgilly in 1782 and Kilmore in 1793. The county boasted almost 30 churches, for in addition to 16 parish churches (Killeavy alone was without) there were 11 perpetual cures with chapels of ease. The parish of Armagh, which was united with the deanery, had four of these: Ballymoyer, Eglish, Grange and Lisnadill. All were endowed with small glebes and parsonages, and had resident curates. While most of the incumbents were also resident in 1804, there were some exceptions. In the two parishes without parsonages, Waring of Shankill resided on his estate in county Down, and McCleland of Killeavy in the precentor's residence in Armagh city – it had, by Special Act of Council, been placed in the parish of Killeavy, so that McCleland was technically resident. Two other incumbents had posts with residences in Armagh, in consequence of Primate Robinson's initiatives. For in 1785 he had appointed Dr William Lodge, rector of Kilmore and chancellor of Armagh, as the first Keeper of the Public Library of Armagh, and in 1790 Dr James Hamilton, prebendary of Mullabrack, as the first Astronomer of Armagh: both resided occasionally in their parishes in summer. Of the remaining non-residents in 1804, Close of Keady lived at Elm Park in Armagh, an estate which his father had inherited from his grandmother, Lady Maxwell, while his curate resided in Keady parsonage, and William Bisset, prebendary of Loughgall, was reported as normally resident in his other parish, Clonmore in county Louth, where at Primate Robinson's expense a glebe house had been provided in 1782 and a church in 1795. If Coote is correct the situation is bizarre, for in 1767 Clonmore had been returned as having only three Protestant families (or 21 souls), while Loughgall had then 464 families, a new church in 1795, and (according to Leslie) no curates during Bisset's incumbency. Primate Stuart, for his part, identified closely with the ongoing progress in the diocese. When a new parish church was built in 1811 for Loughgilly, he presented it with silver plate, as he did a silver chalice to the new Kilmore church in 1814. In 1811 he built St Mark's church in Armagh. Consecrated in 1814, it was the fifth chapel of ease in Armagh parish.

Progress in the diocese was due to the evident co-operation of clergy and laity, and their success in attracting central or specialist funding. In Tartaraghan parish, where the church of 1713 was in ruins, a new church was built in 1816 with a loan of £800 from the Board of First Fruits, while in Ballymore (Tandragee) parish, where the church was rebuilt in 1812 and a tower added at a total cost of £2200, Lady Mandeville gave £700 and the Board the balance. When Acton (Poyntzpass) had been formed in 1789 as a perpetual cure out of Ballymore, 21 acres were given by A.T. Stewart of Acton, and the sums of £390 and £150, for church and glebe house respectively, by the Board. Dr Leslie, the rector of Ballymore (1757-1803), so often host to John Wesley, was instrumental in procuring these several gifts. The Board of First Fruits had also financed the new church (1782) and glebe house (1806) at Newtownhamilton, the parish having been formed out of Creggan by an Order in Privy Council of 1773, with 50 acres of glebe set aside from that parish, and had again financed the new church for Kilcluney (between Keady and Markethill), when it was formed as a perpetual cure out of the parish of Mullabrack in 1792. In the case of Middletown, where another such cure was formed out of Tynan parish, also in 1792, the Stearne trustees provided funds for church, glebe and schoolhouse, and additionally £20 per annum towards the master's salary. At Grange, where a church was built by Primate Robinson in 1773 and a glebe house provided in 1781, the site was given by Sir Capel Molyneux and the building funds raised by parochial assessment. Earlier, Mullavilly 'New Church' had been built c.1737 on the estate of Lord Fane, who gave the ground, at the sole expense of the rector of Kilmore, Dr John Brandreth. 'He loved our Nation, and hath built us a Synagogue', his parishioners recorded, for Brandreth had come to Ireland as chaplain to the Duke of Dorset. Finally, a glebe house was built on land provided in 1812 by Jerome, Count de Salis. Some of the Armagh parishes, as with Ballymoyer, had charter schools, that in Creggan dating from 1737, when it had been endowed with three acres of land, one each by the rector, Dr Hamill, and two of his parishioners.

The Armagh clergy were nothing if not well connected, were pluralists almost to a man, and were at risk of being promoted. Dr Henry Leslie, the son and grandson of clergy, was one of the few exceptions. Thomas Carter, who succeeded him in Ballymore in 1803 (and whose incumbency also lasted for 46 years) was more typical. He had come to Ireland as private chaplain to Primate Stuart, and from 1813 was also Dean of Tuam (without cure of souls). His predecessor as dean, Richard Bourne, had been at the same time rector of Kildress, and resigned the deanery only on succeeding Dr Lodge as chancellor of Armagh. Similarly, Samuel Close resigned his benefice in Meath diocese – he had held it with the rectory of Keady – only on being appointed prebendary of Tynan. One of his predecessors in that dignity, Thomas Quin, held it with the treasurership of Limerick (1791-1808), and another, John Leslie – of the celebrated Glasslough family – with the deanery of Cork (1808-12). Leslie was consecrated Bishop of Dromore in 1812, and translated to Elphin in 1819. Dr James Hamilton, during his years as prebendary of Mullabrack and astronomer of Armagh (1790-1815), also held the archdeaconry of Ross (1790-1804) and the deanery of Cloyne (1804-15). Again, the rector of Killeavy and precentor (1802-34), John Cleland, was also chancellor of Lismore (1796-1834). His predecessor as chancellor, Hon James Hewitt, rector of Derryloran (Cookstown) in Armagh diocese (1776-96), was also rector of a second county Tyrone parish – Dromore, in the diocese of Clogher (1777-1826) – and did not resign it until he had been Dean of Armagh for 30 years. William Bisset, who (as already noted) held the rectory of Clonmore with the prebend of Loughgall, added to these in 1804 the archdeaconry of Ross, in succession to Dr Hamilton, and continued to hold it when rector successively of Loughgilly and Kilmore, and chancellor of Armagh, until in 1822, as chaplain to the Marquis of Wellesley, he was nominated to the see of Raphoe. Bisset and John Leslie had trodden a well worn path from the diocese. For two successive rectors of Loughgilly, William Cope and Richard Marlay, both Irishmen, had become late 18th century Bishops of Clonfert, Cope going on to Ferns and Marlay to Waterford. Again, William Pery, rector of Drumcree (1758-81), and Dean of Killaloe (1772-80), had been nominated (after one year as Dean of Derry) to the see of Killala in 1781 and translated to Limerick in 1784, while the estimable Dr Hugh Hamilton, Dean of Armagh, had been appointed to the see of Clonfert in 1796 and thereafter to Ossory. This record was extended soon after the Union when Nathaniel Alexander, rector of Killeavy, and Hon Percy Jocelyn, rector of Creggan and treasurer of Armagh, both of leading Ulster families, were promoted to the sees of Meath and Ferns respectively.[62]

The Evangelical revival had made inroads into the primatial diocese. Charles Wolfe, on becoming curate of Donoughmore in 1817 – his poem, *The Burial of Sir John Moore*, was first published that year in the *Newry Telegraph* – commented on the 'piety' among the highest orders in both Tyrone and Armagh. In the former county, members of the aristocratic families of Castlestuart and Northland (Knox) had identified with the revival, while among its adherents in the latter county were Sir Capel Molyneux of Castle Dillon, the Count de Salis, Lord and Lady Mandeville, William Brownlow MP, who represented county Armagh in the Irish parliament from 1770 and at Westminster until his death in 1815, and Sir Archibald Acheson (1776-1849), who in 1807 succeeded his father as 2nd Earl of Gosford. A representative peer from 1811, and a Whig, Gosford was to be Governor-in-Chief of British North America (1835-8). Three of the Armagh incumbents in 1804 were Evangelicals. The two pioneers were Hon Charles Caulfield, rector of Killyman (1775-1818), who had been host to Wesley and supported the Methodist preachers, and George Maunsell, rector of Drumcree (1781-1804) – he became resident Dean of Leighlin in 1804 – who supported the Ulster Evangelical Society, an agency of the Calvinist wing of the revival, which sponsored itinerant preaching in south Ulster and in 1802 opened a non-denominational chapel at Moy. The regular Anglican Evangelical tradition was, however, represented by Hon James Hewitt, who in 1789 succeeded his father, 1st Viscount Lifford, Lord Chancellor of Ireland (1768-89), as 2nd Viscount Lifford. In 1796 he was appointed by the Crown to the deanery of Armagh. Educated at Christ Church Oxford, Hewitt had in 1781 married, as his second wife, Alicia Oliver, daughter of Archdeacon John Oliver of Ardagh. Lady Lifford was instrumental in introducing CMS to Ireland in 1814, soon after the Liffords had attended the anniversary of the Bristol CMS Association, when they were the guests of Hon Henry Ryder, Dean of Wells (who, on his appointment to the see of Gloucester in 1816, became the first properly Evangelical bishop). Lord Lifford, for his part, regularly nominated Evangelical curates, some of them relatives, to the perpetual cures in Armagh parish: Silver Oliver, his wife's brother, to Eglish in 1803 (he became prebendary of Loughgall in 1808), Charles Coleman to Grange in 1808, William Lodge Jr to St Mark's on its consecration in 1814, Hon Charles Maude (his elder son's brother-in-law) to Lisnadill in 1818, and Hon John Pratt Hewitt, his younger son, to Ballymoyer in 1818 and to Grange in 1823 – he was to be rector of Desertlyn (Moneymore) for almost 50 years from 1828. The dean also offered the curacy of Armagh to Charles Wolfe when he was recuperating from a serious illness: it was not to be, for Wolfe died of consumption in 1824, at the age of 31.[63]

Daniel Wilson, the future Bishop of Calcutta, visited Armagh in the summer of 1814. His recorded impressions, couched in the codewords of the day, provide a unique insight into the character of church life in the diocese. On dining with Coleman at Grange, he learned that there was a 'revival of piety' among many of the Armagh clergy, and wrote to Josiah Pratt (the Secretary of CMS): 'I am quite charmed with the warmth, activity and prudence of the pious people here.' All about Armagh he observed new churches, glebe houses and schools. He was impressed by the men he met – Hon James Hewitt (later 3rd Viscount Lifford), Silver Oliver, 'a most pious, judicious and amiable man', and the Count de Salis, 'a most lovely man, full of active and enlightened benevolence'. He was the guest of the Liffords at Dean's Hill. There was morning and evening prayer 'in the Servants' place, at which all the family attend', and at the gate of the demense Lady Lifford had a school for 80 children, half of them Roman Catholics. The formation of the Armagh CMS Association was a delicate matter. Coleman told Wilson that, after talking with the Primate, he was confident of his support; but in the event it was not given. Prudently, the inaugural meeting was held in private – in Oliver's parsonage at Loughgall – and 'though very small numerically, was in fact very important in point of influence. Probably the leading persons of 15 or 16 parishes, including a circuit of 20 miles and an immense population, were present'. From parishes in Tyrone, Drs Buck (Desertcreat), Hall (Arboe), and Meredith (Ardtrea), and Meredith's curate, Henry Elrington, son of the Provost of TCD, attended. The Earl of Caledon was appointed president, Lord Gosford, the Dean of Armagh, and Dr James Hamilton vice-presidents, and Oliver and Coleman secretaries of the Association. The respect in which the early Evangelicals were held, and their capacity to attract support for their societies from fellow 'clergymen of the first families and connections' (in Wilson's phrase), are evident here. In Tyrone, Wilson was 'delighted to find that much religious light and feeling are spreading around Dungannon'. He preached in St Ann's Drumglass (which had been built in 1790, and enlarged in 1811). 'The church was a noble structure, and, as the evening lecture had been established three years, a good congregation of 600 or 700 had assembled. The neighbouring clergy were also present in large numbers.' After service he met Lady Castlestuart and Lord Northland's eldest son, Hon Thomas Knox, later 1st Earl of Ranfurly. The latter family was a veritable dynasty of the establishment. Of Lord Northland's seven sons, one became an earl, one a privy councillor, and one (a major-general) a colonial governor, while three others were ordained: Hon Charles Knox (father of Primate Robert Knox), who became Archdeacon of Armagh in 1814, Hon William Knox, then Bishop of Derry, and Hon Edmund Knox, who was to become Bishop of Killaloe. The last named had just resigned as rector of Drumglass, leaving two curates, Richard Murray and Edward Hoare, who 'read prayers' for Wilson. His most awkward moment had come before the service, when they urged him to pass rapidly over what he had to say about CMS and 'to preach the Gospel faithfully'. Wilson did not feel, however, that 'this zealous advice' would best discharge his duty in Ireland, and so 'preached a Missionary Sermon, taking care to press the leading doctrines of the gospel as held by the Church of England.'[64]

### 4. 'By evangelical and religious means'

The extensive operations of voluntary societies in distributing Christian literature and providing education are an important part of the Irish experience in the years after the Union. In his analysis of the early work of APCK, Milne suggests that the commitment of so many Protestants to 'a renewed sense of Christian mission, leading to moral reform, owed much to the growing influence of the evangelical movement'. He discerns that influence within APCK itself, the church society founded in 1792 and incorporated in 1800. While it acted as a pressure group, promoting (like the reformation societies of the 1690s) improved public morality, yet 'the distribution of bibles, prayer books and tracts was from the first the keystone of the Association's work'. Already by 1795 it had distributed 40,000 tracts, and during one quarter of 1825 it circulated 4286 bibles and testaments, 4260 prayer books and 4593 books and tracts. From 1803, APCK also established schools and paid schoolmasters' salaries, attracting increased government funding for these purposes: by 1824 its schools were attended by 9578 Protestant, and 6344 Roman Catholic children. Its policy required the Protestant children to learn the church catechism; no other was allowed. Apart from APCK, four interdenominational societies sprang, in the space of just 12 years, from the evangelical revival: the Hibernian Bible Society (1806), Sunday School Society for Ireland (1809), Religious Tract and Book Society (1817) and Irish Society (1818). They attracted episcopal patronage, were based in Dublin, and largely directed by members of the Established Church. Their first honorary secretaries were, respectively, B.W. Mathias, chaplain of the Bethesda from 1805, and three laymen: the banker, James Digges La Touche, Thomas 'Tract' Parnell, and H. J. Monck Mason. According to the Presbyterian minister in Carlow, James Morgan, the Bible Society developed out of the initiative of a Kilkenny incumbent, Robert Shaw, who had for years drawn cartfuls of bibles from England and distributed them through rural post offices. Although but a fraction of that of the British and Foreign Bible Society (1804), its income in 1824 was £6728. 19s. 4d., and during 1825 it distributed 4059 bibles and testaments in a two-month period. The Tract Society, however, with receipts in 1824 of £3647. 6s. 3½d., enjoyed more than half the income of its English counterpart. By 1826, through its county depositories, it had distributed over two and a half million tracts and 217,000 books, even though, as Parnell informed Lord Roden, 'we sell *only* for ready money; we give away very few tracts'. On its side, the Sunday School Society acted as facilitator for Church of Ireland, Presbyterian and other Protestant Sunday Schools, and by 1825 supported 1702 schools with 150,831 scholars throughout Ireland.[65]

By contrast with these societies, the Society for Promoting the Education of the Poor in Ireland, founded in 1811 and known from 1817 as the Kildare Place Society, drew support from prominent Catholic laity – the Earl of Fingall was a vice president – as well as Protestants. It, too, disseminated literature, almost one and a half million volumes by 1831. By then its literary assistant, Charles Bardin (who in 1820 was curate of St Mark's Dublin), had produced, whether as author or editor, 79 titles in English. The Society also provided schools, 1490 of them by 1825, with some 100,000 pupils, and attracted an annual government grant. Its ecumenical management committee employed two Catholics, Daly and Donnellan, as school inspectors, allowed no distinction of religion in appointments or admissions, and required that only the Bible, without note or comment, be read by those pupils who were proficient in reading – its use as a schoolbook, for teaching, reading or spelling, was forbidden. Nonetheless the Society was charged with proselytism. Its report of 1824 carried Donnellan's denial that its schools engaged in 'proselyting', and his claim that he had never, on enquiry, received proof of such from any Roman Catholic priest who alleged it.

The Commission of Inquiry into Irish Education which reported in 1825 assessed the achievement of all these societies, as relevant. It thus noted that while the Irish Society sought to reach half a million people who used Irish exclusively, and a further million whose native tongue was Irish, though they also used English, 'it forms no part of the design of the Society to preserve and perpetuate the Irish tongue; it is used simply as a medium'. The Commission also reported favourably on the plan adopted by the Sunday School Society, and the results it achieved with limited funds. For it exercised no control, extended its operations easily in that it had no salaries to pay, supplied no catechisms (though permitting their use), and provided only the Bible without commentary; and yet contrived to draw the different classes of society together. In their opinion, it was 'one of the most powerful instruments for raising the character and advancing the general welfare of the people'. Given their terms of reference, however, the Commissioners concentrated mainly on primary education. In general they observed that schools were both better managed and equipped where a local patron – landowner or clergyman – took a committed interest in them. (They found that many schools of the London Hibernian Society, founded in 1806 by English nonconformists, lacked such patronage and were under-resourced.) The APCK's schools, they reported, were 'too few in number, and too Protestant in character' to provide generally for Catholic children, for most of whom the only alternative was the 'country pay school' or 'hedge school'. In the light of their Report, APCK's grant was further reduced – Charles Grant, the chief secretary, had already begun the process – and the Association presently abandoned its provision of schools. As to the Kildare Place Society and proselytism, the Commissioners found no evidence of conversion of children, other than in families of mixed religion. But as the Commission had been appointed in response to a petition from the Roman Catholic bishops, it was obliged to address their misgivings on the character of the education currently on offer to Irish children.[66]

Desmond Bowen's view that, in effect, all was sweetness and light between the Irish Churches until Archbishop Magee's crusading sermon of 1822 shattered this utopian experience, is unsustainable. From the outset the Roman Church had been uneasy about the scriptural schools (as they were called), and sometimes openly hostile to them. On visiting Mrs Robert Shaw's school at Bushy Park, Terenure, the CMS deputation of 1814 found that most of the 210 children in attendance were Roman Catholics, and that the parish priest was 'extremely jealous'; but Mrs Shaw 'acts with prudence, admitting no printed books except the Testament, using chiefly oral teaching, and not having the children on a Sunday'. In 1824 Donnellan himself testified to the Education Commissioners that the object of the priests was to destroy the Kildare Place Society, and that they imposed sanctions on parents who refused to withdraw their children from its schools, including refusal of absolution. The attitude of the Roman Catholic bishops and most (but not all) clergy was in conflict with the choice of many Catholic families, in that they held the reading of the Bible, without note or comment, to be unacceptable, and encouragement of it tantamount to proselytism. Given that the bishops' petition had given rise to their Inquiry, the Commissioners were bound to give due weight to their express stipulation that Catholic children could not attend scriptural schools, or schools where the master was of a different denomination. In the event, perhaps inevitably, they concluded that the Kildare Place Society had 'failed in producing universal satisfaction', and recommended joint secular but separate religious instruction in government aided schools. The Society as a result lost its grant; and the lines of battle over national education from 1832 were thus drawn.

## IV THE POPULAR REFORMATION

### 1. Evangelical laity and clergy

Indications of its influence already given suggest that the development of the church's evangelical revival warrants fuller analysis. Unlike the lost reformation in Primate Marsh's day, it prospered primarily because it won the allegiance, and harnessed the energy, wealth and authority, of significant numbers of laity. For the revival permeated every sphere of society: aristocracy and gentry, commerce, and the professions – banking, law and medicine, politics, armed services and university. Members of prominent families identified with it: Bushe, Parnell and Plunket in public life; Brontë, Synge and Yeats in literary circles; La Touche, Lefroy, Maturin and Trench among the Huguenots. In 1789 Wesley observed 'Honourable and Right Honourable persons' in the Bethesda's congregation, and 25 years later Dublin Evangelicals included one of the lords justices, General Sir George Hewitt; General Thomas Trotter, Colonel Commandant of the Royal Artillery; Major Henry Sirr, the town-major (or chief of the Dublin police, 1796-1826); St George Daly, a judge of the King's Bench, and the banker, Robert Shaw MP of Bushy Park, Terenure.

A photograph taken (as it were) in 1814 marks the contrast with England. There few representatives of either aristocracy or universities had identified with CMS from its formation in 1799. In contrast, Hibernian CMS had as vice-patrons – under Viscount Lorton (formerly Lieut-General Sir Robert

King) as president – three earls, Desart, Gosford and Westmeath, and four Viscounts: De Vesci, Lifford, Northland and Valentia. Its vice-presidents were the Lord Mayor of Dublin, General Hewitt, Judge Daly and David La Touche – all privy councillors; Generals White and Trotter, Hon James Hewitt, Dr Perceval of TCD, Peter La Touche of Bellevue, William Brownlow MP and Alexander Hamilton KC. The 21 committee members included two each from the Disney (of Blackrock), Guinness and La Touche families; Serjeant Thomas Lefroy, Thomas Parnell, Major Sirr, and the academics Henry Monck Mason and P. A. Singer. This patronage is the more remarkable in that no bishop, and virtually no senior dignitary, would countenance HCMS in its early years. The list of speakers at the launch in the Rotunda on 22 June 1814 underlines the discrepancy. The seven clerics were an unlicensed Dublin chaplain, five rural incumbents, and the Dean of Leighlin (Maunsell) – the only dignitary present as such, for the Dean of Armagh pointedly took his place among his peers. By contrast, Lord Gosford, General Trotter, Judge Daly and Arthur Guinness were among the 12 lay speakers. The contrast with England was marked again by 'the old apostle', Charles Simeon, when he attended the spring anniversaries of the societies in Dublin in 1822. Given the 'precise line' which he followed at Cambridge, he was 'astonished to find earls, viscounts and judges calling on me'; and on dining at the Countess of Westmeath's, he met Judge Daly 'and other characters of the highest respectability'.[67]

Women featured prominently in the revival. Simeon's hostess was formerly Lady Elizabeth Moore, daughter of 2nd Marquis of Drogheda. Her contemporaries included two daughters of 1st Earl of Enniskillen, Lady de Grey, the wife of Peel's Viceroy in the 1840s, and Lady Florence Balfour of Townley Hall, and two sisters of Lord Gosford, both of whom married English Evangelicals: Lady Olivia Acheson in 1797 wed Brigadier-General Robert Sparrow of Brampton Park, Huntingdon, and Lady Mary in 1803 Lieut-General Lord William Bentinck, a future Governor-General of India. In Wicklow, three Howard sisters – daughters of Colonel Robert Howard and granddaughters of 1st Viscount Wicklow – married local Evangelicals: Frances, the eldest, William Parnell-Hayes of Avondale – they were C. S. Parnell's paternal grandparents; Isabella, Granville Leveson, 3rd Earl of Carysfort; and Theodosia, as his second wife, Richard, 5th Viscount Powerscourt. Such women became involved with the welfare of the tenants on their estates, the management of schools, and charitable foundations in the cities. Lady Rathdowne and her daughters ran a school at the gates of Charleville in Wicklow, Lady Castlestuart a reading class for poor tenants at Stuart Hall in Tyrone, and Lady Lorton's daughter, Jane, who married Anthony Lefroy MP of Carrig-glass, Longford, assisted the Kiernan sisters in the Retreat at Drumcondra when she was in Dublin. Lady Charlotte O'Brien of Dromoland Castle in Clare was a renowned humanitarian. The daughter of William Smith of Cahirmoyle, a wealthy solicitor who had bailed Sir Edward O'Brien out of debt, she brought to her marriage her father's wealth and business acumen. Praised later by her son, William Smith O'Brien, for her relief work during the Great Famine, she was in 1814 listed as a potential HCMS subscriber by Lady Lifford. That intrepid lady's own finest hour came when, with the CMS deputation in Dublin for the launch of its Irish auxiliary, and the men faltering in face of episcopal disapprobation, she seized the initiative and formed the CMS Ladies Association. Charles Hole praised 'the great Dublin dames' who supported her, but the list of vice presidents reveals that she relied as much on the mettle of her northern friends, Lady Lucy Barry, Lady Florence Balfour, Lady Margaret Molyneux, and Mrs William Brownlow. The unsung heroines of the revival were, however, the clergy wives. They were often both daughters and wives of clergy, or else wives and mothers, or even (like Lady Lifford) all three.

That the revival made such inroads into the upper echelons of Irish society was due to three factors in particular: individual conversions, family networking, and local revivals. The phenomenon of conversion persisted for decades. English influence is discernible, for William Howard, a former major of Drogheda, was converted in Yorkshire, William Smyth of Dublin under Romaine's preaching in London, and Hon Walter Shirley, rector of Loughrea in Galway, through Henry Venn. English publications circulated in Ireland, notably Wilberforce's *Real Christianity* and Thomas Scott's *Force of Truth,* while some Evangelical clergy, like the Maude brothers, were educated in England: Thomas Tighe at St John's College Cambridge – he became a Fellow of Peterhouse – and William Cleaver at Oxford. But there had been indigenous influences also. The hymn-writer A. M. Toplady, who graduated from TCD in 1760, was converted in a barn in Wexford through the preaching of a semi-literate Methodist, and half a century later, H. F. Lyte, when rector of Taghmon in the same county, through the chilling declaration of a dying clerical neighbour that neither of them had found a saving faith. The future Bishop of Cashel, Robert Daly, ordained when he had 'no higher purpose than to slaughter grouse', was himself converted and then instrumental in the conversions of his parishioner, Lord Powerscourt, and his brother Edward Wingfield. Lord Jocelyn, later 3rd Earl Roden, came to faith at an annual meeting of the Bible Society, having out of curiosity followed the crowd into the Pillar Room of the Rotunda. Tom Lefroy, a future Chief Justice of the King's Bench, who had been a youthful paramour of Jane Austen (and reputedly her model for Mr Darcy), came privately to the realization that, although devoutly religious, he had lived 'in the pride of a

Socinian spirit' and not received the faith as a little child. Walter Shirley's frequent preaching in Dublin influenced Irish parliamentary families. Lady Longford and Lady Mountcashel were among his converts, the Pakenhams becoming prominent in the revival's advance. Shirley enjoyed both the protection of aristocratic privilege – he was Lady Huntingdon's cousin – and archiepiscopal support from John Ryder of Tuam. Hence two Bishops of Clonfert failed to silence him, and although he was watched (and heard) by authority in Dublin, he was never inhibited in the diocese. Shirley died in 1786 (aged 60) in the Dublin home of his brother-in-law, George Kiernan, and was buried in St Mary's.[68] His evocative hymn, 'Sweet the moments, rich in blessing, which before the Cross I spend', serves as the epitome of his unique ministry.

The evangelical conversion of Power Trench, when Bishop of Elphin, was perhaps the most remarkable of all. On ministering to his dying sister, Lady Emily La Touche, of Harristown in Kildare, he had become disturbingly aware that he did not share her evident peace and joy, but it was the reasoned letter of his archdeacon, William Digby, in response to his visitation sermon in 1816, that was the instrument of his conversion. Having defended evangelical doctrine from both scripture and the Anglican formularies, Digby told his bishop plainly that 'the true import and meaning' of justification by faith (which Trench had expressly rejected) had not yet been revealed to him, and that the application of the Redeemer's work 'to us individually, that *we may be saved,* is the work of the Holy Ghost, who works in us a *most holy faith*'. Trench pondered his letter for weeks, presently tore up his sermon, and pronounced himself Digby's 'son in the gospel'. Two years later he became the inaugural President of the Irish Society, and next year Archbishop of Tuam.[69]

The revival was, above all, a family affair. A family once influenced by it, whether landed, commercial or clerical, was prone to canvass its several branches, consolidate its new identity through marriage, and carry its faith forward to the next generation. The second Arthur Guinness and his brother Benjamin have been noticed already. Another brother, Grattan Guinness, married a daughter of Alderman Hutton, a Dublin Presbyterian, and two sisters Evangelical clergy: Louisa married William Hoare of Limerick, and so moved from one philanthropic family to another, and Mary Anne married John Burke of Loughrea. If a brewer could produce a mostly Evangelical progeny, it could happen to a bishop. All five sons of Bishop Hugh Hamilton identified with the revival. Alexander, the eldest, became a Dublin lawyer, while Henry returned to his native Ulster and settled at Tullylish House in west Down. Their clerical brothers were Hans, rector of the Ossory parish of Knocktopher, Hugh, rector of Inishmacsaint in Clogher, and George (already, like Hugh, noticed in another context) author of *Codex Criticus of the Hebrew Bible* and other works of international repute. George Hamilton's coded tribute to his father as 'a lover of good men, and of the gospel they preached' serves to make the point that, after John Ryder, he was the first bishop to support Evangelicals.[70] Archbishop Ryder's daughter married Dr John Oliver, Archdeacon of Ardagh, the youngest son of Robert Oliver, MP for Limerick. Their family identified with the revival. Their sons were Robert Oliver of Kilfinnane, Admiral Oliver, who retired to Dublin, and Silver Oliver, rector of Loughgall. Of their daughters, Alicia became Lady Lifford, Anne married William Disney of Blackrock, and a sister married into the Aldworth family of Cork. In another branch of the family, Robert Oliver MP's grandson, Rt Hon Silver Oliver of Castle Oliver, had four daughters: Catherine and Jane married brothers, 1st Baron Mountsandford and Hon William Sandford, both active Evangelicals, Susanna married Dr Hans Hamilton, and Isabella, John Waller of Castletown.

Local revivals were part of Evangelical topography. One of the earliest was in east Down under Edward Smyth. Denied lucrative preferment by the death of his uncle, Archbishop Smyth of Dublin, he became curate of Ballyculter on the nomination of Viscount Bangor. A recent Wesleyan convert, and a fearless eccentric of the type of Grimshaw and Berridge in England, Smyth's ministry, too, was characterized by his care of the people, local itinerancy, and 'ecstatic response' to his preaching. His wife wrote in January 1776:

> I believe there has seldom been a greater revival of religion than in Dunsfort parish. The Lord hath confirmed it by signs and wonders. He seems truly to be pouring out His Spirit upon all flesh. Persons come five miles, and return home in the midst of the snow, to hear the word preached. Many young men have roared out through the anguish of their spirit. Some people were seized with fainting, trembling, contraction of their limbs, and violent crying. Mr Smyth exhorted in a barn in that parish on Tuesday last, and it was thought he had six hundred hearers. Wonders are to be seen almost every time of our meeting.

Smyth alienated his patron when he reproved him for adultery. He was deprived of his house, then brought to trial in the consistorial court of Down for erroneous teaching. The trial was a travesty, back-fired on the authorities, and was abandoned without verdict given. Bishop Trail, however, deprived Smyth of his living. But Lord Bangor's daughter, Hon Sophia Ward, had been converted under his ministry, and the family produced Evangelical clergy in later generations. Smyth was for some years a Methodist itinerant, until in 1786 he settled as co-chaplain of the Bethesda.

The sustained Limerick revival caught up county families and Palatine families alike. In 1778 Wesley returned to Kilfinnane, 'in the neighbourhood of which there is a considerable revival of the work of God', and in 1789 at Pallas he noted that all the Palatine families

> came hither from Ballingarrane, Courtmatrix and Rathkeale; in all which places an uncommon flame has lately broke out, such as was never seen before … all the neighbouring gentry are likewise gathered together.

Castle Oliver and Castle Waller both identified with the revival. Wesley had preached earlier for Jacques Ingram in Limerick city, and Edward Smyth, who was related to the Ingrams, preached there during his itinerant years. In 1796 Averell 'heard Mr Mansell [sic] preach much truth extempore in Johns Church wch was much crowded'. This was probably George Maunsell, on a visit. His father was MP for Kilmallock, and his maternal grandfather Richard Waller of Castle Waller; his son, Thomas, was ordained in Limerick in 1799. The first regular Evangelical Anglican clergy were the Hoare brothers: John was rector of Rathkeale, and William rector of St George's in the city. They were the sons of the philanthropist, Deane Hoare, who had married Susan Ingram. John Hoare married Rachel, daughter of Sir Edward Newenham. When William's wife, Louisa (née Guinness) died in 1809 in her 27th year, the memorial he erected in St Mary's Cathedral encapsulated the faith of these Limerick families, with its emphasis on 'her full assurance of a blessed and glorious resurrection to eternal life through the blood and right-eousness of Him who came into the world to save sinners'. William Hoare, a noted philanthropist, was vicar choral of Limerick, and both brothers served the diocese as vicar general. Neither, however, reached the age of 50: John Hoare died in 1813, William 10 years later.[72]

The revival in Elphin diocese in 1816 was thus described by Archdeacon Digby:

> the word of God, at this time, increased remarkably in the neighbour-hood, and the number of disciples (especially among the gentry) multi-plied … and a great company of the parochial clergy became obedient to the faith.

Clerical meetings were begun on the initiative of George White, a tutor in Lord Lorton's family, and special missions were held in many churches, including Drumcliffe and St John's Sligo, where Digby himself preached with great power. At the same period, Glendalough was transformed into an Evangelical stronghold. James Dunn had pioneered the way, but Robert Daly was the driving force behind it. The son of Rt Hon Denis Daly and Lady Harriet Maxwell, daughter of 1st Earl Farnham, he influenced the many landowning families of Wicklow, both in Enniskerry and beyond it. In 1819 his cousin, the saintly William Cleaver, arrived in Delgany to play Melancthon to Daly's Luther in the diocesan Clerical Society. Meanwhile

Francis Synge of Glanmore Castle had built Nun's Cross church in Killiskey parish in 1817, and appointed J. J. Fletcher as minister. Daly's impact was felt also by the Protestant yeomanry of Powerscourt parish, some 2,000 strong, for he developed Sunday schools, held weekly classes for the young and an evening lecture in church in summer and autumn, published a parish hymnal, and attracted a succession of able curates. In his wider ministry, Daly toured England for the societies each spring, spoke at their Dublin anniversaries, gave vent to his combative nature in print, and published an English-Irish dictionary.[73]

The revival's strength among the laity favoured the Evangelical clergy, whether through family patronage or influence with government. The senior appointments in Clogher in the 1820s (already noted) illustrate the point. Family influence procured the preferment, in the year that each was ordained priest, of William Digby to his archdeaconry at the age of 25, Hans Caulfield as prebendary of Kilmanagh (Ossory) at 22, and James Daly as Warden of Galway at just 19 – Judge Daly's son (and Robert Daly's cousin), he was the last holder of this ancient title. These appointments drew strictures from 20th century chroniclers, but they missed the point that, within an unreformed system, these men were willing to do the work of the ministry. All three served the church faithfully for half a century, Caulfield and Daly in the same post. Again, Evangelicals went to College livings. With reference to Raphoe, Henry Maturin informed Josiah Pratt in 1812 that three former Fellows 'are now settled as Parish Ministers in this Diocese, and are not ashamed of the Gospel of Christ – the number of such Ministers in the Establishment is, I think, increasing'. He himself had gone to Clondevaddock in 1798 – his predecessor, Dr Hamilton, had been murdered by rebels – Joseph Stopford to Conwall (Letterkenny) in 1810, and John Ussher to Raymochy in 1811 (he became archdeacon in 1818); Henry Ussher joined them as rector of Tullyaughnish in 1814.[74] Stopford's former pupil, Dr Thomas Burgh, was his curate before being appointed incumbent of Kilbixy in Meath. Other prominent early Evangelical clergy included Dr John Quarry, now rector of St Mary Shandon, and Dr Thomas Grace of Westport (Archdeacon of Ardfert from 1808). Not all clergy had patrons, however, and some remained curates. Averell came upon three such men in the course of his itinerant ministry. In Kerry in 1799 he noted: 'Sunday, Br Nash preach'd a sound Gospel sermon in the church of Ballymakillicut [sic]'. This was Thomas Nash, curate of Ballynacourty in Ardfert from 1788 – Averell had first stayed with him ('a Clergiman who loves Truth') in 1796. At Bandon in 1795 he had discovered Gilbert Laird, who 'enjoys the life of God in his soul; he believes and embraces all the Truth'. The son of a Methodist, Glover Laird, and ordained in 1790, he was a curate in Cork for 48 years, serving the parishes of first, Desertserges, then Murragh and Brinny. Again, in 1797 Averell found Thomas Wakeham at Midleton 'fully determined for the kingdom'. Cloyne records show that he had been made deacon in 1796, and was ordained priest in 1799, when he was licensed as curate of Ahern and Bretway. In 1803 he became curate of Clonpriest, and in 1807 also schoolmaster at Youghal, and thus continued until his death in 1832. Wesley often referred in England to the 'Evangelical clergy', but they were too few in number to warrant this description in Ireland. Six years after his death, however, the Dublin bookseller Johnston supplied Albert Blest with a list of 29 'principal names' of the Evangelical clergy in 1797.[75] The next 25 years were to witness a marked increase in their number.

## 2. Evangelical Anglicans

The character of the early revival is delineated in the corporate life of the Kilkenny-based Clerical Association founded in 1800 by mostly young clergy of Ossory and Ferns. They included three sons of Armagh parsonages, Hans Caulfield, Hans Hamilton and Thomas Maunsell; Robert Shaw of St John's Kilkenny, cousin of Robert Shaw MP and founder of the Hibernian Bible Society; two men recently converted, Archdeacon Edward Barton of Ferns, and Edward Pidgeon; Edward Carr and his son George, curate of New Ross; Henry Irwin, rector of the colliery parish of Castlecomer, and Peter Roe, curate of St Mary's Kilkenny and secretary of the Association.[76] They met monthly, for service in St Canice's and for study. Their Rule was explicit:

> That our discussions shall be confined to the great and fundamental doctrines of Christianity, as contained in the Articles, Homilies, and Liturgy of our Church ... and that all speculative points, not necessary to our wisdom and salvation, be avoided.

They thus came to a clear perception of what they called the doctrine of imputed righteousness. In a sermon in 1808 Roe quoted Bishop Horsley's assertion that justification by faith was the doctrine not only of the Reformers, but of the apostles, prophets, and patriarchs, and 'the very cornerstone of the whole system of redemption'.[77] They supported one another in ministry. Their priorities were preaching, catechizing, family and parish prayer, and lecturing. Agreeing that they failed their people if they assembled them only on Sunday, they held evening lectures and house groups. They increased the frequency of Holy Communion and raised communicant numbers. They co-operated with Bishop Hamilton in reviving the rite of confirmation. They supported the societies, especially Bible and CMS, and from 1804 corresponded with London Evangelicals. They opened a fund for tract distribution in those places 'where the people do not hear the Gospel', and established lectures in neighbouring counties.[78] They were involved in both parochial charities and emergency relief. George Carr received the weekly sub-scriptions for blankets in the shop which his rector had 'established for the use of the poor', while Shaw spent many hours 'dealing out meal' to 500 families receiving coal, meal and blankets during the severe Kilkenny winter of 1814.[79]

The youngest of them, Peter Roe, became the best known. The son of a medical practitioner who fled from Gorey to Dublin in 1798, he was ordained that year, aged 20. He came to faith gradually, influenced first by his TCD tutor, Joseph Stopford, and while recovering from scarlet fever early in his curacy with Pidgeon, by Wilberforce's *Real Christianity*. His rector allowed him much freedom, and until 1805, when Pidgeon resigned St Mary's in his favour, he exercised a wide ministry. He itinerated in the south-east, and when visiting home (he married in 1806) preached in the Dublin churches.

> The interest excited by his preaching was of the most extraordinary description, and only exceeded by that called forth by Dean Kirwan. Bride's Church used to be crowded to such excess, that the very windows were filled even outside ... St Peter's Church also, and St Catherine's ... were likewise overflowing.

He inherited Kirwan's mantle as the city's foremost preacher of charity ser-mons – on behalf of the Royal Hospital School or the Meath Hospital – and wore it for over 30 years. On visits to London, Roe met Wilberforce and preached for, among others, the aged John Newton and the gentle Richard Cecil, to whom among English Evangelicals he was the closest in type. In St Mary's, he preached at the confirmation of 150 young people held in 1801, and marked the spiritual revival which followed it. He divided the parish into three, and gave a weekly bible exposition in the home of a parishioner in each: 'the people like these lectures very much, and for them have completely deserted the Methodist house'. His work took in the poor-house, asylum, general hospital, gaols and a factory; the charter school, parochial school and poor school; and from 1803 the chaplaincy of Kilkenny garrison. He had an effective ministry to many regiments and kept up a correspondence with offi-cers and men for years. Roe was a quintessential Anglican. He revived tradi-tions long forgotten, writing of 'the two days in the week appropriated for prayers', in Holy week of prayer 'twice a day since Sunday (preparatory to Easter)', and at Whitsun of a week devoted to 'due preparation for receiving the holy sacrament' – it included an address at the daily service. Finding that Saints' days were regarded in a superstitious light, he first gave a sermon on St Barnabas's day, and was induced to do so 'on every succeeding holyday' by the 'vast number which attended the church this day'. He encouraged voca-tions, and 22 men were ordained during his incumbency, some returning to St Mary's as curates. Roe's life style was ascetic – he often dined on bread and cheese and a glass of ale – and his spirit eirenic. These attributes, allied to his personal holiness and his power in preaching, gave him an influence throughout the church.[80]

Not the least significance of the Ossory experience was that it epitomized the revival's Anglican ethos. In observing that 'early evangelicalism had a knack of gathering up the flotsam and jetsam of Ireland's Protestant past', Hempton and Hill point to the problem of identity.[81] Partly one of origins, it was reinforced by undenominational activity: drawing room meetings in Dublin, urban and itinerant evangelism, support of overseas missions, and association with potentially schismatic Methodism. The revival within the church was secured only when Evangelicals dissociated themselves on principle from such activity. The emergence of an Anglican Evangelical identity is variously seen with Tighe's arrival in Drumgooland in 1777, William Smyth's foundation of Bethesda chapel in 1784 (the year of Wesley's first ordinations), the churchmanship of the Hoares, the Raphoe doctors, the Armagh clergy, and the Ossory (and Dromore) Clerical Societies, and the launch of HCMS. Ambiguous undenominational activity was abandoned, while viable interdenominational ventures grew in strength. Thus the short-lived General Evangelical Societies disappeared, the York Street chapel in Dublin (opened as late as 1808) was taken over by Independents, the Belfast City Mission by Presbyterians, and the Dublin City Mission by Anglicans. Realism, and a clearer perception of principle, were both involved. It was the same with overseas mission. Initial support on a general plan was reassessed, and the General Missionary Societies founded around 1810 – in Dublin and Cork; in Antrim, Down, Armagh and Tyrone – to channel support both to the London Missionary Society and CMS, were deserted by churchmen. This was primarily because clear thinkers – notably Shaw in Kilkenny and Coleman in Armagh, in consultation with the wise Josiah Pratt in London – concluded that missionary strategy, involving the growth of new churches, must proceed on an exclusive basis, and convinced their colleagues accordingly. Pratt set out for Dublin in 1814 as soon as this point had been carried. Henceforward, as Roe put it, 'Church money and Church influence will support Church objects' – the very position that Ossory had taken up all along – while support of the Bible and Sunday School societies would continue on an inter-church basis. Thomas Tighe had never taken part in undenominational activity. He supported CMS from its inception, and became chairman of the Banbridge branch of the Bible Society on its formation. His stance came to be adopted generally. By bringing their organization into line with their principles, then, the Evangelicals (at the price of being dubbed 'sectarian') had reinforced their Anglican ethos.

The perceptive CMS deputation of 1814 foresaw 'collateral advantages' for the Irish revival in the formation of its Hibernian auxiliary. It would give its disparate elements a focal point, unite the scattered clergy, and strengthen attachment to the church. That it was, indeed, an engine of progress was due largely to the influence of two men: Edward Bickersteth, Pratt's co-secretary from 1815, whose charisma drew large crowds on his frequent Irish tours, and Joseph Singer (with R. H. Nixon clerical co-secretary of HCMS), who had succeeded to Stopford's fellowship in 1810, and whose organizing genius complemented Bickersteth's popular appeal. In 1818 Bickersteth visited Belfast, Lisburn and Drogheda, and was pressed by Nixon, in view of the general upsurge in interest, to return in 1819: 'Cork must be visited, and I believe Enniskillen and Sligo (see the Map)'. Bickersteth thought that 'upwards of 2000 must have been present' at the 1819 anniversary which, in Roe's words, astonished those dissenters who had not thought there was 'such zeal, exertion and love in the church'. In 1819-20 no fewer than 26 new associations were formed, and another 14 in 1821-2. Senior clerics now appeared on HCMS platforms: Archbishop Trench, Dean Maude, Archdeacon Pakenham. The laity sustained their support: the Earl of Enniskillen, Lord and Lady Hartland of Strokestown, Owen Wynne of Hazelwood, and Charles O'Hara of Cooper's Hill, in the north-west; in Cork, as Bickersteth observed, the Lord Mayor, St Leger Aldworth, Major Greene and John Topp. The traffic was not all one way. In 1817 Guinness and Sirr represented HCMS at the London anniversary, in 1819 Bickersteth proposed to Pratt that Lords Gosford and Jocelyn ('who speaks with much piety and good sense') be invited to speak there, and in 1820 Mathias was honoured as the first Irishman to preach the annual CMS Sermon.[82]

Evangelicals had by now recovered also from the effects of individual secessions from the Church of Ireland. The loss of some of their ablest men – Thomas Kelly, John Walker FTCD, and George Carr – had hurt them in more senses than one, while the zeal of separatist groups to win over church people, rather than the unchurched, was a vexing problem. In response they developed a vigorous Anglican apologetic. Roe's *The Evil of Separation from the Church of England* (1815) – it issued a second edition in 1817– was a proclamation of the primitive origins of Anglican doctrine, worship and government, and an exposition of the biblical basis of a national religious establishment. The secession by 1818 of most Methodists, though ostensibly a more serious loss to the church, was in reality but the formal climax to years of spiritual alienation. By then the revival within the church had come of age, and moved closer to general acceptance. For if, as Pratt and his colleagues had judiciously observed, it had earlier shown 'some of the extravagances of youth', it was handicapped now only by 'the unjust grounds of prejudice' advanced by ecclesiatical authorities.

The essential problem was that Evangelicals were charged with preaching 'new' doctrines subversive of both morality and church. As Bishop James

O'Brien was to put it later, the charge was plausible in that the reformed doctrine of salvation had disappeared from the church's public teaching. Adam
Clarke, a leader of early 19th century English Methodism, provided a local
instance of this general point. He grew up near Coleraine, and attended
Agherton parish church, where the vicar, William Smith, was

> a good man, full of humanity and benevolence, and preached as far as he
> knew it, most conscientiously, the Gospel of Christ; but on the doctrine
> of Justification by faith, or on the way in which a sinner is to be recon-
> ciled to God, he was either not very clear, or was never explicit.

Throughout the church, clergy and people alike were denied, in H. F. Lyte's
words, 'an experimental knowledge of the saving power of Christ as taught
in the scriptures'; did not own themselves – as he put it in his hymn *Praise
My Soul* – 'ransomed, healed, restored, forgiven'. The Evangelicals responded
to this situation both in their preaching and their scholarship. Mathias's
*Inquiry* (1814) expounded the Anglican sources of their soteriology, and as
O'Brien again reasoned in 1866, the charge of novelty had perforce to be
abandoned on the historical evidence, and that of subverting morality on the
contemporary evidence of the moral effects of evangelical preaching.[84] The
point was perceived by men of other traditions. Bishop Jebb paid tribute to
William Hoare's personal holiness and pastoral effectiveness, observing both
that he had been a man of prayer, and 'a preacher of the whole Gospel' who
enforced inward holiness, and also that every charitable institution in
Limerick owed, if not its existence, then its recent prosperity, to him.[85]

That Evangelical clergy kept to the essentials of pastoral care, philanthropy and evangelism; that their preaching dwelt on the themes of sin,
repentance, faith and holiness – was, in a word, Christocentric; that their
love for the church – her sacraments, liturgy, and primitive polity – was genuine; and that they filled the churches to an extent not seen for a century,
came to be generally accepted as authenticating their tradition. Moreover, as
the second Irishman to preach the annual CMS Sermon – J. H. Singer in
1829 – claimed, HCMS had given the Irish church 'a missionary character':
its closest precedent was in the 5th century. While English example and
assistance were available to them – that assistance was always generously
given – the very rapidity of organizational development among the Irish, and
their capacity to sustain the agencies they inaugurated, bespoke the innate
strength, popular appeal, and national character of the indigenous revival. It
was a movement of the grassroots, with strong lay leadership and, although
initially shunned or opposed by the episcopate as a whole, yet able in time to
bring the bishops with it, even before its first representatives were appointed
to the bench. That it was essentially Anglican in ethos, in point alike of its
sources of doctrinal and devotional inspiration, and of its avowed and demon-

strated loyalty to the church, was ultimately the reason for its acceptance. As in so much else, Peter Roe personified the character of a tradition which embodied so much Anglican heritage. His doctrines were those of the Reformers, his asceticism, saintliness and devotional intensity those of the Carolines, and his guides orthodox Anglican divines: his published sermon of 1808 quoted Hooker, Tillotson, Butler, Horne, and Horsley. Modern historians have emphasized the tradition's effect on the church. Beckett observed that its clerical leaders were 'men of great strength of character, and distinguished for learning as well as for zeal', and that they fostered 'a sense of corporate identity embracing the whole membership of the church', by involving the laity in her work. Their influence, in his view, had been exemplary, for by raising the general standard of duty and 'implanting a stronger sense of responsibility' among the clergy, Evangelicals had been able to 'transform the life of the church and give it a new sense of unity and purpose'. Kenneth Milne concurs:

> If the Oxford movement of the tractarians may be said to have left an indelible mark on the *persona* of the Church of England, much the same can be said for the colouring of the Church of Ireland by the influence of generations of evangelicals, lay and clerical, men and women, who, in the teeth of episcopal opposition, eventually made their mark.[86]

As the third decade of the 19th century began, it was in the interest of the establishment to reach accommodation with the Evangelicals; but this would not happen while their flagship, HCMS, was branded as divisive, their doctrines as 'Calvinist', and they themselves (in Singer's phrase) as 'dissenters in disguise'. But if the bishops could not suppress HCMS, they could join it, and they began in the 1820s to patronize the society. While in the nature of the case there would be no formal rapprochement, a piecemeal improvement in relationships is apparent. The bishops, and indeed episcopal households, were not immune from Evangelical influence. The sons of bishops – John Magee in Drogheda, J. S. Knox in Maghera, William Cleaver in Delgany, among others – became leaders among the Evangelical clergy. And in one episcopal palace at least, there was a fifth columnist. Twice within a decade, the Ossory Clerical had to face a bishop antagonistic to them on arrival, John Kearney in 1806 and Robert Fowler in 1813. The latter's lady, however – so CMS was informed – 'is pious, and subscribes to our society'. The antagonism faded. Again, William Knox in Derry was a steady friend and Thomas St Lawrence in Cork, with whom Dr Quarry had a public contretemps in 1810 on the issue of an incumbent's right to dispose of his pulpit, moved from opposition to support. But the paramount influences were William Magee and Power Trench. During his brief episcopate in Raphoe, Magee sought the company of the four former Fellows, and invited young Evangelicals into the diocese: Richard Pope and Hugh McNeile were both curates of Stranorlar, the latter marrying the bishop's daughter Ann. His patronage was given greater scope on his translation to Dublin in 1822. Of the four archbishops then, Magee was the patron and Trench the public champion of Evangelicals.

In true Irish style, however, the old order was not surrendered without a fight. There were skirmishes in individual cases. Primate Stuart blocked Richard Murray's path to promotion from Armagh. Primate Beresford declined the petition in 1821 by a number of eminent laymen to license the Bethesda, as Mathias in his writings 'seems to hold the full Calvinist position'. That reply will have been not so much a disappointment, as an embarrassment, to Lords Wicklow and Roden, Judge Daly, Robert Shaw MP, Robert La Touche and the other petitioners, for theology was not Beresford's forte. The main battle, however, was at hand. The irony of a situation where HCMS enjoyed as yet negligible episcopal patronage, while the Hibernian Bible Society had half a dozen bishops as patrons, was abruptly ended in 1821 when Archbishops Stuart and Beresford resigned from the latter society, alleging that it had come under the control of dissenters and was being directed in ways injurious to the church. Their avowal has been taken at face value by historians. Contemporary perception, however, was that the two primates, uneasy about the strength of an autonomous Evangelical constituency, had chosen to dissociate themselves from it. Their lead was followed by bishops and other dignitaries, so that it took courage for clergy to stay in the Bible Society and, in the case of Edward Wingfield, to take on the vacant office of honorary secretary. At this critical juncture Charles Simeon was invited to Dublin for the spring anniversaries of 1822. Power Trench, long a patron of the Bible Society, took the chair at its annual meeting. He was on delicate ground, and said so. He first examined, and then rejected as untenable, the reasons given by his fellow archbishops for their resignation, and affirmed his own support of the society. Simeon wrote:

> He spoke with a dignity suited to his rank, yet with the meekness of his Divine Master. Perhaps Paul before Festus will give you the best idea of his whole action, spirit and deportment. I doubt not but that he will hear of that speech at the day of judgement.[87]

Trench's courage defused the crisis. Within days Primate Stuart was dead, and Lord John George Beresford nominated to Armagh. If Trench had given the new Primate to think again, he had done his church incalculable service. For only by achieving a rapprochement with Evangelicals might Beresford preside over a united church. That he was able to do so is as clear an indication of statesmanship as was Trench's stand on the platform of the Rotunda.

PART FOUR

# The church in the era of crisis, 1822-1870

In proportion as the Church Established seeks more earnestly to live as a Church, so will her position as an Establishment become less tolerable. – *Maziére Brady, Essays on the English State Church in Ireland, London 1869, p. 154.*

There never was a time when we so much require to cultivate simplicity of object and integrity of purpose. The church can no longer trust to her prescriptive grandeur, opulence and authority. The power of the civil arm is now a very precarious resource. Her fidelity to herself is, under God, her all in all … She must depend on the personal character of her ministry. – *Henry Irwin, Annual Address to the Clergy, 15 April 1831.*[1]

## INTRODUCTION

Primate Stuart and Archbishop Brodrick died on the same day (6 May) in 1822, the former of accidental poisoning. Richard Laurence, the Regius professor of Hebrew at Oxford, was appointed to Cashel, and brought with him his son-in-law, Henry Cotton, sub-librarian of the Bodleian and author of *Fasti Ecclesiae Hibernicae* (1845-78). The primacy might have gone to Power Trench, the son of an earl – such considerations still counted – or to William Magee, academic and orator, but went instead to Lord John George Beresford, the son of a marquis. Trench had put himself out of favour with George IV by taking Queen Caroline's part in a speech of characteristic courage in the Lords during the royal divorce crisis. Magee, by contrast, had come into contention when, during his visit to Ireland in 1821, the king desired to hear him and, at a day's notice, he had preached on the text, 'what must I do to be saved?' As the sermon proceeded, 'the king rose, and coming forward to the front of his pew, appeared to be under a deep impression'.[2] But the government nominated Beresford to the primacy, and Magee to succeed him in Dublin. In the critical half century from then until disestablishment, the church enjoyed stability as well as ability at the highest level, in that only seven men (of five families at that) held the office of archbishop in the four metropolitan sees. For when Laurence died in 1838 and Trench in

138

1839, Cashel and Tuam were reduced to bishoprics; Lord John George served in Armagh for 40 years, and was succeeded by his cousin, M. G. Beresford; and on Magee's death, Richard Whately, Principal of St Alban's Hall, Oxford and a former Fellow of Oriel, became one of the longest serving Archbishops of Dublin (1831-63), his successor in turn being R. C. Trench, Dean of Westminster and another eminent scholar. Marcus Beresford and Richard Trench were to pilot the church through the dangerous waters of disestablishment and reconstruction, being succeeded in the mid-1880s by a Knox and a Plunket, respectively. The leading Anglo-Irish families thus retained their predominance in the church until the last decade of the 19th century.

Effective leadership was needed not least because the Church of Ireland was affected by three national developments. The first was the change in population. Steady increase after 1800 gave over eight million in 1841, and perhaps nine million on the eve of the Famine; then from 1845, as death and emigration took their toll, steady decline set in until 1911. Before the Great Famine, however, famine recurred when the potato crop failed, as in Connacht in 1822 and 1831. Meanwhile the cities continued to grow, provincial towns expanded, and Belfast began its transformation from market town to industrial city. The availability of cheap fares led to an exodus from the 1820s, and by 1851 some half a million Irish had settled in London, Liverpool and other mainland cities. In this volatile situation the church increased her clergy and improved their training, multiplied her churches, strove in the teeth of vested interests to redeploy her resources, worked through her parochial system and specialist agencies to alleviate both urban and rural hardship, and involved herself in famine relief. The second development was the popular crusade, whether the Temperance movement inspired by Father Matthew, or the direct action campaigns led by Daniel O'Connell, that which achieved Catholic Emancipation in 1829, and that in the early 1840s which failed to achieve Repeal of the Union, or again, the crusade, diffuse and sinister in character, which sustained the anti-tithe war of the 1830s. The concomitants of mass action were unrest, intimidation and violence, and the anti-tithe agitation visited great suffering on the clergy and precipitated an appreciable Protestant emigration – it strengthened the young Anglican Churches overseas, particulary in the USA and Australia. The third development was the accession of the Whigs to power at Westminster. Sir Robert Peel's Tory government of 1841-6 was but the longest interruption in their monopoly of office between 1830 and 1874. Church patronage was confined to those who supported (or at any rate did not oppose) Whig policies, particularly in education. Beresford, like most Irish churchmen, was a Tory, Whately a Whig nominee. Partly from conviction and partly for tactical reasons, the Irish Church was targeted by the reforming zeal of the Whigs, and her temporalities reduced, while tithe was converted into a rent charge, and a scheme of national education, unacceptable to the church at large, introduced. Politically, the two decades after 1840 were quieter, but by the 1860s (influenced by the census returns of 1861) disestablishment had become a progressive goal, and when William Gladstone became Prime Minister in 1868, Liberal policy. His Irish Church Act of 1869 duly became law on 1 January 1871.

Throughout a sustained period of crisis, whether precipitated by popular agitation, government policy, or natural disaster, the church held steadfastly to her priorities in mission and philanthropy. As to the former, if the first 'R' of this period was reform, then two others were reformation and revival. Despite opposition, the church adhered to her task of making the Bible available to the Irish people, in English and Irish, engaged in an extensive reformation work through to the 1860s, and in the apologetic of controversy, both academic and popular, which undergirded it, and was deeply involved in the Ulster revival of 1859. At the same time her suffering under duress, and her sacrifice in alleviating human misery during recurrent famine, were heroic. All of these facets of her experience merit analysis here, for although modern scholarship has unfolded much of the public history of the Church of Ireland from the 1820s, when ecclesiastical affairs again came high on the political agenda, exploration of hidden areas has only just begun. Lecky in his day aspired to write 'on the Famine and the Tithe War, so little comparatively is known of them'. The Tithe War is taken up in Bowen's *Protestant Crusade*. The Thomas Davis Lecture Series of 1995 was avowedly 'the first major series of essays on the Famine to be published in Ireland for almost fifty years'.[3] It was also the first to notice the church's involvement in relief work. The centenary histories ignored it.

## I 1822-1839

### 1. 'A choice of evils'

Richard Colley, Marquis Wellesley, and brother of the Duke of Wellington, who had been an able Governor-General of India, was Lord Lieutenant 1821-8, with Henry Goulburn as chief secretary. They faced serious disorder. Adam Clarke, who returned to Ireland in 1823 as President of the Methodist Conference, noted on 18 June that Wellesley had placed the south under the Insurrection Act, while Edward Bickersteth, on advice from HCMS, cancelled his tour that year. With relief for Catholics repeatedly refused by parliament, O'Connell had set out to achieve it by mass action. The new, dynamic force of Catholic nationalism which he unleashed swept aside all obstacles. Previously a supporter of the Kildare Place Society, O'Connell now turned against it and, as Akenson notes, 'used the education issue as a subject on which to bind the clergy to his larger aims'. Rising Catholic expectation was reinforced for some by the quasi-religious excitement induced by folk versions of the prophecies of Pastorini – the demise of Protestantism in 1825 was foretold – and although James Doyle, the Roman Catholic Bishop of Kildare and Leighlin (the 'JKL' of controversy) warned his people in 1825 against 'pretended prophecies which distract your minds and corrupt your hearts and disturb your peace', many Protestants feared for their lives, property and religion. Clergy in isolated locations were menaced by the nocturnal activities of the Ribbonmen, a secret society which Wellesley had suppressed. The church is taken to have opposed Catholic relief, but while Dr Duigenan's violent opposition to emancipation survived him, so support for it survived his contemporary, Henry Grattan. While the matter needs research, it is clear that churchmen in public life were divided, and that, as in England, many Evangelicals supported it. Arthur Guinness, who as Governor of the Bank of Ireland received George IV at College Green in 1821, had been an advocate of emancipation since before 1800. The 'Catholic Question' was to him 'more properly the Irish Question', and until its resolution in 1829 he 'never could look my Catholic neighbour confidently in the face. I felt that I was placed in an unjust, unnatural elevation above him'. Guinness organized St Catherine's parish in support, backed O'Connell's campaign, and joined in public celebrations in 1829. Liberal opinion apart, however, Catholic Emancipation was seen by most Protestants as a desolation, and by Catholics as a triumph. Both understood it, not as the end, but as the beginning. 'Are you prepared, my lords … to transfer from Protestants to Roman Catholics the ascendancy of Ireland?', Primate Beresford enquired of his peers.[4]

While he alluded to the ultimate destiny of land ownership and the Union, his church was the immediate target. The direct action which unnerved Protestants and inflicted suffering on clergy, forced the government, after several failed attempts at reform, to abolish tithe by an Act of 1838. Reinforced by the findings of wide-ranging parliamentary commissions, Lord Grey's ministry also reduced the church's establishment and restructured her administration through the Irish Church Temporalities Act of 1833-4. Meanwhile its scheme of national education, which bore directly on the church's control and understanding of education, had been rejected by most churchmen in 1831.

The experience of this critical decade had far-reaching implications. It demonstrated the government's power to regulate the affairs of the Established Church (and, with 'the church in danger', helped to inspire the

Oxford movement).[5] It also revealed Ireland's capacity to split political parties and topple governments, as with both Whig and Tory ministries in mid-decade. But the Irish achievements of the Whigs were not part of a national plan of reform. They were rather driven by the exigencies of the Irish situation, and above all by the psychological and political significance of 1829.

Catholic triumphalism, the bad harvest of 1829, and Bishop Doyle's support were factors in the widespread refusal to pay tithe. Connacht was spared, Power Trench's reference to his 'plundered brethren' having application particularly to counties Kildare, Carlow, Kilkenny and Queen's, where clergy were deprived of their income. Intimidation was rife, for this 'Tithe War' was waged by secret agrarian societies. Lord Gort cited its statistics in parliament in 1832: 242 homicides, 161 assaults, 723 attacks on houses, 203 riots, 568 burnings, and 280 incidents of cattle-maiming. Terrorism induced emigration from the south-east, deplored by the *Dublin University Magazine* (founded by Isaac Butt in 1833) as 'an evil of awful and tremendous magnitude, threatening to leave this island in a few years without any Protestant population whatever'. In Edinburgh, Dr Thomas Chalmers commented on the irony of the situation where, given the late improvement in clerical standards, men devoted to 'the moral interest of their country' had become the 'martyrs of its misplaced violence'. The English writer, Charlotte Elizabeth, knew well one Kilkenny martyr, Dr Hans Hamilton, rector of Knocktopher, much of whose income went on parochial charity, and who kept a dozen poor girls under his roof to be trained by his wife before going into service. During the excitement of the mid-1820s, Hamilton had received Rockite notices threatening his life, but had been left in peace until in 1831 his glebe was invaded by hundreds of men armed with hurling sticks. A party of police sent to protect the family was ambushed, 13 constables were killed, and a badly wounded colleague took refuge in the rectory. Dr and Mrs Hamilton, 'disguised and in a common cart', fled to Kilkenny, stayed briefly with Lord Ormonde, then left for England. In 1833, broken in mind and spirit, Hamilton petitioned to be a non-resident; he died in 1839. His sometime house guest published her account of this 'affair at Carrickshock' to give the lie (as she said) to reports being circulated in England of the 'oppression' of the people by the clergy.[6]

In 1823 Goulburn had carried a Tithe Composition Act which allowed tithe to become a money payment. An Act of 1832 made this optional provision compulsory, but failed to end the violence. Government first advanced a loan of £60,000 to meet arrears due to the clergy, but in the end (in the 'Million Act') had to write off arrears to a total of £1,000,000. The Primate pointed out that, as a charge on land, tithe would remain payable by the tenant, if not to the incumbent then to the landowner, a more onerous and rigid burden. The Act of 1838 in fact converted tithe to a rent charge, payable by the head landowner and recoverable from the tenantry, but reduced its amount by a quarter. By ending the direct obligation of the Catholic peasantry to the Established Church, however, the Act removed a long standing grievance and ended the Tithe War. During its bitter course, Beresford had given money of his own to relieve distress among the clergy, and encouraged English bishops in raising relief subscriptions. He had also relied much on Lord Roden, whose influence (through the Conservative Association he had founded) led many landowners from 1834 to accept liability for tithe, and allowed the Duke of Wellington, who kept in touch with Roden, to argue the case of the Irish church in the universities and in England generally. Akenson faults Beresford for opposing the reduction in income imposed by the Act, on the ground that the 75 per cent now guaranteed to the clergy represented more than they had actually received in tithe,[7] but the Primate's fears for the future of the establishment perhaps clouded his judgment of pragmatic considerations.

It is reasonable for Akenson to suggest, however, that the church was so obsessed with principle on the education issue that she was unable rationally to appraise her true interest. She sought freedom both to manage her schools, and to provide scriptural education, by which she meant unrestricted Bible reading and religious instruction based on the Bible; and she upheld this freedom as passionately as the Roman Catholic Church opposed it. The latter had, however, carried the day not so much by withdrawing her children from the scriptural schools, as by prevailing upon government to withdraw its subventions from them. State support of the Charter Schools, the APCK schools, and the schools of the Kildare Place Society was ended by 1831, and with the introduction then of Lord Stanley's scheme of National Education, public money was available only to the new national schools. Joint secular and separate religious instruction were prescribed for these, control of syllabus, text-books and 'approved' scriptural material was vested in National Commissioners (of whom Whately was one), and management in practice devolved upon that church which formed the majority in any locality. This scheme was rejected by Archbishops Beresford and Trench, 15 other bishops, and some 1600 clergy, this defiance of the state by the clergy coming at a time when self-interest might have prompted compliance. It is fashionable in the late 20th century to see the national schools as an experiment in integrated education which was thwarted by sectarian animosities as both Anglicans and (initially) Presbyterians turned their backs on it; but it was nothing of the sort. In practice, as Catholics grasped from the outset, and Presbyterians soon tumbled, it was an opportunity for denominational control of state schools, financed from public funds.[8] The Established Church missed out on that opportunity for decades. Instead, at considerable cost, she maintained her own schools on the voluntary principle, and from 1839 co-ordinated this activity centrally through the Church Education Society. The laity gave liberally to the cause of education, but with less passion and more realism the church might have upheld the principle of scriptural education at the state's expense from the beginning, as she was to do later.

If 'a choice of evils' (the phrase was the Primate's) faced the church at every turn, it presented itself to Beresford's mind avowedly in relation to the Temporalities Act. Throughout the months of construction of this complex statute, he was consulted by its architect, Hon E. G. (later Lord) Stanley, the chief secretary. With the Whigs committed to church reform, however, the Primate had little room for manoeuvre. But at least Stanley and he were at one in rejecting appropriation – the application of church income to secular purposes – over against the expectations of the O'Connellites and the wishes of the Viceroy, Lord Anglesey (who even favoured disestablishment). The Primate approved the abolition of church cess, the right of the parish to levy a tax for religious purposes (the right to levy rates for secular purposes had been abolished in the previous decade). As a result, Irish parishes became solely religious bodies, whereas in England they retained their civil powers – it amounted to disestablishment of the Irish parish, as Akenson observes. To make good this financial loss, and generally to redistribute resources in order to augment small livings and provide churches and glebe houses, the government proposed a graduated tax on the incomes of bishops and beneficed clergy, a reduction in the income of the sees of Armagh and Derry, and the suppression of a number of sees. The Primate was able to have the level at which tax on the clergy cut in raised from £200 gross to £300 net of deductions (such as curates' salaries). He accepted the inevitability of the reduction in dioceses, nominating some six sees which he thought most expendable, and accepting with good grace the more severe pruning on which the ministry resolved. The Act reduced the metropolitan sees of Cashel and Tuam to suffragan status, and suppressed 10 dioceses: each was united with a neighbouring diocese on the first death of a bishop in the intended union.

The Church of Ireland was thus in 1833 reorganized into two provinces, Armagh and Dublin, with 10 suffragan sees between them, a total of 12 dioceses compared with the previous 22, organized in four provinces. The process of 'consolidation' was completed when Bishop Tottenham of Clogher died in 1850. In the north, Clogher was now united with Armagh, Raphoe with Derry (1834), and Dromore with Down and Connor (1842); in the south, Kildare was united with Dublin (1846), Waterford and Lismore with Cashel (1833), Ferns and Leighlin with Ossory (1835), and Cloyne with Cork and Ross (1835); in the west, Clonfert was united with Killaloe (1834),

Derry and Raphoe
*1834*

Connor
*1945*

Clogher
*1886*

Armagh

Down and
Dromore
*1842*

Kilmore, Elphin
and Ardagh
*1854*

Tuam, Killala
and Achonry
*1834*

Meath and
Kildare
*1976*

Dublin
and
Glendalough
*1976*

Cashel and Ossory
*1977*

Limerick and Killaloe
*1976*

Cork, Cloyne
and Ross
*1835*

...... Provincial boundary since 1976

—— Diocesan boundaries

Church of Ireland Diocesan structure, 1834–1996

Elphin with Kilmore (1841), and Killala and Achonry with Tuam (1834) – Ardagh was taken from Tuam on Trench's death in 1839 and united with Kilmore. With the suppression of the see of Kildare, the nexus with Christ Church Cathedral was severed, and patronage transferred to the Archbishop of Dublin. And, importantly for the church's administration within a truncated diocesan structure, archdeacons were given the same powers and jurisdiction as they enjoyed in England. Also important for the future was the Act's creation of an Ecclesiastical Commission. Its members were the Primate, the Archbishop of Dublin and four bishops; the Lord Chancellor, the Lord Chief Justice and three laymen. It had a permanent staff. It subsumed the existing Board of First Fruits, and anticipated the functions of the RCB after 1871. The Commissioners were provided with ample funds: the proceeds of the tax on offices (its top rate was 15 per cent on benefices above £1200, and bishoprics above £10,000 per annum); the entire revenues of the suppressed sees; the 'surplus' from the sees of Armagh and Derry; the residual funds from the first fruits; and the income of suppressed benefices – for the old scandal of non-cures, defined as benefices in which divine service had not seen performed for three years, was finally removed. The total funds available to the Commissioners to 1861 was £3 million; already in 1835, the first full year of operation, they had received £168,027.[9] The church could resume the building of churches and glebe houses that had come to an end when the Board of First Fruits ran out of funds. The difference now was that the necessary finance came, not from parliamentary grants, but from the church's own resources as redistributed by the state. It was the acceptable face of erastianism.

Primate Beresford's leadership at a critical period has not been justly appraised. The head of a church on the defensive, he was hampered by a distracted episcopate and harassed by a determined (if often tactically divided) government. He was also handicapped by his perceptions, for he saw the shape of the future in the sufferings of the present, and shared the Irish Protestant penchant for discerning ulterior designs in current policies. He was not helped by Whately's appointment, for the scion of the Irish aristocracy had little personal empathy with the eccentric genius from Oxford, and the Armagh Tory little enough common purpose (as the education issue proved) with the Dublin Whig. He had, however, useful allies: William Howley, Archbishop of Canterbury, an old fashioned High Churchman like himself, Mant and Brinkley among the bishops, Henry Goulburn, the erstwhile Tory minister, whom he had encouraged to become MP for Armagh city, and the erudite Archdeacon Stopford in his own diocese. On 1 February 1830, before the Whigs came to power, Beresford told Howley that pluralities had 'almost ceased to be an evil', with only seven faculties granted in three years, and, pointing to the place of perpetual curacies in meeting 'the wants of the growing population', had said that he wanted the bishops to endow these more amply out of their parent livings, in order to combat 'the evils of disproportionate income'. Clearly evil was not only present to Whig eyes. A copy of an undated letter shows that the Primate refused the Archbishop of Cashel a faculty for his son-in-law Henry Cotton to hold Thurles in plurality: it was left to the Lord Chancellor to decide, and he thought Beresford should grant it. Dr Cotton's case was also raised in Stanley's letter to the Primate of 30 September 1832. He

> holds the Archdeaconry, and two livings, worth above £1000 a year each. On one of them there is not, I believe, a Protestant family, and he never resides. This is one of the glaring blots of which the opponents of the church avail themselves, and which gives the erroneous idea of the general wealth and absence of duty of the church.

Stanley added that if Cotton's £1000 were paid to the First Fruits fund, the parish would be no worse off, the church strengthened by the removal of an 'objection', and the cause of religion advanced by the different application of the money – a neat comment almost on the purposes of the Act he was shortly to introduce. With Beresford's reforming efforts thwarted by vested interests, enforcement required the state's intervention.[10]

If the Primate had the will, the Whigs had the way. Six weeks later Beresford summarized Stanley's privately intimated objectives, in letters to Howley, Mant and Brinkley. These were: to abolish church cess, to settle the question of First Fruits by a tax on benefices, to restrict pluralities and enforce residence, to dissolve unions and pay curates adequately, and to provide a fund for the erection of glebe houses and churches 'and the more equal diffusion of the Established Church throughout Ireland'. Beresford supported the positive outcomes of government policy. He particularly sought a better provision for the incumbents of the populous towns. He was, however, less relaxed about the means. He was aware that there was a lobby at Westminster which sought to overthrow the church, and hesitated to offer it the propaganda of the deed. But he was also tactically aware. To HRH the Duke of Cumberland, who had criticized his stance, he explained that, faced with 'a choice of evils', he had conceived that 'the abandonment of positions which were the least tenable' afforded the only chance of 'securing the permanency of the Establishment'. Here he was at one with the Prime Minister, for Stanley advised him that Lord Grey held that the only way he could 'do something effectual for the security of the Protestant Establishment' was, 'not by conciliating the leaders of the Catholics, but by gaining the power of making a successful resistance' to them. These sentiments hold the key to Beresford's position. Convinced at an early stage that 'the clamour against tithes, however unfounded, is become universal, and that there is no contending against the prejudices of an entire people', he looked for a viable alternative and supported the abolition of tithe. Again, although the reduction of the dioceses was to him an evil *per se*, the alternative as he saw it was 'a ruinous tax on benefices', and with Mant's support he therefore accepted that 'consolidation' was sanctioned by precedent – Mant citing Dromore's union with Down and Connor under Jeremy Taylor. The interests of the church were well served by Beresford's astuteness and resolve, even when her organization in four autonomous provinces imposed severe restraints on his leadership.[11]

### 2. 'To live as a Church'

Adversity seems to have had a salutary effect on the church, or at any rate neither to have diminished her strength nor impeded her progress. Her leadership had been strengthened by Wellesley's appointments in 1823-3. The archiepiscopal changes apart, he had moved Lord Robert Tottenham north to Clogher and Richard Mant to Down and Connor, appointed John Jebb to Limerick on the translation of Thomas Elrington, the former Provost of TCD, to Ferns; and in 1826 he nominated John Brinkley, the astronomer who was President of the Royal Irish Academy, to Cloyne. These were men of ability and stature who exerted a steadying influence, and on whose counsel Beresford (as already shown) relied much at a critical time. Again, the interrelationship with other churches, though confrontational in some well-researched areas, was of mutual benefit in others that receive less attention. The Australian scholar Dr Paul Collins has pointed out that the devotional revolution in Irish Catholicism paralleled the evangelical revival in the Church of Ireland. 'This devotional change flowed into Catholic religiosity and by the 1830s it had begun to permeate Australian Catholicism.'[12] As to the Presbyterians, in his evidence to the Education Commission in 1825 Dr Henry Cooke, then in the throes of his epic struggle with Dr Henry Montgomery in the Synod of Ulster, attributed the decline of Arianism in his own church to 'a visible and increasing improvement in the Established clergy', particularly those in the north:

> their name, their learning, their influence, have in many cases been thrown into the scale of orthodoxy, as well in the Presbyterian as in the Established Church, and from this co-operating power a great revolution of sentiment seems to have arisen in the Presbyterian body.

The *Christian Examiner* returned this tribute by suggesting that the Establishment was indebted to the example of the practical and business-like Presbyterians for much of its zeal and efficiency.[13]

A new divinity curriculum sustained the clergy's improvement. Under the reforming zeal of Provost Lloyd, a systematic two-year course in theology was introduced in the divinity school in 1833. In the first year, which undergraduates could combine with their fourth (senior sophister) year, the Archbishop King's professor, James O'Brien, lectured for two terms on the 'Evidences of Natural and Revealed Religion', and for one term on the Socinian controversy; and his assistants on the Greek Testament, Pearson's 'Exposition of the Creed', and Articles I, II and VIII. In the second year, the Regius professor of divinity – Charles Elrington (1829-50) – and his assistants lectured on biblical criticism and exegesis, the liturgy and the Articles in general, and the church's controversies. The course thus combined emphasis on the church's catholic and reformed tradition with study of the theological fashions inherited from the previous century. In 1837 Lloyd created the chair of moral philosophy for the exceptional Archer Butler, then aged 23 (he was at the same time appointed to the College living of Clondehorkey in Raphoe). In pointing out that CMS entered men in Trinity before its own training institution at Islington was founded, Dr Stuart Piggin suggests that in many respects TCD was a more progressive institution than Oxford or Cambridge, and its theological course the envy of the older universities. He also sees J. H. Singer, one of the divinity assistants (and Donnellan Lecturer 1835-7), as the vital link between the College and CMS.[14]

The scale of the pre-Famine population is outside 20th century experience. In 1840 half a million people lived within a 20-mile radius of Armagh city. Protestants throughout Ireland (including Presbyterians) were rising towards two million, and many rural parishes were hugely populated. Archer Butler found 2000 Protestants in his Donegal parish in 1837. When Hamilton Verschoyle was ordained in 1829 for the curacy of Newton Forbes (in Clongish parish) in Longford, he had the pastoral care of 1200 Protestants.[15] R. S. Brooke's experiences in several scattered curacies between 1827 and 1836 are revealing. His first, at Arva in Cavan with Henry Dalton, who had been his tutor in College, was good for 'professional education; the visiting from cottage to cottage was incessant'. On his way to his second curacy, at Kinnity in King's county, he stayed at Leap Castle with Horatio Darby who told him that among the tenantry were hundreds of Protestant yeomanry – 'and this in the neighbourhood of Tipperary the turbulent'. Finally, at Abbeyleix, first with Arthur Newcombe and then William Wingfield, he took a census of the parish – it had the benefit of a resident proprietor, Lord de Vesci – and found upwards of 1000 Protestants. Of 1293 churches in use in 1832, 697 had been built, enlarged or repaired with funds from the Board of First Fruits. But despite this recent progress, there was still a great want of church accommodation. Much initiative was shown in supplying it. Schoolhouses were licensed for worship, churches built by landed proprietors, chapels of ease provided by individual donors or public sub-scription, and chapels opened in connection with charitable foundations. Under William Bisset, who succeeded Magee in Raphoe, 13 churches were built in as many years. When the new church at Ramelton was opened in 1824, the rector of the parish, Dr Henry Ussher, contributed £900 towards its cost, and gifts of silver plate, a bible, and prayerbooks, and presented 140 of his parishioners for confirmation on the day after its consecration. In Armagh, where Portadown was formed as a perpetual curacy out of Drumcree parish in 1824, Lord Mandeville gave a site for a church and churchyard, First Fruits provided £831, and St Mark's church was built in 1826, while at Richhill, a cure formed out of Kilmore parish in 1837, the new church of St Matthew had previously been the market house.[16]

The needs of the cities varied. Past generations had ensured that church building in Cork kept pace with its growth, and the opening of St Luke's in 1837 and the Episcopal Free Chapel in 1840 maintained the pace. A wealthy city merchant, Samuel Lane, also built a church on his estate at Frankfield for his tenants and those of neighbouring Mount Vernon. By contrast, Limerick had only three churches in 1830, insufficient for its growing church population, particularly in the New Town. The parish of St Laurence had no church, while the sale to the Provincial Bank in 1831 of Lord Limerick's pri-vate chapel left St Michael's, a parish of more than 3000 Protestants, without a place of worship either. As his lordship was unwilling to provide a site, the only legal remedy was a chapel attached to a charity. The lead was taken by E. N. Hoare, John Hoare's son, who collected subscriptions in England, and at a cost of £5273 a chapel and two houses were built, one an asylum for blind females – the counterpart of Dublin's Molyneux Asylum – the other a chaplain's residence. With five clergy as trustees, and Hoare licensed as chap-lain by Bishop Edmund Knox, Trinity Church was opened on 4 May 1834, when Peter Roe preached. The city was to acquire a fifth church when St Michael's in Pery Square was consecrated on 8 December 1844.[17] Dublin, too, was growing, and needed more churches. In 1824 Booterstown was formed into a perpetual curacy out of Donnybrook parish, the prime movers being Dr D'Olier and James La Touche. Anthony Sillery was curate until 1832, R. H. Nixon until 1857. Sandford Chapel was consecrated in 1826. It was built and endowed by Hon William Sandford, who appointed Henry Irwin as chaplain – he had been chaplain to the Royal Artillery at Ballincollig after leaving Castlecomer. On 4 May 1828, when he consecrated the former Wesley Chapel in Great Charles Street as the Free Church, Archbishop Magee observed that as few of the 54 churches in and around Dublin pro-vided for the poor, the chapel had been purchased from the Methodists by public subscription to meet that need.[18]

During the 1830s the provision of trustee churches in Dublin was facili-
tated by the Chapels of Ease Act which Thomas Lefroy, Member for Dublin
University, piloted through the Commons, a measure which simplified a
hitherto tortuous process, and forwarded by the Chapels of Ease Association.
New churches included Christ Church Leeson Park, the Episcopal Chapel
Baggot Street, and Harold's Cross, their first ministers being, respectively,
Maurice Neligan, late of Cork's Episcopal Marine Chapel, Hamilton
Verschoyle, after five years in Ardagh, and R. J. McGhee, the controversial-
ist. The need was greatest, however, in the southern suburbs, which expanded
rapidly after the opening of the Dublin-Kingstown railway in 1834. The
parish of Monkstown, which stretched from Temple Hill at Blackrock to
Loughlinstown, had aquired a new parish church in 1822. Stanford and
McDowell comment, 'In Moorish gothic, with turrets and minarets, it was a
startling sight, but it could seat twelve hundred people'. But it could not
accommodate the new commuter population, for whom no fewer than seven
chapels were built in the parish within 30 years. Two were in Kingstown. The
Mariners' Church was endowed in 1836 by Mrs Trench, the wife of Hon F.
F. Trench, rector of Cloughjordan, who nominated R. S. Brooke as minister;
and 'The Bethel' was built by Dr Thomas Burgh, with James White, a former Army captain, as chaplain — it became Christ Church Dun Laoghaire.
Two other trustee churches merit special mention, the one because it retains
that status in 1995, the other because it was built for Dublin's most celebrated preacher, John Gregg. When St James's Bray, better known as
Crinken, was opened in 1840, there was no church north of Bray nearer than
Killiney. Its founders were two women, Mrs Hannah Magan of Croke Farm,
who donated the land, and Mrs James Clarke of Woodbrook, who gave
£1550 to start a building fund: the £1250 required by the Act for the endowment was raised by subscription. Robert Daly, who preached at the opening,
had recommended John Winthrop Hackett, curate of St Michael's Cork, for
the chaplaincy, and his ministry lasted until 1883: he married a daughter of
H. J. Monck Mason of the Dargle. John Gregg, a native of county Clare, succeeded Mathias at Bethesda Chapel in 1836, but so great were the crowds
attending his preaching that in 1839 Trinity Church — in Lower Gardiner
Street, near the Custom House — was built to accommodate them, W. H.
Krause, a former Army officer, succeeding Gregg at the Bethesda. Archbishop
Whately regarded consecration only in its legal aspect, and 'came down one
day in his carriage, walked through the church, signed the deed of consecration, and drove away again'. A district had been assigned to Trinity from the
parish of St Thomas, the requisite endowment provided, and the church's
temporal affairs placed in the hands of a committee of laymen, so freeing
Gregg for his unique preaching and pastoral ministry.[19]

One expedient seen in both Cork and Dublin was adopted in the north also. Bishop William Knox built the Free Church in Derry at his own expense in 1830: its dedication was Christ Church. In Belfast, where neither St Anne's nor St George's provided seating for the poor, the initiative in building a Free Church was taken by the vicar, Arthur Macartney. The lay rector of the parish, Lord Donegall, gave the site, Bishop Mant procured £2500 from First Fruits, Macartney nominated Thomas Drew, a native of Limerick, as minister, and Christ Church in College Square North was opened in 1833. As curate of Rathcavan (Broughshane), Drew had built parochial schools and begun a clothing club and dispensary. The district assigned to Christ Church needed his energy and vision, for its teeming population was unchurched, largely uneducated, and much given to whiskey drinking: it shared, in short, the degradation of the industrial cities of northern Britain. Drew launched a campaign of reclamation. He preached, catechized and visited relentlessly. In his first five years he introduced a clothing society, a dispensary, libraries for adults and children, a day school and Sunday school, an adult class, a weekly singing class with 220 members, and the 'Christ Church Psalm and Hymn Book'. By 1838, his Sunday congregations exceeded 1000, daily attendance at the schoolhouse was 400, and the main Sunday school, with 1000 enrolled, had an average attendance of 400 children and 60 teachers. Drew had also begun Sunday classes and weekly lectures in the cottages of artisans and farmers, and out of this initiative came the Wickliffe schoolhouse Shankhill, the Luther house of prayer at Whiterock, and the Huss schoolhouse on Bower's Hill. Also in 1838, as secretary of the trustees, Drew laid the foundation stone of the Magdalene Asylum and attached chapel. Appalled, however, by apathy over this project, and judging that it sprang from ignorance on the part of 'the friends of the Establishment', he published a pamphlet – *The Church in Belfast* – in which 'a few hints and a few facts [were] respectfully offered' to them.

The parish of Belfast, 32 miles in circumference, Drew observed, stretched from Lisburn to Carnmoney, and its church population – shown as 16,338 at the 1834 religious census – was now probably 20,000: but it had only three churches and four clergy. Drew pleaded that many were dying in rural areas with no minister to attend them, and in reference to his schoolhouses, wrote: 'this plan (which was only had recourse to in the last extremity) does not supply the lack of ministers'. He pointed out that Limerick, with less than half the church population of Belfast, would soon have five churches, and Cork, with about the same as Belfast, had nine churches and 15 clergy: 'and shall Belfast, with all its wealth and spirit, leave the poor to perish?' Acknowledging that affluent churchmen were involved in general community progress, but had done nothing for their own people, Drew recommended a church extension society similar to those in many English dioceses, and to that end a Memorial to the bishop from the nobility, gentry and other laity of the diocese. In company with Archdeacon Walter Mant he had undertaken a fact-finding tour and reported on the want of churches, and he was active in the diocesan Clergy Aid Society, founded in 1837 initially to sponsor itinerant ministry and ultimately to provide more resident clergy. He spoke to his published proposals at its first annual meeting, and the upshot was a Memorial to Bishop Mant in November, followed on 19 December 1838 by the 'Great Meeting of the Diocese of Down and Connor for Church Extension', held in Christ Church with 1500 attending. Speakers drew attention to the recent achievements of the Presbyterians in church extension, and amid great enthusiasm it was agreed to form a diocesan Church Accommodation Society – Drew had done much advance lobbying. It raised £32,000 for church building in four years. In April 1839 Mant licensed the Wickliffe schoolhouse as St Matthew's Chapel Shankhill, and in December consecrated the Magdalene Chapel, Hamilton Verschoyle preaching the first sermons. Here, although as with St George's, most pews were reserved to provide rents for the chaplain's salary, one-third was set aside for the poor.[20]

## High Churchmen and Evangelicals

In the early decades of the 19th century, the old High Church tradition of the Church of Ireland experienced a revival. Its continued progress during the 1830s was independent of (though initially linked with) the Tractarians, for it was an indigenous tradition with its roots in the 17th century. It had come down from Bramhall and Jeremy Taylor, through the later Caroline divines, through King and Berkeley, Swift and Skelton; but by 1800 it had been in danger of withering away. Its revival owed much to Archbishop Brodrick, but its best known exponents were John Jebb, his examining chaplain and from 1809 rector of Abington in Cashel, and Jebb's lifelong friend and correspondent, the layman Alexander Knox. While the revival of High Church principles was strengthened by the arrival from England of Richard Mant in 1820 and Richard Laurence in 1822, native episcopal leadership was provided by William Magee in Dublin and Thomas Elrington in Ferns. Primate Beresford himself identified with this tradition, as did George Miller, Headmaster of Armagh Royal School from 1817, and Dr O'Callaghan, Master of Kilkenny College; and in TCD, Archer Butler, Charles Elrington, and later James Henthorn Todd. Under Jebb, the diocese of Limerick became a High Church centre for both clergy and laity: the de Veres, William Monsell of Trevoe, son of Lord Emly, and Lord Adare, son of the Earl of Dunraven, were prominent lay adherents. The tradition propagated its tenets both in its publications and through personal influence: Professor Stokes pointed out that Knox was consulted by government ministers, bishops, scholars and London publishers.

High churchmen stressed the primitive and catholic aspects of their church's heritage, and generally taught what they called 'church principles' or 'sound churchmanship'. Distinctive doctrines and practices, many of them anticipating the Tractarian movement, were recovered in the early 19th century church. The daily offices, early Communion, Lent and Holy Week observances, sung Eucharist and choral evensong were restored to the church's life. The younger John Jebb (the bishop's nephew) pointed later to Canon John Fitzgibbon (d.1831) who introduced a surpliced choir and Choral Eucharist in St John's Limerick (some 20 years before their introduction, under Jebb's own influence, in Leeds parish church). As to doctrine, Mant had upheld baptismal regeneration in the Bampton Lectures of 1812, and this doctrine was held as strongly by Laurence. Magee, for his part, urged his Dublin clergy to contend for 'the apostolical origin and succession of the Christian ministry'; and Archer Butler gave a positive statement of the doctrine of apostolic succession with an absolute refusal to unchurch any body of Christians who did not possess it. But the influence of Jebb and Knox was paramount. Dr Bolton cited the claim of Archbishop Brillioth of Sweden (the Donnellan lecturer in TCD in 1949) that they were the 'real though forgotten pioneers' of 'the Anglican Renaissance', which is 'not identical with the Oxford Movement'.[21]

Jebb had preached in Cashel Cathedral in 1807 a series of sermons which have been described as 'among the best expositions of Anglican liturgical theory'. An appendix to a volume of his sermons published in 1815 stressed Anglican adherence to the first four General Councils, the Vincentian canon, and the Early Fathers. And Knox published in 1826 his treatise on the *Use and Import of the Eucharistic Symbols:* to Knox, the Eucharist was an extension of the Incarnation. Jebb again set a high standard for his ordination candidates (as Magee did): the syllabus included the evidences of Christianity, liturgy, ecclesiastical history and Greek Testament, and Burnett's *Pastoral Care;* and, additionally for priests, Butler's *Analogy* and parts of Hooker's *Ecclesiastical Polity.* The precedent for the divinity school reforms of 1833 is obvious. Jebb's candidates were examined for three days. One of them was William Palmer, later Fellow of Worcester College Oxford, whom Newman acknowledged to be 'the most thoroughly learned of the Tractarians'. Bolton suggested that Palmer's influential *Origines Liturgicae* 'may be regarded as one of the fruits of Jebb's ordination courses'. Jebb died in 1833, the year in which Keble's sermon launched the Oxford movement. Bolton saw him 'as standing for something larger than Tractarianism, and as representing the Anglican spirit at its best', with his synthesis of catholic tradition, evangelical fervour and sound learning. Addleshaw and Etchells concurred. Observing that Jebb had learnt his theology from the Fathers and the Carolines and their successors, they added: 'his High Churchmanship had about it a warm-heartedness, a depth of spirituality and devotion, which were distinctly evangelical in tone'.[22]

On the memorial which he erected in Lisburn Cathedral, Mant recorded that Jeremy Taylor had been 'a powerful asserter of episcopal government and liturgical worship, and an able exposer of the errors of the Romish Church'. Old High Churchmen rejected Roman Catholicism both as schismatic and erroneous in doctrine, and engaged at once in controversy with the Roman Catholic Church and in attempts to convert Roman Catholics to the purer faith and sounder church which they believed Anglicanism represented. They were inclined to look askance at Evangelicals and to dub them 'the puritan party'. They did less than justice, however, to men such as Roe and Digby who had upheld primitive church principles in their resistance to separatism, who took their pastoral standards from the Ordinal before Mant recommended it to his Down clergy, and who were prominent in restoring observance of the sacraments and rites of the church.

For Evangelicals generally, it was a period first of consolidation. They developed a central organization to support their societies. The anniversaries of these (except that of the Irish Society on St Patrick's day) had become known as the 'April Meetings', and with an attendance from all parts of Ireland were in effect an annual convention. From 1822 clergy met for breakfast on the Friday (the CMS anniversary) at the premises of William Curry, the publisher, and soon introduced their Annual Address. An initial attendance of around 50 trebled by the 1830s (it was 138 in 1831), and by the 1840s some 500 clergy were meeting on four mornings, with an advertised subject for study on three of them. Evangelicals were also much into print. In 1830 the first volume of the *Irish Pulpit,* a collection of sermons, appeared, but the launch in 1825 of their monthly magazine was of greater significance. Biblical, scholarly, at once Irish and Anglican, the *Christian Examiner* both epitomized and stimulated the movement which gave it birth. Its editors were Dr Singer and Caesar Otway, a cleric with literary flair and a passionate love for Ireland, who was also co-author with Dr George Petrie of the short-lived *Dublin Penny Journal.* As literary editor, Otway published the early work of the novelist, William Carleton ('Wilton'). As Susan O'Brien points out, 19th century Evangelicals used such periodicals to promote revival, and their very publication 'reflected the growth of denominationalism and the concomitant decline of ecumenical protestant evangelicalism'.[23] It was the case here. Support was extended both to the older societies and the new missionary agencies: the Scripture Readers Society (1822), the Church Home

Mission (1828), and the Island and Coast Society (1833). The Home Mission promoted itinerant preaching. Its best known evangelist was John Gregg, a fluent Irish speaker, who preached in all 32 counties during his years as incumbent of the rural parish of Kilsallaghan. Meanwhile, the new denomination which became known as Brethren was formed in Dublin in the late 1820s, mainly by professional people who had been members of the Established Church. Their secession took place a decade after the formal Methodist secession. The motives, aspirations, and subsequent history of the new movement are not relevant here. But it is the case that the majority of early Brethren had come to faith in the Church of Ireland, and that they seceded at a time when the vitality of the Evangelical revival in the church was most marked, and its evangelistic zeal at its most effective.

The revival also grew in strength. Primate Alexander recalled that in his boyhood (he was born in 1824) it had begun 'to lay a strong hand on the younger clergy', and that his father – Robert Alexander, a former Army officer – had been fortunate to have several as his curates in the Derry parishes of Errigal (Garvagh) and Aghadoey. In 1840 the *Christian Examiner* claimed that half of the 2000 Irish clergy were Evangelicals, and paid tribute to the divinity school as a principal source of 'the present good', in that it supplied annually 'the demand for a spiritual and enlightened minstry'. Another inspiration was James O'Brien's *The Nature and Effects of Faith* (1833), a trenchant exposition of the reformed doctrine of justification which became a prescribed text in the divinity curriculum. First preached in ten sermons in the College chapel, the work was dedicated to the students of Trinity. But the period saw Evangelicals advance not only in strength and coherence, but also in point of relations with church authority. In this William Magee's influence was paramount. In his analysis half a century later, Wills pointed to the disorder in Dublin on Magee's arrival in 1822: the diocese had been virtually without a bishop for 20 years, as Cleaver had long been insane and Beresford's stay very brief. A lax discipline had combined with 'the corruptions of a gay metropolis' to secularize the clergy, and the strong reaction of the laity had tended to spiritual dogmatism. The diocese needed (in high Victorian terms) 'a man of genius, unbending resolution, sound discrimination, and uncompromising fidelity', who would both awaken slumbering consciences and moderate excitement. Dublin's example before 1822 had done nothing to help during 'a season of vast movement' in the church, where religious enthusiasm plunged too readily into 'theological metaphysics' and needed firm and kindly handling, and where the bishops – 'many of them not chosen for their spiritual qualifications' – saw clearly 'the evil of irregularities', but not as clearly 'the spirit which really troubled the stagnant waters of the church'. Many of them had therefore made it a rule to refuse to ordain men 'professing what were called Evangelical opinions', and commonly labelled Calvinist.

The archbishop thought differently: he saw these demonstrations in their true light. He believed he recognized the hand of God, and knew that all the earnest devotion, the large mixture of genuine faith working by love, was not to fall to the ground; and though his own views were not at all identical with those called Evangelical, he did not reject, but even preferred those young men who held them. He saw that they had in them all the zeal that was then to be found in the church, and that they had at least the spirit of true religion.[24]

The biographer's judgment is corroborated in a contemporary source. Soon after Magee had succeeded Beresford, now in Armagh, George Hamilton related a conversation with one of Magee's 'young men', his son-in-law, Hugh McNeile:

The Archbishop he is convinced will direct all his attention to the irregular and dissipated clergy – and leave those who wish to do their duty alone. McNeile seems very anxious that those who were objects of the Primate's jealousy should treat the Archbishop with confidence and consult him.[25]

In 1825 Magee licensed the Bethesda and other proprietory chapels, thus vindicating the long wait of these Anglican foundations for official recognition, and conferring legitimacy in particular on Mathias's ministry after 20 years of rejection. He encouraged church extension by Evangelicals, and consecrated their new churches. He also gave his patronage to the Home Mission on its formation. Magee had only six active years before he was, like Cleaver and Jebb, incapacitated by illness. In that time he integrated the Dublin Evangelicals into the Establishment.

Magee's influence at the centre was complemented by Power Trench's leadership in Connacht. Though he, too, would lay a strong hand on younger clergy – he ordained 56 priests in 13 years from 1826 – initially he drew in experienced men. Several of his former Elphin clergy came into Ardagh, the much loved William Digby becoming incumbent of Killashee, where Trench stayed during his visitations of that diocese. Charles Seymour, however, as an Irish speaker, was appointed to Ballynakill in Tuam, the vast union that covered much of Connemara. Trench also welcomed men who were disowned elsewhere for their principles. When W. B. Stoney's licence was withdrawn by Bishop O'Beirne, he had brought him to Elphin: now he gave him a curacy in Tuam, and later the living of Newport. Dr Thomas Burgh, who had written an account of Stoney's experience, himself left Meath for the incumbency of Ballinrobe, Trench needing his gifts for 'a poor, enslaved and ignorant population'. He appointed other men on trusted recommendation: Edward Synge, at the request of his father Francis Synge, to the curacy of Tuam, J. D'Arcy Sirr, son of Major Sirr (and Trench's biographer), to the living of Kilcoleman, at the request of Lord Wellesley, and Joseph Leathley to Street on Robert Daly's recommendation. He also ordained men recommended by Mathias and R. H. Nixon. An autocrat by background and temperament, Trench demanded a total commitment from his clergy, and his didactic but affectionate relations with them are apparent in his published correspondence. He supported them by prayer, counsel and friendship. Together they broke up unions, built churches, glebe houses and schools, developed clerical meetings and diocesan societies for education and outreach, gathered up a lost generation of church people, and laid the foundation for the missionary advance in Connacht under Bishop Thomas Plunket. When Killala was united with Tuam in 1834, the archbishop (then aged 64) was unsparing in his oversight, though managing only two and a half miles per hour on horseback (as on the long road to Belmullet). He was gratified by the numerical strength and vitality of many Achonry parishes, and held in high regard laymen such as Major O'Hara with whom he stayed at Annaghmore, and John Wynne of Hazelwood. Trench fired his clergy with his own passion. He read Simeon's *Horae Homileticae* to them, urged them to preach the 'fundamental doctrines' of the gospel, and dwelt on their accountability for souls: 'who can reflect on this and not tremble?' His confirmations, and his celebrations of Holy Communion, were always regarded as moving experiences, and when, assisted by Bishops Leslie of Elphin and Beresford of Kilmore, he consecrated one of his clergy, James Arbuthnot, for the see of Killaloe in 1823, he was visibly affected by the solemnity of the occasion, at which Warden Daly preached. His passion derived from the perception which he enunciated in his Charge of 1835:

> God's imputation of righteousness to as many as believe in him ... is not a fiction, but a blessed reality. What he speaks is done, and what he commands stands fast, and the righteousness of our Lord Jesus Christ becomes as truly ours (for we are made the righteousness of God in him) as our sin became His, who knew no sin.[26]

A movement advanced by archbishops and embraced by increasing numbers of clergy and laity could neither be rejected nor misrepresented indefinitely. By 1840 there were few residual problems at diocesan level. Some bishops had invited Evangelical clergy into their dioceses, as with Brinkley of Cloyne, others had reached a *modus vivendi* with them. By then, too, Evangelicals had clerical societies in many dioceses and considerable influence in several chapters, and generally were co-operating with orthodox churchmen over a range of common interests. Their contribution to progress under Mant in Down and Connor was appreciable, whether on the part of Archdeacon Creery of Connor, Hon Henry Ward and Thomas Drew among the clergy, or of Sir Robert Bateson of Belvoir, John McNeile of Parkmount, and William Traill of Ballylough, among the laity. Such co-operation ultimately informed the vexed question of church order, and compromises evolved during the 1830s bespoke growing tolerance and mutual respect. During that decade controversy shifted from doctrine to discipline. With many bishops now patrons of HCMS, and the Bible Society controversy dead, the Home Mission became the focus of contention. Precisely it was the *Clerical* Home Mission Society, both managed and staffed by clergy (and using no lay preachers). Its missioners were, however, charged with departing from the liturgy and entering dioceses without permission (in practice they sought that of the incumbents). The wider issues of the respective jurisdictions of diocesans and beneficed clergy, and of innovations in worship, were involved here. To put the latter into perspective, hymn-singing which Evangelicals had introduced 50 years earlier was still dismissed as un-Anglican. Again, the Mission's committee was made up of men whose churchmanship was not in doubt: three became bishops in the next generation. Even so, senior bishops, notably Elrington and Mant, opposed its operations, Mant holding in his Charge of 1834 'that the order of the church was broken, and her discipline abrogated, by these unlawful ministrations'. Its supporters retorted that the same accusation had once been levelled at HCMS. They had a point, but they protested too much: they had become used to independent action. A revealing light is thrown on the scene from Tuam, where in 1836 Trench approached the Home Mission – one of his former clergy, Charles Fleury, was now its secretary – with a view to instigating missionary activity in his dioceses. But as Fleury was to recall:

> The brevity of our rules and regulations, the liberty apparently assumed by our committee, arising from the then indistinct and undefined nature of pastoral and episcopal jurisdiction, startled his grace, and caused him to fear, naturally enough, that if our committee should ever pass the bounds of law in their proceedings, he would become a partner in our reproach were he to join us formally.

Trench instead formed his own Connacht Home Mission Society, laying down that there was to be no unauthorized intrusion and that only liturgical prayer was to be used. True to his principles, and with good grace on both sides, he desisted from involving the diocese of Clonfert (united with Killaloe form 1834) when Bishop Sandes informed him that he did not want to place upon his clergy 'any restraint which may not appear essential to the maintenance of episcopal authority.'

In the end, compromise was thrust on the Evangelicals. In March 1838 judgment given in the Consistorial Court of Armagh declared the Home Mission's intrusive operations to be opposed to the church's discipline. There was much heart-searching at the April Meetings. Drawing on the experience of co-operation in his own diocese, Drew berated the clergy for going it alone and taking it for granted that the bishops 'would oppose such a work, if properly proposed to them'. Singer supported him, and a Memorial to the bishops was agreed in principle. It was the Down and Connor pattern on a national canvas. The sequel was the formation, under episcopal patronage, of the Additional Curates Society for Ireland, the Clergy Aid Society for Down and Connor merging with it.[27] This episode ended the 'splendid isolation' of Evangelicals. Their tacit acceptance that they could achieve more in evangelism by working with the bishops than through independent action, was a new and encouraging situation for the church. William Magee could rest in peace.

### 3. 'The Reformation begun'

Much ink has been spilled on the so-called second Reformation, which retains a fascination for students of the period. It has, however, yet to receive detailed assessment and sympathetic treatment from the standpoint of the Church of Ireland, which tends to be pilloried in much historical writing. The relevant chapter in Phillips's History, by Dean Norman Emerson, did take up the subject – indeed, devoted disproportionate space to it –[28] but its polemical character has detracted from its usefulness. The 'Roman Controversy', sustained by the church with erudition and intensity for half a century, has yet to receive authoritative analysis. It is not possible here to do other than introduce the subject, explore it further in the second half of the chapter, and indicate the lines on which a definitive study can be developed. Asked by the Education Commissioners in 1824 if there had been many converts of late, Archbishop Magee replied that the spirit that must lead to Protestantism was active, and added: 'in truth, with respect to Ireland, the Reformation may, strictly speaking, be said only now to have begun'. He thereby indicated the effect of the widespread reading of the Bible both by the adult population and in the scriptural schools. Magee publicly espoused this hitherto unobtrusive, but now openly contested, popular movement. He enjoined controversial preaching on his clergy, engaged in public controversy with Dr Doyle ('JKL'), advised converts to take the oaths prescribed for them by law, and on the occasion that Roman Catholics, including a priest, were received into the Established Church at Christ Church Cathedral, preached on building 'on the foundation of Jesus Christ'. The Irish Society, of which Hon James Hewitt and H. J. Monck Mason were secretaries, published an edition of the New Testament in Irish at the instigation of one of its founders, Thadeus Connellan, and together with his own primers and vocabularies, it was widely used. In its Kingscourt district, which comprised six midland counties, 375 masters and scholars resolved in 1826 'that the reading of the Holy Scriptures is our right as men, our duty as Christians, and our privilege as Roman Catholics'. The resolutions were presented to Earl Annesley, who presided at the society's annual meeting of 17 March 1826.[29] Next year the district superintendent – Robert Winning, a Presbyterian minister – wrote that in counties Cavan, Monaghan, Meath and Louth, 'thousands are in the constant habit of reading the Bible, who are the poorest and were till lately the most ignorant of the Roman Catholic population'. Although the Primate confirmed 43 converts in Ballymachugh church in 1827, the great majority of Bible reading Catholics remained committed to their church. It was the same in other districts. The superintendent of schools in county Leitrim, Charles Johnston MD of Dromahair, wrote in 1827 of the general 'hungering after knowledge', and instanced one Roman Catholic parish which had memorialized the bishop to provide a priest who would preach from the Bible.[30] The Irish Society reached more remote places also. In 1826 it established a schoolmaster on Tory island off the Donegal coast, which had had no priest, place of worship, school or copy of the Bible when Robert Daly had visited it earlier. In 1827 Bishop Jebb indicated the progress of the Reformation in general:

> I have learned that in almost every part of Ireland inquiry and a thirst for knowledge and in some instances a degree of religious anxiety are gaining ground amongst Roman Catholics. Numbers in neighbourhoods predominantly popish are thinking and inquiring and reading the Scriptures.[31]

But George Hamilton returned home to Killermogh to find all the Catholic children 'withdrawn from the School – tho' with many tears'. Some said that they would read the Douay Testament, and he asked his relatives in Dublin to send six copies.[32] This is interesting evidence of the use made of the edition of the Rhemish Testament, without note, comment, various reading or marginal reference, which had been printed in 1820 by Richard Coyne, the principal Catholic bookseller in Dublin, at the request of some eminent men – among them the Earl of Fingall, Lord Lorton and John David La Touche. Some 20,000 copies had been struck off from stereotype plates for general distribution, but particularly for use in schools, hospitals and prisons. Each copy bore the 'Approbation' of Dr Troy, the Roman Catholic Archbishop of Dublin, and also his certification that the text was conformable to that of the Douay English version which he had sanctioned, and R. Cross had printed, in 1791. (Cotton pointed out, however, that the text of Coyne's edition differed from Cross's edition in at least 500 places, and was rather the text of Dr Challoner's second edition of 1750.)[33] The fact that Coyne's edition was printed at the request of a society formed for the purpose by leading Catholics and Protestants is evidence of the contemporary resolve to make the Bible as widely available as possible. This whole matter warrants detailed research.

The reformation provoked a counter reformation. An Encyclical of Leo XII condemned the 'effrontery' of the Bible Society in translating the scriptures 'into the vulgar language of every nation', and urged the bishops 'by all means in your power to turn your flocks away from these pernicious pastures'. As part of the more aggressive stance now adopted under Catholic nationalist inspiration as much as papal direction, meetings of the Bible Society were disrupted from 1824 – at Loughrea, Power Trench refused to yield the chair to intruders 'unless I'm forced out of it, *unless I'm forced out of it*' – anathemas were pronounced against scriptural schools, and public controversy sought. At venues north and south, Roman Catholic priests and Protestant clergy debated for days the principal doctrines and historical disputes which divided their churches: those at Downpatrick and Londonderry in 1828 were organized by the new Irish Reformation Society (Magee had taken the chair at its first meeting in Dublin). The 'controversy with Rome' was variously developed by the Established Church. Elrington, like Magee, encouraged his clergy in Ferns to preach controversial sermons, the Ardagh clergy preached a series of such in Longford church, and the first in Dublin were preached by Edward Wingfield and the novelist C. R. Maturin, curate of St Peter's. Again, while the Regius professor of divinity had long lectured on the Roman Controversy, the editors of the *Christian Examiner*, Singer and Otway, were instrumental, in conjunction with R. J. McGhee, in founding the College Theological Society in 1830, with the object of training ordinands in ecclesiastical history and polemical divinity. McGhee, in Emerson's view, 'apparently knew all there was to be known about the teaching of the Church of Rome', and published both major works of scholarship and popular pamphlets on the subject.[34] Again, in 1827 Mathias published his *Vindiciae Laicae*, an inquiry into the unrestricted access to the scriptures which the laity enjoyed in the primitive church: Canon T. J. Johnston judged that his work stood comparison with that of the German patristic scholar, Adolf Harnack.[35]

The phenomenon of public recantation was prominent in 1827, particularly in Dublin and Cavan. With reference to 'the weekly notices of conversion in all parts of the country', Jebb thought that there was too much readiness 'to make public displays'. But this aspect soon faded. In east Galway, many Roman Catholics were won over through Robert Plunket's 'quiet and unobtrusive work' at Headford, and through the influence of the Irish schools at Ballinasloe, which Lord Clancarty's family supported. In west

Cork, which had been free of 'public displays', and where Beamish preached widely in Irish, new churches were opened in the parishes of Caherah, Ballydehob and Kilcoe, while Knockavilly and Killowen, previously without Protestant parishioners, had two resident clergy in 1831 and congregations assembling in lofts and barns. In the Dingle peninsula in county Kerry, George Gubbins arrived in 1831 as curate of a district which comprised four parishes but had only five Protestants and neither church nor school. He was supported in mission by the Irish Society and the Scripture Readers Society, and also by Lord Ventry and his chaplain, Charles Gayer. The latter persuaded the Irish Society to send an ordained convert, Thomas Moriarty, to take charge of the Irish-speaking congregation that became consolidated at Dingle itself. After 1840 three other Irish-speaking clergy came to the district, and by 1849 it was to have four places of worship, four schools and two residences for clergy. Further north, Connemara and the islands off its coast had been neglected by the churches. In 1830 Power Trench placed two curates at his own expense in the vast Ballynakill union, Mark Foster at Tully and Brabazon Ellis at Roundstone, and in 1837 sent two Irish-speaking clergy, Joseph Duncan and Thomas De Vere Coneys, to preach throughout the region. Coneys also preached in Irish to hundreds of Roman Catholics in St Nicholas's Galway, as John Gregg had done earlier. Meanwhile the Connemara Christian Committee, founded in 1836 with Hyacinth D'Arcy of Clifden Castle as its treasurer, appealed for public support in providing schools, scripture readers and literature. The Island and Coast Society was also busy. In 1839 William Pennefather visited Port Murray on the Aran Islands, to find its schoolmaster, Hogan, who had been converted through the Irish Bible, and both Protestants and Catholics 'anxious about religion'. He learned that the Society was also sending a master to the island of Inisturk, where the people had 'neither priest nor Protestant pastor'. The Church of Ireland and her agencies could call on resources which the Roman Catholic Church was then unable to command.

This versatile scriptural work sometimes aroused violent opposition. Ellis wrote of the vilification of his wife and himself at Roundstone, whence 60 converts had had to flee, Pennefather of the persecution endured by Hogan. Winning reported from Cavan that, two nights after the priest of Ballytrane had denounced from the altar the reading of the Irish Bible, and said it must be stopped, a party of 30 men broke into the homes of the Irish scholars between Carrickmacross and Ballybay and beat them with stones. Opposition to converts led to the formation of colonies both at Dingle, and on Achill island, where Edward Nangle's mission had been founded with Trench's support. The colony at Dingle sheltered 190 families: farms were taken on lease, and a church, school and houses built. Even clergy were not spared. On 13 November 1829 Bishop Leslie informed Magee of the shooting of his curate at Roscommon.

> He had established a flourishing Sunday school and infant school in the town, which the people would send their children to in spite of the denunciations of the priests, who from their altars openly cursed him and the schools, and all who frequented them. From this it seems that Mr Day was doomed to destruction, at least no other cause can be assigned.[36]

Modern value judgments mostly stress the reformation's disruption of accepted communal norms and conventional inter-church relationships. There were certainly clergy and gentry who would not countenance the missionary work, while its supporters placed too much reliance on the Irish language when, of its own accord and through the anglicization policy of the National Schools, it was fast disappearing. Again, the several colonies inculcated a siege mentality and were dominated by an ugly paternalism. Nonetheless, the church had been reproached in the past for failing to do what a significant part of the church was now doing to such effect. Charged then with neglect, she was condemned now for proselytism. But her duty was clear. As the Established Church, she was bound to bear witness to the Irish people; as a reformed church, to 'banish strange doctrine'. Her integrity of purpose here stemmed from an evangelical imperative, for her objective was, not to win converts, but to teach faith in Jesus Christ. Conscious that he was addressing many Roman Catholics in St Peter's, Charles Maturin counselled:

> Say to your priests, we reverence your functions, we respect your persons – but we will think for ourselves. We will read the Scriptures … we will read history … we will compare, we will judge, *we will decide for ourselves.*[37]

There was nothing disingenuous in this advice. But because, like the church's scriptural work, it inculcated 'the spirit that must lead to Protestantism', it must needs be countered by those whose peculiar 'function' it was to quench that spirit. The reformation, then, experienced the tensions arising from the clash of two opposed imperatives.

### 4. 'In time of famine'

The normal parochial activity of the revitalized church represented a near-universal philanthropy, for the parishes were providers. Many had their own dispensaries, schools and libraries. The large urban parishes had a network of support, with the laity acting as district visitors and, in effect, as parochial welfare officers. There are instances of clergy wives running dispensaries, and of clergy daughters staffing soup kitchens during famine. In extremities of weather and epidemic, clergy in poor parishes organized material aid such as blankets, coal, clothing and medicine; in famine emergencies they distributed relief supplied by outside agencies. Two future Primates grew up taking it for granted that the local church was a centre of care. Robert Gregg's account of the welfare agencies in Trinity Church matches his appraisal of his father's pastoral work in inner city Dublin; and William Alexander knew that his father's visiting book in rural Derry was as assiduously filled as that of any London hostess, and that the involvement of both parents in the concerns of the parishioners achieved as much as later organizations. Women generally contributed much as carers: titled ladies ran schools and managed charities, the wives and daughters of commercial and professional families were involved with asylums for the sick and disabled, for orphans or for prostitutes. In many rural areas the rector's family were the only resident gentry, and dedicated service was expected of them. The clergy were trusted by the entire community: seasoned travellers noted that the Catholic emigrants often sent money home through the rector rather than the parish priest. Primate Beresford, dwelling on the local influence rather than the office of a bishop, bemoaned the impending loss of 10 diocesans whose spending and charities touched a wide circle. The resident landowners strove to raise the living standards of their tenants. Their 'moral agents' – like W. H. Krause on Lord Farnham's estates in Cavan – both superintended the work of the estate schools and also attended to the material needs of the tenantry. At Clifden in Connemara, John D'Arcy built up a prosperous community of some 300 houses, a church, school, dispensary, and fever hospital; he also developed port facilities.[38] The reinforcement of the tradition of Georgian benevolence by the philanthropic drive of the Evangelical movement made for action. Church people were exhorted from the pulpit to demonstrate their love for God by loving their neighbours also, and to express that love in action. The beautiful window placed in Abbeyleix church by the Queen's County Protestant Orphan Society encapsulates that spirit in its tribute to Hon John Vesey as 'one who from love to his Saviour devoted his best interests to that Society'.

The church's commitment to caring was tested to the limit by disease and famine. The clergy were often victims of epidemics, as with the group of young clergy whom Brinkley had attracted to Cloyne. In the winter of 1831-2, Thomas Walker, rector of Buttevant, died of typhus fever at the age of 29, and his curate, Robert Disney, six weeks later. A third victim, at the age of 33, was Henry Brougham, rector of Tallow and cousin to the Lord Chancellor of England.[39] In 1832 Dr Robert Traill noted that the cholera reached Skibbereen on the same day (7 July) that an anti-tithe meeting was held there. While it ravaged the district he kept his churches open, and held services of intercession. The wife of one of his two curates in Schull parish fell victim to it. January 1834 saw the cholera in Castletownshend, and brought

news that it was also in county Antrim: in March Traill recorded the death of
his sister-in-law at Ballylough, the first wife of William Traill (whose second
wife was to be the mother of Provost Anthony Traill of TCD).[40] In 1833 Dr
Charles Boyton, rector of Conwall, wrote to Lord Roden from Letterkenny:

> We have that 'Scourge' the cholera in Raphoe (8 miles) and are expecting
> it in the town – so stir I cannot. I had a converse with the RC Bishop
> today, who has left orders with his people to support me at the vestry
> respecting precautionary measures (last year they were refractory with my
> predecessor) – his Lordship himself goes to Dublin. However they are
> behaving wonderfully well.

His predecessor, Joseph Stopford, had laid victims of the cholera in their
coffins. Times of crisis, however, exposed the failings of the non-resident gentry. A petition of Armagh clergy to parliament in 1834 attributed anti-tithe
agitation to an attack on all property, occasioned by the greed and exploitation of absentee landowners.[41] Earlier, during the 1822 famine in Connacht,
Bishop Jebb had pointed in his speech in the House of Lords to the absentee
proprietors of Mayo, who abstracted £83,000 from the county each year but
between them had donated only £83 to a relief subscription. He drew a contrast with the clergy who in some parts of Mayo, and especially where they
had least professional employment, were 'the chief, frequently the sole moral
prop and stay; and … are indefatigable in every social and civil service'.

The potato crop of 1821 had failed in Connacht, so that famine and distress were general in the spring of 1822. On 8 June Archbishop Trench
toured Mayo, describing it as more wretched than any other area except
Connemara. He wrote to the London Tavern Committee:

> In my progress from place to place I travelled through hundreds and
> thousands of weak, emaciated, unfed human creatures, just kept alive,
> and no more. Many, very many, not having one ounce of wholesome food
> per day. I saw people at Newport, who had come fifteen miles to receive
> four quarts of oatmeal for one week, for the supply of a family.

He added that fever, dysentery and cholera were prevalent. He had presided
at all the local committees, on which his own clergy served. His hope was to
keep as many alive as possible for another two of three weeks, 'when I was
assured large further supplies would be sent from the strong representatives I
made to the government' – in fact, to Goulburn. He dismissed talk of
employment, insisting that the people in general were too weak to work, and
must be fed. In starkly logical terms he stressed the urgency of a situation that
could not be met by ordinary rules: 'if we are not supplied, we must die; if
we are promptly supplied, many yet may be saved'. When Trench was not on
tour, he was active in Tuam. He provided a soup kitchen, where his family

assisted, and when fever reached the town, went out with a horse and cart and brought its victims to a temporary hospital which he supplied with beds and nurses. He rose at 4 am, setting aside 'many important duties of my station for this paramount one'. He was mostly on the move. As Jebb told the Lords, he was,

> from morning to night, from extremity to extremity of his province, at once the mainspring, the regulator, the minute-hand of the whole charitable system. As distress deepened and spread abroad, he multiplied himself with a sort of moral ubiquity.

When the crisis was over, the province expressed its thanks to him. One Roman Catholic priest wrote that he had acted 'without distinction of creed', another that he had accompanied him to 'the cabins of misery and disease' in Bohermore parish. The Roman Catholic Warden of Galway, Dr Edmond Ffrench, of whom Trench said that relief money 'could not be put into more honest, more impartial, more humane hands', hailed the archbishop's work as the exercise of 'a sacred ministry' in which he had 'interposed between the victims of contagion and the grave'. Ffrench added that he now returned home with 'the benedictions of a grateful and affectionate people'. Trench would only allow himself to say: 'By the grace of God our efforts to preserve the lives of our people have been crowned with success.'

The Tuam clergy were stretched even in the good years. Edward Synge's glebe at Kilkerran was constantly visited by the sick, to whom he dispensed medicines. John Gorges of Hollymount sacrificed his life 'by his unguarded visits in inclement weather to the cabins of the sick and needy'. The diocese was ready for the next crisis – the famine of 1831. Though not as severe as that of 1822, it was bad enough. Storms and bad weather destroyed the potato crop in the coastal regions of Galway, Mayo (and Donegal), and Trench wrote in June that parishes which he had thought provided for until harvest were 'in bitter want: notwithstanding all the exertions making in this county, in London and various parts of England'. He sat in London with the Exeter Hall's Western Committee for Relief of the Irish Poor, and recommended that the cargo of 100 tons of Bengal rice which it had purchased be sent, half to Warden Daly in Galway and half to W. B. Stoney in Newport. (Donegal was supplied through an Army officer there.) As in 1822, the archbishop kept himself informed: 'I opened a correspondence with my clergy and some other gentlemen residing in the most distressed districts, on whom I could rely' – Crossmolina, Achill, Newport, Westport, Louisburgh, Renvyle, Clifden 'and all Connemara' were specified. From Renvyle he had 'the cheering account' that the new crops – 'very fine and in full bloom' – would be ready before the end of July. The crisis of 1831 passed. In the recurrent, but less severe, scarcities of later years of this decade, Trench was again involved in

directing relief. He did not live to see the Great Famine. But the policy which
he devised in Connacht was his legacy to the church in the more extensive
crisis which struck Ireland six years after his death. He worked on two fixed
principles. One was that only famine distress, as distinct from normal necessity, might be relieved by emergency aid; the other that relief be provided
impartially, according to need. His application of his principles merits brief
scrutiny. With its lack of industry and employment, Connacht had ordinary
wants, indicated in Trench's graphic comment, 'we are naked, bedless, blanket-less'. He set his face against the application of relief funds to these permanent needs. 'A year of this kind,' he wrote in 1831, 'does us great mischief.
Starvation is now become a trade, and provisions are sent in abundance
where no calamity occurred.' He returned fully half the funds entrusted to
him by the Exeter Hall committee, and led it to invest the surplus for future
emergencies. His policy here cut him off from the London Cornhill
Committee with which he had worked closely in 1822, and from the practice of the Roman Catholic authorities in Connacht, through whom
Cornhill continued to distribute provisions. His approval of aid for the victims of cholera in 1833 seems to have been the sole exception he allowed in
this decade. As to his criteria for the distribution of famine relief, he apprised
the Western Committee of one method of control:

> When I have given money of my own, I have directed each clergyman to
> call upon the Roman Catholic priest to assist him in the distribution, and
> that they should once a week, or fortnight, publish in the newspapers
> what they are doing, requiring them both to sign the statement, or to signify to the public the reason for declining to do so.

The point here is not the remarkable authority which Trench asserted over
the clergy of both churches, but rather that he should have leaned over backwards to ensure that Protestants were not favoured in the distribution of
relief. One of his oldest friends, Charles Seymour, now rector of Ballinrobe,
conducted a spirited correspondence with some Roman Catholic priests in
the Mayo newspapers, but a public debate about partiality is a far cry from
the popular mythology of famine relief.[42]

## II 1840-1870

### 1. The Victorian Church
The final phase of the Establishment was paradoxical. Assured in her integrity
and vitality as a religious communion, the Church of Ireland was insecure as
'the Church Established'. Efficiently administered by a virtual department of
state, she was increasingly actuated by the voluntary principle. The very
prominence accorded to disestablishment and its aftermath, then and since,

has obscured the real strengths of the Victorian Church: her leadership, her influence at home and abroad, her scholarship, philanthropy and spirituality. While these facets of her life are briefly explored here, three themes merit separate treatment: the Great Famine of 1845-8, the Ulster Revival of 1859, and the continuing Reformation.

The normality restored in 1838 was short-lived. The Famine took its toll of the clergy, emigration of the laity. Ireland was changed utterly. The young, vibrant pre-Famine society gave way to an ageing, listless society, apparently dead to public issues. Bitterness lurked beneath its surface. As J. H. Newman noted, when rector of the new Catholic University from 1854, the phrase 'the bloody English' was on everybody's lips. The countryside changed. Holdings were no longer divided, marriage was delayed, and impoverished landed proprietors were deprived of their land under the Encumbered Estates Act. The gap between north and south widened as north-east Ulster developed railways, industries, and a manufacturing base in Belfast. The ecclesiastical balance of power shifted. Many of the poorest Roman Catholics had perished, the Catholic middle class prospered, and the majority church had money enough to build churches, schools and hospitals. By the 1860s the authoritarian Cardinal Cullen was demanding disestablishment and land reform. The Ulster Presbyterians, numerically strong, commercially wealthy, politically liberal, supported Gladstone's Irish Church Act and first Land Act, their agenda matching Cullen's. The Establishment was both isolated and vulnerable. The religious census of 1861 (the first since 1834) was the expected *coup de grace*, for although the Church of Ireland's share of the reduced population had risen, her membership had fallen from 853,160 to 693,357. In some dioceses losses were severe: a third of 33,507 members in Raphoe, more than a third in Ossory and Killaloe, almost 40,000 of 104,359 in Clogher – in 1834 it had been, after Armagh, the second most populous diocese. But in the east Kildare was down by only some 1500, Cloyne by 2000 and Dublin by 6000 – with 100,267 members Dublin was now the most populous diocese. And there were gains in the north-east: almost 13,000 in Connor, to 80,125 (still short of Armagh's 85,583, a drop of almost 18,000 for the primatial diocese), and almost 3500 in Down (with 28,868) and Dromore (44,474).[43]

The church had changed in other respects also. Leaner and fitter after the Whig reforms, she was well managed by the new Ecclesiastical Commission. Its *ex officio* members left business to the salaried government nominees, J. C. Erck, the former secretary of the Board of First Fruits, and Francis Sadleir, later Provost of TCD. From their annual six-figure income they were responsible for the expenses of divine service and for church repairs. When belated reform abolished 'Ministers' money' in 1857 – an impost levied on ratepayers in southern towns and paid to churchwardens for maintenance – they

replaced it from their revenues. They also relieved the bishops of estate management, so that as salaried officers rather than landed magnates they could
now concentrate on their episcopal (and until 1870, parliamentary) duties.
With Joseph Welland as its sole architect (1843-60), the Commission was
able by 1865 to build 90 churches and rebuild 198 others, to give a total of
1579 churches, many of them voluntary, as against 1293 in 1832. (To keep
these figures in perspective, in 1834 there were 2105 Roman Catholic
churches for some six and a half million people.)[44] Belfast acquired some of
the new churches as its population rose from 87,000 in 1851 to 120,000 in
1861, of whom some 30,000 (24.6 per cent) were members of the Established
Church. Drew's herculean efforts of the 1830s were continued by the diocese. In 1843 Holy Trinity was opened, and in 1853 St John's Laganbank,
Hugh Stowell of Manchester preaching at its consecration. St Mark's Ligoniel
followed in 1856, and at November 1858 there were 16 churches and licensed
places of worship and 18 clergy within the parish of Belfast. Five more
churches were built during the 1860s: St John the Baptist (Upper Falls), St
Luke (Northumberland Street), St Stephen (Millfield), St Mary (Crumlin
Road) and the Mariners.[45] Bishop Knox's Church Extension Society, founded
in Messrs Ewart's office in 1862, was proving effective, and a further four
churches were begun before 1870. When Drew died in that year – he had left
Belfast for the living of Loughinisland in 1859 – one of these, St Philip's
(Grosvenor Road) was designated the 'Drew Memorial' church.

Church architecture changed. Influenced by the Cambridge ecclesiolo-
gists, notably J. M. Neale, and by the younger Jebb and Dr Theodore Hook,
vicar of Leeds, a new style replaced both the concept of the auditory church
and the austere simplicity of the tower-and-hall church. Its inspiration was
mediaeval, with a long chancel separated from the nave by steps as its characteristic feature. Box-pews were discarded, three-decker pulpits were
replaced by a simple pulpit, a nave lectern, and a litany-desk above or below
the chancel steps, and the 'lightsome' Georgian windows by stained-glass.
The font was moved to the west end, and the choir from the western gallery
to the chancel.[46] Victorian churches in Belfast and other developing towns
were built in the new style, and many older churches re-arranged to accommodate it. Holywood parish church, built to (Sir) Charles Lanyon's design in
1844, and enlarged to that of his son John Lanyon in 1869, is a fine example of the former, Holy Trinity Ballycastle of the latter. But the old style survived in the country. In St Matthew's Scarva, built in 1850, the nave came
up to 'the communion part', with the choir situated centrally on the south
side. Public worship also underwent change as hymns were gradually introduced. With the Sternhold and Hopkins, and the Tate and Brady versions of
the metrical psalms still predominant, early parish hymnals had, somewhat

defensively, listed precedents – New Testament practice, the early Christians as recorded by Pliny, the Reformers – as with Power Trench's preface to the Westport collection of 1837. But as late as 1858 the *Christian Examiner* was insisting, 'if antiquity be a plea, hymns can claim it', while in 1855 J. H.Todd had published his *Book of Hymns of the Ancient Irish Church*. General hymnals were by now being published. An edition (c. 1855) of *Two Hundred Hymns* listed 70 churches which already used it, and observed that the hymns were 'in general use' in 12 Dublin churches which had their own hymnals. Some of these highlight Victorian habits in worship. The Episcopal Chapel's 1844 edition called for more hearty singing and deplored the 'reproach which rests upon many congregations' – failure to join audibly in the responses. In 1849 the Molyneux chaplains urged their people to stand for praise and kneel for prayer, and appended an Admonition (published by SPCK) critical of the custom of sitting during psalms. Finally, in 1856, APCK published *Hymns for Public Worship*, a compilation of 180 hymns by Hercules Dickinson, vicar of St Ann's Dublin. Dickinson believed that Whately's formal recommendation of the new hymnal was 'the first episcopal authorization of hymns' in the church's public worship. A new and enlarged edition was issued in 1864 as *The Church Hymnal for Use in the Church of Ireland*.[47]

Increasingly a shared tradition, by 1870 hymn-singing was a unifying influence in the church. Keble's 'Blest are the pure in heart', Newman's 'Lead, kindly Light', J. M. Neale's translations of Latin office hymns, and hymns from ancient Irish sources were adopted alongside the familiar hymns of the evangelical revival. Bishop Mant wrote 'Bright the vision that delighted', and J. S. B. Monsell (rector of Ramoan 1847-53), 'Fight the good fight', 'Worship the Lord in the beauty of holiness' and other hymns. (Monsell published his first in 1850, but like Lyte before him, left for England in 1853.) But supremely, with 'Once in royal David's city', 'There is a green hill' and other much-loved hymns, Cecil Frances Alexander popularized hymns and established their value in teaching the faith to children. As with so many facets of Victorian church life, the development of hymnody needs fuller research, but it is clear that most parishes had taken hymns into the liturgy before disestablishment.

What of the church's essential being? Lord John George Beresford discerned in 1845 'a state of spiritual health and life and order and devotedness' without precedent in her history. With disestablishment in prospect, Marcus Beresford in 1868 blamed external causes, pointing out that even opponents had testified to the exemplary character of the clergy; and Ball wrote in retrospect that political considerations had prevailed, and that no charge of neglect had been made against the church or her clergy. Gladstone himself said that the church was free of those abuses which depend on clerical conduct, and praised the clergy as 'a body of zealous and devoted ministers'. And in 1867 Bishop Moriarty of Kerry saw them as 'not only blameless but inestimable'.

> They are peaceful with all, and with their neighbours are kind when they can, and we know that on many occasions they would be active in beneficence but that they do not wish to appear meddling, or incur the suspicion of tampering with poor Catholics. In bearing, in manners, and in dress they become their state. If they are not learned theologians they are accomplished scholars and polished gentlemen.

Their influence was real enough. Sir William Wilde pointed to the more 'Protestant' tone of Irish society, as seen both in its literature and the very 'conversation and manners' of Catholic priests, and also in the decline of pilgrimages (Lough Derg apart) and veneration of holy wells.[48] It was at this period, too, that some 100 former Roman Catholic clergy sought the support of the Priests' Protection Society. This pervasive influence was complemented by academic achievement. The early, romantic interest which the *Christian Examiner* had fostered in the early Celtic Church was taken up with erudition and authority by the School of Ecclesiastical History in TCD, and notably by James Henthorn Todd and William Reeves. In Fergal Grannell's judgment, 'the improved character of Early Irish ecclesiastical studies during this period was due almost exclusively to a high standard of Anglican scholarship'. Moreover, the campaign for the preservation of Ireland's ecclesiastical antiquities, 'sponsored almost exclusively by members of the Established Church', resulted in 137 primitive churches, monastic sites, Round Towers, High Crosses and the like (most dating from pre-Norman times) being preserved as National Monuments under the provisions of the Irish Church Act.[49]

The voluntary principle was hard at work. By 1868 a total of £188,000 had been raised for CMS and SPG, £126,593 for the CMJ, and over £400,000 for the 35 Protestant Orphan Societies. Mostly by placing them in private homes, the latter had provided for some 10,000 orphans, many more than had entered the workhouses. The Crimean War stimulated interest in the welfare of soldiers. The Soldiers Friend Society for Ireland was founded in 1857, the Soldiers Institute in Dublin in 1858. Elsie Sandes a convert of the 1859 revival, was to develop this work worldwide in the Sandes Soldiers Homes. The charitable foundations of earlier generations were sustained, and new agencies founded. Large urban parishes were centres of social support. Dr Thomas Miller, the vicar of Belfast (1848-72), was in 1860 presented with an Address which commended his oversight of a parish which embraced the entire town and had many civic charities devolving upon it. Much philanthropic activity centred on Dublin, and devolved on the Protestant middle class. Dr Charles Orpen founded the Claremont Institution for the Deaf and Dumb. The Adelaide Hospital, which had been opened in 1839 in Bride Street primarily for the Protestant poor of the Liberties, was re-opened in Peter Street in 1858, with Lord Roden as President. Work among prostitutes was disguised in Victorian euphemisms, as with the Dublin Mission for Friendless Females, which helped the poorest class of them. The general poor of the city, many drawn from the provinces in search of employment, were supported by Ragged Schools – the earliest, begun by the Kiernan sisters, predated those of Lord Shaftesbury – by night asylums, such as that adjoining St Michan's parochial schools, and by agencies such as a Shoe-Black, Broomer and Messenger Society which found casual employment for boys. The Association for the Relief of Distressed Protestants, founded in 1836, gave grants of money, coal, food, clothing and household necessities to poor families. The Fleet Market soup kitchen was establshed in St Mark's parish in 1847 to feed the poor during the Great Famine. In that year also, the Dublin Parochial Association was founded to relieve 'the poor of this City of every denomination.' Its clerical founders were influenced by

> the great Amount of distress existing at all times in the City of Dublin, and so unevenly distributed through the several Parishes, [and] the fact that persons of all religious denominations apply to the Parochial Clergy.[50]

Philanthropy apart, prominent churchmen were exemplary employers and landlords. *The Times* in its obituary in 1870 noted Lord Roden's integrity as a landlord, while the *Newry Telegraph* pointed out that since 1845 no ejectment process had been issued in his name on the Dundalk Estates, 'and that the rents are low is proved by the fact that there is not a shilling due by the tenantry on the entire estate.' Guinness's brewery was a major employer and contributed much to the Irish economy. Its stout offered the working class both an affordable alternative to whiskey and, as Michelle Guinness observes, a more reasonable option than that of the total abstinence preached by Temperance crusaders. The second Arthur Guinness – 'our leading citizen' to the Catholic *Freeman's Journal* – and his son, Sir Benjamin Lee Guinness, were public spirited men. They served the Bank of Ireland, the Dublin Chamber of Commerce, the Meath Hospital, the (Royal) Dublin Society and St Patrick's Cathedral; their own workforce above all. The historians of the brewery note their capacity to choose men wisely, and add:

> Those whom the Guinnesses had chosen were treated well. From earliest times, they appear to have paid good wages, and by the 1860s they were in the vanguard of good employers, taking an enlightened interest in their workmen's health, housing and old-age, in the welfare of their families, in the regularity of their employment and in their hours of work.[51]

Education was a major preoccupation. In 1854 the Institution for Collegiate,

Professional and General Education was founded by Evangelicals to prepare pupils for the universities and services, the civil professions and commerce: Dr Fleury was President, and Bishops Daly and Singer, Lords Enniskillen, Mayo and Roden, and Sir Joseph Napier, patrons. Most effort was, however, expended on primary education. In county Armagh, the Gosford and Manchester estates had a network of schools in rural locations and in Tandragee and Portadown – the two families were linked through Lord Mandeville's marriage to Lord Gosford's niece. Large resources were absorbed by the Church Education Society. Lord de Grey, the Viceroy from 1841, advised Peel's government to fund its schools, but left Ireland in 1844 unheeded. Early in 1845 the Primate was petitioned by a majority of bishops, 1700 clergy, 1635 landowners (including 35 peers) and 60,000 laity, and on 13 May Beresford informed the Prime Minister that the society's schools were educating 103,833 children, of whom 32,900 were Roman Catholics and 13,500 Protestant dissenters, at an annual cost of £30,000. Peel, however, refused his appeal for a grant, and pointed to the success of the National Education scheme. Thereafter the Society's schools, pupils and costs expanded steadily. During the 1850s the financial burden became insupportable, and in 1860 the Primate accepted that many local managers must transfer their schools to the National Board. He was supported by Bishop O'Brien and Hamilton Verschoyle, hitherto the Society's secretary – with emotions running high, all three were dubbed traitors.[52] This was the turning point. The Society's schools now declined in number, and with many parochial schools under National Board auspices by 1870 with Marcus Beresford's support, the church was to be largely spared the prohibitive cost of providing primary education after disestablishment. By a nice irony her dependence on government support was greatest after she had ceased to be the state church.

Lord John George Beresford served in Armagh until 1862, Richard Whately in Dublin until 1863. The Primate, an ecclesiastical statesman of patrician style, committed to his church and caring of his clergy, was honoured by churchmen of all traditions when in 1855 he celebrated the 50th anniversary of his consecration. Whately, respected but unpopular, was regular in his tours of confirmation, trenchant in his episcopal charges, and prodigious in his writing. John Pentland Mahaffy was much influenced by his *Elements of Logic* and his methods as a teacher and conversationalist, but 'deplored his deliberate ruggedness', while W. E. H. Lecky saw 'the love of truth for its own sake' as his outstanding characteristic, but perceived also his inability to comprehend men of a different cast of mind.[53] Of the two archbishops in 1869, Marcus Beresford had been Bishop of Kilmore from 1854, and Richard Trench Dean of Westminster: a Beresford was still a Beresford, and Trench was of a Whig branch of another leading Irish family. The point is not without its significance, for the post-reform episcopate was recruited from men of academic distinction and spiritual gifts, subject to constraints avowed by mostly Whig governments. While appointments to 1867 reflected the still predominant place of both aristocracy and academe in the church's life, from 1842 they also fairly represented (if initially from these same sources) the strength of her Evangelical tradition. As men of that tradition mostly supported the Church Education Society, and as Lord Clarendon, the Viceroy in 1847, announced that Whig church patronage would be confined to supporters of the National Board, their early opportunities of promotion were limited to the intermittent periods of Tory administration. During the longest of these, Peel's government of 1841-6, Lord de Grey appointed James O'Brien to Ossory in 1842 and Robert Daly to Cashel in 1843; and in 1852 Lord Eglinton appointed J. H. Singer to Meath. There were five Evangelical bishops from 1862, when the Earl of Carlisle (previously Lord Morpeth) appointed John Gregg to Cork and Hamilton Verschoyle to Kilmore: Gregg had kept clear of the education controversy, and Verschoyle had changed sides.[54] Four of these five were on the bench at disestablishment (Singer died in 1866), the Hon Charles Brodrick Bernard joining them as Bishop of Tuam from 1867. With O'Brien and Daly, the third episcopal survivor from the 1840s was Robert Knox, of the Whig family of Lord Northland of Dungannon. More creative than Mant, whom he succeeded in Down in 1849, Knox prepared his dioceses for disestablishment, founded the Belfast Church Extension and Endowment Society, convened diocesan conferences, and gave wise leadership during the Ulster revival. The other bishops in 1869 were academics. William Fitzgerald, one of Whately's aides, had had a brilliant career in TCD before his appointment to Cork in 1857; he was translated to Killaloe in 1862. Charles Graves, the able mathematician who was the President of the Royal Irish Academy, was appointed to Limerick in 1866, and Samuel Butcher, Regius Professor of Divinity, to Meath in the same year, by the Conservative Lord Derby. William Alexander, appointed to Derry in 1867 when an incumbent of that diocese, had just narrowly missed the Chair of Poetry at Oxford. At the age of 43 his great gifts as leader, preacher, and scholar were duly recognized.

The church was also well served by senior clergy and laity. Francis Sadleir and J. C. MacDonnell were able Provosts of TCD, George Salmon, who succeeded Butcher in the chair of divinity, a mathematician and theologian of international stature. Archdeacon Edward Stopford of Meath, with whom Gladstone corresponded, and the High Churchman, Archdeacon William Lee of Dublin, previously Archbishop King's lecturer in divinity, were erudite apologists for the church as the pace towards disestablishment quickened; so, too, was A. T. Lee, who in 1857 came from England to Ahoghill in the diocese of Connor, and in 1863 published his *Present Case of the Church of Ireland* as part of his prolific defence of her cause. Robert Gregg, who was for three years minister of Christ Church Belfast after Drew, went to the diocese of Cork on his father's becoming bishop, reorganized its finances, and provided a model for the post-disestablishment church. Among the laity, the ecclesiastical lawyer, J.T. Ball of Dublin, was in 1862 appointed vicar general of the province of Armagh by Marcus Beresford, and with his support also became MP for Dublin University and a member of the ritual committee in England, and in 1868 an Ecclesiastical Commissioner for Ireland. With their love for the Irish church unabated, other men made their mark in England. William Connor Magee, one of the most powerful preachers of the day, grandson of Archbishop Magee and soulmate of William Alexander, had been rector of Enniskillen, Dean of Cork, and Dean of the Chapel Royal in Dublin before becoming Bishop of Peterborough in 1868. Hugh McNeile of Ballycastle, whose wife was Magee's aunt, became Dean of Ripon and, in Eugene Stock's judgment, 'unquestionably the greatest Evangelical teacher and preacher in the Church of England'.[55] His county Antrim contemporary, Hugh McCalmont Cairns (1st Earl Cairns) held in rapid succession the principal law offices at Westminster, and was Lord Chancellor of England before he was 50. Other devoted churchmen gave distinguished service overseas: Lord Gosford as Governor-in-Chief of Canada, and Lord Mayo, who had been Chief Secretary for Ireland in several governments, as Governor-General of India from 1868 until he was assassinated four years later. Lord Caledon and Sir Lowry Cole were Governors of Cape Colony; Sir Robert Montgomery, cousin to William Alexander, was Governor of the Punjab during the Indian Mutiny; Sir Richard MacDonnell, son of the Provost, was Governor of Hong Kong; and his successor, Sir Arthur Kennedy, to whom there is a memorial window in Holywood parish church, was Governor also of Queensland. The contribution of Irish clergy and laity to the development of the Commonwealth needs extensive research. The part played by the sons and daughters of episcopal palaces and country rectories is alone worth investigation. The record of the family of the late Georgian bishop, William Foster, is not untypical. While, conventionally, one son became, and one daughter married, an Armagh incumbent, and, more ambitiously, another son became, and another daughter married, an Irish judge, their sister, Agnes Foster (apparently unlisted by Leslie) became engaged, when visiting Rome, to Giovanni Mastai Feretti, later Pope Pius IX. Two grandsons of Bishop Foster became colonial judges. William John Foster, a son of Loughgilly rectory, was a Judge of the Supreme Court of New South Wales, and his cousin, Sir William Foster Stawell, for 29 years Chief Justice of the Supreme Court of Victoria: both were involved in church synods in Australia.

Lecky's opinion that 'the Irish establishment became by far the most evangelical section of the Anglican Church'[57] has reference not only to Evangelical strength as such, but more generally to the church's reformed and Protestant ethos. Faced with this situation, biographers tend to type men who were not of 'the Evangelical school' – Dr Salmon is a case in point – as 'liberal evangelicals'. Churchmen of other traditions were anxious to stand well with Evangelicals. Thus W. C. Magee was gratified, when invited to preach the CMS Annual Sermon, not only because it was the 'blue ribbon' of the Evangelical pulpit, but also 'an identification of myself with the best of Evangelical Churchmanship, and a kind of *testamur* from them that I should have been glad of.'[58] Bishop Robert Knox, for his part, presided at the inaugural meeting in Belfast of the London-based Evangelical Alliance.

Relationship was based on mutual trust and respect: Lord John George Beresford's appointing Alexander Irwin as his private secretary in his last years is a good example.[58] But there was much convergence of interest also. Having pioneered areas now occupied by the church at large – as with clerical societies, church journalism and the revival of traditional usages – Evangelicals were content to share, or even surrender, the field. The *Christian Examiner* ceased publication after 45 years once the *Irish Ecclesiastical Gazette*, published monthly from 1855, was soundly established. They had long held a high doctrine of confirmation; now W. H. Krause welcomed Whately's practice of combining the rite with first communion as 'the right administration of this ordinance', and in accordance with 'the mind of the Church of England'.[60] Again, they had restored the doctrines of atonement and justification to prominence; now Provost MacDonnell, in the Donnellan Lectures of 1858, made it possible 'to strengthen evangelical doctrine' – against F. D. Maurice and others – 'by softening its more retributive and forensic aspects'. Lord Carlisle, who apparently came to faith in America after the Whig defeat of 1841, and who as Viceroy made Evangelical bishops, praised the interpretations of the atonement by Magee earlier and by MacDonnell – his 'excellent friend' – and also admired Alexander Knox's emphasis on the incarnation as the focus of faith.[61] But beyond trust and convergence, a common mind was evinced in biblical theology and conservative scholarship. It shared a conviction in the centrality of the atonement (however interpreted), in the reality of 'that wonderful change called "conversion"', in Alexander's words, and above all in the plenary inspiration of the Bible and – prominent in Whately's thinking – its unique authority in essential matters of faith and practice. Out of this last conviction came biblical scholarship, expository teaching and preaching, and family piety. Mahaffy had, by the age of 14, been taken through the Bible six times by his mother, 'without losing sympathy for the Christian tradition'. As a young Fellow of

TCD, he regularly heard the Evangelical preachers – Krause, Day and Gregg – and as Provost was still conscious of their power half a century later. In midweek lectures it was usual to work through one book after another, as with Theophilus Campbell of Holy Trinity Belfast, the epistles being much favoured. Perhaps too much: for in an Annual Address to the clergy McNeile criticized those who professed belief in plenary inspiration but neglected the minor prophets. The laity shared this expository approach. Dr Crawford of Belfast described Lord Mandeville as

> a partial investigator of the word of God, diligently comparing Scripture with Scripture till he come to a satisfactory meaning. I have got a great many passages cleared up through him.[62]

In the field of scholarship, R. C. Trench's *Notes on the Parables* and *Notes on the Miracles* were published long before he came to Dublin, Alexander's various commentaries – on the Johannine Epistles and for the *Expositor's Bible* and the *Speaker's Commentary* – when he was still Bishop of Derry. Together with Salmon's *Introduction to the New Testament*, these works reveal the depth of biblical scholarship over 50 years, Whately's four-volume *Scripture Lessons*, written for the National Board, its skill in application, and William Lee's Donnellan Lectures of 1854 its apologetic. In *The Inspiration of the Holy Scriptures: its Nature and Proof*, Lee expounded the tension between the divine and human in inspiration. He rejected the 'mechanical' theory, but yet sought

> to establish, in the broadest sense, all that its supporters desire to maintain – namely, the infallible certainty, and indisputable authority, the perfect and entire truthfulness, of all and every the parts of Holy Scripture.

He classified under three heads the 'defective views' of inspiration held by liberals: first, that the Bible contains, rather than is, the Word of God; second, that the divine influence was universal, but unevenly distributed; and third, that of Schleiermacher and his school, whose shibboleth was, 'the letter killeth, the spirit giveth life'.[63] This, then, is the background to the declaration of the General Convention in 1870:

> The Church of Ireland doth, as heretofore, accept and unfeignedly believe all the Canonical Scriptures of the Old and New Testament, as given by inspiration of God, and as containing all things necessary to salvation.

A theological consensus inhospitable to its principles thwarted the progress of Tractarianism among Irish churchmen. Though content to be 'Catholic without the popery', they could not comprehend, much less countenance, R. H. Froude's Anglicanism 'without the protestantism'. The episcopate, the university, and most of the clergy were therefore united in rejecting Tractarian tenets as un-Anglican. James O'Brien's Primary Charge of 1842, like his Charge of 1845, was a refutation of Tractarianism, and was widely read in England and America. But Whately, with his bitter hatred of the 'Tractites', was their principal antagonist, with the assistance of William Fitzgerald, 'the Archbishop's shadow'. His Charge of 1843 held that, in exalting tradition, the Tractarians implicitly denigrated scripture, for in practice they made tradition equal to revelation in determining belief. In the early 1850s his *Cautions for the Times* – modelled on *Tracts for the Times* and largely written by Fitzgerald – were inspired by the growth of ritualism in England and his fear of its spreading to Ireland. There were other Irish antagonists. When in 1846 the rector of Tandragee, Mortimer O'Sullivan, published his *Theory and Developments in Christian Doctrine*, the *Christian Examiner* opined that Newman had 'fallen into hands powerful enough to expose him to himself'. That journal, for its part, kept its readership well informed. It provided in 1838 analyses of Froude's *Remains* and of Newman's *Lectures on Justification,* and in 1840 printed the condemnation of Tractarian principles by the Heads of the University of Oxford.[64] Positively, it carried a series of articles by Robert Daly on 'the Authority of the Church' (an exposition of Article XX), treatises on episcopacy, sacraments and liturgy, and information on the Parker Society, founded in 1843 to reprint the works of the Anglican Reformers.

The experience of two men of Tractarian background, the one the guest, the other the son of an Irish rectory, is instructive. On coming down from Oriel, the future historian and man of letters, James Anthony Froude (R. H. Froude's brother), spent some months with William Cleaver at Delgany and as a result lost confidence in his Oxford teachers. Two considerations influenced him. The first was his discovery that Anglican clergy 'of weight and learning' could hold reformed principles, and 'the Church to which Newman and Keble had taught us to look as our guide did not condemn them'. The second was that these principles had observable effects in Christian character and spirituality. For, as evinced in their sermons, hymns and conversation, the 'cultivated circle' among whom he moved – the Glendalough clergy and laity – were as full of the Spirit of Christ as 'the most developed saint in the Catholic calendar'. He found in particular a quiet good sense and an intellectual breadth of feeling in his host's household, which to one 'who had been brought up to despise Evangelicals as unreal and affected was a startling surprise'. The long family devotions, the business of relating these to the duties of daily life, and the quality of the devotional literature, were also a revelation to him.

> Evangelicalism had been represented to me as weak and illiterate. I had found it in harmony with reason and experience, and recommended as it was by personal holiness in its professors, and general beauty of mind and character, I concluded that Protestantism had more to say for itself than my Oxford teachers had allowed.[65]

Froude's contemporary, F. R. Wynne, the future Bishop of Killaloe, was brought up by his father Henry Wynne, a rector in county Wexford, on Keble's *The Christian Year* and Manning's sermons. His biographer – his son-in-law J. O. Hannay (better known as George A. Birmingham, the novelist), a severe critic of the later Evangelicals – records that his Evangelical friends in Trinity, including E. C. Stuart of Edinburgh, the future colonial bishop, were 'men of real piety' whose companionship 'deepened and strengthened his personal religion'. It was the same when Wynne left College. As curate of Carnteel (Aughnacloy) from 1850, he found in his rector, Archdeacon Stokes, 'a kind and sympathetic friend and a true spiritual father'. By the time he moved on to a curacy in Queen's County, and was appointed by Sir Charles Coote to the chaplaincy of Ballyfin House, he had lost all his Tractarian traces. McDowell sees him as a 'liberal evangelical'.[66]

But Irish opposition to the Tractarians was not confined to the Evangelical and Broad traditions. It came from the old High Church tradition also. As Dr Nockles has established, that tradition was damaged by Tractarianism, which 'diverged both spiritually and theologically' from it, and so had 'a negative impact on the fortunes of native High Church traditions' in both Scotland and Ireland.[67] This impact was accentuated for the Irish Church in that Newman and other Tractarian leaders attacked her in the *British Critic* as 'uncatholic', and condemned Irish High Church attempts to win converts from Roman Catholicism. For that reason they mostly withheld their support from St Columba's College, which was founded in 1843 by William Monsell, Lord Adare and the English clergyman William Sewell, under the patronage of Primate Beresford, expressly to educate converts from Roman Catholicism in church principles. For their part, although they had welcomed the early *Tracts for the Times*, Irish High Churchmen parted company with the Tractarian leaders after they embraced extremes of doctrine and abandoned the Anglican Reformers. An example was W. A. Fisher, rector of Kilmoe in west Cork (1840-80). He had at first 'delighted' in the Tracts, but after Newman's *Tract No. 90* (1841) was published, tied up all his copies of them, 'and put them out of reach on top of his bookcase, and never more opened them', convinced 'that he was being led away from Christ to external things'. Primate Beresford read the Tract 'with deep concern and I must say with considerable indignation', and condemned it publicly in his charge of 1841. Nonetheless, their early association with the Tractarian leaders was used by their opponents as a stick with which to beat men of old High Church tradition, and their progress in the church was retarded. The monthly *Irish Ecclesiastical Journal* which they founded in 1840 was forced to cease publication in 1850. St Columba's abandoned its early missionary purpose and became instead a public school on explicitly High Church lines. The tradition suffered also both from defections – Aubrey de Vere, Monsell and

Adare became Roman Catholics – and lack of political patronage: Evangelicals were appointed bishops from 1842, but not High Churchmen.[68]

Despite the difficulties, however, the old High Church tradition proved indestructible. Men of intellectual stature continued to identify with it. Todd was now librarian and professor of Hebrew in TCD, Samuel Butcher became Regius professor of divinity in 1852, and William Lee professor of ecclesiastical history in 1857. In the decade before disestablishment, High Churchmen joined the Evangelicals and Broad Churchmen on the episcopal bench: Richard Trench in 1863, Butcher in 1866, and William Alexander in 1867. High Church influences were seen in worship. Todd developed the choral traditions of St Patrick's Cathedral after he joined the chapter in 1837, and Mant published his *Church Architecture Considered* in 1843 (the same year as the younger Jebb's *Choral Service of the United Church of England and Ireland* was published). Dublin churches of High Church tradition became well known: All Saints' Grangegorman, where William Maturin became incumbent in 1843; St John the Evangelist Sandymount, founded by Sidney Herbert MP in 1850, with Dr William De Burgh as its first incumbent, and Butcher and Todd among its trustees; and St Stephen's and St Bartholomew's. The tradition provided the Church of England and Anglican Churches overseas with able priests. Its passion for work among the urban poor was to find magnificent outlet in the work of Father Robert Dolling (1851-1902) in the slums first of Dublin, and then of Portsmouth and Poplar. Its influence, out of all proportion to its numerical strength, was to be exerted in the Revision debates after disestablishment in order to safeguard (in alliance with conservative Evangelicals) the church's catholic heritage, and not least by the saintly, scholarly Canon Richard Travers Smith, vicar of St Bartholomew (1871-1905). It was strong enough also for Todd and Maturin to found in 1866 the Irish Church Society; and resilient enough to survive ugly Low Church demonstrations, inspired by fear of rampant ritualism in England, such as that at St Stephen's in 1870.

Relations with the Presbyterians were strained during the period, particularly in Ulster. Indeed, with southern detachment, the *Christian Examiner* deplored a 'civil war' which distracted both churches there from their common purposes, and urged them to concentrate on their essential unity. The journal's point that Presbyterians were only 'technically' dissenters, in that their church was established in Scotland, was just as unrealistic. For the technicality involved legal disability, highlighted when the Consistorial Court of Armagh declared mixed marriages to be void when performed by Presbyterian ministers. It required Acts of Parliament, first in 1842 to confirm the validity of such existing marriages, and then in 1844 to authorize their celebration in future. Again, Presbyterians ended their opposition to national education at the very time the Church Education Society rejected it. Emerson attributed the tension in relationships to these marriage and education issues; but it went deeper than that. Presbyterians shared the revived antagonism of English nonconformists to the Established Church and, with Dr Henry Cooke as a notable exception, wanted disestablishment. They outnumbered Anglicans in Ulster, and the union of their Synods in 1840 enhanced their confidence. They also held a high doctrine of their church's polity in government and worship, and were wont to dismiss episcopacy as 'prelacy' and liturgical worship as 'popish'. The moderate episcopacy traditionally professed by the Church of Ireland was, ironically, seen as provocative when publicly avowed in rejecting the exclusive episcopacy of the Tractarians – there was a particularly acrimonious controversy in Derry; and in the 1860s the Anglican baptismal and burial services came under attack from Presbyterians. There were instances of mutual support at local level in church extension and charitable endeavour, and there was co-operation between many ministers of the two churches during the 1859 revival. But these exceptions neither counteracted the penchant of a lively theological age for public controversy, nor disguised the antagonisms of Ulster's communal relationships, rooted as these were in history, folk memory and statute.[69]

The period of Evangelical ascendancy in the church (c. 1845-95) lasted for some 25 years each side of disestablishment. In 1905 Primate Alexander regaled General Synod with his memories of the revival's influence before 1870. It had been 'almost everywhere', its parochial activity incessant, its saintliness evident, its preaching earnest and simple, warm-hearted and often extemporaneous, with few sermons of the sort that 'a much-loved bishop described as "not having enough gospel to save a tit-mouse"'.[70] Its clergy were in demand, as early advertisements in the *Irish Ecclesiastical Gazette* reveal. The Archdeacon of Elphin sought a curate for Carrick-on-Shannon 'of proved evangelical piety and active habits'. Another rector specified: 'evangelical views, love of pastoral visiting from house to house, a measure of real pulpit ability, and an aptness for cottage lectures indispensable'.[71] Some clergy stood out: Charles Leslie of Holy Trinity Cork, Dr Traill of Schull, Charles Seaver, minister for 54 years of St John's Laganbank, Prior Moore, Headmaster of Cavan Royal School. At Cloughjordan in Tipperary, the Hon F. F. Trench was renowned for his holiness and asceticism, his apostolic intensity, his Whig politics, and his preaching from the dickey of a carriage during revival in his parish. At Kingstown, where in summer the Mariners' Church boasted one of the largest congregations in Ireland, R. S. Brooke had a 'class system' (evidently in more senses than one).

We had large classes for the children of the gentry; a class of beggars; one for converts from Romanism; one for servants, men and women; one for young men preparing for the ministry; one for pauper old women; a great class of young ladies … but the most prized was our adult seaman's class.

Evangelicals were in the van of progress. During the April convention at the Rotunda, the clergy (over 600 on occasions) spent four early mornings studying subjects of pastoral and topical moment. William Cleaver was the first incumbent to administer baptism during public worship, William McIlwaine of St George's the first in Belfast to hold an early morning celebration and a Harvest thanksgiving service. Sir Benjamin Guinness, at a personal cost of £150,000, restored St Patrick's Cathedral from virtual ruin, and John Gregg, who preached at his funeral in 1868, built the new St Fin Barre's Cathedral. In TCD, Singer gave informal lectures on pastoral theology years before they were introduced into the divinity curriculum. Again, the laity purchased corporation livings when the Municipal Reform Act abolished all but 10 of the town corporations and, by making these elective, transferred control of most to Catholics. Thus in Limerick the trustees of Trinity Church bought at public auction the advowson of St Laurence's parish, which had no church, and appointed their minister as rector – Benjamin Jacob (1839-62), 'a man of outstanding abilities and of deep spiritual power who left his mark upon Limerick'.

In Dublin a fund was raised to buy up livings, with Singer, Roden and Arthur Guinness among its trustees. Hitherto Evangelical strength had resided in the city's voluntary churches, but by the 1850s they held the parishes of St Nicholas (Halahan), St Luke (Burroughs) and St Michan (Charles Stanford, the last editor of the *Christian Examiner*); and Hon Henry Pakenham was Dean of St Patrick's. Nonetheless, two-thirds of Dublin's church population are estimated to have attended the voluntary churches. Preachers of renown were Hamilton Verschoyle at Baggotsrath, Krause at Bethesda, Charles Marlay Fleury, tenth in a line of Huguenot pastors, at the Molyneux chapel, John Gregg at Trinity Church, and Henry Irwin at Sandford. Gregg said of the last that no man 'influenced a greater number of the educated, thinking and reading portion of society', and when in 1857 Irwin celebrated the 60th anniversary of his ordination, a testimonial was signed by almost 1000 clergy.[72] Maurice Day came among these pulpit giants, most of whom preached extempore, when St Matthias's was opened in 1843. Canon T. W. E. Drury, recalling in 1950 that he had heard Day preach in old age, wrote of him:

> This young man, who always wrote his sermons and preached from his MS, whose sermons were chiefly on doctrinal subjects, who cultivated no tricks of oratory … soon built up one of the largest and most influential congregations in Dublin.

The young Charles F. D'Arcy belonged to it.[73] In 1867, when Day became rector of Enniskillen, Achilles Daunt succeeded him, as William Pakenham Walsh had Irwin in 1858. McDowell and Stanford point out that these were men of learning and breeding, loyal to their church and its liturgy, who 'treated the sermon as a vital force and preached with tremendous vigour and emotional earnestness'. Here John Gregg was pre-eminent. Though Trinity Church seated 1800, it attracted congregations of over 2000, some sitting on the pulpit steps and TCD students standing in the aisles. Gregg preached extempore for more than an hour, out of his long concentration on the text and his general reading in works of oratory, classical authors, poetry, history and biography. Mahaffy might 'escape' College chapel, and hear Newman at the Catholic University chapel, or Maturin ('of the early Tractarian school') at Grangegorman; but he regularly heard Gregg. Lecky might hear Dr Anderson at the Catholic University; he, too, heard Gregg.[74] Lord Carlisle might admire Knox and MacDonnell as theologians; but he attended Trinity Church, and appointed Gregg to the see of Cork. Two other features of these voluntary churches need remark. Their ministers received as such no emolument from the Established Church (though Irwin was also Archdeacon of Emly and Gregg from 1857 Archdeacon of Kildare). And no fewer than four of them became bishops, Gregg and Verschoyle before disestablishment, Day and Walsh after it.

Irish Evangelicals gave much to the Church of England, and to churches overseas. Brooke, McGhee and Sirr went to rural English incumbencies, Capel Molyneux became minister of London's Lock Chapel, and William Pennefather founded the Mildmay Conference and various East End charities. The diocese of Chester under J. B. Sumner attracted many Irish clergy: of these, Joseph Baylee was the founder of St Aidan's Theological College, Birkenhead, and Hugh McNeile incumbent of St Jude's Liverpool. Similarly, the American diocese of Ohio under Charles McIlvaine attracted clergy and laity from Ireland. Much interest was also shown in the Protestant Churches of France and Italy, especially the Vaudois Church through the Dublin Waldensian Aid Society. Anthony Sillery toured the Piedmontese valleys on several occasions, Lord Roden in 1844, when he wrote home accounts of the work there of Colonel John Beckwith, a nephew of Sir George Beckwith who had commanded the Forces in Ireland. In 1852 Roden also led a European deputation to Italy to secure the release of Rosa and Francesca Madiai, who had been imprisoned in Tuscany for reading the Scriptures.[75]

*Irish Clergy in Anglican Churches overseas*
The strengthening High Church tradition, like the Evangelical tradition, contributed hugely to the growth of Anglican churches overseas: the Dublin

churches of All Saints, St John and St Bartholemew evinced a strong missionary zeal from their foundation. With CMS concentrating in Africa and the East, SPG sponsored missionaries from both traditions in its work in Canada. Of the 106 Irish clergy sent overseas in the period 1824-70 by SPG, 67 (more than half) went to Canada, 19 to Australia, and six to South Africa. One of the remaining 14 was George Hunn Nobbs of Dublin, who settled among the Pitcairn Islanders and later joined their migration to Norfolk Island. Edward Synge was outstanding among early SPG-sponsored clergy in New South Wales. Bishop Frederic Barker of Sydney wrote in 1863 that Synge

> by his unwearied patience and zeal has planted, and by his prayerful and repeated visits has watered, the seed of Divine life in every part of that vast region, which from the Darling to the coast, requires the traveller to pass upwards of 1000 miles. The Society, by the continuance of its grants to Mr Synge, has conferred a great and lasting blessing on the Colony.[76]

Bishop Barker, who had family connections in Ireland and had worked with the Home Mission, received 18 Irish clergy as against 42 trained in Sydney's Moore College. The first incumbent of Wollongong, Devenish Meares, was a TCD graduate. So was the first Colonial Chaplain in South Australia, Charles Howard (who had been ordained by Sumner). On his early death, another TCD man, James Farrell, married his widow, succeeded him in Holy Trinity Adelaide, and in 1849 became the first Dean of Adelaide. The first Bishop of Melbourne, Charles Perry, might speak of 'the zeal and somewhat of a wrong-headedness' of his Irish clergy, but he relied much on them, none more so than Hussey Burgh Macartney (1799-1894). Descended from Irish orators, one time curate with William Digby, and rector of Kilcock, he had gone out with Perry in 1847, outlived several bishops, built St Paul's Cathedral, and was Dean of Melbourne until he was 95. His service was commemorated in Dean John Paterson's sermon in St Paul's in 1994. Irish laity also made their mark down under. Sir Richard MacDonnell was Governor of South Australia (1855-62) at a formative period in the colony's development. That of the Swan River colony was forwarded by a soldier, Frederick Irwin, son of a Headmaster of Raphoe Royal School, who recruited clergy in Ireland, built a 'rush church' near the site of Perth's modern Anglican cathedral, and wrote prophetically on the responsibilities of colonial powers to aboriginal peoples.[77]

To 1878 the Irish Church provided 87 CMS missionaries: five were women, the majority clergy (including five non-Irish TCD graduates). Robert Trench of Cloughjordan, a Cambridge man like his father, 'full of zeal, overworked himself in India and died of fever, and was followed to the grave by his beautiful young wife' – a daughter of Francis Hewson, rector of

Dunganstown. India also attracted T. H. Fitzpatrick from St Matthias's, H. M. M. Hackett from Crinken, who became Principal of Allahabad Divinity School, and Robert Bruce of Charleville, a brother of Dean Bruce of Cork.[78] In West Africa, John Bowen became Bishop of Sierra Leone. He had emigrated to Canada in 1835, but returned to enter TCD in 1843. Influenced by Krause, Bowen visited CMS stations in 1848-51, and was consecrated in 1857, only to die two years later – a tragically normal span in the swamps of West Africa. Colman Hammond, father of T. C. Hammond, also served in Sierra Leone in the 1850s, his first wife dying there of fever. The later concentration of Irish CMS missionaries in East Africa, particularly in Kenya and Uganda, was complemented by the influence of Irish SPG missionaries in South Africa. William Wright, the first of them, had arrived at the Cape on 8 March 1821: the first celebration of Holy Communion in South Africa took place in his church on Christmas Day 1822, with 16 communicants. Wright's strong opposition to nascent racism led him into trouble with the Irish governor, Sir Lowry Cole: he left the Cape in 1829. The Dublin philanthropist, Charles Orpen, was ordained at the age of 57 for work in South Africa, and a former Roman Catholic priest in Clonfert, John Quinn, also worked there. Two other Irish clergy, Dean Williams of Grahamstown and Canon St Leger of Capetown, founded newspapers, the (*Eastern*) *Star* and *Cape Times*, respectively. All these men were identified with the church of the Province of South Africa, whereas Robert ('Paddy') Lamb from Cork became a founder of the small independent Church of England in South Africa (with which Sydney diocese has retained links).[79] The first Irishman to go to New Zealand with CMS was R. Maunsell of Limerick. He spent 59 years there, and became Archdeacon of Waikato. His son G. Maunsell translated much of the Bible into Maori. Another TCD man, E. C. Stuart, became Bishop of Waiapu in 1877.

In Canada, Bishop John Inglis of Nova Scotia proved as indefatigable as his father Charles. In his first visitation, which took in Bermuda, he travelled 5000 miles, consecrated 44 churches, and confirmed over 4300 people. He reminded his clergy in 1839 that the Church in Canada owed its existence under God to SPG. The voluntary principle was to become prominent, for during the 1830s government financial aid to the church was phased out, with clergy in post guaranteed 75 per cent of their stipends (similar to the Irish tithe settlement of 1838). John Inglis died in 1850. The Irish episcopal succession was resumed when Benjamin Cronyn became Bishop of Huron in 1857. He was the first elected bishop in Canada, legal standing having been given to Anglican Synods in 1857. An Evangelical sponsored by SPG, Cronyn had been ordained by Power Trench in 1827, and served the Longford parish of Kilcommick until he emigrated to Canada in 1832. After his consecration in Lambeth Palace, he made for Dublin and recruited three young men in Dr Fleury's Bible class. In their early years in Canada they were known as 'the three musketeers': all three became bishops. Initially they did much to provide the Canadian Church, in Philip Carrington's words, with 'strong, magnetic leadership rather than perpetual controversy'; and to create – as in Dublin – 'the big city church with its substantial lay support and its popular preacher'. Edward Sullivan assisted in St George's Montreal, then became rector of Trinity Church Chicago; James Carmichael succeeded him in St George's, and later became Dean of Montreal; and John Philip Du Moulin became rector of St James's Toronto. Of Cronyn himself, Carrington wrote:

> The new diocese of Huron, under its energetic and forceful bishop, became a powerhouse for the whole Canadian Church. He was a great fighter, and a great fisher of men.

John Travers Lewis, who came from an aristocratic background in Cork, was a bishop of a different churchmanship. He was loyal to his Evangelical clergy, many of them Irish, but careful not to add to their number! Lewis, too, achieved a first, for his consecration as Bishop of Ontario in 1862 was the first to take place in Canada (in St George's Cathedral Kingston). At the third Provincial Synod of Canada, in 1865, Lewis proposed that the Archbishop of Canterbury be requested to convene a conference of bishops representing the entire Anglican Communion. The idea had previously been mooted by an American bishop, but it was the formal proposal from Canada which was taken up and which led to the first Lambeth Conference in 1867. Lewis became Archbishop of Ontario in 1893: his episcopate lasted for 40 years.[80]

## 2. The Great Famine

The Famine of 1845-8 differed from previous famines both in geographical extent and duration, but like them drew a heroic response from the Church of Ireland. If, as Louis Cullen has it, 'the Famine was less a national disaster than a social and regional one', then there is evidence that clergy (and sometimes landed families) mitigated its effect in particular regions, as they had done in Connacht in 1822 and 1831. With so many absentee landlords, the weight of responsibility fell on the clergy, the *Freeman's Journal* noting as early as 17 November 1845 their 'zeal to obviate the impending miseries'. They had no monopoly of that zeal. William Carleton wrote at the time of the 'exertions of the clergy of all creeds', and Patrick Hickey thinks that the churches emerge 'with fair credit' from the Famine: 'the number of victims among the clergy testifies to their efforts'.[81]

In the Church of Ireland's case, in 1847 alone 40 clergy died of exhaustion or of fever contracted in the course of relief work. In Canada, in the same year, five Anglican clergy died of famine fever at the quarantine station on the St Lawrence. Archer Butler, who as rector of Raymochy (from 1842) experienced the Famine's 'appalling intensity' in Donegal and superintended the distribution of food in his parish, saw one good result of the crisis: 'it has tended to remove prejudices … which, in some degree, existed towards the clergy of the church, on the part of their poorer Roman parishioners'. His biographer, Thomas Woodward, vicar of Mullingar, noted that 'the inestimable value of our parochial system, even in a temporal aspect, in districts which could be reached by no other machinery', had been widely acknowledged.[82] Desmond Bowen's researches have tested that claim for three western counties. In Galway, Mayo, and Sligo the local Relief Committees were usually staffed by clergy, and with the Roman Catholic priests seldom 'out of the saddle' as they ministered to the dying, they were usually glad to leave the organization of relief to the Protestant clergy. Hence most of the applications for aid received by the Quakers in Dublin came from, and most relief grants were made to, the latter. Although often in hardship as well as danger – incomes were withheld by absentee landlords whose rents had been stopped – the clergy organized soup kitchens. Their presence meant the difference between life and death. Thus at Renvyle in Connemara a resident curate fed the people, whereas at Bundarragha on Killary Bay the people starved for want of a clergyman. It was the same when *HMS Scourge* landed two boilers on the Mullet in Mayo, Bowen noting that there was no one to 'set up a food station, the boilers could not be operated, and the people died'.[83]

The presence of the clergy was as vital elsewhere. In the parish of Donaghmore in Derry diocese the rector was an absentee and there were no resident gentry. The curate, Edward Maguire (later Dean of Down), applied for food and was supplied first with meal by the Quakers, then with Indian corn imported by the government. It 'fell to my lot', he wrote, 'to distribute the foodstuffs at reduced prices, and to account for all the money received. Hundreds of starving people passed weekly through my hands.' In south Ulster the efforts of the future Dean of Connor, Charles Seaver, curate of Mullabrack, made him a household name in the countryside. He personally supervised the distribution of food at the great soup kitchens in the district – there were 5000 names on his relief list – and no death from starvation was recorded.[84] Further south, but still in Armagh diocese, William Pennefather was incumbent of Mellifont near Drogheda. As emphasis moved nationally from the provision of relief works, to that provided by voluntary agencies, to outdoor relief (under the 'Soup Kitchens Act' of early 1847), he tried forlornly to keep pace with it. The sufferings of his community are reflected in his letters. Money sent to him, he wrote in November 1846, was timely

> for even here the poverty is great. It is wages the people want; food there

is at present, if there were money to purchase it. On Monday I was at the Relief Committee and pinching hunger was too plainly written on the faces of many of the people. I am going to drain a field I have, make walks, etc. to try to find employment for a few. But it is always difficult to *close* such works, and of course I could not long continue them.

The situation deteriorated, and although in the winter of 1847-8 he was able to distribute Indian meal and rice supplied by Dublin friends, he saw it as but 'a drop in the ocean of misery'. As supplies dwindled, he restricted this relief to the children at his school, but was afraid he would have to close it. (Normal expenses of mistress, house, fuel and food came to £60 out of his annual income of under £84.) In January 1848 he appealed to Richard Nugent in Cavan to 'do anything for my wretched people'. Some 3000 (out of 4500) were paupers, in great destitution: 'my door is besieged by half-starving creatures, just out of fever, craving for food'. The two vital components of relief were an adequate supply of food, and agencies to administer it. Both appear to have been missing at Mellifont, and Pennefather, for all his great philanthropic achievement in the East End in later years, seems to have been unable to influence the provision of them.[85]

The suffering of west Cork is well known, the heroism of the region's clergy not so well. When in 1862 Dr Caulfield was consecrated as Bishop of Nassau in Lambeth Palace, the rector of Durrus, James Freke, recalled in his sermon how as rector of Skibbereen he had 'laboured in the midst of famine and pestilence with an energy which only great physical power, sustained by great spiritual zeal, could have supplied'. His neighbour in Schull, Dr Robert Traill, though his equal in calibre, did not survive. A classical scholar who had dwelt on famine deaths in beleaguered Jerusalem in his translation of Josephus, he died himself as a result of his work among the 18,000 starving people in his parish. Hickey's research has established Traill as a key figure in the regional emergency. He designed a pit to save the potato crop. He wrote to Lord Bandon, and his letter was read in the House of Lords. James Mahoney of the *Illustrated London News* saw him visiting the dying and his daughters distributing food – one was to marry John Synge, and become the mother of J. M. Synge. Traill also escorted Capt Caffin of *HMS Scourge*, which had landed 90 tons of supplies, in a tour of the region, where children were dying with 'an awful rapidity'. Caffin's report shocked Charles Trevelyan in London, and moved F. F. Trench in Tipperary to come to Schull 'out of charity'. On 14 March 1847 Trench met with the Ballydehob Relief Committee and outlined his plan to establish 'eating houses'. His aim was to provide 'a meal of substantial Indian meal stirabout or porridge' a day, rather than just soup.

There is no want of food in any place (delightful consideration) but there is a most deplorable want of *available agencies, and a consequent want of suitable measures to bring the food and the medicine within the reach of the people.*

Trench therefore sent to Dublin for doctors, and appealed for volunteers. One of those who responded was his cousin, R. C. Trench, the future Archbishop of Dublin, then professor of divinity at King's College, London. At the height of their effort, he and his helpers gave out 10,000 meals a day at less than 11/4d each in the nine eating houses in Ballydehob, and on 23 April 1847 he was able to write that 'the mortality … had been arrested'. Ironically, Traill had died on 21 April.[86]

It was not only the clergy who cared. From exile in Tasmania, Smith O'Brien noted the contrast between the 'depopulators' who turned the poor out to be 'absorbed (or exterminated)', and his family in county Clare, who 'in the most disastrous period of Ireland's calamities cherished the children of the soil'. Patsy Adam-Smith observes that Charlotte O'Brien not only concerned herself with the estate population at Dromoland, but also with 'feeding the general starving and homeless', and that, as 'a great organizer and humanitarian herself', she denounced incompetence wherever she found it. Thus on hearing of the extremities to which starving people at Bantry had been driven, Lady O'Brien wrote on 13 February 1847 that, with resident gentlemen there and 'a good harbour to bring provisions direct from America', there must be great mismanagement which ought to be enquired into. By contrast, 'in our neighbourhood the people are so well taken care of that there is nothing like starvation'. Her practical approach is clear from another of her letters:

> I am setting up Mary Grady as a seller of food at Mohane and she says it is the greatest comfort for the people around her to be able to buy supplies for supper and breakfast without having to go to Newmarket or Ennis, both of which places are often without bread or meat. I am encouraging them to make rich porridge and sell it out to their neighbours at a penny a quart.[87]

The experience of Killala and Achonry during the Famine has been researched in detail by Bowen. Of their 40 clergy, only one was non-resident, while in the case of several others service to the dioceses went back a long way. Three Mayo incumbents had been involved in famine relief in 1822 and 1831. They were Joseph Verschoyle Sr of Ballysakerry, nephew of Bishop James Verschoyle, George Birmingham at Lacken, and James Burrowes, tutor to Bishop Stock's family in 1798, who had held the living of Castleconnor from 1804. Robert Noble, vicar of Athboy in Meath, came during 1847 to assist this 'aged vicar' – Burrowes was then 78 – 'in his onerous duties of feeding the hungry, attending the dying, and burying the dead'. He noted that for five months past 400 families had received food weekly at the glebe house at the hands of his family, and that one daughter had died, and his wife become ill, of fever. Advised to get medical help from Sligo, Burrowes replied, 'my income is stopped, and I cannot afford it'. His wife died, and he soon after her. In many parishes there was co-operation. The Dean of Achonry, E. N. Hoare, who elected to live in the Ox mountains of Sligo, worked with four Roman Catholic priests in setting up seven soup kitchens in the district, while Archdeacon Trulock of Killala, who was rector of the coastal parish of Skreen, served as a magistrate, made representations to government, and also worked with the parish priests in famine relief. He died (aged 55) from exhaustion in September 1847. Again, when Francis Kinkead, the gentle, humane Evangelical curate in Joseph Verschoyle Jr's parish of Kilmoremoy (Ballina), who had fed 1100 people from a soup kitchen during the last weeks of 1846, died of 'road fever' on 27 January 1847, the Roman Catholic bishop and people 'offered united supplication for his soul's repose', and the *Tyrawley Herald* opined that 'his life was sacrificed to his love'. The same newspaper reported (on 20 March 1848) the death of another clergy wife of famine fever, 'caught in the discharge of a charitable duty which she was always foremost in performing'. This was Jane, wife of Francis Little of Dunfeeny (Ballycastle), whose clerical father, James Little of Lackan, had kept a diary during the French invasion of 1798. William Tyndall, however, had arrived only in 1835, to the mountain parish of Kilmacteigue. In the spring of 1847 he did the work of the local doctor who had fled to Dublin, and with the assistance of two sisters and a brother, worked also in the soup kitchens. In July he caught famine fever and died. The parish priest, James Higgins, wrote of him to the Quakers as his 'charitable and good friend'.[88]

Criticism of the Church of Ireland's role in the Famine was implicit, first, in allegations that Protestant north-east Ulster, which escaped its severity, had done little for starving people elsewhere. Thomas Drew, who was prominent in the Belfast Relief Committee, said publicly in Tuam in 1853 that Belfast had sent £20,000 for relief in Connacht, adding – hand raised – that £7000 had 'passed through that right hand alone'. The more serious allegation, however, was that of souperism. Its myth rests on the assumptions that the Church of Ireland engaged in proselytism during the Famine, and promoted it by selective distribution of food. Souperism, in fact, was more often alleged in relation to the church's missionary work after the Famine (and is taken into account later). Its application to the Famine is misplaced, and evidence of it is seldom offered. Hickey observes that it 'distracted attention not only at the time but ever since from the heroic charity' of men such as Traill and the Trenches, and quotes the Roman Catholic priest who told J. F. Maguire, the editor of the *Cork Examiner*, of 'the noble and God-like exertions' of F. F. Trench, who had not made 'the least attempt to interfere with the religious faith of the people'.[89] But had anyone in west Cork? Robert Traill had long 'waged war on popery in its thousand forms of wickedness'. But not in 1847, when he was working himself to death relieving famine. In his play, *Souper Sullivan*, Eoghan Harris took up the story of William Fisher, rector of Kilmoe or Goleen (one of the six parishes profiled by Hickey): 'his critics do not deny that he was an Irish scholar, that he fed the poor, that he saved many lives. They think that a charge of proslytism [sic] is enough to distract attention from his epic achievement.'[90] Interestingly, both Harris and Hickey use the phrase, 'distract attention'. Is the intention of the myth as applied to the Famine to distract and discredit? Pennefather at Mellifont noted that the priests were furious because he fed the Catholic children at his school. But was he to let them starve on account of their religion? Bowen has established that charges of proselytism and souperism were made against only four of the 40 clergy in Killala and Achonry. His investigation of these takes account of the character of the clergy, their specific refutation of the charges, and the motives of 'political priests' in making them; and concludes both that the charges are 'not proven', and that the clergy of the two dioceses 'were not guilty' of either souperism or proselytism during the crisis of 1847'.[91] In the context of the Great Famine, then, souperism is an intrusive irrelevance. The Church of Ireland can recall without distraction the unremitting efforts of her clergy and their families to save lives, and with pride the sacrifice of those men and women who in love laid down their own.

### 3. The 1859 revival

'Now, my dear bishop, may the Lord strengthen you and your clergy, and give you all wisdom and grace to carry forward, as His instruments, by His power, this glorious work'. So Charles McIlvaine, Bishop of Ohio, wrote to Bishop Robert Knox of Down during 'the '59 revival' in Ulster. That visitation profoundly affected the Church of Ireland, the Presbyterian Church, and the smaller denominations of evangelical Protestants. But although documentation of its impact on the church is prolific, most accounts lean heavily on Presbyterian sources and tend to present the revival as primarily a Presbyterian experience. That impression was heightened when in 1959 the Presbyterian Church celebrated, and the Church of Ireland largely ignored, the centenary of the revival: Dean Emerson's booklet *The Church of Ireland and the 1859 Revival* was published at the time to counter the impression. But even a cursory glance at contemporary records serves as a corrective.[92]

In November 1859, the incumbent of St John's Laganbank, Charles Seaver, wrote of the experience of Down, Connor and Dromore:

I am in a position to state that above seventy parishes in these dioceses have felt the power of the Holy Ghost. Vice and immorality have greatly decreased, Sunday schools have had the attendance nearly doubled, the houses of God have been crowded, and the communicants greatly increased.

He added that the bishop had to date held confirmations in the Belfast churches of Ballymacarrett, the Magdalene chapel, St John's and Trinity, 'instead of all in the parish church, as in former years'. Bishop Knox himself, after hearing 'the report of men of sober minds and sound judgements', had written in July:

I felt that God was shedding abroad, in many places, a spirit of knowledge and fear of the Lord, inducing in many cases, reformation of life. I speak not now of the physical and bodily prostrations – to them I attach little importance – but of that strong conviction of sin, prayer for mercy, calling upon Christ for pardon, and the testimony of a reformed life – and who can scoff at such fruits as these?

Knox had earlier called his clergy to a conference on the revival. Perplexed by some aspects of the movement, he had first written for advice to his brother bishop in Ohio, and he read McIlvaine's reply to his clergy, with its encouragement of the movement's spiritual good and its counsel as to its undesirable concomitants. The vicar of Belfast, Dr Miller, noted that the assembled clergy were unanimous in their desire to continue active in the revival work 'in a calm and prayerful spirit', and in their resolve 'to avail ourselves of every practicable opportunity, at all times and in all places, to preach and teach Christ'. The attitudes of Knox and his clergy to the revival, then, are explicitly clear, as is their alertness to any evil tendency which might injure their people.[93]

Churchmen had studied revival. The *Christian Examiner* had earlier carried analyses of its history and characteristics in America and Scotland. Awareness was heightened when news of the translatlantic revival of 1857 reached Ireland. The General Assembly heard reports at its meeting in Derry in 1858. The Church of Ireland had no such formal convocation, but during the April Meetings of 1859 the theme of the clergy conference on the third morning was 'Spiritual awakenings', and the hundreds of clergy present heard eyewitness accounts from America.[94] In many Ulster parishes sermons and prayer groups dwelt on revival, expectancy increased, and, after the revival had claimed its first converts, Seaver suggested that 'a work of grace, silent but deep and progressive, had been going on for some time, gradually leading them to the Saviour'. From April to the end of the year, the revival's progress was monitored monthly by the *Christian Examiner*, while visiting clergy recorded their experiences – notably Dr Salmon, Archdeacon Stopford of Meath, Maurice Day, Achilles Daunt and the ubiquitous F. F. Trench. Their consensus was that no new agencies were being employed, and that the church's ordinary means of grace – communion services, worship in church and the open air, preaching and prayer groups, now often multiplied – were being visited with extraordinary power. The Hon Henry Ward, rector of Killinchy, said that those who had undergone 'a saving change' in the past had been numbered by tens, or even twos; 'but now, blessed be God, they can be counted by hundreds'. Clergy in other dioceses concurred. Robert Smyth, who had succeeded Robert Alexander in Garvagh in 1832, had 'never before witnessed even the most remote approach to what is now going on'. Two Clogher clergy applied to the Religious Tract Society in London for literature, the one reporting that 250 parishioners had come to faith, the other that the revival had affected almost every family in his parish of 5000 souls. Some saw in the unwonted unity of Anglican and Presbyterian proof of the revival's divine origin. For, with but few exceptions – recent animosities proved too durable in Londonderry – the major towns experienced such unity. In Enniskillen a united service was held under General Cole's monument, in Lurgan clergy and ministers went 'hand in hand', in Newry the Dean of Dromore, Dr Daniel Bagot, presided at a 'union meeting'; and the harmony in Coleraine was the wonder of the world, attracting clergy from London, ministers from Edinburgh, and church leaders from as far as India and Malta.[95]

There was a dark side to the revival movement which its chroniclers have not always appraised. It did not consist in the physical prostrations as such, but rather in giving undue prominence to these, or any other, concomitants of revival – later in its course, visions and stigmata were common phenomena. In Seaver's view, the tendency of the 'bodily affections' was not necessarily evil, and they were common during the early intensity of the revival; but where they were discouraged they did not occur, as in Trinity Church under Theophilus Campbell, or the Presbyterian congregations of Henry Cooke and James Morgan. Men and women under conviction of sin, as Bishop Knox had noted, often experienced great emotion, but no more so, as Henry Ward put it, than the liturgy allowed in its confession that the memory of past sins is 'grievous unto us, the burden of them intolerable'. What men of discernment set their faces against, however, was 'revivalism', which sought to induce emotion and to contrive physical reaction through excitement. They saw it as Satan's 'counterwork' to the work of God, and opposed it as counterfeit. The sermon published in 1859 by one of the church's leading intellectuals, the egyptologist Edward Hincks of Killyleagh, was typical of their attitude: 'The devices of Satan as they respect a great work of God which is now going on in this country'. This attitude was shared by the Presbyterian minister, Isaac Nelson, out of his understanding of an earlier Ulster revival, and by Bishop McIlvaine, out of his experience of earlier

American revivals.[96] The latter warned Bishop Knox that God's work was marred when inventions of men to promote excitement were introduced, when even prayer became 'an auxiliary of excitement', preaching became a caricature of truth to the same end, and 'Christ was preached exceeding little'. Such features were present in Ulster, and are well documented. They were exposed by, among others, Archdeacon Stopford, Dr McIlwaine of St George's Belfast, Professor McNeece, the Archbishop King's lecturer in TCD and rector of Arboe, and a Coleraine layman, Stephen Gwynn. Dr Salmon also used his great authority to hold the revival movement under Scripture, and was at pains

> to distinguish from the real work of God those human elements which, in my judgement, disfigure this movement. If the clergy pet and encourage what they ought to suppress, thereby inducing false tests of the presence of God's Spirit, and giving occasion to the enemy to blaspheme, it is a Christian duty to labour to correct those errors.

Nonetheless, as with the others, Salmon kept the negative aspects in perspective, and trusted that, when all deductions were made, much would 'remain to the praise and glory of the Lord in the day of His appearing'.

The more immediate outcomes of the revival cannot be as confidently assumed. Clergy in England, influenced by reports of its darker side, were generally not supporters of revival. John Venn, who out of his first hand experience in Ulster was a supporter, became discouraged when the revival did not immediately deliver Irish recruits to CMS: Eugene Stock, assessing the position later, realized that delivery had only been delayed – a tribute to the permanent effects of the revival.[97] In Ulster itself, fringe Protestant groups grew during the 1860s, particularly the Brethren, mainly at the expense of the Presbyterians. Otherwise, historians tend to mistime the laity's new prominence in the Church of Ireland: it had been a feature of the Evangelical revival for two generations, and was not a result of the 1859 revival. Not least, it has become fashionable to attribute the Ulster revival, in sociological terms, to a predisposition which was common to insecure societies. Whatever the validity of that attribution, however, it is not incompatible with the contemporary understanding of clergy and laity that Ulster had experienced spiritual revival in which good and evil were intermingled, and in which also 'all wisdom and grace' were given to its human 'instruments', so that through their teaching authority and pastoral sensitivity the good might prevail. As Patrick Collinson, with reference to an 18th century Scottish revival, has cautioned those concerned with Church of Ireland history: 'the spirit bloweth where it listeth and the social scientist may be able to account for everything except that'.[98]

*4. The Reformation continued*

That appreciable numbers of Roman Catholics joined the Church of Ireland in the two decades after the Famine is not in dispute. Disagreement arises over the circumstances. Historians tend to distinguish 'ultra-Protestants' and their ' proselytizing agencies' from other churchmen; but most bishops supported home mission and leading men in the Establishment were among its apologists. Again, the myth of souperism at once alleges that conversions were procured by material means and by implication denies conscientious reasons for converting; but it ignores the persecution to which converts were often subjected and the testimony of outside observers as to their integrity. That such controversial matter is uncongenial to the mindset of the late 20th century is not in doubt; but the Victorian Church can be justly appraised only in terms of her own convictions. She conceived that it was her duty to proclaim evangelical truth and confute Roman error. As William Conyngham Plunket put it, her 'mission' to Roman Catholics did not imply that they were heathen, for she had a 'mission' to her own nominal members also. Rather it was her place

> to approach them as Christian brethren, and to adjure them in a spirit of love for the sake of our common Lord and Master, to escape from out those dark clouds of human tradition whereby His glory is obscured and His Gospel well-nigh hid, and to enjoy in all its fulness the light which His holy Word reveals.[99]

That adjurement was variously sustained. In 1852 a number of academics, unhappy with 'the prevailing tone and spirit of religious controversy in Ireland', launched their periodical, *The Catholic Layman*. They included Butcher and Salmon, E. A. Stopford and J. H. Todd. Their aim was to improve the temper of controversy, their object to promote

> such a knowledge of controversial theology and ecclesiastical history, as is necessary to enable a man of ordinary intelligence and education to form an independent judgment between the rival claims of the Churches of England and Rome.[100]

Rivalry is the *mot juste*. Its essence was discerned by Salmon. One of the church's profoundest intellects since the Reformation, his *Infallibility of the Church* was a remorseless critique of Roman Catholic dogma. But his analysis went beyond dogma. Convinced that 'Rome is against the Scriptures because she believes the Scriptures are against her', he explained why he was 'not ashamed of the object aimed at' in controversy.

> I believe that the Church of Rome teaches false doctrine on many points which must be called important … [and that] they who submit to her are obliged to surrender their understanding to her… I count it, then, a very good work to release a man from Roman bondage.[101]

This attitude informed the Church of Ireland's reaffirmation in 1870 – in the Declaration adopted by the General Convention – of her 'constant witness against all those innovations in doctrine and worship' which had defaced or overlaid the primitive faith, and which she had rejected at the Reformation. They also influenced the church's extensive home missionary effort before 1870. By 1853 the Irish Society supported six national supervisors – four clergy and two inspectors of schools; 60 resident clerical superintendents; 26 ordained missionaries; 104 Scripture readers (151 in 1854); and 580 teachers with 26,232 scholars. It also had at Ventry a collegiate school which prepared men fluent in Irish for entry to TCD. It worked 'silently and steadily through the district' around Doon, with missionary clergy at Doon, Pallas and Cappamore. In 1851 Bishop Daly confirmed 375 persons in Dromkeen church, and 183 in 1854 – there had been under 10 in 1848. Progress in Connemara began at Castlekerke (near Cong) in 1842, and in 1847 Bishop Plunket ordained the Irish-speaking Scripture reader there, J. B. O'Callaghan. By 1849 services in Irish were being held at Errislanon, Ballyconree, Sellerna, Glan and Rooveagh, where Roderick Ryder, a converted priest, worked. O'Callaghan wrote in 1851:

> My congregation on Sundays is now greater than those of the two next Romish chapels put together, and this without holding out any earthly inducement to a single person to change his faith. There is no manner of employment for those who can work, and there is no fund to relieve the sick, the persecuted or the aged.

Plunket ordained Hyacinth D'Arcy after his lands were forfeited under the Encumbered Estates Act, and so gave impetus to the work, for D'Arcy was a strong leader who built many churches and schools. Exactly how Thomas Plunket, Bishop of Tuam (1839-66) was transformed from an absentee, incurring the wrath of both Primate and Viceroy, into a resident diocesan whose courage and resolution sustained the missionary effort, is not clear; but his conversion was as real as his predecessor's, and he saw himself as gathering the fruits of Trench's work. The Society for Irish Church Missions (ICM), founded in 1848 – after the Famine – by Alexander Dallas, an English clergyman, became active in Connemara. While its work depended on indigenous leaders, it was able to deploy resources from England, and by 1852 eight churches and six schoolhouses had been built, 6000 converts were attending church (of whom 1948 had been confirmed since October 1849), and 3000 children attending the schools. Nationally, those same resources allowed ICM to provide missions in 21 counties, with a network of 37 local committees covering 500 parishes, under the sanction of the bishops. At the height of its effort it supported 37 missionary clergy, 98 schoolteachers, 221 Scripture readers and several hundred Irish teachers. The Bishops of

Rochester (Wigram) and Winchester (C. R. Sumner) toured the missionary districts, the former noting that he had

> stood in the districts of Moyrus, Derrygimla, and Clifden, on the Hill of Doon [and] in the island of Inisturk, and found myself surrounded with poor, earnest, intelligent converts who had suffered hardships and proved their sincerity under persecution for the truth's sake.[102]

Ironically, the Irish church was charged in England with neglecting the Roman Catholic population,[103] and in refuting that charge in his paper to the 1863 Church Congress, W. C. Plunket armed himself with evidence from the missionary areas. A clergyman in west Cork, Spring, informed him that whereas he could recall but six churches and clergy in the coastal regions of Skibbereen and Bantry, there were now 14 churches and 16 clergy. In west Connacht – Connemara, Erris and Achill – where in 1848 there had been 13 congregations, 11 clergy and seven churches, there were now 57 congregations, 35 clergy and 27 churches. Tuam diocese alone, in fact, showed an absolute increase of the Protestant population in the 1861 census, and Connemara had become 'characteristically Protestant'. Another clergyman, Lewis, wrote from Dingle that 1100 children of converts had been educated in the Mission's schools and 21 converts ordained. He added that Dingle was now 'a great centre of emigration', as many converts had left for other parts of Ireland during the previous 20 years, 'and five hundred at least emigrated to America'. Plunket also quoted the report of Dr Foley, himself a Dingle convert, that he had met 'hosts of Dingle converts' during a recent visit there, and that of 400 persons whom he had addressed at Boston, most were converts from Kerry 'or had become converts since they removed to America'.[104] Fergus Pyle pointed out that converts also left Connemara for Belfast, Scotland and America, and cited the experience of one convert family. While John Conerney was ordained in Clifden in 1851 and served for many years at Sellerna, his brother Thomas moved to Belfast and worked as a coach fitter. Of Thomas's two ordained sons, John Pirrie Conerney (who died in 1940) became Dean of Raphoe and Patrick Pirrie Conerney bursar of the Church of Ireland Training College.[105] This trend is relevant to the sea change which came over the missionary scene from about 1865, Plunket observing that the 'disheartening drain' of emigration had become a major discouragement. Apologetic support dried up at the same time, and in 1884 – the year he became Archbishop of Dublin – Plunket was to find himself obliged to defend the church's very involvement in 'proselytism', a far cry from the charge of neglect just two decades earlier. Salmon, too, although he continued to lecture on the Roman Controversy, noted that the College Theological Society seldom debated topics bearing upon it. As for missionaries, Bowen notes that they had lost their pioneering zeal and settled into routine parochial ministry. The tide, in short, had ebbed quickly, but its high water mark was to be visible for generations.[106]

The complexities in this area are illustrated in Richard Whately's experience. His archdiocese was affected by the reformation, the Roman Catholic *Tablet* observing in 1851 that 'the seats of successful proselytism' were not Tuam or Cashel, but Dublin. In that year some 700 persons attended a weekly class for inquirers in St Michan's schoolroom, and controversial lectures were given weekly in that parish and in those of St Thomas, St Michael, St James and St Nicholas Without.[107] Whately himself was a controversialist: when in 1854 the dogma of the Immaculate Conception was promulgated, he responded with *Thoughts on the New Dogma of the Church of Rome* (1855), in which he argued that it gave official approbation to a popular cult and an unscriptural doctrine already widely approved in the Roman Catholic Church. Whately did not support the missionary societies, questioned their influence, and even curbed the activity of ICM in one Dublin parish. Here, however, his own household was against him, for his wife was in sympathy with ICM, and several of his daughters were involved in its mission in Dublin. The archbishop did accept the genuineness of conversions in general, and believed that many poor Catholics converted out of gratitude for the sacrificial love shown to them by the clergy and their families during the Famine. He appreciated, too, the influence of the Irish language in promoting biblical education. His modern biographer sees him also as 'convinced of the coercive nature of rural Catholicism', and he was a founder in 1850 of the Society for the Protection of the Rights of Conscience, which supported poor Protestants, including converts, who were victimized on account of their religion. The supreme irony, however, is that Archbishop Cullen saw him as a proselytizer. Whately had prepared scriptural extracts for use in the national schools. Archbishop Murray had approved of these, but not so Paul Cullen. The latter's disapproval was justified by Whately's privately stated belief that these extracts contain so much that is 'inconsistent with the whole spirit of Romanism', even though he could not 'openly support' the National Board as 'an instrument of conversion'. If he differed in style both from his predecessor and from the 'proselytizers', Whately was yet at one with them in essential attitude. It was for that reason that Cullen challenged, and in the event overthrew, his influence in the national schools. If his defeat left Whately embittered, it was but an earnest of the overthrow of the Established Church herself.[108]

PART FIVE

# The independent church, 1871-2001

God make our Church of Ireland to be herself the saviour of the warm-hearted, kindly, impulsive people who form the great mass of our fellow-countrymen.
– *Archbishop J. B.Crozier, addressing the General Synod, 1912.*

For what is the Church? The Church is not the clergy: the Church is the clergy and laity. Administratively, you have all learnt that lesson since the Disestablishment: but, from the point of view of what the Church exists for, the lesson waits to be learnt.
– *Archbishop J. A. F. Gregg, addressing the General Synod, 1942.*

What is the Church's mission today? Is it not to bring men and women into a true and real relationship with Jesus Christ? If our General Synod is not doing that, then we've got to ask ourselves, 'Why are we meeting?'
– *Bishop Edward Darling, preaching at the Eve of Synod Service, 1993.*[1]

## I PROLOGUE: THE GENERAL CONVENTION, 1870

The Irish Church Act received the royal assent on 26 July 1869. The Liberal majority in the Commons had ensured its passage, under Gladstone's masterly guidance, during the spring; and, despite the impassioned eloquence of Bishops Alexander and Magee (in a maiden speech), and the formidable presence of Lord Cairns, the Conservative majority in the Lords did not vote it down. It was an Act, first, of severance. The church ceased to be established by the state, which would no longer appoint her bishops or prescribe her worship. It was an Act also of spoliation. The church lost her endowments, the bishops their lands and palaces, the clergy their incomes and rectories. (Correspondingly, Presbyterians were deprived of the *regium donum*, worth £69 annually to every minister; and Roman Catholics of the annual grant for Maynooth.) The church retained only her churches, churchyards and schools, and the services of her clergy, who were to receive life annuities from the state. She was given the option of purchasing the glebe houses and up to 10 acres of the glebe lands at market value, and compensation of £500,000 for recent private endowments. It was, finally, an Act of self-government. The church became responsible for finance and property, doctrine and discipline, and appointments of bishops and incumbents. Before January 1871, when the Act would become fully operative, she had therefore to address a daunting agenda. But by removing all restrictions on her right to assemble in synod (provincial or diocesan), the Act had restored her freedom of action, and by referring to such a scheme, had in effect recommended her adoption of synodical government by bishops, clergy and laity.[2]

The joint meeting of the Synods of Armagh and Dublin, each summoned by its metropolitan, took place in St Patrick's Cathedral Dublin on 14 September 1869 – the first national clerical assembly since 1711. By definition, the laity were excluded. A general convention of the church would, however, be another matter, and the clergy supported it. The archbishops had already been requested (by a meeting of lay representatives in Dublin) to convene a Lay Conference to decide on the mode of their representation – there were no precedents. When it met in October, chaired first by the Primate, and then by the Duke of Abercorn, it decided that the lay delegates to the general convention should be elected by the new diocesan synods. (The clergy had decided on the same procedure for their delegates, and refused *ex officio* membership to deans and archdeacons.) The Conference also found it 'expedient' that there should be two lay delegates for every clerical delegate. That decision, together with the decision of the clergy not to restrict matters of doctrine and worship to their own order, determined the character of the General Convention (and of the General Synod from 1871). Again, where the clergy were spirited, the laity were practical. The clergy recorded that theirs was 'not to originate a constitution for a new communion, but to repair a sudden breach in one of the most ancient churches in Christendom'. The laity got down to the repair of that breach. They proposed that an organizing committee, made up of the bishops, four representatives (two clerical and two lay) from each diocese, and co-opted members, should draft a constitution for the church. The bishops 'cheerfully acceded', and the Organization Committee – it had five judges among its co-opted members – worked from 5 to 28 January 1870. Its *Draft of an Act of Constitution, with Standing Orders and a Finance Report*, formed the basis upon which the Convention proceeded during more than nine weeks of business.[3]

The General Convention met on 15 February 1870, before its lawyers would become involved in the Assizes, and its parliamentarians with the Irish Land Bill. It sat continuously until 2 April, a total (including Saturdays) of 41 working days; its second session, of 16 days, took place in the autumn.[4] The first session was held in the Antient Concert Rooms, Great Brunswick Street (later Pearse Street), the second in the Metropolitan Hall, Abbey

Street. The Constitution adopted by the Convention consisted in the celebrated Preamble and Declaration, and a series of statutes. These covered the General Synod, diocesan synods, parishes and parochial organization; the Representative Body; the election of bishops and appointment of ministers to cures; and (at the second session) ecclesiastical tribunals.[5] The RCB was constituted during March, and its 60 members appointed in April: the 12 bishops, one clerical and two lay representatives from each diocese, and 12 co-opted members. (Membership rose to 65 when Clogher was separated from Armagh in 1886.) On the first day of the second session (18 October), the General Convention formally received the Charter of Incorporation – under the Act's provisions it had been procured from the Crown and was dated 15 October 1870. The Convention adopted the definitive powers of the RCB by resolution also on 18 October.[6] Thus the church now had both 'an ecclesiastical Parliament' to make her laws, and 'a Corporation to hold and manage' her property.[7] Her status was not unique. As the Primate acknowledged, she had had the example of the churches of Canada, Australia, and New Zealand to guide her, as they in turn had been guided by that of the American Church; and also a Report of the recent Lambeth Conference embodying the experience of all the voluntary Protestant Episcopal Churches. The General Convention, for its part, expressed itself both gratified and cheered by the resolution passed on 8 July 1870 by the Diocesan Synod of Sydney, declaring its 'cordial attachment' to the Church of Ireland, and its 'admiration of the wisdom and ability' which she had displayed in adversity.[8]

Of the 655 delegates to the General Convention, 209 (rather less than one-third) were clergy, and 446 laymen – there were no women delegates. In some southern dioceses clerical representation was greater than a third – in Cloyne it was 41.7 per cent; conversely, clergy were under-represented in some northern dioceses, with 25.0 per cent in Armagh and only 22.2 per cent in Down. The lay representatives were drawn, as circumstances in the Victorian Church dictated, from the aristocracy and gentry and the learned professions. There were 42 peers: two dukes – Abercorn and Manchester – 15 earls, five marquises, seven viscounts, and 13 barons. A further 53 delegates bore other distinguished titles: seven were Right Honourable, 12 Honourable, and 30 baronets; and four heirs to peerages had courtesy titles. These titled delegates apart, representation was distinguished overall, as the extrapolation below indicates.[9]

|  | Armagh | Dublin |
|---|---|---|
| **Professional men:** | | |
| Generals | 1 Chesney (Down) | 1 Dunne (Kildare) |
| Army officers (Captains and above) | 26 | 26 |
| Senior Fellows and Fellows of TCD | 1 Traill | 3 |
| QCs | 3 | 6 |
| Doctors of Divinity | 11 | 17 |
| Doctors of Laws | 7 | 4 |
| Doctors of Medicine | 3 | 1 |
| | | |
| **Public Representatives:** | | |
| Deputy Lieutenants | 81 (14 titled) | 52 (14 titled) |
| MPs | 20 | 8 |
| Justices of the Peace | 107 | 97 |
| Total | 208 | 157 |
| Total lay delegates | 255 | 191 |

The range of experience and skills among the delegates to the Convention both ensured that its complex legal and financial business was competently handled, and also determined the parliamentary format which it devised for the General Synod.

Among the outstanding men in the Convention (and its successor Synods) were Provost Humphrey Lloyd of Trinity College (1867-81), and his successors, J. H. Jellett and George Salmon; the President's two regular assessors, Judge Longfield and Dr Ball, and their fellow-lawyers, Sir Joseph Napier and Judge Warren; the honorary secretaries of the RCB, Joseph Galbraith and William Digges La Touche; prodigious scholars in the future bishops William Reeves, the antiquary, and Charles Reichel, the son of Moravian parents; Colonels Ffolliott of Elphin and Saunderson of Kilmore; Deans Dickinson of the Chapel Royal, MacDonnell of Cashel, and West of St Patrick's; and clergy whose authoritative knowledge bore directly on the challenges facing the church, Archdeacon Stopford of Meath, Richard Travers Smith of Dublin, and Alfred Lee of Ahoghill, who edited the Convention's two journals. There were able apologists in the High, Low and Broad traditions of the church. And, as their strength warranted, Evangelicals were well represented: through third generation members of such pioneer families as Guinness, La Touche and Lefroy, and the aristocratic families of Pakenham and Trench; and in the persons of such influential senior clergy as Henry

Ward, Alexander Irwin and C. S. Stanford.[10] Four Evangelical delegates became bishops by 1878: Maurice Day (Cashel 1872), Robert Gregg (Ossory 1874), Hon W. C. Plunket (Meath 1876), and W. Pakenham Walsh (Ossory 1878), after Robert Gregg had succeeded his father in Cork. Two became archbishops. Lord Plunket – he became 4th Baron Plunket in 1884 – was Archbishop of Dublin, 1884-97; and Robert Gregg, whose financial acumen was vital to the work of reconstruction, was elected Primate in 1893, only to die three years later at the premature age of 62.

Marcus Beresford, whose primacy (1862-85) spanned disestablishment and its aftermath, carried authority both as a man of affairs and a chairman of consummate ability. His direct style of speech and wise counsel informed his opening address to the Convention:

> Our Church still retains all that is essential to its life as a living branch of the Church of Christ. We still abide in the Apostles' doctrine and fellow-ship; we remain planted in the firm basis of scriptural truth; we retain our form of Divine worship, and the three-fold Apostolic Order which the Church of Ireland has professed for more than fourteen centuries. In doc-trine and in discipline we are unchanged. We have not, therefore, to cre-ate, but restore; not to build up a new church but to supply such supports as the State has taken away from the old. This is a work which can only be done by the cordial co-operation and united effort ·of the whole Church. Mutual forbearance, mutual goodwill, mutual respect for each other's feelings and opinions, are necessary to a successful issue.[11]

At the end of its first session, the Convention's journal claimed that it had forwarded the 'future prosperity, stability, and unity of the ancient and Apostolic Church of Ireland'. But the reality belied the rhetoric. For the church's future was threatened at once by financial uncertainty and doctrinal restlessness. 'Poverty is advancing upon us like an armed man,' Beresford himself warned. As 1870 ended, it was not certain that the church could command the resources necessary to her survival, or that even then, she could avoid what the RCB called 'a purely congregational system'.[12] Again, the Convention had appointed committees to draft new canons, and to advise on Prayer Book revision: both were to report to the General Synod in 1871. But Archdeacon William Lee of Dublin had withdrawn from the Convention in protest, and the bishops had declined to serve on 'Master Brooke's Committee' (named after its chairman, William Brooke, Master in Chancery). As if that were not enough, a Low Church party, in which the Butlers – Lord James of Dublin and the Hon Henry Cavendish of Clogher – were prominent, was aggressively anticlerical. It had sought at the Lay Conference to deny the clergy the right to vote as a separate order, and at the Convention to deprive the House of Bishops of the power of independent action. Both attempts had been thwarted by the adroitness of the Duke of Abercorn, but the menace remained.[13] What was clear, as 1871 began, was not so much (*pace* Mrs C. F. Alexander) that it dawned on 'a churchless nation', as that unless both her solvency and her catholicity could be secured, the independent church's very survival would be at stake.

## II 'PROSPERITY, STABILITY, AND UNITY'

### 1. Finance

Financial security, in the form of life annuities, was guaranteed only to those bishops and clergy who were in office at 26 July 1869 and living on 1 January 1871. Of its nature, this was an arrangement between the state and individuals and not a re-endowment of the church. Government would, however, make over to the RCB the capitalized value of the annuities of those clergy who were willing to commute them, with the church accepting responsibility for paying such clergy. A bonus of 12 per cent would be added for every diocese where not less than three-quarters of the clergy commuted: it was calculated partly on actuarial grounds, partly to cover administrative costs. In the event, the bishops and all but 45 clergy commuted, and the RCB received £7,581,075 as commutation capital. (Multiplied by a factor of 20, the amount is over £150 million in 1996 values.) But with £597,000 (or almost £12 million in 1996) initially due to the annuitants each year, the capital would be expended wholly for that purpose – and, inclusive of interest, had been so calculated. Meanwhile, with but £500,000 of her own in compensation, the church had to find the funds to purchase clergy residences and glebe lands (an Act of 1875 increased the maximum holding to 30 acres), to pay the stipends of clergy appointed after 26 July 1869, and to meet all other operating expenses.[14] The substantial sums needed for these purposes would be raised from two sources: voluntary giving by church members, and profits accruing from prudent management by the RCB of the commutation capital.

The importance of voluntary support, and guidance as to its organization at both diocesan and parochial levels, were set out in an appeal to the church. Distributed under cover of a letter from the archbishops, it was read in all churches on 8 May 1870. It advised the creation of the Central Sustenation Fund, and invited special donations to establish, and regular subscriptions to sustain it. Parishes would pay assessments into this fund, and parishioners were urged both to donate two per cent of their incomes or property values, and also to subscribe a penny a week.[15] The response was generous. The total raised voluntarily in the two decades to 1889 was £3,733,180, an annual average – it included legacies – of £186,659 (or £3 ¾ million in 1996).

Primate Gregg noted in 1895 that voluntary giving had reached £4 ½ million (or £90 million) in 25 years, 'exclusive of the amount expended on the fabrics of the churches' and of giving for missionary and philanthropic purposes. The church had thus 'set in order her machinery, while she fulfilled her mission.' The same level of support was sustained during the next two decades, so that to the end of 1915 a total of £8,008,329 was raised voluntarily, a yearly average of £177,962 over 45 years.[16]

The church's property before 1871, however, had had an annual value of some £680,000, and the discrepancy now was made good from another source. The commuting clergy were allowed to compound their annuities, wholly or in part, in certain circumstances: on retirement, on leaving Ireland, or if they wished to raise a lump sum for a specific personal reason, such as marriage. The residual capitalized value in such cases was divided between the RCB and the compounding clergy, according to a fixed scale which took age into account. This composition (as it was termed) yielded appreciable sums, for 1102 clergy compounded, and the 'composition balances' which came to the church amounted to £1,651,097. The RCB was able for years to invest the commuted capital at a higher rate of interest than that at which it had been calculated, so that profits from commutation itself also accrued. This gain was enhanced in respect of parishes which had annuitants as incumbents, for the RCB was able to accumulate their parochial assessments as permanent endowments, instead of having to apply them to stipends. At the end of 1889, therefore, there remained £3,550,320 of the commutation capital, or almost half the total originally received, while at the same time, with fewer annuitants still alive, the annual outlay on annuities had fallen to £94,342.[17] It naturally continued to fall during the next decade, Primate Alexander noting in 1897 that only 275 annuitants remained of the original 2043, with the yearly payment to them now reduced to £51,000.[18] In 1926, Primate D'Arcy observed that 15 annuitants only remained, whose average age was 83, and of whom but two were still serving.[19] (The last annuitant, Canon Somerville Large, died in 1939.)

These trends, taken together, released appreciable funds for general investment. Already at the end of 1889 the RCB held investments of £3,057,785, apart from the commutation moneys and the glebe lands. By then, too, most of the 1521 clergy (including the 342 curates) were receiving stipends rather than annuities, and were therefore a principal charge on the church's resources. In 1915 the Stipend Fund stood at just over £4 million. It had been built up from two sources: the early accumulation of parochial assessments from parishes with annuitants; and the regular transfers to it both of the profits of commutation and of the composition balances. There was Canadian precedent for Irish experience. In the settlement of the 'Clergy Reserves' question in 1854, the principle of commutation had been recognized by the government, and clergy in post permitted to claim a capital sum calculated on their life expectancy, in lieu of a guaranteed stipend. The Canadian clergy who commuted agreed to hand the money over to the diocesan Church Societies as an endowment for future clergy stipends.[20]

The healthy state of her finances in 1915 does not disguise the Church of Ireland's perilous financial situation in 1870. That it improved so assuredly was due to the confidence of the clergy, the commitment of the laity, and the competence of the Representative Body. If the arithmetic of 1870 had been precise, the risk had been awesome. As Primate D'Arcy recalled more than half a century later, the clergy had surrendered the security offered to them by the state, and entrusted their capitalized life interests to the untried RCB. 'By that act of self-sacrifice was laid the foundation of our whole financial system.' As a later historian put it, 'clerical trust in the RCB would be a major factor in future unity'.[21] That trust was vindicated both by the generosity of the laity's response and the management skills of the RCB. Primate Crozier told the General Synod in 1914 that Lord Ventry's death left only two men in whose names the Charter of 1870 had been drawn up: the Earl of Courtown and the Provost of TCD (Anthony Traill). Noting in 1915 that both had since died, Crozier observed that five current members of the RCB were the sons of men who had drafted the Constitution in 1870.[22] The RCB, in short, had become as much a dynasty as the 20th century dynasties of Croziers, Days, and Peacockes among the clergy.

## 2. Revision

The outcomes of the General Synod's revision efforts were the Canons enacted in 1871 and the Prayer Book published in 1878. Disestablishment had made certain technical changes in both canon law and liturgy necessary, and a lively pamphlet debate had shown that doctrinal change was widely desired. The fires of the Revision debates in the early Synods had long been stoked, so that points of doctrine were fiercely contested. Principle clashed with passion. Concern for the integrity of the BCP contended with fears aroused by the ritualism then rampant in England, and by its doctrinal connotations. But the General Convention had reaffirmed the church's 'constant witness' against 'innovations in doctrine and worship', and the new Canons of 1871 were 'designed to forbid innovation and preserve the *status quo*'.[23] If the church could not be moved in a Catholic direction, however, would she yet be pulled in a Protestant direction? The attempt was made: some even looked to the 'Book of Common Prayer Revised', a recent Low Church production in England. In the Primate's words, debate 'roved over the whole circuit of the Hampton Court and Savoy Conferences' of the 17th century.[24] The new Canons would preserve the church from the liturgical chaos prevalent in

England; but could she also protect her catholic heritage in doctrine and sacrament? That aged Evangelical theologian, Bishop James O'Brien of Ossory, was afraid lest 'in raising bulwarks against Ritualism and Popery', she should herself be 'converted from a tolerant and comprehensive church into a narrow and exclusive sect'. He warned that such an outcome might be achieved without material alterations, merely by authoritative definitions which limited to one sense only expressions of which various interpretations had hitherto been allowed. (The term 'regenerate' in the baptismal offices was a much debated instance of the bishop's point.) But this peril was avoided. John Henry Bernard, who held the Archbishop King's chair in TCD once occupied by O'Brien, was able in 1903 to reassure the Anglo-Irish Church Society at Westminster that to suggest that the Irish Church had 'fallen into heresy, or that she had protested herself out of her catholic inheritance, is to suggest what is, happily, not true'.[25]

That happy outcome had, however, come out of conflict. It was not defined strictly in terms of churchmanship, though some generalizations are valid. In the terminology of the day, High Churchmen were conservatives, Low Churchmen ultra-revisionists. Evangelicals were divided, though the majority, including most bishops (O'Brien was an exception), were moderate revisionists. Broad Churchmen – Bishop Fitzgerald, Dean Dickinson and John Jellett (the future Provost) among them – were pragmatists first. But there were pragmatists in every tradition: men who, whatever their personal predilections, contended that the church's interest required that revisionist concerns should be fully expressed, and then drawn into compromise. Dr Salmon's wisdom was seen in his insistence that the pent-up emotions in the church needed outlet in synodical debate. While accepting that there were risks in revision, he urged that 'the danger attending the course of doing nothing is vastly greater'. And while he also understood the risk of 'weakening English sympathy' for his church – a consideration which weighed heavily with Archbishop Trench – Salmon yet held that 'we could live and work without it; but what we cannot do without is the complete and hearty sympathy of our own laity'. Forty years later, Archdeacon Sherlock recalled that Salmon's 'learning and moderation gained from the Synod an extraordinary trust and affection', while Dean Hercules Dickinson earned its gratitude for his 'keen sense of the ridiculous' which 'often restored good humour to a heated debate'.[26] And a modern historian has seen Lord Plunket as 'one of the great eirenic figures' in the Revision debates, in that he had sensed 'the need for courage, restraint, and fundamental optimism', and been a realist also in finding 'formulae which would preserve unity and comprehensiveness'.[27]

The battle, nonetheless, was intense while it lasted. Controversy raged around the Holy Communion and Ordinal, the baptismal formularies, the form of absolution in the Visitation of the Sick, the Apocrypha, and the Athanasian Creed. As to the last, an era which seldom hears the Litany or even the Commandments may find it difficult to fathom the Victorian obsession with 'The Creed (commonly called) of St Athanasius'; but the debate, in which the chief protagonists were Reichel and Travers Smith, was complex and protracted. In the end, the rubric requiring the Creed to be read in churches was simply deleted, and its text (even the hotly disputed damnatory clauses) left unaltered. The offending absolution formula was substituted by another from within the BCP, and the Apocrypha removed from the lectionary. Significant change in the services was avoided. In response to one current controversy, an addition to the catechism taught that, in the Lord's Supper, the Body and Blood of Christ were received 'only after a heavenly and spiritual manner, and the mean whereby they are taken and received is Faith', so neatly conjoining the Evangelical and Caroline understandings of the sacrament. Again, the liberty hitherto allowed in expounding the baptismal formularies was affirmed, and expressly avowed in the 1878 Preface. With changes kept to a minimum overall,[28] that Preface had, as Gabriel Daly put it, to be 'a heavy-duty instrument which would please no one': both archbishops and two of the bishops in fact voted against it. Its most famous clause opined that 'what is imperfect with peace, is often better than what is otherwise excellent, without it'. The identity of the author is uncertain. It is not easy to reconcile Plunket's recollection that these words came to him while he was dressing, with that of Bishop Fitzgerald that the clause containing them had remained (despite the Revision Committee's attentions) as he himself had written it.[29] But the point is immaterial. For their sentiment was shared by all the men who had guided the Synod into the ways of peace.

Various influences, then, ensured that the 1878 revision would be, in Bishop Stephen Neill's words, 'characteristically conservative, and characteristically intelligent'. The ubiquitous lawyers, including Evangelicals like Sir Joseph Napier, were mostly conservatives, and argued their case tenaciously. The procedural device which they had influenced earlier, namely that any alteration in doctrine or liturgy must be supported by two-thirds of the clergy and laity in Synod, voting separately, also worked against radical change.[30] Many proposals failed to meet this crucial requirement. The 20th-century church has seen the Canons of 1871 as the the epitome of Victorian conservatism. As noted earlier, Bolton observed that they codified the actual practices common among all traditions of Irish churchmanship. Seventy years after their enactment, Primate Gregg judged them to have been 'framed with the object of preserving a reasonable standard of uniformity in the church's public worship'. Gregg stressed also the continuity achieved by the first

General Synod: the 'present Canons' had substantially reproduced the language and principles of the Canons which had been of legal authority from 1634 to 1870.[31] Where Gregg could only assess, Marcus Beresford had been able to influence. His role in revision has seldom been noticed. But his shrewdness and direct interventions in debate were often decisive. Primate Alexander, who was in a position to know, judged: 'To him more than to any other single person we owe the integrity of our Prayer Book. The smell of fire has scarcely passed over it.' It had, however, passed over the church herself. In his sensitive analysis a century on, Gabriel Daly perceived that through her trial by fire the Church of Ireland had preserved her faith and unity intact, and in doing so, acquired 'a newly authenticated identity'.[32] That identity derived essentially from accommodation of the two Anglican traditions which had informed the Irish Church since the early 17th century: that of Bramhall and Taylor, handed on through the later Carolines and the indigenous High Church revival, and that of Ussher and the Irish Articles of 1615, revived by the Evangelical movement.

### 3. Episcopate

Before entering on its work, the General Convention had 'solemnly declared' that the Church of Ireland would 'maintain inviolate the Three Orders of Bishops, Priests or Presbyters, and Deacons in the sacred Ministry'. The first election of a bishop was therefore an occasion for proclamation. It arose in 1872. Maurice F. Day was elected by the united synods of Cashel on 19 March, and consecrated in St Patrick's Cathedral on 14 April. The sermon was preached by Achilles Daunt, who had earlier succeeded Day in St Matthias's, and was Dublin's most renowned Protestant preacher. (St Matthias's congregation worshipped during 1870 in the great hall of the Exhibition Palace: it seated 3000, and was filled to capacity.) Thousands had attended Daunt's preaching during the General Convention, and the American evangelist, D. L. Moody, invited him to preach in his place during his Dublin visit, Daunt matching his humility by declining. Taking Eph 3:10 as the text of his consecration sermon, Daunt observed the church in its mystical aspect, then enunciated a high doctrine of episcopacy in considering the church's visible aspect. The three-fold ministry was not only 'a convenient system of human expediency, but an Apostolic, and therefore a Divine institution ascertained by the sure warrant of God's Word', and historically there had been 'an *episcopal succession* in the Church of Christ from the earliest times'. Daunt was also sensible that the freedom which the Irish church had enjoyed at the Synod of Cashel in 1172, exactly 700 years earlier, had been restored to her; was clear that her adoption of synodical government (and episcopal election) had patristic precedent – he quoted Cyprian's resolve to do nothing without the counsel of his presbyters and the consent of his laity (*sine consensu plebis*); and was convinced that if Protestant truth was ever 'to gain ascendancy in Ireland – it can only be through a Church that is Episcopal'.[33]

The Constitution provided that the primate would be elected by the bishops, and the bishops by the diocesan synods. If a synod failed to elect, the bishops would elect instead. The method of election by diocesan synods was replaced in 1960 by an Electoral College in each province. The record of the original method over some 90 years may conveniently be given here. Between 1872 and 1959, there were 100 episcopal elections, eight to Armagh and 92 to all other dioceses. Diocesan synods elected 'decisively' on 53 occasions, that is by the requisite two-thirds majority of clergy and laity, voting by orders. The bishops elected on 38 occasions where synods had failed to elect (once through lapse). The remaining election was at the option of Bishop Charles Irwin, who chose Connor rather than Down and Dromore when his united diocese was divided in 1945 (he had been bishop since 1942). The Synod of Derry and Raphoe alone failed to elect a bishop, but with only four in 90 years, that diocese had the fewest vacancies. Kilmore, by contrast, elected a bishop at eight of nine vacancies – the Armagh Synod elected for Kilmore at that of 1939. Dublin elected an archbishop on three of seven, Cork a bishop on five of seven occasions (the Armagh Synod elected once for Cork, and the bishops once). The respective diocesan synods elected at six of nine vacancies in Down, and six of 10 in both Meath and Killaloe. Derry, as the statistics indicate, had the longest episcopates, both William Alexander (1867-96) and J. Irvine Peacocke (1916-45) serving for almost 30 years. Before 1960, with no mandatory retiring age, bishops normally died in office. In the 48 years from 1872 to 1920, only 12 of the 50 episcopal vacancies arose through resignation, compared with 17 of the 50 vacancies in the 39 years from 1920 to 1959.[34] In the late 20th century bishops must retire at 75. By contrast, Bishop Darley, a former Headmaster of the Royal School Dungannon, was 75 when elected to Kilmore in 1874, and for 10 years 'amazed men by his mental and physical activity'. William Alexander was in his 87th year when he resigned Armagh in 1911, doing so only because 'he wanted once to possess his soul before he died'.[35]

Alexander's election in 1896 (at the age of 72) had brought the first scholar to the primacy in the 19th century. Others followed: Charles F. D'Arcy, a Fellow of the British Academy, in 1919, J. A. F. Gregg in 1938, and George Simms in 1969. Notably, too, each of the three was translated from Dublin, as against only three such translations in the 216 years to 1919.[36] The scholarly tradition of the see of Dublin was maintained also by J. H. Bernard (1915-19), who on his election to Ossory in 1911 (by the bishops), had been the first ex-Fellow of TCD to make the bench since 1866, and who resigned the archbishopric for the provostship;[37] and by H. R. McAdoo (1977-85), a theologian and ecumenist of international stature. With the notable exception of Archbishop Robin Eames, who was 48 on his election in 1986, most primates since 1886 (when Robert Knox succeeded Marcus Beresford) have been older than their predecessors in the Established Church, their tenure shorter, and their previous episcopal experience longer – D'Arcy had been bishop of four several dioceses. Thus whereas there were 11 primates during the 180 years 1691-1870, there were again 11 in the 110 years 1886-1996, and whereas the average tenure of the primacy before disestablishment was 19 years, after 1886 it was only 10 years. Interestingly, six of the 11 post-disestablishment primates had been Bishops of Ossory. Two had gone first to Dublin (D'Arcy – by way of Down – and J. A. F. Gregg), and two to other dioceses (R. S. Gregg to Cork, and John Baptist Crozier to Down). Both Godfrey Day in 1938, and John Armstrong in 1980, were translated direct from Ossory.

With the bishops electing the primate, an arrangement had been devised otherwise to involve the Armagh Synod in the elections arising from each vacancy in that diocese. The procedure was that the synod elected an *ad interim* Bishop of Armagh, who thereupon took part in the election to the primacy, and thereafter became bishop of the diocese made vacant by that election – unless it was Dublin, when he instead became bishop of the diocese vacated by the new Archbishop of Dublin. Though intended to be fair, this arrangement had unfortunate consequences. By 1896, three of the 13 dioceses had had bishops elected by the Armagh Synod – Down (Reeves 1886), Cork (Meade 1893), and Derry (Chadwick 1896). Meade and Chadwick were still in post when Primate Alexander resigned in 1911, and under a new provision limiting bishops so elected to two at any one time, D'Arcy was elected Bishop of Down – the diocese vacated by Crozier's election to the primacy – by the Down Synod, and not that of Armagh. Again, Ossory received two successive bishops elected by the Armagh Synod, Day in 1920[38] and, on his election to the primacy in 1938, Ford Tichborne. This contingency was also unwelcome. Hence at the two later vacancies in the primacy before the Electoral College was instituted, the bishops elected the *ad interim* Bishop of Armagh: in 1938, on Godfrey Day's death after only five months in office, and again in 1959. The *ad interim* Bishop of Armagh, however elected, was popularly known as 'the floating bishop'. But as in the Established Church, not all dioceses had the same appeal, and two 'floaters' elected by the bishops in 1938 refused appointment in circumstances which suggest that, when it came to self-interested intrigue, the independent church could hold its own with the Establishment.

On Primate Day's death, Dean R. G. S. King of Derry was elected *ad interim* Bishop of Armagh amid general expectation that Bishop Peacocke of Derry would succeed Day in Armagh, given that J. A. F. Gregg, the Archbishop of Dublin, had declined the bishops' offer of the primacy at the first vacancy in 1938. Dean King was on his way to Dublin by train, however, when his friends there learned from the new Bishop of Cork, R. T. Hearn, a close friend of the archbishop, that Gregg had changed his mind and would accept the primacy if it were offered to him. As the Earl of Belmore was to recall, Bishop Peacocke therefore dispatched Bishop W. H. Holmes of Meath (his former archdeacon, and secretary to the House of Bishops) 'to way-lay King on his arrival, and give him the tip that Derry might not be the vacant Bishopric!!!' On King's refusing the appointment, the bishops offered it the next day to Archdeacon John Crozier, 'who asked for time to consider it (i.e. to see which way the Tuam cat would jump!)'.[39] In the event, Crozier was elected to Tuam by the diocesan synod, the 'floatership' was finally accepted by Canon A. E. Hughes, and on the next day Gregg was duly elected Primate. Arthur Barton, the Bishop of Kilmore, succeeded Gregg in Dublin, so that Kilmore – now filled by Hughes – turned out to be the diocese which King and Crozier, each for his own reason, had refused.

## III 1871-1938

### 1. 'The principle of self-reliance'

The independent church had created a network of controls. General vestries elected select vestries, diocesan synods elected diocesan councils, and the General Synod established (in 1883) a Standing Committee, its non-episcopal members being elected triennially. Under such controls many matters previously subject to private initiative were centrally co-ordinated: the creation of the Board of Missions in 1881 is a good example. If greater uniformity was achieved, however, creative diversity tended to be lost, and the church in time to be less comprehensive and tolerant. The new scheme of patronage illustrates the point. The 1869 Act ended episcopal patronage, and bought out most private patrons. Every vacancy was now subject to a diocesan board of patronage, with the bishop, clerical and lay diocesan nominators, and parochial nominators as members.[40] As all the trustee churches (except ultimately Crinken and St John's Sandymount) applied to come within the parish system, they lost their power of appointment, and ultimately risked their founding tradition. Uniformity was achieved in other ways also: one church, one newspaper, one hymnal. In 1871, the monthly *Irish Ecclesiastical Gazette* argued that, with church members voicing opinions in synods and vestries, it was expedient to report weekly on all church assemblies, and 'as the only church paper now published' – the *Christian Examiner* had ceased publication in 1869 – volunteered itself for this role.[41] The APCK's hymnal of 1864 was taken up by a joint General Synod-APCK committee, enlarged to 475 hymns, and published in 1873 as the *Church Hymnal*: its music edition was prepared by the composer, Sir Robert Stewart, professor of music in TCD and organist (since the age of 19) of Christ Church Cathedral. With the new hymnal achieving a 42nd edition by 1885, private collections disappeared from public worship. An appendix in 1891 took the total of hymns to 642, the new edition of 1915 to 721 and 16 carols, and an appendix in 1935 to 767 hymns and 21 carols. With carols now popular, the St Patrick's Cathedral Carol Service on Christmas Eve had been introduced early in the century.[42] After the excitements of the 1870s, liturgical revision had gone into remission. But a new committee in 1909 'gave promise of enriching the Book of 1878', and after 17 years' work delivered 'a more logical arrangement of the contents'. Moreover, as 1878 had introduced a popular Service of Thanksgiving for the Blessings of Harvest, so 1926 provided an Order for the Public Institution for a Minister to a Cure. Recommending its adoption in 1914, Primate Crozier observed that the custom of public institution had become general – 'no other service is more popular, none so largely attended on a weekday' – and had helped convince the people 'of the reality of episcopal oversight'. Two alternative forms of Evening Prayer were added in 1933.[43]

Training of both teachers and clergy was given high priority. The Church Teachers' Training School, which the Church Education Society had founded in 1847, received government funding from 1884. The General Synod had endorsed the school in 1873, but had difficulty in financing it. Many synodsmen feared the consequences of associating it with the National Board, but Synod was persuaded to agree by far-seeing men, and notably Lord Plunket (author of 'For Christ to learn, for Christ to teach'). Dr Kingsmill Moore, a Balliol man, was the first principal of the newly constituted Church of Ireland Training College, and worked closely with Plunket after he became Archbishop of Dublin. The public statue in Plunket's honour was, appropriately, erected beside the College in Kildare Place. The question of the church's involvement with the TCD Divinity School was long in contention with the Board of Trinity College. Control of endowments, curriculum, and staff appointments were legitimate concerns of the church, given that most of her clergy were trained in the Divinity School. The College, on the other hand, supplied large numbers of clergy to England and overseas. The matter was not resolved until a government enquiry – the Fry Commission of 1907 – reported, the General Synod rejoicing that it had accepted the church's right to 'a share in the control of the Divinity School'. Major constitutional changes were embodied in the King's Letter of 1911 establishing a Divinity

Council, with three bishops as members, and powers that could not be altered unilaterally by the College. While the bench could influence courses and appointments, the board was guaranteed the continuation of divinity training within Trinity: the arrangement would last until 1980. Finally, on the initiative of the bishops, the General Synod resolved to provide a hostel for divinity students, and in 1914 the divinity hostel in Mountjoy Square was opened: it would suffice for 50 years.[44]

Diana McFarlan has revealed that there was much innovative energy in the late Victorian Church. Choral festivals became popular. The earliest took place in Ramoan church in 1866; Ballymena held its third choir festival in 1883. Armagh diocese had three choir festivals from 1879, one for each of counties Armagh, Tyrone and Louth. In 1889, the annual Dublin Choir Festival was held in St Patrick's Cathedral, with choirs from Swords to Bray and all the city parishes, those from St Ann's, St Peter's, All Saints' Grangegorman, and St Bartholemew's being robed. Harvest services also became very popular. Derry diocese held them in 1875 on the same day, an arrangement which would not have suited the Belfast woman who had 'done' 13 harvests for a shilling (11 pennies and two ha'pennies in collections). Fêtes, bazaars and fairs also flourished, the earliest again in 1866, when Mrs Humphries of Ballyhaise House held a bazaar in Cavan in aid of the Irish Clergy Sons Education Society. The great 'Bazaar at the Kildare Place Training College' in 1886 lasted for several days. In other respects, the Church of Ireland was literally on the move. Services prior to embarkation were held at Londonderry and Queenstown for church members who were emigrating, and cards of introduction to clergy in America and Canada distributed. The Missions to Seamen (founded in 1873) was also at work in Irish ports, and opened a Sailors' Home at Waterford. The chaplain for the open roadsteads in Belfast Lough was able in 1883, with the Mission's launch *Primrose*, to visit most of the 200 ships which took shelter during the February gales, to hold thanksgiving services aboard some, and to sell Bibles. The growth of the railway network facilitated church activities. Excursions, many under the auspices of the Church Temperance Society, became popular. In both Limerick and Cashel and Emly, diocesan councils and clerical societies met in Ryan's Hotel at Limerick Junction. Travel by water was still common, and preferable to road travel by dog-cart, outside car, pony trap or bicycle. The coming of the motor car was to transform 20th century church life, even if the *Gazette* could not see bishops choosing to travel 'at the rate of 30 miles in 2 hours'. Its caution was confounded when D'Arcy of Ossory, Crozier of Down, and other bishops began to 'adopt' motor cars from 1906 onwards.[45]

At the reopening in 1878 of the restored Tuam Cathedral, Bishop Bernard pointed to much recent 'adorning, beautifying and altering' of churches out of 'the principle of self-reliance'. As few new churches were needed outside of Belfast, resources could be committed also to the cathedrals in which the church took such evident pride. In 1878 also St Fin Barre's in Cork was completed, Bishop John Gregg laying the top stones of its western spires shortly before he died. Christ Church Cathedral Dublin was reopened in the same year: Henry Roe bore the cost of the restoration at £250,000, and provided a new Synod Hall, in which the General Synod was to meet for over a century, on the site of the ancient St Michael's church. The project was supervised by the eminent English architect, George Edmund Street. Then on 22 September 1896, St Brigid's Cathedral Kildare was reopened after its restoration by Street, a project 'zealously supported' by Archbishop Plunket. The preacher was Archbishop Benson of Canterbury, who promised in Belfast several days later to return for the consecration of St Anne's Cathedral. (It was not to be, for he died suddenly two days after leaving Ireland.) It had been decided to build St Anne's, to a Romanesque design by the church's leading architect, Sir Thomas Drew, on the site of the old parish church, which continued in use as the cathedral was built around it. A charter was granted by an Act of General Synod, and the foundation stone laid on 9 September 1899. Dean O'Hara had launched the project, and on his becoming Bishop of Cashel, Dean D'Arcy had carried it on. Before he in turn became Bishop of Clogher, D'Arcy was able to announce that the pulpit from the nave of Westminster Abbey, where Archbishop Trench had preached as Dean, had been presented to St Anne's. When he was Primate, D'Arcy preached on 2 June 1927 at the dedication of the west front of the cathedral.[46]

'Belfast,' William Alexander wrote to D'Arcy, 'is the great hope of the Church of Ireland in the future'. Its population, 87,000 in 1851, was 387,000 at the census of 1911, of whom 118,000 (30.5 per cent) were Church of Ireland members. Although many large churches had been built in the inner city (for example St Mary's Crumlin Road) and the suburbs (St Mark's Dundela) by 1900, the 34 parishes had only 37 churches and some 65 clergy. The rights of pew-holders deprived the poor of seats, many clergy were absorbed in building projects, and pastoral care often neglected. The problem which had persisted since the 1820s, of a church population far in excess of resources, was at its most acute. When D'Arcy returned to the diocese in 1911 as bishop, he found two Belfast parishes with more than 10,000 people, and 10 others with over 5,000 each. All were 'woefully understaffed', only four had 'more than a rector with a single curate to do all the work'. The bishop paid tribute to Sir William Ewart's generosity in endowing city parishes; but he berated the establishment. Its *modus operandi*, he wrote later, could not cope with a problem without precedent in the church's history. For, in a financial system 'rigidly connected' with the old parochial and diocesan structures, 'all our funds –or nearly all – were "ear-marked", to use the catchword which met us at every turn'. When he went to Armagh, D'Arcy – like Alexander and Crozier before him – kept the General Synod focused on the needs of the region. He expressed amazement that some knew 'more about Fuh Chow or Uganda than they did about Belfast or Lurgan or Portadown', and urged the Synod 'to pour men into the North' and to send ordinands there for training.[47] Such advocacy was heeded. Two future Archbishops of Dublin 'trained' in Belfast, Arthur Barton as Head of the Trinity College Mission which had begun work in St Mary's parish in 1912, and Alan Buchanan as Head of the Southern Church Mission which worked in the east Belfast parish of Ballymacarrett from 1930 – it was supported by the RCB and every southern diocese. The General Synod allocated £2000 a year from 1922 to the Additional Clergy Fund, and £75,000 in 1928 for the provision of new churches. In 1938 a further £40,000 was provided for more churches and halls, in response both to a request from the diocesan council, and a report from the secretary of the RCB and the Provost of TCD, who had toured the various building projects in Belfast parishes.[48]

Women contributed much to church life. Archbishop Crozier said in 1914 that in some remote parishes the Sustenation Fund owed its success 'to women's zeal and self-denial', and that he knew parishes in Ossory and Ferns where parochial funds were 'altogether collected' by women, and one or two where 'ladies of rank' were the main support. Women brought to Ireland two organizations which had originated in the diocese of Winchester: the Girls Friendly Society and the Mothers' Union. The former had been founded in England by an Irishwoman, Mary Townsend, daughter of a Kilkenny rector. A principal aim was to 'help lonely girls from the country, working in cities'. Its Irish branch was founded in Bray in 1876, its first Dublin office started in 1878 with Louisa La Touche as registrar, and its first hostel opened in Molesworth Street in 1880. It soon spread to the main towns, and in 1885 formed an emigration department to help girls going to North America. The Mothers' Union was introduced in 1887 by Annabelle Hayes, wife of the rector of Raheny. Archbishop Plunket chaired the meeting at the Palace in St Stephen's Green at which the Dublin Association was formed in 1892.[49] Pledged to support marriage and family life, not least by example, the Mothers' Union was to exert significant influence in the church throughout the 20th century. Women were involved also in overseas mission. HCMS sponsored women missionaries from 1874, and by 1934 had sent 165 women overseas. Also in 1874, Charlotte Pym of Monkstown hosted a drawing-room meeting at which the Mission to Lepers was founded: as the Leprosy Mission, it was to become a worldwide, interdenominational organisation in the 20th century. A Missionary Conference in Alexandra College Dublin was attended by 300 women in 1879, and a women's missionary society, the Church of England Zenana Mission, formed its Hibernian auxiliary in 1897: its first two missionaries, both clergy daughters, left for India a year later. In 1892 also a Deaconess and Missionary Training Institute was opened in Mount Pleasant Square in Dublin (in connection with the YWCA), and in 1902 a Women Workers' Settlement, to train women for poor city parishes, was established in Belfast. It was, then, with good reason that Crozier should thank God that women were

> the chief glory of our land. They provide most of life's atmosphere. They do the larger voluntary part of our church work. They fill today the same office as Mary Magdalene on the morning of the Resurrection – they are *apostolae apostolorum.*

But their status was another matter. The Primate's tribute was made in support of the attempt at the General Synod of 1914 to permit women to hold parochial office. This right had been taken from them in 1870, when the General Convention confined all such offices to men, and rejected proposals that women – including property owners and householders – should be eligible for even the general vestry. In 1914, some 1400 women petitioned the General Synod to change the law. Canon J. A. F. Gregg (who presented the petition) and Mr Justice Madden moved that women be eligible both to register for the general vestry, and for appointment to all parochial offices. The Primate pointed out that prior to disestablishment women could attend and vote at vestry meetings and fill the office of churchwarden, 'as women do today in England'. He added that in the Presbyterian Church women could vote in all matters of importance, including the election of a minister. Crozier was countered by Bishop Bernard's politically correct argument that the rights which women had enjoyed in an aristocratic church were not appropriate in a 'democratic' church. The motion was lost. During the Great War, however, a committee (appointed on the initiative of Madden and Gregg) collected evidence of the work of women in parochial administration. Its report was received by the General Synod of 1919, when the proposal lost in 1914 was again debated, Gregg – now Bishop of Ossory in succession to Bernard – asking: 'why this unjust sex discrimination in the church?' (Women over 30 had been admitted to the parliamentary franchise in 1918.) But Bernard, whom Gregg was about to succeed again in Dublin, still opposed change, and in patronizing terms: he wanted, for example, to see 'the great lady of the parish on the Vestry, but not the gardener's wife'. The clergy supported the proposal; a majority of laymen rejected it. It was finally carried in 1920.[50] All parochial offices were now open to women; but not yet the church's synods.

In November 1920, a special session of the General Synod addressed for five days problems which had become acute during the war. The tide of emigration had risen, and inflation, already present before 1914, had become severe, subjecting many clergy, in Primate D'Arcy's words, to 'the grinding tyranny of an abject poverty'. The special session aimed to provide the clergy with adequate remuneration, and to regroup parishes into viable units: to assure, as the Primate put it, 'not only a living wage, but a man's work'. Although the General Synod of 1919 had created an emergency fund and authorized payment of a war bonus to clergy, a clerical defence union was formed to secure increase in stipends, amalgamation of parishes, and investigation into the 'ear-marked' funds of the RCB. That body had meanwhile been busy, and in 1920 presented the report of its Committee on Retrenchment and Reform, which recommended substantial increases in minimum stipends for incumbents and curates, groupings or unions of parishes and a commission with power to enforce them, the designation of 'light duty' parishes for older clergy, and a clergy superannuation scheme geared to compulsory retirement of bishops and clergy at age 70. D'Arcy was openly critical of the report as failing to identify how the church might best employ 'the great resources of men and money which she possessed' – he meant that the North was under-resourced. At the opening of the November Synod, however, he urged the adoption of Bills designed to eliminate 'the great waste of resources'; and he later pronounced its achievement 'a reform which amounted almost to a revolution'. (Compulsory retirement was not considered; in 1961 it was fixed at 75.) The commission worked for five years, and by 1926 had reduced the number of incumbencies from 1114 to 974, and of clergy from 1361 to 1162: in Limerick, Kildare, and Tuam (worst hit by emigration), the reductions were 151-111 in incumbencies, and 179-122 in clergy. A pattern which was to recur throughout the 20th century was thus established.

Aside from its central agenda, the special session of 1920 also considered a Bill to provide for a reduction in the number of dignities and canonries – it proposed that a proportion of one in seven of the clergy in each diocese should be dignified. With the Cathedrals of Armagh and Down and the two Dublin Cathedrals unaffected, 12 cathedral establishments only were to continue, and 16 deaneries were to be suspended – they included Connor, Dromore, Elphin and Raphoe; Ardfert, Lismore, Cloyne and Ross. As well, 16 archdeaconries (all in the southern province) were to be reduced to eight by pairing. Decision was, however, deferred to the ordinary session of 1921. It was then proposed to reduce the number of suspended deaneries to four, with 10 others to be held instead by bishops of united dioceses; two deaneries were spared either fate, and four archdeaconries were also spared. But the proposal was lost.[51] By the late 20th century, the desired ratio had been achieved in some dioceses – in inverse proportion – and a southern clergyman without a dignity or canonry had become an endangered species.

Finally, the Evangelical tradition went into relative decline during this period. Its history after 1870, like that of the Catholic tradition, has yet to be studied, so that analysis is necessarily speculative; but several points seem established. Whereas seven Evangelicals had become bishops in the generation after disestablishment, none was elected after 1900. These bishops had charged their clergy to 'preach Christ', the movement's central emphasis for more than a century. But the standard of preaching had declined. Already in 1882, in his *Decay of Modern Preaching*, Mahaffy saw it as stereotyped, formulaic, and unworthy of educated congregations, and preachers as needing to learn the art of rhetoric. Moreover, after the deaths of Archbishops Robert Gregg in 1896 and Lord Plunket in 1897, Evangelicals had no national leaders, clerical or lay: their support among the aristocracy does not appear to have survived the Victorian era. Their missionary zeal and pastoral commitment were unabated, but they appeared to be in retreat from scholarship, failing to come to terms with developments in theology and modern thought, and tending to retire into quietism. The church was also less congenial to men of conservative scholarship: T. C. Hammond left for Sydney in 1935 at Archbishop Mowll's invitation, to become Principal of Moore Theological College. Many Evangelicals also became preoccupied with Low Church practices foreign to their tradition. Mahaffy, for his part, wore the old-fashioned white tie of the early 19th-century cleric all his life, 'to keep aloof from a new kind of clericalism which he disliked', evinced in the adoption of the 'Roman collar'. But in their aversion to clericalism, Evangelicals only created their own, tending to elevate secondary matters to primary importance. Primate Alexander, who paid a moving tribute to the old Evangelical revival at the General Synod of 1905, had perhaps alluded to such in his poetic lament three years earlier:

> Heaven is waiting for the advance of the army of God, and earth listening to catch the music of its march. Yet multitudes spend their time in quarrelling over the uniform and the colours.

Again, Evangelicals withdrew gradually from situations which they felt unable to influence, and associations which they no longer controlled. Although in 1922 Bishop Patton could refer to CMS as 'the glory of Evangelical Christendom', even that society was abandoned by many Evangelicals, who in that year founded the Bible Churchmen's Missionary Society (BCMS). This tendency to move apart, into an isolation unknown for 90 years, left Evangelicals open to misunderstanding, and diminished their influence in the church. Ideological isolation was reinforced by social segregation. For the middle-class removal to the Dublin suburbs had changed the attitude of Evangelicals (and other churchmen) to poverty. A new attitude, born of ignorance, was – so Martin Maguire argues – expressed in moral superiority and coercion, as personal and spontaneous almsgiving gave way to 'bureaucratized and prying charity'. The coercive approach was seen in both the Church of Ireland Temperance Society, which aimed to restrict access to drink as well as evangelize, and the Labour Home and Yard at Ringsend run by the Church Army. It was left to Patterson Smyth of St Ann's to reject emphasis on individual salvation and plead for a more social religion. He founded the Church of Ireland Social Services Union 'not to mitigate the results of poverty but to attack poverty itself'. Maguire concludes: 'Religion alone, even Protestant middle-class evangelicalism, could not resolve the social problems of late Victorian Dublin'. The result was that the state and local authorities took over public welfare, so forcing a reduction in the social role of the churches in which Evangelicals had predominated.[52]

## 2. 'A missionary Church'

The independent church deepened the commitment to overseas mission which she had inherited. In 1873, HCMS was supported by 555 parishes, SPG by 318, and both societies by 123 parishes; by 1897 the parishes which gave no such support had fallen from 461 to 156. To the three older societies (CMJ was the third), the Established Church had added the South American Missionary Society (SAMS) in 1844, and the Colonial and Continental Society ('Col and Con') in 1851. Another five societies were launched on the high tide of missionary interest after disestablishment. (They included the Mission to Lepers, the Missions to Seamen, and the Zenana Mission, already mentioned.) Two Dublin University Missions (DUM) were founded. Robert Stewart, a Dublin clergyman on leave from China, founded in 1886 the DUM Fukien Mission (later the Far Eastern Mission) in connection with CMS. Then in 1890 several TCD men offered to SPG on condition that they could live and work on community lines. The society assigned them the northern part of the Indian diocese of Chota Nagpur, centred on the city of Hazaribagh. After a special ordination held in TCD chapel by Archbishop Plunket, five men and a nurse with experience in mission hospitals in Southern Africa, Fanny Hassard, sailed for India in 1891. To 1913, the DUM to Chota Nagpur attracted 23 men and 29 women from Ireland, many of whom worked in St Columba's Hospital.[53]

The receipts of all the missionary societies of the Church of Ireland (and of the Hibernian Bible Society) totalled £51,760 in 1912 and £54,504 in 1913, and they deployed in total 297 missionaries in 1914. Hibernian CMS, which had for the first time sent £20,000 to London in 1900, had 133 missionaries. It had provided three bishops for China and two for Japan; and the DUM to Chota Nagpur later provided five bishops to the church in India. There were Irish martyrs also. Dublin was shaken by the murders of Robert and Louisa Stewart in China in 1895. George Pilkington, the son of a Dublin QC, was killed in 1897 in Uganda, where he had done much to found the church. The Irish church's commitment to mission was appreciated throughout the Anglican Communion. The Secretary of CMS claimed in 1898, in a letter to the honorary secretaries of the General Synod, that Irish zeal 'had been at once an example and a stimulus to other churches', and in 1900 the Archbishop of the West Indies wrote of 'the magnificent work' done by the Irish both at home and in the colonies. The tributes were deserved. At the Christmas ordinations in 1878, 23 TCD men had received English orders. McDowell gives a total of 1044 TCD graduates (averaging 26 a year) ordained for English dioceses between 1873 and 1913; and observes that 45 per cent of all TCD men in orders were working either in England or overseas.[54]

Canada continued to rely on Irish clergy as its frontiers extended. Manitoba became a province in 1870, British Columbia in 1871; and immigration in 1907 was estimated at 300,000. Most new dioceses were missionary areas, pioneers in demand. Bishop Bond of Montreal, a Cornishman himself, declared that Englishmen were no use in Canada. Bond had recalled the Irish 'musketeer' Edward Sullivan from Chicago to succeed him as rector of St George's Montreal, and in 1882 Sullivan became the second bishop of the missionary diocese of Algoma in northern Ontario. His fellow musketeers were raised to the episcopate also. John Philip Du Moulin became Bishop of Niagara in 1896. (Sullivan, whose health had broken down through constant travel, took his place in St James's Toronto.) James Carmichael, who had been Bond's coadjutor, succeeded him as Bishop of Montreal in 1906. There were other well-known Irish clergy. 'Father Pat' (W. H. Irwin) worked among settlers, miners and railwaymen in British Columbia, and ministered to the Mounties at Fort Steele, until his tragic death in 1902. Wycliffe College Toronto had in 1914 three Irish staff supplied by the 'Col and Con'; and that society had founded Emmanuel College Saskatoon to train clergy for western Canada where many Irish had settled. Irish ordinands received free training there, provided they then gave five years' service to the church in Canada.[55]

The Irish auxiliary of SPG celebrated its bicentenary in 1914 (as HCMS did its centenary). It had long lagged behind HCMS both in appeal and efficiency. Its first diocesan associations dated from 1824, but a general secretary was not appointed until 1855 – he was assisted by an 'Organizing and Travelling Secretary for Ireland' from 1861 – and the auxiliary became representative of all Ireland only in 1892. Contributions to the parent society came to £4356 in 1894 and £6841 in 1912, though an additional £5100 was raised for its bicentenary (in 1901) and £1700 for the Indian famine fund in

1897. The High Church revival, with its strong missionary emphasis, ensured a steady recruitment for Anglican Churches overseas. The 106 sent out by SPG from Ireland in the 46 years to 1870 were followed by 108 – 92 men and 16 women – in the 43 years to 1913 (in addition to the Chota Nagpur contingent). The Irish pioneered work in Burma, Korea and Japan. In India, George A. Lefroy joined the Cambridge Mission to Delhi in 1879. He became Bishop of Lahore in 1897 and Bishop of Calcutta and Metropolitan of India and Ceylon in 1913. Marie Elizabeth Hayes, a daughter of Raheny rectory and one of Ireland's first women doctors – TCD had refused her admission – went out in 1905 to St Stephen's Hospital Delhi; she died tragically in 1908.

In South Africa, 26 Irish missionaries began work with the Church of the Province between 1869 and 1919. Several became bishops. Francis Balfour from Townley Hall near Drogheda was the first resident Anglican bishop in Basutoland (modern Lesotho) and Nelson Fogarty the first in Namibia; William Gaul from Derry became Bishop of Mashonaland in 1895. Although no Irish missionaries belonged to a religious order, Balfour and Gaul encouraged the work of Anglican religious orders in their dioceses. Two clergy, David Croghan and John Darragh, had been Dr Maturin's curates at Grangegorman. Croghan introduced choral services and (on 29 April 1874) a daily celebration in Bloemfontein Cathedral – the first cathedral in the Anglican Communion to have a daily Eucharist.[56]

There was also an Irish branch of the Spanish and Portuguese Church Aid Society. Its support of the Protestants in the Spanish and Lusitanian Churches reached its zenith in 1894, when Archbishop Plunket, accompanied by the Bishops of Clogher (Stack) and Welland (Down), went to Madrid and consecrated Senor Cabrera as the first Bishop of the Spanish Reformed Church, despite initial misgivings at home and hostility from Anglo-Catholics in England. Thereafter the Irish church exercised a general oversight, Archbishop Gregg visiting the two churches four times between 1924 and 1934.[57]

The work of the societies was until 1928 co-ordinated by the Board of Missions, thereafter by the new Missionary Council of the Church of Ireland. The Council considered mission 'a primary duty of the church'. It was able to report total receipts by the societies of £65,993 in 1935-6, and of £62,628 in 1936-7 (they now included BCMS). The annual day of intercession for missions was held on St Andrew's Day. In 1938, the service of intercession took place as usual in Christ Church Cathedral, the culmination of 'an unbroken chain of prayer from Matins to Evensong', a course of missionary lectures was given in TCD for the third successive year, and the Missionary Council set about attracting to Ireland up to 12 of the overseas bishops expected at Lambeth in 1940.

A new statute of 1938 extended the benefits of the the the clergy superannuation scheme to clergy who had served overseas. Archbishop Day, who had himself served with the Cambridge Mission to Delhi, commended this measure to the General Synod with the comment that missionary work had never been more urgently needed. Then, conjoining the names of Robert and Louisa Stewart, George Pilkington, George Alfred Lefroy, Frances Hassard, and Marie Hayes with those of Saints Patrick, Columba, Gall and Canice, the Primate charged his church to be true both to 'her glorious ancestry' and to her Saviour's supreme purpose for her – 'to preach His Gospel to all mankind'. Day took up this theme again in his peroration, his imminent death adding poignancy to his words.

> This brings me to the last thing I want to say. In all the great periods of the history of the Church of Ireland, when she has been most vigorous, most truly alive, she has been a missionary Church. The noblest of her sons and daughters have gone forth from her shores to proclaim the Eternal Gospel.[58]

By this criterion the period 1871-1938 was among the church's greatest. And for the future, the annual TCD missionary lectures would become, appropriately, the Godfrey Day Memorial Lectures.

### 3. Church and country

Loyalty to the Crown was a unifying factor in the Church of Ireland until the mid-20th century. Thus the General Synod sent an address of loyal greeting to Queen Victoria at her Diamond Jubilee in 1897, sang the National Anthem at its special session of 1912, and after George VI's accession, adopted in 1937 a resolution of 'loyal and dutiful greeting' to the King.[59] This loyalty properly survived partition, for both jurisdictions from 1921 were under the Crown, the Irish Free State as a self-governing dominion and Northern Ireland as a continuing part of the United Kingdom; and the Prayer Book of 1926 accordingly retained the state prayers for use in both jurisdictions.

Support for the Union with Great Britain also united the Church of Ireland during the long Protestant retreat before the Great War. Primate Beresford's prophecy of 1829, that 'the ascendancy of Ireland' would pass to the Roman Catholics, was gradually fulfilled from the 1870s. Protestants perceived the transition at work in disestablishment, transfer of land ownership to tenants, the campaign for Home Rule, and electoral reforms which both delivered majority rule in local government and transformed Ireland's representation at Westminster – 86 (of 105) Irish MPs elected in 1886 were Nationalists. Although the first leaders of the Nationalist Party were churchmen – Isaac Butt was the son of a Donegal incumbent and Charles Parnell was a Wicklow landowner – their church exhibited virtually unanimous

Synod Hall and Christ Church Cathedral

Archbishop Lord Plunkett

George Salmon, Provost of TCD

William Alexander

John Baptist Crozier
(See House, Belfast)

Archbishop George Otto Simms

Ecumenical gathering: Archbishop Simms
with (L-R) Archbishops Alan Buchanan,
Michael Ramsey and Dermot Ryan

Kathleen Young, the first incumbent

Canon Ginnie Kennerly on the occasion of her ordination, with Fr Romuald Dodd OP

RUC graves, Scarva churchyard

St Elizabeth's Dundonald: the old and the new

Summer Madness

Robin Eames and Donald Caird

Walton Empey

Bishop Paul Colton with (l) Lyndon McCann, Chancellor of the United Dioceses of Cork, Cloyne and Ross, and (r) Wilfred Baker, Diocesan Secretary.

Bishop Richard Henderson with his wife Anita and their children (l to r) Pippa, Cicely and Jack.

Mrs Helen Clarke and Bishop Ken Clarke

Dean Houston McKelvey and Monsignor Tom Toner at St Anne's Cathedral, Belfast

opposition to their political objective. The special sessions of the General Synod in 1886, 1893 and 1912 – the years in which the three Home Rule Bills were introduced – revealed a reawakening of the 'sense of danger' of 1689-91: it was reinforced by the ugly agrarian violence which attended the Plan of Campaign in 1879-81. While most churchmen believed that self-government would not be in Ireland's material interests, their opposition was driven rather by the emotional fear that Protestants would be imperilled under Home Rule. This fear united bishops, clergy and laity, and initially gave common cause to church people in every province. The Home Rule issue, in short, provided a focus for the mounting unease within the Church of Ireland over the transformation of Ireland's social and political landscape, and the concomitant threat from the Catholic revival which began around the 1880s.

With the primacy vacant, Archbishop Plunket presided at the special session of the General Synod held on 23 March 1886. As though anticipating late-20th century criticism, he asked whether they had 'any right to deal with a question of politics. If we distinguish politics from party, I say unhesitatingly we have'. Plunket pointed to the practice of debating government policies (as in education) which affected their people, to the Prime Minister's request for expressions of minority opinion on Home Rule, and to the fact that opposition was not confined to 'one political party'. The church had 250,000 people in the three southern provinces, 100,000 of them in Dublin diocese, Plunket observed, and many synodsmen 'who do not come from Ulster, who are not Orangemen, and who are not Tories'. The Synod concurred. As 'a body of Irishmen holding various political opinions', it declared 'unswerving attachment' to the Union, denounced Home Rule as potentially separatist, and determined 'to resist it as tending to impoverish, if not extirpate' Protestants. These convictions were expounded in speeches by, among others, Bishop Alexander, Dr Salmon, Judge Warren and Provost Jellett. At the Synod's ordinary session six weeks later, Plunket (again presiding) reported that 20,000 copies of the earlier resolutions had been distributed, and 2000 of the full record sent to peers, MPs, and newspapers.[60] The Standing Committee circulated a Protest against Home Rule before the Synod's special session of 1893: it was endorsed by 1203 parishes out of 1229, with but 21 dissentient vestrymen in all Ireland. Primate Knox, an old-fashioned Whig, described the second Home Rule Bill as 'bristling with dangers' to the Empire, to Ireland, and to his church. Though intended for the better government of Ireland, 'it would be better to call it a Bill to suppress the Protestant faith – a Bill to subjugate this country to Papal dictation'.[61]

This was strong language. It was inspired by the perceived threat from a triumphalist Catholicism. This perception ended Presbyterian antagonism to the Church of Ireland and allegiance to the Liberal party; swelled the ranks of the Orange Order; gave Protestants a common cause in Unionism; and drew two leading churchmen, Colonel E. J. Saunderson, the Cavan landowner, and W. E. H. Lecky, the historian, away from Whig and romantic ideals, and turned them into Unionist MPs. It also led some of the church's ablest minds, during the next 20 years, to question whither Ireland was bound, and to counsel their people to resist pressures, such as that of the *Ne Temere* decree of 1908, to convert to the Roman Catholic Church. Thus Mahaffy published *The Romanization of Ireland* (1901) and *Will Home Rule be Rome Rule?* (1912); and a young Cork clergyman, J. A. F. Gregg, preached in St Fin Barre's Cathedral a series of six Lenten sermons – their titles included Papal Infallibility and The Cult of the Blessed Virgin Mary — which he published as *The Primitive Faith and Roman Catholic Developments* (1909). Gregg's purpose was 'to give information, and so strengthen conviction', the Dean of Cork's hope (in his Foreword) that the sermons would 'tend to the confirmation of our people in the primitive Catholic Faith'.[62]

But there were already fewer church members. Primate Alexander spoke in 1900 of 'the melting away of the church population' in many rural districts, Crozier in 1912 of the loss of resident clergy, the closure of churches, and the church's 'dwindling population' outside of north-east Ulster. Of his visitation of Tuam diocese in 1911, Crozier observed that in parishes

> where, a few years ago, our people were numbered in hundreds, now they have diminished to a few score or even less. Our Protestant people are seeking in Canada and elsewhere a freer atmosphere and fuller scope for their energies where no religious disabilities bar their progress.[63]

As for Ulster itself, Patrick O'Farrell has shown that Protestant strength there posed a challenge to Catholic revivalists:

> There was much in renascent Catholic Ireland that was vigorously intolerant, repudiated industrialized Protestant Ulster, denied diversity and sought religious homogeneity. There was a strong element in Irish Catholicism, which saw the achievement of Home Rule as a signal for the conversion of the North. A writer in the *Catholic Bulletin* of March 1912 put this objective without equivocation: 'The time has arrived for action … To bring into the bosom of Holy Church the million of our separated brethren is a most attractive programme…' The attraction of this programme was less obvious to Irish Protestants.[64]

It was against this background that the third special session of the General Synod met on 16 April 1912. With five members only (out of 403) voting against, it reaffirmed the church's opposition to Home Rule. But with the Lords' veto, effectual in 1893, now removed, the 'resistance' pledged by the

General Synod in 1886 had begun to materialize in Ulster. In his presidential address, therefore, Crozier said that he had spent most of his life among Ulstermen – he had been vicar of Holywood (1880-97) and Bishop of Down (1907-11) – and knew them well. His assessment, which ran counter to opinion at Westminster that they were bluffing, was that having rejected 'the bribe' of a parliament of their own, Ulstermen were 'desperately determined' to 'defend their freedom and their birthright with their lives'.[65] That determination was evinced both in the signing by 471,414 men and women of Ulster's Solemn League and Covenant, and in the recruitment, training and arming of the Ulster Volunteer Force (UVF). Bishop D'Arcy's influence was significant. He had consulted Lord Macnaghten, a Lord of Appeal in the House of Lords, and been persuaded by that distinguished Ulsterman to sign the Covenant, their joint resolve in turn influencing Primate Crozier.

In D'Arcy's words, 'a truly religious conviction animated the opposition to Home Rule'. The will of the Protestant people was reinforced by the support of their churches. On 14 January 1914, Lord Londonderry wrote from Mount Stewart: 'A great churchgoing has been arranged for today, the Primate and the Bible to sanctify our cause'. Church services preceded the signing of the Covenant throughout Ulster on 28 September 1912. In Belfast D'Arcy preached to a packed congregation in St Anne's Cathedral before signing in the City Hall. As bishop of the diocese, he was fourth in precedence, after Sir Edward Carson, Lord Londonderry, and the Moderator of the General Assembly; the Dean of Belfast was the fifth signatory. D'Arcy also spoke regularly to gatherings of Volunteers, and dedicated their colours. He was motivated by two convictions (which he avowed in several letters to *The Times*). The first was that the order and discipline of the UVF saved the province from anarchy at a time of high tension; the second that its strength (particularly after the 'gun-running' of April 1914) made it unlikely that the government would use force against Ulster. In the tense spring of 1914, however, that was not yet certain, and when the General Synod met in Dublin, Primate Crozier deplored the 'cruel tragedy that there should be the real danger of drenching the fair fields and towns of Ulster with the blood of their fellow-countrymen to create "a united Ireland"'. But the danger was averted. Despite the failure of the Buckingham Palace Conference to reach formal agreement in July 1914, an accommodation which involved the exclusion of most of Ulster from the jurisdiction of an Irish Parliament had been identified as the most realistic solution on the eve of the First World War .[66]

Together with Roman Catholics, Presbyterians, and other Irish people, members of the Church of Ireland, both men and women, volunteered for service in the Great War. Already in the spring of 1915, Crozier acknowledged that 'few families' represented in the General Synod had 'not felt the cruel pain the war has brought about. Home after home has been left desolate'. Two members of the RCB had each lost an only son, Bishop D'Arcy's only son had been 'desperately wounded' at Ypres, and Bishop Bernard's younger son was to be killed at Gallipoli 10 days after the Synod had ended. The Primate spoke also of the 'many thousands' of church members – official figures late in 1916 indicated 21,000 – who had 'gallantly responded all over Ireland to their country's call'.[67] Crozier noted elsewhere that 'all the young men of military age' from the rectories of Armagh diocese had joined up, 'and the daughters of the clergy have found their calling in munitions works, hospitals and elsewhere'. He himself visited Irish troops on the Western Front early in 1916, and preached five times each Sunday to companies of two or three thousand. He said on his return: 'I went out to teach them; they have taught me – the patience of hope, and the joy of sacrifice and service'.[68] There was much individual heroism. Outside the church in the Louth village of Collon, a simple memorial records that James Samuel Emerson VC, 2nd Lieut Royal Inniskilling Fusiliers, was killed in action at Cambrai in 1917. A memorial in the chancel of Holywood church honours another soldier who won the Victoria Cross, John Dunville of Redburn, who was also killed in France in 1917. In all, 42 Holywood parishioners had given their lives; and the new vicar of the parish in 1920, Charles Manning (later Archdeacon of Down), had been awarded the Military Cross in 1918. Other Great War chaplains also served with distinction. Of the bishops in the 1950s, McNeil Boyd of Derry had won the MC, and like John Crozier of Tuam, had been mentioned in despatches.[69] Not all clergy in uniform were chaplains. Berkeley's biographer, A. A. Luce, served as a combatant with 12th Royal Irish Rifles and won the MC in 1917.

Common war service had forged a unity among Irishmen upon which John Henry Bernard set much hope, but it was shattered in the wake of the Easter Rising. The Convention of 1917, at which Archbishops Crozier and Bernard and Provost Mahaffy represented the church, failed to reach agreement, Sinn Fein – committed to withdraw from Westminster and to establish Dáil Éireann – won a majority of parliamentary seats in 1918, and armed conflict began in 1919. The northern bishops, who had held that Irish unity would best be preserved within the Union,[70] shared their people's desire to opt out of the secessionist Irish Free State, and supported the creation of Northern Ireland and its defence against armed rebellion. The scattered church population elsewhere suffered cruelly in the fighting of 1919-23: two members of General Synod were murdered, other lives lost, and fine houses destroyed. Speaking to the General Synod of 1921 of the murders of synodsmen Sir Arthur Vicars and George Frend, Primate D'Arcy said that members of the church 'in several parts of the country – quiet, defenceless farmers for the most part – have been most cruelly killed'.[71] Gregg, now Archbishop of Dublin, described a massacre of Protestants in west Cork during the Civil War as 'a declaration of war upon a defenceless community', and led a deputation to ask the leaders of the Provisional government, Cosgrave and Collins, if they were 'desirous of retaining Protestants in the country'. On its fourth day of meeting, the General Synod of 1922 adjourned to Christ Church Cathedral for 'a solemn service of Intercession for the Church and Country'. It had heard Primate D'Arcy speak on the first day 'of the shocking deaths recently inflicted on some members of our Church, and of the expulsion of many others'.[72]

The Church of Ireland population in the 26 counties of the Irish Free State in fact fell from 249,535 in 1911 to 164,215 in 1928, a loss of 85,230 people in 15 years. The apocalyptic warnings of the special sessions of the General Synod seemed to have found statistical justification. But whereas Protestant emigration from rural Ireland had been appreciable before 1914, the decline of the Protestant working-class in Dublin was precipitated by the Great War. Martin Maguire comments: 'As rural Ireland prospered, Dublin became an industrial graveyard as war-time controls strangled non-essential industries.' This crisis was the more serious in that working-class Protestants – some 10,000 men – had in 1911 constituted 38 per cent of all Protestant males working in Dublin. Moreover, the census report for 1926 indicated that 25 per cent of the church's loss arose from the withdrawal after 1921 of the Crown forces – police, army and navy – and their dependants.[73] Nonetheless, with the church's population at 145,030 in 1936, the decline continued. In an analysis given to the General Synod of 1939, his first as Primate, Gregg attributed it to three factors: emigration, mixed marriages, and the practice of late marrying. With characteristic directness, he advocated 'the replenishment of our human stock through a fuller development of family life', and every effort (as he was to put it again in 1946) 'to discourage and prevent mixed marriages'. As to emigration, he saw it as inevitable when 'the two communities' were 'outside one another' – a situation reinforced by the state's adoption of a new Constitution in 1937.

> It is the fact that we are outside the close-knit spiritual entity which the majority constitutes, and are not homogeneous with it, that decrees our decline, unless we can effectively protect ourselves. Our two communities repel one another, and the smaller – on sociological grounds – tends to suffer. Individuals transfer themselves to a more sympathetic environment.[74]

## IV 1938–2001

### 1. The states of the church

#### Traditional and conservative

Primate Gregg's towering presence held the church steady until 1959, but did not encourage change. With her bishops mostly elderly and cautious, and her mission crushed by her institutional weight, the Church of Ireland was in need of renewal. But the later Anglican perceptions of renewal for mission and of the missionary role of the episcopate[75] were confined to a few visionaries. When George Simms became Bishop of Cork in 1952 at the age of 42, to Henry McAdoo (who succeeded him as Dean of Cork) it was 'like a springtime' in the diocese, and of great spiritual impact. Simms held Lenten Bible classes in the cathedral parish which hundreds attended, led city and diocesan missions, and invited his clergy to the palace for a three-day Bible school. His responsibilities as Archbishop of Dublin from 1956, however, largely precluded this gifted teacher from such ministry, for his energies were absorbed in civic duties and scores of church committees.[76] Simms's vision for recovery of the church's spiritual mission, linked to reform of her structures, found practical expression later in *Administration 1967*, a report prepared by a small committee under his chairmanship. But its radical proposals for change were rejected by the General Synod. Ironically, the report listed various Commissions – in 1919-20, 1936-41, 1943, and 1947-52 – the reports of which had been 'quietly pigeon-holed'.[77] For their part, most clergy served their parishes conscientiously. As a curate in Derry in the late 1940s, Victor Griffin was required to make a minimum of 40 house visits a week, and these were recorded in a book.[78] But leadership, in point of delegation, or the spiritual development of their people, or equipping the laity for ministry (another of Simms's emphases) was outside the experience of most incumbents. Curates trained in mid-century carried these limitations forward until they retired as senior clergy in the 1980s and 1990s. Clericalism resulted in spiritual deprivation. When he became Bishop of Cashel in 1968, John Armstrong found that Roman Catholics after Vatican II were turning to Anglicans for guidance in Bible study: 'but sadly our people have not learnt how to study the scriptures'.[79]

In populous northern parishes they had not learnt to communicate either, except at the major festivals. It was not that the Eucharist was infrequently celebrated. In suburban and town parishes during the 1950s, the early Sunday celebration was thinly attended, the conjunction of Morning Prayer and Holy Communion on the monthly Communion Sunday encouraged most parishioners to leave at the break, and the early celebration on Saints' days attracted few communicants. Inappropriate arrangements were only part of the problem. Victorian architecture had made the altar remote from the people. Sacramental life was generally at a low ebb, with font and holy table seldom at the centre of congregational experience. Baptism was normally administered out of sight rather than in the presence of the congregation. Witness to the Eucharist as the central service of the people of God was maintained only in the High Church tradition. Nonetheless as Vincent Ryan pointed out in 1970 church people were not comfortless:

> One of the most attractive features of Anglican worship is the celebration in cathedral and parish churches of Morning and Evening Prayer. Here clergy and people unite their voices in what is truly the prayer-service of the whole community. The simple structure of the twin offices, together with their rich biblical content, has with good reason been admired by Roman Catholic liturgists.[80]

As at earlier periods, however, the pulpit was out of harmony with the liturgy. The root problem was that good men, confusing the church's evangelical purpose with institutional propriety, had substituted a vague sacramentalism for experimental religion. With characteristic bluntness Gregg quoted Mazzini to the General Synod of 1946: 'When anyone says to me, "Behold a good man", I ask, "How many souls has he saved?"'[81] And Bishop W. S. Kerr of Down (1945-56) thus expressed his exasperation after a service in his diocese: 'The Church! the Church! When are we going to hear a sermon on the Church's Lord?'[82] Herbert O'Driscoll, a native of Cork diocese who became Dean of Vancouver, recounted in his autobiography *The Leap of the Deer* his conversion from institutional religion to personal faith. Preaching in Holywood (his wife's home parish) in the late 1950s, O'Driscoll had referred to conversion – 'that word that sends shivers up and down the spines of loyal Anglicans'. Gregg was instrumental in the appointment of a Dean of Residence at Queen's University in 1951, dedicated the new Students' Centre in 1955, and supported the institution of the annual theological lectures.[83] The foundations were well laid. But they were rocked by Canon Bryan Green, whose mission in 1958 was sponsored by the Church of Ireland, Presbyterian, and Methodist deans of residence, both through his ancillary lectures on courtship and sex, and his preaching of justification by grace through faith.

Repudiation by the establishment of the Church of Ireland's Evangelical tradition compounded the problem. Patronage which it had once dominated now worked against that tradition and the theological climate was inhospitable to it. Many able clergy left for the Church of England. Those who remained did not provide leadership, which fell instead to Dr J. S. McCann of Belfast and other laymen. BCMS provided some cohesion, but (like HCMS from 1814) lacked episcopal patronage. Many laity looked to pan-evangelical organizations. They were in good company. David Sheppard, Bishop of Liverpool 1975-97, was helped in his search for faith by the ladies of the Sandes Soldiers Home in Palace Barracks Holywood during national service. By 1969, a more positive, forward-looking, and church-centred emphasis was discernible among Evangelicals: but it needed to be nurtured.

The church remained conservative also in point of her anti-Roman Catholic apologetic and associations. In 1950, the bishops in a Pastoral Letter – it was written by Gregg – refuted the dogma of the Assumption,[84] and Kerr published his scholarly *Handbook on the Papacy*. APCK reissued Gregg's *The Primitive Faith and Roman Catholic Developments* in 1957. The church's symbiotic relationship with the Orange institutions was unquestioned in the northern province. In Belfast, the Bishop of Connor until 1969, Cyril Elliott, walked in the annual Twelfth procession. Orange affiliation retained its importance for Church of Ireland people in the border counties of the Republic. Robert Heavener, rector of Monaghan and an Orangeman, was elected Bishop of Clogher in 1973. An historian and Grand Chaplain of the Orange Order, Dr M. W. Dewar, joined the Chapter of St Patrick's Cathedral Dublin in 1983. But this very association, traditional though it was, tended in time to widen the gap between church members who were citizens of two states. That process had been hastened by the Second World War and the departure of the Republic of Ireland in 1949 from the Commonwealth, even if traditional loyalties served both to delay and to disguise the process.

Despite the neutrality of the southern state, the Second World War drew volunteers from all over Ireland into the forces of the Crown. If not in the same numbers as in 1914-18 – three Holywood parishioners fell in 1939-45 as against 42 in the Great War – Church of Ireland members again gave their lives. They included a son of Primate Gregg and two sons of the Prime Minister of Northern Ireland, Sir Basil Brooke (later Lord Brookeborough). Abbeyleix church has a memorial to Major General F. W. Warren, CBE, DSO, Commanding 5th Indian Division of 14th Army, who was killed over Assam in February 1945, aged 47: he was the son of Canon H. E. Warren. Clergy again served as chaplains. Of the episcopate in the 1970s, Archbishop Alan Buchanan of Dublin had been taken prisoner at Arnhem in 1944 while serving with the 1st Airborne Division, and Bishops Arthur Butler of Connor and Cuthbert Peacocke of Derry had also been army chaplains. At home, air-raids in Belfast killed and injured many Church of Ireland people, in common with their fellow citizens. Four churches were destroyed, and 12 others damaged in the Easter raid of 1941. Primate Gregg told the General Synod of churches, halls and rectories, as well as people's homes, reduced to ruins; of parochial entities collapsed, and their people scattered.[85]

The General Synod of 1949 met, in the Primate's words, 'under strange conditions, with the Republic of Ireland an established fact'. Gregg hoped that 'two diverse loyalties' would never 'be allowed to mar the essential oneness of the Church of Ireland'. But there were yet inescapable consequences. *The Gazette* had carried a protracted correspondence in the early months of 1949 on the expediency of retaining the state prayers in their customary form. Part sentiment, and part semantics, the case for retention was silenced by Gregg's blunt observations 'that the Republic is a fact', and that 'in our prayers, above all, there must be reality'. Though with much sadness of heart, he concluded, the state prayers would be adapted 'to fit the Republican form of government'. A residual royalism, however survived in Dublin into the 1950s. A memorial service for George VI was held in St Patrick's Cathedral in 1952. On Trinity Sunday 1953, and 'in accord with the desire of Queen Elizabeth', a pre-Coronation civic service took place in Christ Church Cathedral, at which Dean Lewis-Crosby preached.[86] Archbishop Barton of Dublin rather than the Primate attended the Coronation (as he had the Royal Wedding in 1947 at Gregg's request). Again, at the pre-Synod service in St Patrick's Cathedral in 1954, prayers were said for both HM The Queen and President Sean T. O'Kelly.

A new Church of Ireland generation in the Republic, however, moved away from inherited West Briton loyalties. Tacit acceptance of the state gave away to positive support, and southern church members, particularly in the cities, became more confident in their citizenship. The intellectual basis for their fuller involvement in public life was laid by W. B. Stanford in *A Recognized Church* (1944) and H. R. McAdoo in *No New Church* (1945). The *Church of Ireland Gazette*, for its part, carried at various times Fine Gael election notices, and an election address by De Valera (partly in Irish, but mostly in English). Dublin had from 1956 an Irish-speaking Archbishop in George Simms.[87] A major influence in helping Church of Ireland youth to become culturally integrated in society was that of Coláiste Móibhí, the preparatory college established in 1927 (initially at Glasnevin) to train future primary teachers. It supplied the Church of Ireland Training College with students who were fluent in Irish, so ensuring that the church's primary schools would survive. To safeguard its own identity in a theocratic environment, while at the same time identifying with the state, was no mean achievement on the part of the small Church of Ireland population in the Republic.

The situation of church members in Northern Ireland was very different. Though also a minority – they formed the third largest denomination after the Roman Catholics and the Presbyterians – they were part of the Protestant majority which had sustained the Unionist party in government since 1921. But Protestant unity was political, not religious. The Church of Ireland was involved in a power struggle with the Presbyterians over, for example, school appointments – a sectarian aspect of Ulster life which had been little noticed. Gregg had at first refused the primacy partly because he did not 'think that at 65 I should ever be able to find N. Ireland anything but a strange land spiritually and politically'. Archbishop Lang of Canterbury agreed then that 'the political Protestantism of the North' would have made his position difficult. These misgivings may have inhibited Gregg once in Armagh, and nullified his renowned independence of mind. He had always refused to join either the Orange or the Masonic institutions because he knew from experience that their members 'forfeited independence of judgment'.[88] Moreover, he had for two decades spoken fearlessly about the shortcomings of the Irish Free State. He seldom commented, however, on public affairs in Northern Ireland, evidence in itself that later claims of widespread social injustice and discrimination on religious grounds were unwarranted.

In socio-economic terms, working-class Protestants were as deprived as their Catholic counterparts, while both had the same entitlement to state-provided health and social security benefits. Within both communities, however, corruption and local abuse of power were not uncommon. Out of his 22 years' experience as a priest in Londonderry, Victor Griffin demolished allegations about religious inequalities, identified the nepotism prevalent in both Derry communities, and highlighted the Belfast government's neglect, for political reasons, of the north-west region.[89] The real danger inherent in the Northern Ireland arose from the monopoly of power by one tradition. Under Lord Brookeborough's tenure as Prime Minister (1943-63), things appeared stable enough, but the massive vote for Sinn Fein in the British General Election of 1955 and the IRA's campaign of violence (1957-62) were ominous signs. Confrontation and conflict lay in the future, after Gregg's time. He was made a Companion of Honour in 1957, and resigned the primacy in 1959.

In the period 1936-61 Church of Ireland membership fell from 490,504 to 448,816. Of the total fall of 41,688, almost all (98.4 per cent) was in the Republic, in the context of a fall of 150,079 in the population of the state. In Northern Ireland, by contrast, the population rose by 145,297 over 25 years while that of the Church of Ireland remained static. As recorded by census in each jurisdiction, the details are:

### Church of Ireland Population: 1936-1961

| Republic of Ireland | Northern Ireland |
|---|---|
| 1936  145,030 (4.9 per cent) | 1937  345,474 (27.0 per cent) |
| 1946  124,829 (4.2) | 1951  353,245 (25.8) |
| 1961  104,016 (3.7) | 1961  344,800 (24.2) |

The decline in the Republic came on top of the heavy fall in membership between 1911 and 1936. It meant that the proportion of the Church's membership living in the Republic fell from 29.6 to 23.2 per cent by 1961. Although, correspondingly, the proportion in Northern Ireland rose from 70.4 to 76.8 per cent, the Church of Ireland alone of the churches failed to increase her actual numbers there: that is, experienced a decline in real (and relative) terms between 1936 and 1961. The Roman Catholic and Presbyterian Churches gained most, with increases of 69,257 and 22,722 respectively; but the Methodists increased also by 16,100 and 'Others' by 38,002.[90] Whatever the reasons for the Church of Ireland's failure here, her disproportionate allocation of resources as between north and south, a disparity which was steadily worsening, and her inability to redress this situation, would seem to bear much of the blame.

Internal membership records show a discrepancy with the government figures. In 1947, the Church of Ireland claimed only 457,100 members compared with the 1946-51 census aggregate of 478,074; and in 1965, only 403,500 compared with the 1961 census total of 448,816. The figures for each diocese indicate that the discrepancy related largely to Northern Ireland. In other words, there were in 1951 over 20,000, and in 1961 over 45,000 people who declared that they were members of the Church of Ireland, but of whom the church had no record. Many of these were in Belfast. That city in 1965 had 60 parishes and 116 clergy for an apparent church population of 124,781: the most populous parish, St Mary's Crumlin Road, had 6258 parishioners. The clergy had on average pastoral responsibility for 1075 known church members. These figures compare with the diocese of Dublin, which in 1947 had 154 clergy for a membership (both urban and rural) of 51,000, an average of 331; and the diocese of Cork, which had 77 clergy for 11,600 people, an average of 150. Overall in 1965, the Church of Ireland had 796 clergy, 648 incumbencies, 1248 churches in use every Sunday and 121 less often; and supported also in 14 dioceses no less than 31 cathedrals, 29 deans, 27 archdeacons and 142 canons. The Church in Wales, with six dioceses, had 984 clergy and 854 incumbencies; with only six deans, 14 archdeacons and 65 canons.

While the conservative character of the Church of Ireland itself militated against radical change, the situation was exacerbated because of the domination by the smaller, mostly southern dioceses of representation in the General Synod, and of the Standing Committee and the RCB. Nine dioceses, with an aggregate population of 61,000, had 318 Synod representatives, clerical and lay; the remaining five dioceses, with a population of 343,000, had 330 representatives. When Armagh, Dublin and Derry are isolated within the latter group, the two dioceses of Connor and Down, with a combined population of 224,500, had only 135 representatives (45 clergy and 90 laity). That is to say, 55 per cent of the Church of Ireland's known membership had only 20.8 per cent of the representation on the church's decision-making bodies.[91]

### 'An open church'

The stability which Gregg represented in his convictions and style, and which continued under his successor James McCann (1959-69), was ended by two developments, the one in the Anglican Communion and the other in Ireland. The first consisted in liturgical renewal, changes in pastoral practice, and rapprochement with the Roman Catholic Church after the Vatican II decree on ecumenism and its sequel in the meeting of Archbishop Michael Ramsey with Pope Paul VI in 1966. The Church of Ireland was fully involved. General Synod appointed a Liturgical Advisory Committee (LAC) in 1962. Ramsey appointed Archbishop Simms as Anglican co-chairman of the joint Commission on the Theology of Marriage and its application to mixed marriages. The Church of Ireland supplied also, in Dr Henry McAdoo, the Anglican co-chairman of the Anglican-Roman Catholic International Commission (ARCIC I) on doctrine, which worked from 1970 to 1981.[92] McAdoo, who had become Bishop of Ossory in 1962, and was to become Archbishop of Dublin in 1977, was an outstanding scholar and linguist. He lectured on the Continent in both French and German; and at President Hillary's inauguration was to read the gospel in Irish. He was an authority on the Carolines. As a rector in Cork, he had published *The Structure of Caroline Moral Theology* (1949), and after his election to Ossory, *John Bramhall and Anglicanism, 1663-1963* (1964) and *The Spirit of Anglicanism: a survey of Anglican Theological Method in the seventeenth century* (1965).

It was ironical that the second development – in Ireland – should date from 1966 also. The 50th anniversary of the Easter Rising heightened tensions in Northern Ireland which fuelled the street disorder and political violence of 1968-69. The Ulster situation was far removed from the civilities of ecumenical dialogue, and the historic first meeting in 1969 of the leaders of Ireland's four main Churches – Roman Catholic, Church of Ireland, Presbyterian, and Methodist – was occasioned, not by theological debate, but by inter-communal strife.

Internal change marked the 1960s, even if it sometimes came slowly. Women had become eligible for all lay offices in 1949, but only one was elected to the General Synod in 1951, and still only 18 in 1969 (six of them from Connor).[93] Favourable property movements in central Dublin prompted the transfers to Rathmines of the RCB from St Stephen's Green in 1964, and the Training College – it became the College of Education – in 1968: Coláiste Móibhí moved to an adjoining site. Both the divinity hostel and the RCB library (founded at Gregg's instance in 1932) were relocated at Braemor Park in Rathgar. The King's Hospital moved from Blackhall Place to Palmerston. Simms and Bishop Mitchell of Down (1956-69) directed the church's attention to her early Celtic heritage, Mitchell inaugurating an annual St Patrick's Day pilgrimage in his diocese. In 1963, a crew of 13 men skippered by Wallace Clark rowed a curragh from Donegal to Iona in the wake of St Columba 1500 years earlier. Simms and Mitchell organised diocesan conferences also with a view to encouraging vocations to the priesthood – these had fallen dramatically since the 1930s – and out of their initiative came in 1960 the Central Advisory Council for Training for the Ministry (later the Bishops' Selection Conferences).[94]

The Episcopal Electoral College was created in 1960. Its record can conveniently be given here. There were 46 episcopal elections between November 1960 and December 2001, nine by the House of Bishops and 37 by the College. The former chose a new Primate on the three occasions that the see of Armagh fell vacant, George Simms in 1969, John Armstrong in 1980, and Robert Eames in 1986. The bishops elected to other vacant sees also, on the six occasions (out of 43) that the College had failed to elect: Richard Hanson to Clogher in 1969, Samuel Poyntz to Cork in 1978, William McCappin to Connor in 1981, Bishop Poyntz to Connor in 1987, Harold Miller to Down in 1997, and Michael Jackson to Clogher in 2001. The unions of Killaloe with Limerick in 1976 and of Cashel with Ossory in 1977 left 12 sees. (Kildare was separated from Dublin and united with Meath, also in 1976, and the diocese transferred from the province of Armagh to that of Dublin.) Apart from translations, all but three vacancies arose from retirements: Bishops de Pauley of Cashel (1968) and Pike of Meath (1976) died in office, and Hanson resigned (1973).[95] Dublin University ceased to confer the Doctorate of Divinity *iure dignitatis* on new bishops. It mattered less in that many had doctorates in their own right, and that the BBC bestowed the title on those who had not.

Changing patterns of worship restored both sacraments to the heart of congregational experience, and found expression in Parish Communions, family services, and modern hymnody. The Eucharist became central rather than peripheral to the worship of urban parishes (many rural parishes kept to a monthly celebration); and 'Publick Baptism' began to be administered during Morning Prayer. More urban parishes introduced the Three Hours Devotion on Good Friday and a midnight Eucharist on Christmas Eve, and many rural parishes extended their harvest thanksgiving from Friday evening through Monday. Innovation was often spontaneous, with legislation some way behind. The emphasis was on freedom and flexibility. Thus the Canons adopted in 1974 were devised by a select committee sensitive to 'what ministers and people may do, rather than what they are forbidden to do'. That they were already doing it was noted also, whether in respect of new hymns and prayers, or of plain stoles of various colours the use of which was 'now widespread and should be recognized'.[96] As the stole had no post-Reformation precedent, General Synod resolved that its now authorized use had 'no doctrinal significance'.[97]

In this environment of change, the 1955 edition of the *Church Hymnal*, revised in 1960 and containing 181 new hymns and carols,[98] soon became inadequate and the use of some modern hymn collections was authorized. Meanwhile liturgical revision proceeded apace. Services drafted by the LAC were authorized for use on an experimental basis, and modified in the light of criticism. While the Communion Order of 1967[99] was a conservative revision of the 1662 BCP service, *Holy Communion 1972* (with an Irish translation by Canon Coslett Quin) was more radical, after the framework drawn up by an Anglican liturgical consultation after Lambeth 1968. It incorporated new versions of the Lord's Prayer, the Nicene Creed, and other texts also by the International Commission on English Texts.

After 13 years in Dublin, George Simms was elected Primate of All Ireland in 1969. His decade in Armagh was marked at once by more focused change in the church, and by relentless terrorism in Northern Ireland. In a situation dominated by fear, Simms's eirenic spirit drew abuse upon himself. He responded with courage and dignity, while his sensitive nature suffered from the indiscriminate violence inflicted on innocent people. As a diocesan, although his pastoral style was non-directive, he had the capacity to influence his clergy to reach the right decision themselves. With his unfailing recall of names and faces, his unaffected interest in people, and his humility, Simms was 'a man greatly loved' throughout the church. His presidency of the General Synod revealed his character. Intimate and good-humoured, he asserted a gentle and subtle authority, his evident exasperation at times held under a control that allowed him to express no more than a tone of disapproval. His expertize served the church well. A fine liturgical scholar, he chaired the LAC (and served as its consultant after he retired in 1980). The journal *Search* – with Elizabeth Ferrar as editor, it replaced *New Divinity* in 1978 – was published under his chairmanship until his death in 1991. Simms hoped that it would help to create 'an open church, with the humility to listen and learn'.[100] He was conscious of her need to communicate also, and as well as contributing his weekly column 'Thinking Aloud' to the *Irish Times*, encouraged training in media skills at Braemor Park, the role of the Central Communications Board, the appointment of a press officer, and the creation of an information centre in St Anne's Cathedral. During his primacy the Georgian palace in Armagh was sold, and a new (and very inadequate) see house built in the cathedral close. Simms was unsparing of himself. As President of the International Leprosy Mission, he undertook with Mrs Mercy Simms[101] an arduous tour of India in 1974 to mark the centenary of its founding in Ireland. His *In My Understanding* (1984) revealed the richness of his devotional life and his gift for communicating his spirituality, best seen in his lectures on the Book of Kells. That given at Campbell College Belfast on 18 October 1974 was described by the Headmaster, Robin Morgan, as 'an experience in controlled rapture'.[102]

Simms had done much to improve the ecumenical climate in Dublin, and in Armagh developed personal friendships with Cardinals Conway and Ó Fiaich, ensured that the first meeting of the four church leaders (held before his arrival) should evolve into a regular pattern, and encouraged the launch of the inter-church process. He was co-chairman of the annual conference held at Ballymascanlon from 1973 between representatives of the (Protestant) Irish Council of Churches and the (Roman Catholic) Irish Episcopal Conference. In 1973 also, on the initiative of Archbishop Alan Buchanan of Dublin, the chapel in TCD ceased to be affiliated to the Church of Ireland and became shared by all churches which had a chaplain accredited to the college. With the lifting of the self-imposed ban on its students in 1970, these included the Roman Catholic Church.[103] Simms maintained a strong commitment to ecumenism. In 1970, the centenary of disestablishment and his first General Synod as Primate, he invited the Methodist Lord Soper to preach at the pre-Synod service in St Patrick's Cathedral. It was a significant signal. Gregg's rigidity had killed formal discussions with the Presbyterians and Methodists in 1935, and the lead in resuming them was given by McCann and Simms in 1964. (Mitchell had initiated informal discussions at Murlough House in 1958.)[105] Outside Ireland, the church entered into full communion not only with the Lusitanian and Spanish Reformed Episcopal Churches (in 1963), but also with the Church of South India, a union of episcopal and non-episcopal churches (to which Gregg had been opposed).

But doctrinal consensus impinged only indirectly on the consciousness of church members. The value of ecumenical dialogue lay primarily in the justification given to joint services, pulpit exchanges, and local intercommunion. All traditions in the Church of Ireland removed the denominational fence from around her altars, variously welcoming all baptized Christians, (as with St John's Sandymount), or all 'who love the Lord Jesus' (St Patrick's Coleraine) to communicate at the Lord's table. The new, formal relationship with the Roman Catholic Church encouraged private initiatives. The best known of these was the founding of the Christian Renewal Centre at Rostrevor in 1974 by Cecil and Myrtle Kerr. Here Christians from all churches lived together in community, and reached out in ministry through-out Ireland. In many localities, Christians worshipped together during the annual week of prayer for Christian unity or the women's world day of prayer, shared in Bible study and prayer groups, and co-operated in sending material help to the persecuted church overseas: Kill o' the Grange parish and its three neighbouring Roman Catholic parishes in Dublin sent containers of clothing and household goods to Sudanese Christians. The coming together of church leaders had both symbolic and practical value. For the first time since the Reformation, the Church of Ireland openly affirmed Roman Catholic Christians. Bishops preached in one another's cathedrals and spoke in unison in tragic situations. For his part, Pope John Paul II received Church of Ireland bishops (including the Orange Bishop of Clogher) during his visit to Ireland in 1979. At Ballymascanlon representatives of all the churches dis-cussed contentious issues openly. In 1974, when rational debate was being overtaken by the emotions engendered by internment, Archbishop Buchanan restored calm with characteristic courtesy and candour: 'I was a prisoner – without trial. And therefore I sympathize with *all* prisoners.' He went on to insist that a state facing armed rebellion had the right to defend itself – an assertion which was not challenged.[105] Opportunity for such plain speaking across a wide spectrum of opinion was rare in the 1970s.

In several important respects the episcopate of George Quin, Bishop of Down (1969-80), was pivotal for the northern province. He excelled in blending the conventional and the vital. As vicar of Ballymacarrett from 1951, he had drawn his working-class parishioners to informal Sunday evening epilogues. He had appointed men – he had five curates in 1956 – who 'taught publicly and from house to house repentance towards God and faith in our Lord Jesus Christ', as James Mehaffey claimed in his farewell ser-mon. Quin went on to be rector of Bangor and was appointed Archdeacon of Down by Mitchell, whom he succeeded as bishop in 1969. Quin's appraisal of the future was shrewd. He saw that the church's leadership would remain with men of Broad tradition, and that evangelical and charismatic influences were vital to her renewal. He set out to equip the leaders, and to encourage renewal. Three of his curates became bishops and one, Jack Shearer, Dean of Belfast. Quin advised Robin Eames not to accept a southern dignity, and in 1975 (at the age of 38) Eames joined him on the bench as Bishop of Derry. He appointed Mehaffey as diocesan missioner and Gordon McMullan as Archdeacon of Down, and in 1980 (the year he retired) they became Bishops of Derry and Clogher respectively, Eames and McMullan in turn succeeding Quin in Down. James Moore, who had followed Eames in St Mark's Dundela in 1975, became Bishop of Connor in 1995. It was a trib-ute to Quin's influence, then, that in 1996 all five northern bishops, including the Primate, were Down men. (Bishop Brian Hannon of Clogher spent his ministry away from Down.) The legacy was still effective in 2000 when Ken Clarke, a protégé of Quin, was appointed to the see of Kilmore.

But Quin's influence was wider still. He emphasized the ministry of the entire church, and particularly of the laity. In Bangor he had identified with the annual conference of young Church Evangelicals, and as bishop influenced the restoration of patronage to Evangelical clergy. He became a founding trustee of the Christian Renewal Centre, and in 1977 took the platform at the National Charismatic Conference in Dublin. He linked his diocese with St Michael-le-Belfry in York, encouraged lay leaders to go there, and in 1978 invited David Watson and his team to conduct a diocesan mission. It was marked by ministries in mime and dance and by Watson's powerful preaching, and culminated in praise in St Anne's Cathedral. (The Presbyterian minister Ken Newell has written of the value of Watson's mission for his own spiritual development.) Quin inspired devotion by his large-hearted friendship and pastoral strengths. By embracing charismatic renewal, he stamped it as authentic; and by nurturing Evangelicals he restored their self-confidence and provided them with a diocesan base. His achievement was comparable with that of William Magee 150 years before.

The church's historic link with TCD was transformed when, in John Bartlett's phrase, the Divinity School was disestablished. The College terminated the courses leading to the divinity testimonium in 1978, suspended the three divinity chairs as they fell vacant 1978-82, and enrolled ordinands in the new, non-denominational faculty of theology. Meanwhile, the divinity hostel became the Church of Ireland Theological College in 1980. Canon James Hartin was its first principal, Canon John Bartlett FTCD, associate professor of biblical studies in Trinity, succeeding him in 1989.[106] The structure of the ordained ministry changed. With numbers of clergy falling in the 1970s and many due to retire during the next two decades – the problem was exacerbated by earlier retirement – it became imperative to recruit a part-time auxiliary ministry. The non-stipendiary minister (NSM) soon became a familiar figure in every diocese. The shortage of stipendiary clergy resulted also in men being appointed to incumbencies after one curacy, and instituted by bishops who had typically served three curacies. The obvious disadvantage in this trend was offset by an increase in the number of mature ordinands, many with managerial experience. Most of them were married, and the lack of suitable accommodation at Braemor Park bore hardly on their families. Incumbencies, too, tended to be of shorter duration, reflecting at once the increased mobility in society, the ending of the former rigidity over diocesan boundaries, and the new perception (first seen with George Simms) that many incumbents were less effective after 10 years in the same post.

The long period of liturgical experimentation ended when the *Alternative Prayer Book 1984* (APB) was published by Collins. It comprised Morning and Evening Prayer, Baptism and Holy Communion; litany, collects, and weekday intercessions and thanksgivings; psalter and lectionary; and the text – in the modern translation of the New International Version – of the Old Testament reading, epistle and gospel for Sundays, festivals, and holydays for two years. The work of revision begun in 1962 was finally completed with the publication of *Alternative Occasional Services 1993*. It included confirmation, marriage, funeral, ordination, and institution services; a new Service of Thanksgiving after Adoption; a section on Ministry to the Sick which provided for the laying on of hands and anointing with oil; and an alternative order of the eucharistic thanksgiving, reproduced from *An Australian Prayer Book* 1978 (AAPB). Given the Irish church's links with the Anglican Church of Australia and the Church of England, which published *The Alternative Service Book 1980* (ASB), comparisons were interesting. The compact AAPB did not include the text of its prescribed readings, while the voluminous ASB did so for one year only. But both included the pastoral services and the ordinal, which the Church of Ireland published separately in 1993. Again, unlike AAPB, the APB did not include the 39 Articles, and unlike ASB, made no reference to them in its preface.[107]

This liturgical achievement warrants some comment. In the first place, no market research was undertaken before APB was published, and its unexpectedly large sales, whatever the profit to the publisher, yielded some £10,000 annually to the General Synod's Royalties Fund through a well-written royalties clause. Secondly, the alternative services enriched the worship of many parishes, through fuller congregational participation and greater intimacy in, for example, the sharing of the Peace at the Eucharist. On the other hand, devotion to the BCP and reassurance derived from it were strong, and it often required courage on the part of the clergy to introduce their people to new idioms of worship. In many parishes a realistic if uneasy compromise was achieved by using APB at some services and the BCP at others. Thirdly, despite the disclaimer in its preface that it was replacing the BCP, the use of the *Alternative Prayer Book* on almost all official church occasions tended to relegate the BCP to second class status. Uneasiness on this score, and opposition to the APB in conservative parishes (many, but not all, in rural Ulster) highlighted the loss of the unity which the Church of Ireland had for so long derived from a common prayer book. Finally, the very weight of material – in hymnology as well as liturgy – presented a problem which some urban parishes overcame by compiling their own selections, and using these in conjunction with weekly service sheets. This expedient at once drew upon all available material, albeit often in a hybrid manner, and dispensed with the use of all books – a local refinement of the loss of common prayer.

Commitment to the church overseas remained strong, while support became more versatile. The Mothers' Union had sent £3 to its overseas fund in 1932, and over £1000 for the first time in 1958: giving was £40,000 in 1985, doubled to £79,000 in 1994, and reached £104,000 in 1999. Several Irish missionaries worked under MU auspices, the first being Irene Lockett from Belfast. The older societies changed their names. SPG joined with UMCA to form the United Society for the Propagation of the Gospel (USPG). HCMS became CMSI: Church Missionary (later Mission) Society Ireland. BCMS became Crosslinks. In 2001, CMSI and Mid-Africa Mission (formerly the Rwanda Mission) merged, the better to deploy resources in the Great Lakes region of mid-Africa. In 1972, before the onset of hyper-inflation, 15 societies had aggregate income of £294,779 from direct giving and legacies; it rose to £552,249 in 1980, to £1,212,663 in 1994 (with almost £1 million in direct giving), and to more than £1½ million in 1999. CMSI was still the best supported society. Crosslinks was in 1994 within £14,000 of the general income of CMSI, but fell away in the late 1990s as CMSI increased its income from £322,874 (1994) to £585,251 (1999), an increase of 55.2 per cent in five years. Meanwhile SAMS enjoyed a fivefold increase from £11,855 in 1980 to £65,224 in 1994, and a further increase to £116,156 in 1999.[108]

The church's approach to the developing world was influenced by new perceptions of mission. One was the concept of mission partnership in the Anglican Communion. While full-time missionaries were still being supported, indigenous churches in Africa and elsewhere were provided with short-term partners also: CMSI supported 131 (mostly short-term) mission partners to 1994. Another innovation was the annual projects undertaken by CMSI. These helped Nairobi Cathedral to lay a water pipe for Kayole in 1995, raised over £40,000 in 1996 to buy hoes and beans, and so help the church in Rwanda to support stricken families, and in 1997 supported mission partners from the church in Sudan in their work in Zambia. The concept of mission partnership was further enhanced by the appointment of an Overseas Resource Person for the Church of Ireland. Canon Jerome Munyangayu, who had experience in Rwanda and Tanzania, held this appointment 1995-7, and enriched the church through his many insights. (In 2000 he became rector of the Down parish of Killyleagh.) Charles Irwin, a clergyman with experience of the Church of South India, was appointed Overseas Resource Person in 2000, his remit being to assist the church towards 'a greater commitment to mission'.[109]

*Change and decay*

Robert Henry Alexander Eames was elected Primate of All Ireland in March 1986, on the retirement after a brief primacy of John Armstrong. Eames invited comparison with William Alexander, under whose primacy the century had begun. Alexander was a widower of 72 on election, Eames 48 and married; both had been Bishop of Derry. Alexander was a High churchman bred in an Evangelical rectory, Eames a Broad churchman brought up in a Methodist manse. Both were scholars, with strong pastoral inclinations. Both stood high in Anglican estimation, Alexander for his eloquence and the clarity of his theological insights, Eames for his conciliatory skills and leadership both in Ireland and in the Anglican Communion. Ulstermen both, they had spent their entire ministry in the North (Eames having taken his law degree and his doctorate at Queen's University). Each ended a sequence of five predecessors who had – with the exception of Robert Knox's brief primacy – come to Armagh from outside the province. Like Alexander, Eames was from the outset of his primacy forthright on public issues, fearless in avowing conviction, and (on matters about which he felt strongly) at once passionate and plain spoken. Alexander had noted: 'It is sometimes convenient to erase Ulster from the map of Ireland'.[110] Eames believed that the Anglo-Irish Agreement of 1985 ignored the interests of Ulster's Unionist majority. Finally, whereas Alexander had retired on the eve of the Ulster crisis of 1912-14, Eames was elected to Armagh after almost two decades of violence in the province.

In 1990, there was both press speculation in Britain and general expectation in Ireland that Eames would be appointed to Canterbury (and again, in 1995, to York). But these derived rather from popular perceptions of his abilities and prominence in the Anglican Communion than of realities in the Church of England. Eames had been a member of the ACC from 1982, figured prominently in the Lambeth Conference of 1988 and chaired two inter-Anglican commissions: Communion and Women in the Episcopate 1988-9, and the Theological and Doctrinal Commission from 1991. It was more appropriate that in 1995 Eames should have been made a life peer, as Baron Eames of Armagh. With world attention focused on Northern Ireland, with violence unabated, and with his background and immediate diocesan responsibility, he had become a principal spokesman for Northern Irish Protestants. Until 1996, Donald Caird complemented him in style and in the scope of his pronouncements as Archbishop of Dublin, while Walton Empey's succession in 1996 ensured that the outlook of a generation which had grown up with the Republic would be more vigorously expressed. The ultimate question for the church was whether the particularism of her leadership would reinforce a tendency to evolve two *de facto* autonomous provinces – in effect, two national churches.

While the Ulster situation became a major concern of Archbishop Eames (and is considered later), purposeful ecumenical activity and internal change characterized his primacy also. With the Church of Ireland involved in the Porvoo Declaration, the consensus of Anglican and Lutheran Churches in northern Europe, Eames preached at the service to celebrate its signing in Tallinn Cathedral, Estonia, on 8 September 1996.[111] At home he was, like his immediate predecessors, fully committed to the inter-church process (he had attended Ballymascanlon from its inception), and to the regular meetings of the leaders of the four main churches also. He developed a close understanding with Cardinals Ó Fiaich and Cahal Daly; and through his advice and encouragement was supportive of an incoming Moderator of the General Assembly, Dr A. W. G. Brown.[112] But noting in 1992, 'we are in danger of creating a denomination of ecumenists',[113] Eames advocated more local understanding. He dedicated the extension to the Christian Renewal Centre at Rostrevor in 1986. As Primate, Eames alerted the Church of Ireland to the dangers that her distinctiveness might be eroded either by accommodation to a minority situation, or through complacency – he called for 'new thinking on the deployment and movement of clergy'; and warned that resistance to change might become 'an ingredient for decay'.[114]

It is clear that Eames pursued twin strategies from the outset of his primacy. The first was to find workable answers to residual theological and pastoral dilemmas, as with the ordination of women and the remarriage of divorced persons. The second was to equip the church for the 21st century, by identifying her episcopal needs, managing her ministerial resources, making her central administration more efficient, reassessing her spiritual and social priorities, and providing her with a single, comprehensive book of common worship. At the same time, the familiar historical pattern of informal initiative reinforcing formal agenda was again apparent in the church, arresting decline, inspiring youth, and enhancing her local effectiveness.

The Church of Ireland decided in 1990 to ordain women to the priesthood. The bishops had pronounced in 1970 that there were no theological barriers, but the General Synod was not ready then for such a radical departure from tradition. During the next two decades the church became accustomed to women's public ministry as readers and deacons, and convinced of the case for the ordination of women. Her right, as an independent church, to use her catholic and apostolic authority in this matter was not seriously disputed. She took her historic decision (as Bishop Roy Williamson reminded the English General Synod) before the Church of England, the Scottish Episcopal Church, and the Church in Wales decided to ordain women. The first two women were ordained by Bishop Poyntz of Connor in St Anne's Cathedral on 24 June 1990 (37 days after the General Synod's enactment on

17 May 1990). They were Kathleen Young and Irene Templeton. Young later became the first woman incumbent in Armagh province, as Ginnie Kennerley did in Dublin. Canon Kennerley was also the first woman to be elected to a cathedral chapter, that of Christ Church Dublin in 1996. Opposition to women's ordination had been driven partly by prejudice, mostly by caution, and only rarely by principle. Except for a few individuals in Ulster, no-one seceded: the defections from the Church of England had no parallel in Ireland. In the period 1990-2001, the priesthood of women in both the stipendiary and auxiliary ministries commended itself in every diocese. The calibre of the women ordained, the character of their service, and their commitment above all to pastoral work, set new standards in ministry and stamped the seal of approval on the church's initiative. Nor was there any subsequent move to ordain homosexuals (alleged elsewhere as the inevitable consequence of women's ordination). The Primate declared in 1992 that there were no practising homosexuals among the clergy, and that he could not see how an active homosexual could become a priest in the Church of Ireland.[115]

From 1992, the General Synod's Committee on the Ordained Ministry considered terms and conditions of service for both stipendiary and non-stipendiary clergy, husband/wife ministries, maternity leave and benefits, and the concept of local ordained ministry. As the Commission on Ministry from 1996, its terms of reference were extended to lay ministry also, including that of readers and licensed workers, and to the deployment of clergy. It aimed to bring control and consistency into an increasingly complex and versatile professional sphere. Modern trends affected clergy and their families. There were more divorced clergy, many clergy wives had their own careers, and generally rectory families were subjected to increased pressure and stress. These problems attracted regular analysis, but not always action. The diocese of Dublin, however, formed a Clergy Support Group in 1995 to help in the pastoral care of clergy and their spouses. Its three members were specialists in the causes and treatment of stress and independent of the clerical structures of the diocese. Details of the new service were sent to the clergy and their spouses separately.[116]

In 1996 the General Synod regulated the marriage in church of divorced persons. This matter had been debated under the guidance of a select committee 1973-93, and of a committee of Standing Committee for a further three years, and its legal, pastoral, and theological aspects exhaustively examined.[117] The church's practice since disestablishment had been inconsistent. In 1895, Judge Warren had clarified (in his *Laws of the Church of Ireland*), and General Synod had accepted, the statutory right of incumbents to marry divorcees in church. (The Synod had recognized also that bishops might refuse to exercise their discretion to grant special licences.) Incumbents retained this right in both jurisdictions after 1921, and in the southern state were obliged, under the protection of the law, to discharge it. The church at no time passed a law forbidding remarriage in church, and both Gregg and Kerr publicly upheld the right of clergy, in certain circumstances, to marry divorcees, Kerr (and some other bishops) allowing licences to be issued. After their deaths, however, the bishops issued a Pastoral Letter in 1966 expressing an indissolubilist position – the first formal document to do so. Thereafter episcopal influence was often exerted to uphold that position, and so to discourage remarriage in church. In 1980, the select committee summarized the historical position, and sought leave to introduce regulations which would bring 'order and discipline into a confused and unsatisfactory situation in the life of our Church.'[118] But the necessary two-thirds majority was narrowly missed and the impasse continued.

During the early 1990s, however, it became clear that General Synod members had become overwhelmingly disposed in principle to legislate 'for the regulation of marriage discipline in the Church of Ireland'. The bugbear now was penitence (which had been dealt with in detail as early as 1977). In 1993, the Synod rejected the proposed penitential regulations, summarily dismissed the select committee, and directed Standing Committee to take the matter forward, only to regard as too severe the preferred penitential service proposed by its committee in 1994. A service of preparation, to be used in all cases, was instead approved in 1996, and regulations at last enacted. They required clergy to consult with their bishop and to seek his advice in every case. They came into force on 1 September 1996.[119]

The General Synod itself underwent change. After the Synod Hall was sold, it met first in the premises of the Royal Dublin Society (RDS), and then in the years 1995-9 in the magnificently restored Royal Hospital at Kilmainham. Here the Eucharist was celebrated in the beautiful Caroline chapel, and the business of the Synod loftily overseen by Primates Boyle and Marsh from the portrait gallery. With the disposal of the old Synod Hall, however, there was no reason for the General Synod to meet in Dublin exclusively. Accordingly, its sessions of 1986, 1991 and 2000 took place in Belfast, and that of 1994 in Cork. As Belfast, unlike Dublin, offered no Royal venues, the first two sessions there were held in the City Hall, and that of 2000 at the splendid Waterfront Hall. The Cork venue was the congenial Silversprings conference centre where, uniquely, all the members who attended were united in a most moving celebration of Holy Communion. Away from Dublin, the traditional pre-Synod service - it was to lose its moorings in 2000-01 - was held in St Anne's and St Fin Barre's Cathedrals respectively. After the Belfast meeting of 2000, Standing Committee in its wisdom decided that the General Synod should be of no fixed abode on its return to Dublin.

The session of 2001 was therefore held at the O'Reilly Hall, University College Dublin, and that of 2002 planned for the Stillorgan Park Hotel conference centre. In point of membership, there was less innovation. In 1991, there were 80 women among the 432 lay delegates (18.5 per cent), and in 2001 still only 104 women (24.1 per cent). More than a decade after women were first ordained, there were in 2001 only 11 women among the 216 clerical members of the Synod. Its Standing Committee failed to lead by example. It had eight women among its 30 lay members in 1993 and the same number in 2001 (with no woman among the 30 clerical members). Standing Committee was evidently shy of using its power of co-option to improve the representation of women, preferring to co-opt up to seven men, some of whom had lost their seats in the triennial elections: a case of missed opportunity compounded by travesty. The limits of the progress made by 2001 were covered in Archbishop Empey's comment (shades of Crozier in 1914) that women were the backbone of parochial life, but poorly represented in the Church's decision-making bodies.[120] Analysis was one thing, however, action another.

The Fifth edition of the *Church Hymnal* was published in 2000. Bishop Edward Darling was general editor and Dr Donald Davison music editor, supported by a revision committee which was appointed by the General Synod in 1994. *Irish Church Praise*, published in 1990, had introduced modern hymns and songs in preparation for a revision of the 1960 edition of the hymnal. But the 'hymn explosion' since 1960, an avowed sign of a 'new reformation' in the Christian Church, made the committee's task 'much more complex than anything previously undertaken'. It wisely ascertained from parishes (well over half responded) what hymns they sang and wanted to sing, and compiled a data-base of all suggested material. In the event, the new edition provided 'a greater range of different styles and sources' than that of the 1960 edition: old evangelistic mission hymns used afresh, Taizé chants, Iona worship-songs, charismatic choruses, Irish hymns (with English singing translations), canticle substitutes and other liturgical material. It was innovative in other respects also. It provided indexes of composers and arrangers, and of tunes; of themes and subjects, and of biblical references. It included 17 plainsong melodies and some 40 descants. It scrapped the Carols section of two previous editions, integrating Christmas hymns and carols in the body of its 719 hymns. It made language 'as gender-inclusive as possible', but with exceptions indicated by commonsense. In a major innovation, both full music and melody editions were published. The practical difficulty with the melody edition – apparently unforeseen by the clergy and organists who made up the committee - was that the book was too heavy for many in the pews to hold, use readily, or set down easily. Its print was also inconveniently smaller than the available space allowed. The LAC, meanwhile, began preparing a 'Sunday services book' to complement the new hymnal. Planned as a 'unifying book', its stated aim was to present BCP services in a 'user-friendly' way, and APB services 'lightly revised' both to allow greater flexibility and to take account of criticisms made since 1984. It would include such 'historical documents of faith' as the 39 Articles and the Preamble and Declaration of 1870. By 2001, the intended new book had, confusingly, been identified as The Book of Common Prayer 2004. The plan may prove to be too voluminous to win back parishes which have given up worshipping from books. Liturgical policy will in any case end the life of the APB just two decades after its publication. Its usefulness was impaired when the Revised Common Lectionary came into use in Advent 1995. The new lectionary was already in use in Anglican Churches at home and overseas, and – with slight variations – in the Lutheran and Roman Catholic Churches. Its scheme reverted to the BCP pattern of a systematic reading of the scriptures. These welcome features were offset by the fact that pages 319-752 of the APB were made redundant after only 11 years in use, though it continued to be reprinted and sold at full price. It was proposed in 2001 to subsidize (from the Royalties Fund) an interim paperback edition of the APB; but this misguided plan was effectively scuttled by retailers.[121]

Experience of worship became more diversified. The Council for Mission in Ireland pointed to 'the recovery of *intimacy* among Christians', instancing fellowship in small groups.[122] Some of these were house-based, others held in church halls, whether prayer, Bible study, or healer groups. Extempore prayer became increasingly common. Some older churches replaced their pews with chairs, so allowing freedom in patterns of worship.[123] The church's Youth Council organized the largest annual youth festival held in Ireland during the 1990s. Staged initially at Castle Archdale and then Gosford Park, 'Summer Madness' had by 1993 expanded to 2400 campers and 600 day visitors, and invested in a big top which accommodated 3000. This Christian Arts Festival, 'offering young people the chance to explore their faith through contemporary music, drama and mime', developed teaching and recreational programmes, and culminated in the Eucharist on Sunday morning. Emphasis on youth became more pronounced generally. Diocesan youth officers supported clergy and parish youth leaders, assisted with nurture groups, and arranged spiritual development weekends. The annual diocesan youth camp for Dublin diocese attracted 124 young people in 1995. In 'the year of youth 1996-7', Connor diocese appointed two field workers, a man and a woman, to work with parishes, and organized a training day 'to help the whole church understand the way young people think these days'. A well publicized Youth Forum held in Dublin in 1996, with the Primate in the chair and most bishops present, was trenchantly critical of the Church of Ireland's style and priorities.[124]

The diocese of Cork sustained its active reputation in many facets of its life. The Lord Mayor of Cork told delegates to the General Synod in 1994 that the Church of Ireland had made a great contribution to the city in law, medicine, the arts and sport, and was greatly respected in Cork. That respect was practically expressed when the city's business community undertook in April 1995 to raise £350,000 towards the £4 million required to move St Luke's Home, catering for 90 elderly residents, from its Victorian building to a modern complex at Blackrock. With good reason Bishop Warke boasted: 'There is life outside Dublin. There is even youth work outside Dublin.' The diocese canvassed opinion among its young people through a questionnaire, identified worship, education, training, and Bible study and prayer as their main concerns, and began to reach out to its young people in a more professional way, initially through modern methods of communication in the secondary schools, and then nurture groups which emerged from this approach.[125] Cork maintained, too, its record for initiative. Under the leadership of Harold Miller, the Church of the Resurrection at Blarney, at one time threatened with closure, was restored at a cost of £180,000 and re-ordered, all the architectural features of the Georgian (1776) church being retained. The font (as recommended by Bishop Mant in 1843) was for total immersion; the holy table set precisely in the centre of the church and surrounded on three sides by the congregation, so emphasizing the 'gathered' people of God.[126] Owning itself the 'happy diocese', Cork had the distinction of providing the Church of Ireland with five of the nine bishops newly elected between 1993 and 2001: Michael Mayes (Kilmore), Richard Clarke (Meath), Harold Miller (Down), Richard Henderson (Tuam), and Michael Jackson (Clogher). Clarke and Jackson had been successive Deans of Cork. Moreover, Cork featured in two of the other four appointments. Paul Colton, a Dublin incumbent, returned to his native Cork as bishop; and Ken Clarke (Kilmore), a Down man himself, had married Helen Good from Cork. The election of Archdeacon Ken Good (Helen Clarke's brother) to the see of Derry in March 2002 reinforced the Cork record.

The Church of Ireland in the 1990s, then, had many strengths. Practical response to human need, whether in Ireland or overseas, was a particular strength. The Bishops' Appeal fund, begun in 1979 to channel aid to developing countries, had raised IR£1,772,830 by 1989. During the 1990s, the Appeal struck a balance  between its response to recurring humanitarian crises and its original commitment to longer-term strategies, in projects related to medical work and healthcare, education, rural development , and refugees. An emergency appeal throughout the church on the same day was made for Kurdish refugees in 1991, for famine relief in Somalia and its region in 1992, and for the suffering people of Rwanda in 1994: IR£225,000 was received for this last crisis. In the years 1990-4, the annual income of the fund exceeded IR£600,000 in one, and IR£500,000 in two other years - one individual contributed £100,000 sterling in two of these years. Support in both currencies continued steady in the late 1990s, until core income in punts surged by 30 per cent in the two years after 1998. The total for 1999 was IR£321,000, of which the diocese of Dublin contributed IR£120,000. Income for 2000 was boosted also by two large bequests and by emergency appeals to a total of IR£513,000. The administration of the Appeal was meanwhile taken over in 2000 by Church of Ireland House (at a fee of 1.0 percent of the fund). Until she retired in January 2001, Mrs Bet Aalen had worked for seven years on a part-time basis as the Dublin-based education adviser with the Bishops' Appeal. She recalled it to its founding principles, with emphasis on justice in international development and trade central to its activities: the Jubilee Year call for the lifting of the burden of debt on the world's poorest people was a high profile example. Mrs Aalen's salary was financed in part by an annual grant of IR£6,000 from Christian Aid. For its part, the Appeal distributed its crisis funds and much of its normal allocation through Christian Aid, with its 'readily verifiable use of resources' and its work in 60 countries. Otherwise, it used the services of Anglican mission societies, and especially CMS.[127]

At home, the church tackled social problems. Archbishop Eames spoke in 1994 of the counselling service of the Church's Ministry of Healing, the many parishes north and south which had schemes to alleviate unemployment and provide skills training, and the care of the elderly in the Republic through residential homes and provision of housing. He called, too, for a special ministry to socially deprived urban districts and for church action on drug and alcohol abuse, homelessness, and care of single parents.[128] Choice Housing Association Ltd, founded in 1977 in Belfast, provided housing both in small clusters and sheltered accommodation for clergy, widows and others in need. Eligible for state grants and enjoying charitable status, Choice complemented the work of the older Church of Ireland Retirement Trust. By 2001, Choice had evolved a new design concept, in conjunction with a local health trust, for people in the early stages of dementia. The board of social responsibility in each province and the families' department of the Mothers' Union, did valuable work; and in 1995, the diocesan committee for social action in Dublin organized seminars on the family, violence in the home, and planning for retirement. In the Republic, too, many church renovation projects were generously supported by the local Roman Catholic community, in the capital by Dublin Corporation, and there and elsewhere by the FAS scheme. Here again the inter-church family was a new phenomenon, for the problem of mixed marriages was increasingly resolved, not by the theologians, but by lay people making up their own minds and couples choosing in Christian love to share their faith. Other brave initiatives were taken. In central Dublin, where upwardly mobile young people were pouring back into new flats and apartments, Willie and Ruth Stewart developed a creative ministry in City Outreach for Renewal and Evangelism (CORE); but it was Archbishop Caird's vision which had 'planted' them in St Werburgh's in the first place.[129] They were later able, with both civic and voluntary support, to restore St Catherine's church at a cost of some £1½ million and to make it, after its rededication by Archbishop Empey, a vibrant centre of faith and versatile social activity.

In Northern Ireland, Bishop McMullan adapted the St Patrick's Day celebration to give recognition in Down Cathedral to carers of disabled people and victims of terrorism, and led his diocese to avail on a pioneer basis of the marriage counselling services provided by Relate. The Sit-out for Charity on the steps of St Anne's Cathedral every Christmas by 'Black Santa' (the Dean of Belfast) both caught the public's imagination and channelled support to local and overseas charities. The Sit-out was begun by Dean Samuel Crooks and carried to new heights by his successor Jack Shearer. At Christmas 2000, Dean Shearer raised the remarkable total of £400,000, completing his Sit-out a week before his untimely death. The 25th anniversary of the Sit-out was celebrated in 2001 under his successor Houston McKelvey. In the diocese of Connor, 27 churches and halls were built 1968-93 in response both to demographic realignment arising from intimidation and the more normal movement of communities from inner city areas. Again, many northern parishes were at last learning (in Archbishop Gregg's phrase) that 'the church is the clergy and laity', as clergy perceived their role as equipping their people for ministry and teaching them to use their gifts for the common good. A score of volunteers from Clogher diocese worked alongside the Ugandan Church in 1994 in medical and rebuilding projects. And the Two Cathedrals' Festival in Derry, begun by the organists of St Eugene's and St Columb's, celebrated its fifth anniversary with a broadcast service on BBC Radio 4 on 20 October 1996. In the autumn of 1996 also, Mrs Thelma Mehaffey, all Ireland president of the Mothers' Union, was instrumental with Lady Mayhew's support in bringing about the first Women of Faith Conference, held at Hillsborough Castle. Attended by Catholics and Protestants, the conference celebrated the work that women in the churches were doing overseas and at home, and challenged women of faith to devise and implement ideas for building a more harmonious society in Northern Ireland. In 1996 again, church administration in Belfast relocated to the former *News Letter* premises in Donegall Street. The enhanced facilities provided for the diocesan offices of Connor and Down and Dromore, CMSI and APCK, the press office, the diocesan library and other organizations.[130]

But the Church of Ireland's strengths were offset by evident weaknesses. On his election as Archbishop of Dublin, Walton Empey was denied a period of quiet preparation, and wrote of the inappropriateness of being thrust into Dublin (and out of Meath) without notice. In his enthronement sermon, Empey insisted that the clergy should be free to do their priestly work 'rather than be burdened with further expectations for which they were never ordained'.[131] Their anachronistic involvement in educational management was a case in point. In Northern Ireland, in-service appraisal and training of clergy needed higher priority. Some clergy still did everything in their parishes; a few did very little. Promotion of some of the latter to canonries, apparently on the basis of seniority, meant that clerical indolence was still being rewarded.

The church's expectation of her bishops needed rethinking also. While most were able chief executives and communicators, their definitive role of providing pastoral support to hard-pressed clergy was sometimes neglected, whether from personal limitations or preoccupations in the wider church. Moreover, the 'management model' of episcopate, as the Commission on Episcopal Ministry observed in 1996, entailed loss of theological skills: 'The primary role of the bishop is not that of an administrator or a manager but of one who teaches with vigour and clarity.'[132] The church's central administration was severely criticized. At the General Synod of 1992, clerical speakers accused it of both ignorance of VAT legislation and its bearing on listed buildings in Northern Ireland, and of sharp practice in relation to the Church's specialist officers. But a layman, Hilary Morrison, had written years earlier that the RCB and especially its Finance Committee had

> moved from a supportive financial and administrative role to the centre of gravity in the affairs of the church, almost overshadowing the General Synod, the chief legislative authority in the church. As it were, the financial tail has been wagging the spiritual body.[133]

As chairman of the RCB's new Executive Committee, Morrison became a key player in the 1990s in managing change in the organization; but the need for greater openness and accountability remained. The experience of the Select Committee on Marriage 1992-96 was revealing. Appointed by, and supported with evident enthusiasm from the floor of the General Synod, and with Bishops Empey and McMullan as its episcopal members, the committee's treatment by the establishment was formally correct, actually obstructive, and arguably cynical.[134] The church's greatest weakness, however, was the continuing decline in her membership.

### Church of Ireland Population: 1971-91

|      | Republic of Ireland | Northern Ireland         |
|------|---------------------|--------------------------|
| 1971 | 97,741              | 334,318 (22.0 per cent)  |
| 1981 | 95,366              | 281,472 (19.0)           |
| 1991 | 89,187              | 279,280 (17.7)           |

In 1961-71, the church lost 16,757 members, 6275 of them in the Republic. The population there rose by over 150,000, more than reversing the falls of 1926-61. That of Northern Ireland rose by a further 51,310: the census revealed that 142,511 people (9.4 per cent) had refused to state their religion, so that the number outside the main churches inclusive of the smaller denominations totalled 230,449 (15.2 per cent). In consequence, despite the population growth in Northern Ireland, the loss to the main churches was: Roman Catholic 19,626, Presbyterian 7398, Church of Ireland 10,482 and Methodist 630.

In 1971-81, Church of Ireland membership fell by a hefty 52,846 in Northern Ireland. By contrast, the fall of 2571 in the Republic was the lowest of the century. The 1970s were the most violent decade in Northern Ireland's history, and the official figures support the anecdotal evidence that many Church of Ireland members left the province at that time. But the drop in membership was apparently influenced by other factors also (these would be notably operative in the Republic also in the 1980s). Small denominations gained some 25,000 members in 1971-81, while the numbers stating no denominational affiliation almost doubled to 274,584 – whether of people refusing on principle, or preferring to state 'Protestant' or 'Christian'. (The number was swollen by an estimated 74,080 persons who were 'under-enumerated' in 1981 for political reasons: the 1991 census revealed that most were Roman Catholics.) During the next decade, however, the Church of Ireland's position in Northern Ireland steadied, and a loss of only 2192 members was recorded in the 1991 census. But the relative position had weakened significantly. The numbers given as 'none' (a new category in 1991) and 'non-stated' aggregrated 174,061, and together with 'others' (the members of smaller denominations) totalled 296,508, or 17.8 per cent of the population. These figures compare with the Church of Ireland's 279,280, or 17.7 per cent. Again, Roman Catholics had increased from 477,921 in 1971 to 605,639 in 1991 (from 31.4 to 38.4 per cent). In 1971 the Church of Ireland population had been 69.9 per cent of the Roman Catholic population; in 1991 it was 46.1 per cent.

In the Republic in 1981-91 Church of Ireland membership fell by 6179. Of that number, 3071 (49.7 per cent) were in the 20-29 age group (the 10-19 age group in 1981).[135] Archbishop Caird said publicly that Church of Ireland numbers were probably understated, when almost 100,000 people stated no denominational affiliation, including 16,329 who were categorized as 'Christian' (unspecified). He believed that many church people refused to answer questions about denomination as 'intrusive on their personal life and freedom', and that this was true in particular of inter-church families, many of whom worshipped in the Church of Ireland. Caird suggested that the 'Anglicans' and some of the 'Protestants' could also be claimed,[136] but did not comment on the 'Other Stated Religions' category, which had grown from 12,970 to 40,324 since 1981. One significant finding of the 1991 census was that, unlike 1981, the fall in Church of Ireland membership in Dublin city was not matched by an increase in counties Dublin, Kildare, Meath and Wicklow.[137]

The situation overall, if not critical, yet presented the Church of Ireland with a serious challenge. Primate Eames spoke variously of the movement of population from west to east, of the vibrant churches on the outskirts of all cities, and the fact that 'That great traditional strength of the Church of Ireland, the rural diocese, is changing'.[138] Total membership of 368,467 throughout Ireland at the 1991 census compared with the figure of 346,015 provided by diocesan secretaries in 1996 to the Commission on Episcopal Ministry. (The diocesan office in Belfast did not respond: figures for Connor and Down were estimated.) The Commission gave shape to the statistics. It described large areas of the south and west as 'denuded' of Church of Ireland people; the area north of a line from Clew Bay to the mouth of the Boyne as having seen 'severe depopulation'; and the area within it comprising Elphin and Ardagh diocese as possibly 'in the process of collapsing'. (In May 1994 no incumbent had been living in Roscommon, and the county had no stipendiary clergy in 1996.) The number of parochial units and stipendiary clergy in 1996 was overall almost half that of 1947, with incumbencies down from 882 to 458, and clergy from 1033 to 550. In the same half century the number of dioceses had fallen by two. The Commission proposed a further reduction of two, by amalgamating existing dioceses to create a diocese of the west (an enlarged Tuam), of the south west (Cork and Limerick) and of the midlands (Meath and Kilmore). It commented that the Church of Ireland had 'an enormous potential for staggering on until a system totally collapses', adding that it had not been helped by the immediate summoning of an electoral college for Meath at the vacancy of 1996. The loss of 6179 church members in the Republic 1981-91 was in fact equivalent to the size of a rural diocese. Bishops were appointed to Kilmore in 1993 and Meath in 1996 when their total population in 1996 (including Kilmore's Northern Ireland complement) was 12,015 – a total matched by aggregating three or four northern parishes.[139] With translations from south to north apparently ended, the southern dioceses had at the end of 1996 several younger bishops with nowhere to go.

At a time when the non-Roman Catholic population was growing in the Republic, the fall in her membership had other significance for the Church of Ireland. In some provincial towns where she closed churches during the 1980s, thriving independent churches with strong leadership and a sense of mission replaced them. Dublin, too, saw a growth of such churches. At Michaelmas 1996, 55 cathedrals and churches of the Church of Ireland advertised their services, as against 44 other Protestant churches. Most of the latter were historic bodies such as Presbyterians and the Society of Friends; some were new independent churches.[140] Leaving aside the special case of the inter-church family, the Church of Ireland did not appear to be attracting many of the increasing numbers leaving the Roman Catholic Church.

There is an apparent correlation between the Evangelical recovery in the northern province, and the Church's being spared a more serious decline. Like the revival at the end of the 18th century, the recovery came just in time. It bore other similarities to it. It was a popular movement. It placed in Evangelical hands the great parishes of the 'English road', from Carrickfergus to Portadown. It was innovative and resourceful. It pioneered new styles of worship, new methods of parish management, and a new concept of every person ministry. It increased church attendances, communicants, numbers of ordinands, and commitment to the church overseas. It revived the old tradition of 'cottage meetings' in the modern house groups. It developed strong, imaginative leadership, including that of women. Until 1999, Evangelicals led the two high profile reconciliation communities in Ulster, Trevor Williams at Corrymeela and Cecil Kerr at Rostrevor. Their agencies, such as the Church Army and the Church Pastoral Aid Society, served the wider church. Their support, in both the clergy and laity, carried the vote for women's ordination in the General Synod. This point had a fuller significance. For Evangelicals in the Church of Ireland generally did not confuse church order with biblical essentials, as did many in England and Australia, and eschewed also the rigid, systematic theology revived in other reformed traditions in Ireland. Again, they did not organize on party lines, for their primary loyalty was to the Church of Ireland. Their younger clergy were apolitical, were mostly not identified with the Orange institutions, and in some cases gave a firm lead against Masonic influence in the church. Generally (though by no means universally) Evangelicals shed the arrogance previously exhibited towards men and women of other traditions, and abandoned their earlier isolation. Their new strength and confidence were, however, not yet reflected in patronage; promotion of Evangelical clergy appeared at the end of 1996 to be capped at deanery level. The situation was made worse when in January 1997 rearguard action blocked the election of an Evangelical to the see of Down by the Electoral College. It behoved the House of Bishops, to whom the appointment to Down now fell, to deal wisely with the thwarted claim of Evangelicals to the episcopal office. The response of the bishops was appropriate. On 18 February 1997 they elected Canon Harold Miller as Bishop of Down. It was a turning point. Later that year, Dean Richard Henderson, who like Miller had trained at St John's Nottingham, was elected Bishop of Tuam; and in 2000 Archdeacon Kenneth Clarke, rector of St Patrick's Coleraine, was elected Bishop of Kilmore – both by the Electoral College.[141] With two of their most able, energetic and innovative northern clergy now bishops, Evangelicals perceived that their long wait for acceptance was over. Ironically, however, the simultaneous emergence of Reform Ireland, a pressure group more low church than evangelical in its emphases, threatened to divert the Evangelical recovery, sustained under notably creative and charismatic influences, from its essential purposes.

At the end of the 20th century a reformed General Synod was perceived as vital to the church's future effectiveness. Its annual meeting was increasingly seen as a wasted opportunity. In part annual general meeting of a non-profit organisation, part legislative body, and part religious convention, its priorities needed to be reassessed. Archbishop Eames, in his presidential address in both 1991 and 1994, and Bishop Darling in his pre-Synod sermon in 1993, questioned the relevance of its business to the church's mission. Criticism centred on its cumbersome parliamentary format, unchanged in essentials since 1871. A reduction in its size, and payment of members' expenses (as for members of Synod committees), were also proposed by Barry Deane of Cork, an honorary secretary of the General Synod 1970-94. But the exceptional attendances at Cork in 1994 – with totals of 515, 512, and 390 clergy and laity over the three days[142] – were a telling (and ironic) rebuttal of his case. With so many members paying their own travel costs, and so many families in the host city – whether Dublin, Cork or Belfast – providing hospitality, the Synod's value lay not least in its capacity to unify the church.

Adapting its procedures was a different matter. In his reply to the debate on Standing Committee's report in 1993, Deane was dismissive of speakers who had strayed outside its ambit, failing to recognize that *faute de mieux* they sought to raise matters of general interest. There were other models which the church might consider. Primate Eames professed his admiration for the procedures of the Australian General Synod which he addressed in Melbourne. But as that body did not meet annually, and had greatly circumscribed powers, a more apposite model might be the annual synod of one of the autonomous Australian archdioceses. The Sydney Synod in 1989, for example, sat until late in the evening over five days, included in its formal business interests usually consigned to fringe meetings in Ireland, and through a simple procedural device allowed members to raise and, where agreed, Synod to debate a range of topical concerns in church and society. The General Synod came close to that model in 1996, when it suspended standing orders and received a vibrant presentation from the Youth Council. Whatever devices it might in future adopt, it had become widely accepted that the General Synod should debate contemporary issues more fully, give clear direction to the executive, and determine policy in ordinary as well as special situations.

Finally, the Church of Ireland's marked influence upon the Anglican Communion carried through to 2001. Archbishop Eames's unique role in leadership is noticed elsewhere. Archbishop McAdoo continued to publish erudite works of Anglican scholarship after he retired. Dr Stephen White, Dean of Raphoe, published *Authority and Anglicanism* (1996). Lady Eames was worldwide president of the Mothers' Union 1995-2000, and Rt Hon David Bleakley national president of CMS 1983-97; Roy Totten of Lisburn became national chairman of the Church Army in 2001. Among expatriates, David Ford became Regius professor of divinity at Cambridge in 1991, and Alister McGrath principal of Wycliffe Hall, Oxford in 1995, and titular professor of historical theology at Oxford in 1999. Irish clergy had continued to serve the Church of England as incumbents and bishops. William Gordon Acheson (1890-1966) was the epitome of a faithful parish priest of Catholic tradition. Ordained in Ossory in 1921, he served with the Bush Brotherhood in Australia before settling into his 40 years' incumbency of St Stephen's Lewisham. Richard Hanson, a prolific author, held chairs of divinity in both Durham and Nottingham and, after his brief tenure of the see of Clogher, was a theology professor and assistant bishop in Manchester. Roy Williamson, a son of St Donard's in East Belfast, was successively Bishop of Bradford and of Southwark, Henry Richmond principal of Lincoln Theological College and Bishop of Repton. The line continued. Wallace Benn became Bishop of Lewes in 1997. George Cassidy was Archdeacon of London when he was appointed Bishop of Southwell in 1999. Irishmen continued to serve as Army chaplains. Ivan Neill, born in Templeharry rectory in Tipperary, was chaplain general 1960-66; and Gervase (Gerry) Murphy served, after he retired from the Army, as both rector of Sandringham and chaplain of HM Tower of London. Douglas Graham, after wartime service as a chaplain in the Royal Navy, became Headmaster of Portora Royal School in 1945, and then Headmaster of Dean Close School, Cheltenham (1954-68). The distinguished service of Irish women in India continued also. Elizabeth Ferrar (1912-2001), who went there in 1939 with the DUM to Chota Nagpur, was first head of St Kieran's Girls High School, then from 1956 head of the community – the first woman to hold that position – and finally bishop's representative at the thriving Christian community at Kandara.

The succession of overseas Irish bishops remained unbroken. Henry Le

Fanu, of a distinguished Dublin family, was Co-adjutor Bishop of Brisbane, from 1929 Archbishop of Perth, and Primate of Australia 1935-46: he was chaplain general of the Australian forces at the outbreak of the Second World War. John Jagoe, chaplain in chief of the Royal Air Force late in the War, became Bishop of Bermuda after it. John Curtis had been Bishop of Chenkiang until the communist victory in 1949 forced him to leave China, and Brian Herd, another son of St Donard's, was Bishop of Karamoja until he was expelled from Uganda by Amin. Fred Willis was Bishop of Delhi and William Manning of George in South Africa. In the Canadian Church in the late 20th century, Kenneth Maguire was Bishop of Montreal and John Conlin of Brandon in Manitoba. Percy O'Driscoll from Cork became Bishop of Huron, then Archbishop of Ontario. His brother Herbert was Dean of Vancouver, and Desmond Carroll from Dublin, Dean of the Yukon and chaplain to the Royal Canadian Mounted Police until 2001. Moreover, of the 12 Irish bishops in 2001, six had served as priests in other Anglican provinces: Walton Empey in Canada, Michael Mayes in Japan, and Ken Clarke in South America; and James Mehaffey, Harold Miller and Richard Henderson in England.

One feature stands out in any roll-call, however brief – the steady contribution of Portora Royal School to the leadership of the Church. Of the above, Conlin, Graham, Richmond and Walton Empey were educated there. Donald Caird, Empey's predecessor in the see of Dublin, had been chaplain at Portora. John Crozier of Tuam, and two successive Bishops of Connor, Samuel Poyntz and James Moore, were also educated at Portora. So, too, were Dr Michael Jackson, who returned to Ireland from Oxford as Dean of Cork in 1997, and was elected Bishop of Clogher in 2001; Dr Adrian Empey, who was appointed principal of the Church of Ireland Theological College in 2001; and Dr Ian Ellis, who became editor of *The Church of Ireland Gazette*, also in 2001.

### 2. The state of the Protestants

To compare 1996 with 1691 is to experience the sensation of 'where we came in'; yet with perceptible differences. In 1691 Irish Protestants had emerged – united – from a political and military crisis which had threatened their very survival. During its course the future Archbishop of Dublin, William King, had famously written *The State of the Protestants*. Three centuries on, Archbishop Robin Eames saw the tragic summer of 1996 as 'one of the most defining moments in the history of Ireland'. For behind its dire events he discerned the deeper issues for Ulster Protestants as insecurity, uncertainty about the future, and

frustation caused by events over which people felt they had no control.

Many in the Protestant community felt they were being slowly but surely led into a future which would see an erosion of their ethos and way of life.

That summer was critical for the Church of Ireland also, in that it exposed starkly the division which had developed through the divergent experiences and loyalties of her members in the two states of Ireland since the 1960s. The division expressed itself, in Bishop Mehaffey's words, in 'diametrically opposed' views which needed greater understanding. Or was it too late for that? The Provost of Tuam, Robert MacCarthy, declared that 'the danger existed of a serious split in the church', as her members in the Republic had 'lost all sympathetic understanding of the North, heightened by the events at Drumcree this summer'. And the religious affairs correspondent of the *Irish Times*, Andy Pollak, in writing of 'the tensions in the Church of Ireland', suggested that her Southern members 'now have far more in common with their Catholic fellow-citizens than with their Northern co-religionsts'.[143]

The Church of Ireland population in the Republic had become culturally and politically integrated into the state while preserving its denominational identity: *Irish and Anglican* by Victor Griffin, the Dean of St Patrick's, served as its apologia. Gregg's two communities of 1939 were no longer outside one another. The ecumenical movement, in Kurt Bowen's view, had provided a 'religious rationale for greater harmony, toleration, and cooperation' between them; and liberal Catholics had allied with Protestants in a 'shared opposition to the forces of conservative Catholicism'.[144] Bowen's analysis extended to the early 1980s. In a submission to the Forum for Peace and Reconciliation in Dublin – its chair was Judge Catherine McGuinness, an Anglican – the Church of Ireland welcomed both the change in the political and social climate which had helped to make the Republic 'more acceptable to Protestants', and the efforts of successive Dublin governments to create 'a more inclusive society'. For its part, the Church of Ireland community was loyal to the state, and posed no threat to it. Its views on social issues, as the submission to the Forum claimed, were 'sought by policy makers, politicians and the media'. In short, as Archbishop Caird said in 1995, it was 'a confident minority well understood and well accepted'.[145] That influence derived in part from the informed responsibility which the church had cultivated on controversial issues. The work of the Role of the Church Committee, instituted by Archbishop Simms in 1969, facilitated well-researched advocacy on, for example, contraception, divorce and mixed marriages. The committee's influence was asserted through its annual reports, its 1980 publication *Issues in Ireland Today*, and its off-the-record meetings with the Dáil All-Party Committee and senior Dublin politicians – among them Jack Lynch, Garret Fitzgerald, Patrick Cooney and Brian Lenihan.

This new-found confidence emboldened the Church of Ireland in promoting Protestant interests in general. Her assertiveness was demonstrated at the General Synod of 1993. Archbishop Caird claimed that Anglicans 'on both sides of the border' would support the board of the Adelaide Hospital in the campaign 'to preserve its identity and ethos' as the last remaining Protestant teaching hospital in the Republic. The Synod gave its support, and in the event the Dáil changed the constitution of the Adelaide in order to entrench Protestant rights, and made the Church of Ireland their custodian on behalf of the state's entire Protestant population. At the same Synod meeting, Archbishop Eames rejected the Irish government's proposals to devolve to local secular bodies powers in relation to the management, funding and staffing of Church of Ireland schools, emphasizing (in terms which echoed the European Convention on Human Rights) the 'fundamental right' of members of 'a minority community to have their children educated within their own tradition and ethos.'[146]

Kurt Bowen concluded that Protestants in the Republic had long sought integration rather than assimilation, and perceived that that stance had its exclusive as well as its ecumenical side. Thus the extent of integrated schooling was checked by the imposition of quotas on the admission of Catholic applicants to Protestant schools, and public intermingling was balanced by 'segregation in the more private areas of social life.' But although by 1980 Protestants were angry over the lack of progress with the mixed marriages issue, they yet adhered to 'the rhetoric and public rituals of ecumenism.'[147] For Church of Ireland people, their achieving integration as citizens meant, paradoxically, that their denominational identity was more closely guarded. In her analysis at the mid-point of the Anglican Decade of Evangelism, Canon Ginnie Kennerley deplored a policy of separateness:

> Perhaps the real, natural, Decade of Evangelism in Ireland was the 1970s when Charismatic Renewal swept the country and brought many denominations together to rejoice in their rediscovery of the freshness of God's Word and the activity of God's Spirit. All too soon the renewal movement was tamed by our denominational structures, as church leaders clawed back their sheep from the RDS gatherings and the house-groups round the corner.[148]

The Church of Ireland's experience in Northern Ireland was very different. Northerners had found it difficult to speak of their tragic circumstances during the tense General Synods of the early 1970s, and the Role of the Church Committee had been less effective in addressing these than it had Southern concerns. By the 1990s the position had been transformed. In an emotional farewell speech to the General Synod in 1994, Bishop Poyntz – for many years chairman of the Role Committee – dwelt graphically on the privation of the working class communities in West Belfast. There was much reappraisal after the hot summer of 1996. In a sermon in Christ Church Cathedral, the Archdeacon of Dublin, Gordon Linney, observed that it was only in Northern Ireland that the Church of Ireland had 'a significant contact with people in all the social and economic categories', and questioned whether Southern members, who often distanced themselves by condemnation from those in the North, knew or cared about them. 'Do we really understand their frustrations and fears, which are not only political, but cultural and economic and religious as well?' Despite competent articulation of these, there was what Primate Eames called 'a credibility barrier'. In a powerful address to the General Synod of 1997, Eames identified the lack of a sense of direction among Northern Protestants as productive of fear, frustation, susceptibility to violence and sectarianism. His point was illustrated by a Belfast rector, Kathleen Young, who spoke of her community as one 'with no confidence in its own identity'.

> In Lower North Belfast, sectarianism, fear of the opposite community, finds expression in physical violence and rioting, because people do not have the skills to put a polite face upon it. People who are fearful, who see their community disappear, who are constantly condemned – who feel they have no stake in the community – do not think twice about pulling it down.

The rot had set in 30 years earlier. Working class Protestants were angered then by allegations that they were privileged; Protestants generally at being, as Lord Monson put it, 'aggressively vilified'. Worse was to follow. A populist reform cause had taken to the streets in 1968, and out of the interaction which it provoked a classic revolutionary situation had emerged. Its core was the Provisional IRA's campaign to destabilize, and ultimately destroy, the Northern Ireland state. Although British soldiers, Roman Catholic policemen, and innocent civilians were its victims also, it was directed primarily upon the Protestant population. It involved both economic destruction and targeting of selected victims: businessmen, politicians, retired servants of the state, and off-duty members of the RUC and UDR, both men and women. In every county, but particularly Armagh and Fermanagh, many of the IRA's victims were members of the Church of Ireland. They included young men on isolated farms, killed in the chilling pursuit of 'greening the border'. At his retirement in January 1997, Gordon McMullan published his sermons and public statements as Bishop of Clogher (1980-6) and of Down. They included addresses given at some 24 funerals in Clogher of murdered men: most of them farmers killed as they worked the fields, crossed the farmyard to feed stock, or returned from market. In one sequence the bishop assisted at the successive funerals of three brothers. He twice returned home from the Lambeth Conference to bury terrorist victims.[150] It fell to McMullan also to bury several casualties of the operational irresponsibility of Northern Ireland Command, senior members of RUC Special Branch who died in the helicopter crash on the Mull of Kintyre in 1994. Archbishop Eames spoke to the General Synod in 1993 of the 'unbelievable attitudes of forbearance, fortitude and forgiveness from people in the most unlikely circumstances', and later that year said to the Standing Committee: 'Bearing in mind our relative size as a church, the Church of Ireland has carried a burden in the troubles far exceeding any other denomination'. In acknowledging, during the bicentenary of 1988, their church's debt to the Church of Ireland, Sydney Anglicans noted the 'steadfast Christian witness … in difficult and distressing circumstances' of bishops, clergy and people in Northern Ireland.[151]

But that witness was impaired by two factors: reporting priorities and politically correct language. What Senator George Mitchell has called 'the twin evils of violence and intransigence' so dominated that little notice was taken of the good. Many Church of Ireland people worked, for example, in education and medicine. But the achievement of school heads and staffs in preserving an atmosphere of normality and fostering cross-community relationships was ignored, as was 'the value, integrity and professionalism of the medical profession' during 25 years of violence – to quote Archbishop Eames's maiden speech in the House of Lords. Again, the slogans in which the several phases of 'the troubles' were encapsulated were prone to misinterpretation, as with 'civil rights' or the 'peace process'. Dean Griffin, who had preached prophetically about the powder-keg that Derry had become by the late 1960s, and warned that the ensuing explosion would engulf the entire state, was dismayed on moving to Dublin in 1969 at the widespread belief there that Northern Catholics were 'totally disenfranchised', and angry when he 'heard the RUC', whom he knew to be doing a difficult job well, 'described as thugs and Fascists'.[152] Insidious use of language involved also, as Conor Cruise O'Brien has shown, the 'non-sectarian unity' preached by Republicans. While their prime objective was to break the connection with England, that of Northern Ireland Protestants was to defend it.

> In that case, with respect to Republican doctrine, the relevant characteristic of these people is not that they are *Protestants* – in which capacity Republicans theoretically welcome them with open arms – but that they are *Unionists*. Unionists can be regarded either as British, part of the occupying forces, or as Irish traitors. In either case Republicans derive warrant from their ideology to shoot these people down, whenever opportunity occurs.[153]

Dialogue within the Church of Ireland was hampered by a language barrier. In the *Gazette* inaugural lecture of October 1996, Martin Mansergh, a Southern churchman and special advisor to Fianna Fáil on Northern Ireland, hailed 'a new era of understanding and trust.' The phrase, taken from the

Downing Street Declaration of December 1993, defied realities in Northern Ireland. Bishop McMullan saw the era differently. It was conditioned rather by the Anglo-Irish Agreement of 1985 which, by its exclusion of Unionists and its involvement of the Dublin government in decisions affecting their lives, was a conscious trumping of 'the Orange Card'. Echoing Archbishop Plunket in 1886, McMullan commented: 'in fact what was being put down was not just Orange opinion but the deep convictions of the entire unionist population, many of whom had nothing to do with Orangeism.'[154] The Anglo-Irish Agreement, in short, shifted the balance of power in Northern Ireland, put paid to any last vestige of Protestant triumphalism, deepened misunderstanding and distrust, and made a political settlement difficult. And in Dublin, Senator Mary Robinson resigned from the Labour Party in protest at the treatment of Unionists.

Ceasefires were announced by the IRA and loyalist paramilitaries in August and October 1994 respectively. But there was a perception that the IRA had called theirs both to preempt increasingly deadly loyalist violence, and for other tactical reasons. In the spring of 1995, the Church of Ireland informed the Forum for Peace and Reconciliation that there was much suspicion in the Unionist community 'of motives in respect of the peace process', and a distrust of some of its principal figures 'including politicians and government ministers from both administrations'. Tension persisted. As *The Times* discerned: 'The belief that London bends towards Dublin, which in turn follows a pan-nationalist agenda, has done much to create this tension.' The Canary Wharf bomb in February 1996, and the bombs in Manchester and at Thiepval Barracks in Lisburn later in the year, aroused fears that secret concessions were being made to terror tactics. As so often, Eames put the situation into perspective:

> People have got to realize that if you come through 25 years of mayhem and immense suffering, and if in that period the perception has been that it has been your community, your religion and your political outlook that has [sic] been the real target, then it is only natural that there will be suspicions and talk of hidden agendas.[155]

The perception of other astute observers went deeper still. In the spring of 1997, John A. Murphy saw it as 'obvious' that as long as there was appeasement of Sinn Fein/IRA, the terrorists would continue to apply pressure on both governments until their long term objective was achieved.

> At present such pressure is being applied to get Sinn Fein into talks, then it will be used to promote cross border institutions, after that to force the pace to a united Ireland, next to move towards a 'socialist' (really a fascist) republic.[156]

It is against this background that the leadership of Archbishop Eames needs to be assessed. His involvement in public affairs from the outset of his primacy in 1986 was motivated by several concerns. One was his perception of the early years of tension: 'Few people saw or heard a moderate or reasonable Protestant case; few if any could detect a moderate Protestant voice.' He did much to change that situation, and after 'weeks of intense terrorist activity' in 1993 could claim that the Church of Ireland was 'a voice of integrity, reconciliation, and moderation in this tragic scene'.[157] Initially, his task had been the more delicate in that Cardinal Ó Fiaich, with whom he continued the cooperation fostered by his two predecessors, had by his perceived Republican sympathies reinforced traditional fears and so strengthened Protestant extremism.[158] Again, Eames was sensible that 'Protestantism needs a new confidence in itself. In many cases Protestants see themselves as the real casualties.' The limited value of private dialogue had been brought home to him when as Bishop of Derry in 1980 he was reduced to open anger and grief by the vacuous arrogance with which a senior government minister in Dublin dismissed a delegation from the Role of the Church Committee.[159]

In his *Chains to be Broken*, Eames dealt trenchantly with the role of the media, the security dilemma, and the penal system in Northern Ireland. He showed understanding of the psychologies of both Ulster communities, and of their interaction during, for example, the Civil Rights marches of 1968 and the hunger strike of 1981. In 1987, he called for a plan to supercede the Anglo-Irish Agreement, and in 1990 called on the Dublin government to reconsider the irredentist Articles 2 and 3 of the Irish Constitution. His considered judgment was that the Anglo-Irish Agreement had brought the fears of Ulster Protestants to the surface, reinforced their siege mentality, and given them a sense of betrayal. Eames believed that the pendulum in redressing grievances had swung too far. He told the General Synod in 1993 that it was 'essential that *both* the British and Irish governments' should recognize 'the legitimacy of both traditions in Northern Ireland'.[160] The two governments, for their part, acknowledged Eames's authority when they involved him in redrafting their proposed joint statement, and as influenced by him the Downing Street Declaration of December 1993 corrected the imbalance of the Anglo-Irish Agreement by strengthening the Unionist position. Again, in the summer of 1994, after the Provisional IRA had announced its first ceasefire, the Archbishop had a pivotal role in persuading the Combined Loyalist Military Command to announce a like cessation. He received its deputation, represented in person to the Prime Minister in Downing Street its fears that a deal had been done with the Provisionals, was reassured by John Major that 'there has been no secret deal with the IRA', and reported this assurance back to the leaders of the loyalist groups. At his meeting with them, Eames made two conditions: first, that they would express regret for the suffering which they had caused, and second, that they would not bluff him in any way about their agenda. The loyalist ceasefire was announced (with the agreed note of regret) six weeks later. [161]

In 1996, however, Eames identified two 'perceptions' in the Unionist community: first that its future was unsure, its position being eroded, and its views ignored; second that Nationalists had never accepted the validity of the Northern Ireland state. He believed that the latter perception continued to influence the attitude of Protestants to their Catholic neighbours. That summer *The Times* noted 'the all-pervasive sense that the link with Britain is being undermined', and the perception that the peace process was a vehicle for that purpose. It observed that in 'an atmosphere of insecurity and impotence, the attachment to Orange institutions that reinforce the identity of loyalists becomes much stronger.'[162] But as the need to march became more insistent, so the countervailing urge to prevent marching became more imperative. Ruth Dudley Edwards noted that Sinn Fein/IRA were 'the driving force' behind various attempts to block traditional parades, and added: 'the Southern Irish have not the faintest idea that Orange marches are a vital safety valve for beleaguered and insecure Ulster Protestants'. In this situation, as the Primate told the General Synod in 1997, 'what happened outside Drumcree Church could just as easily have occurred outside any Protestant Church in Northern Ireland'.[163] Fintan O'Toole observed that Orangemen were 'the bearers of a venerable, tolerant and distinctively Irish tradition'. Their right to march was upheld in televised interviews in August 1996 – in relation to the Apprentice Boys' parade in Derry – by John Bruton and John Hume. Parades had not been at issue when Archbishop Eames published *Chains to be Broken* in 1992, and he barely noticed Orangeism in his book. It was different now. In his address to the Armagh Synod in October 1996 – Drumcree parish was in the primatial diocese – Eames observed first that 'a multitude of ordinary, decent, law-abiding men and women' had embraced the Orange Order 'as a social and cultural expression of their identity'; and doubted that the agenda of peace would be advanced by 'general demonisation' of the Orange Order. He pointed out that it had 'no official or structured connection' with the Church of Ireland. Rather, as with all the main Protestant Churches, many church members were also:

> members of the various Orange Institutions. This is their freedom of choice, and freedom of association. There is hardly a Church of Ireland parish in Northern Ireland which does not contain members of those Institutions. They view their membership as part of their culture. They view their membership as a traditional part of their lives. Their fathers and grandfathers before them were members. They do not see any con-

flict between Church allegiance and Orange membership. There are many members of this Diocesan Synod who would represent such a dual allegiance. Those of us who have worked in the Church of Ireland for most of our lives recognize this as a fact.[164]

That measured statement contrasted with calls for the Church of Ireland to dissociate itself from the Orange Order, even to expel its members from the church. Such calls came out of what Archbishop Empey, at the Dublin and Glendalough Synod, identified as 'a groundswell of anger, frustation, bitterness and hurt' among Southern members of the church over the televised images of Drumcree. Archbishop Eames's primary duty, however, was pastoral and prophetic. He dissociated the rector, select vestry, and worshipping community of Drumcree parish from the events which followed the church service (in both 1995 and 1996). He paid tribute to his clergy, under pressure from 'the hardening of attitudes, the interpretation of events, and the uncertainty of the political situation'. He condemned the encouragement to violence and the abuse, some of it directed at himself, heard at Drumcree, the orgy of destruction which damaged the province after it, and what he called 'the naked face of sectarian hatred' which manifested itself in the burning of churches and intimidation of churchgoers during the months that followed it. He recognized, too, that the Orange Order was 'engaged in a profound debate about its ethos and future', and urged encouragement for those seeking to 'influence its life in a realistic and Christian manner'. In seeking toleration within the Church of Ireland the Primate was helped by the positive stance of fellow bishops. Bishop Mehaffey – who had worked tirelessly as a peacemaker in Derry during August – referred at the Derry and Raphoe Synod to the simple solutions of those 'far removed from the coal face of confrontation and conflict'. He asked how the Church of Ireland could 'speak about a pluralist society and the accommodation of differences' unless she could 'hold together in one church family people of very diverse political and religious opinions'. It was significant that Bishop Darling, whose entire ministry as a priest had been in the North, should have spoken in conciliatory terms to the Limerick and Killaloe Synod. He said that it was futile for those who were 200 miles from the scene and 'living in a different cultural setting' to apportion blame, when they could not know all the facts or understand all the tensions that had led to Drumcree. Moreover, Darling commended the Combined Loyalist Military Command for 'exercising great restraint in the face of such provocation' and maintaining its ceasefire. He thus echoed the Primate's earlier commendation of the loyalist paramilitaries, and his acknowledgment that 'the maintenance of their ceasefire under great provocation' had not always received due recognition.[165]

*3. At the turn of the century.*

At the outset of the 21st century, several questions were being asked of the Church of Ireland. First, a question of identity: how to define herself in the light of profound changes in post-modern society, in, for example, the sphere of sexuality; and how to preserve her unity in the face of divisive pressures arising both from the conflicting perceptions of purely Irish phenomena such as *Drumcree*, and from the deepening divisions in the Anglican Communion. Liberal fundamentalism in America, and conservative fundamentalism in Africa, Asia, and parts of Australia, notably Sydney, threatened both orthodoxy and Anglican unity, and were insidiously influencing some Irish Anglicans. Again, with institutional religion, as Bishop Michael Jackson saw it, 'now fighting for its survival and changing rapidly in the process', with 'the trend towards sporadic church attendance and congregationalism', and with the collapse of the parochial system in many areas, the church was forced to begin to consider new models of ministry and in particular to conceive of her cathedrals in more creative terms than 'the theology of stay-as-history'. The 'engaged role for cathedrals' which was developed in both Dublin and Cork in the last years of the 20th century, with 'people – irrespective of denomination – gravitating towards them on a daily basis', went, in Jackson's view, far beyond statistical arguments about size of congregation and parochial viability.[166] Second, a question of communication: how to share the thinking of the few – whether theological, prophetic or ecumenical – with the many. There were not wanting high quality publications. *The Passion of Christ* (1997), reflections on the Good Friday reproaches, by Dr William Marshall, vice-principal of the Theological College, represented devotional writing at its best. The volume of essays edited by Dr Stephen White, *A Time to Build: Essays for Tomorrow's Church* (1999), was erudite and thought-provoking, but deserved a wider readership. But many parishes had no bookstall, and even the *Gazette* was virtually unknown to many regular churchgoers, a situation which it sought to improve by opening its own website. Third, a question of authority: how to hold in tension, in a context of increased specialism, a tendency towards oligarchic control and a tradition of formal democratic process. Calls for greater openness and accountability at all levels of experience in the church came up against the reserved categories – matters over which the House of Bishops had, tacitly but comprehensively, decided to maintain exclusive control. These included selection of candidates for the ordained ministry, both regular and auxiliary, and the training of these candidates; and the sensitive area of the church's episcopal establishment. Lack of disclosure on episcopal expenses was an anachronism. In 2001, the RCB advised the Connor diocesan council that its annual contribution to the central fund for financing the episcopacy had been increased by £7532 (15 per cent) to £61,724. The council passed this charge on to parishes in increased assessment for the diocesan general fund. But no details were supplied to either diocese or parish. This policy of non-disclosure contrasted with that in the Church of England, where full disclosure on episcopal stipends and related expenses was provided, and where in 2001 a working party made proposals for the disclosure and use of information about working costs and expenditure on bishops' houses. The report *Resourcing Bishops* claimed that the advantages of transparency outweighed any disadvantages, and that most bishops were in favour of it: experiences which the Church of Ireland had yet to test.[167]

The failure of the General Synod to reform itself was instructive. A working group on synodical structures had spent some years on the task, only to have its proposals rejected in 2001. The group had assumed on the basis of incomplete evidence from 2000 that the Synod supported its approach in principle and, just as fatally, showed some insensitivity in its presentation. Its chief failing, however, was to devise an elaborate scheme before it had secured its primary objective – a much smaller Synod. Detailed plans for new synodical procedures, residential sessions, and payment of members' expenses, both travel and accommodation costs, were therefore redundant. It was ironic that, at the very time when the Church of England reduced the size of its General Synod in order to cut expenditure, the Church of Ireland should be recommended to do the same in order to incur expense: a proposed abandonment of the voluntary principle which had served so well since 1871. The principle of democracy was also imperilled under the proposals, in that a smaller Synod with more than one-third of its members holding office or serving on permanent committees, would have been a creature of the establishment. And not least, the proposed redistribution of seats would have left smaller southern dioceses with meagre representation, and given a preponderant power to the northern laity, given that the 2:1 ratio of laity to clergy was proposed to be retained. Much of the thinking behind the rejected scheme would therefore need critical reappraisal when the issue of General Synod reform was revisited.[168]

The Church of Ireland Theological College at once experienced change and attracted controversy. The principal change was the creation of a College Council, with Bishop Richard Clarke as chairman, and Bishop Miller as chair of its academic committee. The Council was appointed by, and accountable to, the House of Bishops, and not the General Synod. There was also a change of principal. Professor Bartlett retired in 2001, and the Council elected as his successor Dr Adrian Empey, vicar of St Ann's Dublin, a mediaeval church historian and author of repute, whose combination of pastoral effectiveness, academic distinction, and teaching ability (he had been a part-time lecturer in the College), augured well for his tenure as principal. In determining the most appropriate training models for ordained ministry in the 21st century, the new regime in the College faced a difficult choice: whether to maintain academic rigour to a high standard, or to develop training patterns which focus more fully on pastoral and practical preparation for ministry. Controversy centred in part on the suitability of the residential accommodation at Braemor Park in the circumstances prevalent at the turn of the century. Built in the 1960s when most of its students were unmarried men in their early twenties, the College's cramped and claustrophobic conditions were inappropriate 40 years later for men and women who were, typically, of mature age, married, and experienced in other occupations. A select committee of the General Synod identified the problem, but failed to inspire a solution to it. Again, the diocesan council of Connor deplored in 2001 'the inadequate level of maintenance grants' for ordinands, and pointed to 'the financial plight of married students with dependant children, living and maintaining their households in Northern Ireland'.[169] Generally, too, there was criticism of the requirement for graduates over the age of 30 to spend three years in the College, and recognition that the strain so imposed was a factor in the breakdown of clergy marriages. The absence of recreational facilities at Braemor Park, and the neglect of an emphasis on the physical fitness of students, meant also that some at least of the Church's many overweight clergy could trace the roots of their condition to their experience in College.

Controversy of an ideological nature also surfaced in the late 1990s. It related to curriculum, prescribed texts, and, allegedly, questions of orthodoxy. It was taken up publicly by Reform Ireland, both on its website and through its adherents among newly ordained clergy and in the student body. Persistent and partial criticism distressed staff, poisoned the atmosphere in College, and undermined discipline. The alliance of conservative thinking and low church practice was an old and not dishonourable tradition in the Church of Ireland; but it did not inform the College ethos. The problem was compounded by the abandonment of the convention, more than two centuries old, of retaining Evangelical representation at faculty level, and that at the very time that ordinands were required to train at Braemor Park, rather than continue to enjoy the option of training at theological colleges in England – an option which, ironically, some members of the College Council had themselves exercized. Bishop Miller, who trained at St John's Nottingham, acknowledged publicly after he became a bishop that he had been unwilling to consider training in Dublin. From the understanding implicit in that admission, the College Council might be guided to remove the causes of a sense of injustice which, out of frustration, had found expression in inexcusable and intimidatory fashion.

Late in 2001, Andrew Furlong, the Dean of Clonmacnoise, was given leave of absence for three months by his diocesan, Richard Clarke of Meath. Furlong had disseminated unorthodox doctrinal opinions on his parish website in Trim, and was invited by Bishop Clarke to engage in quiet reflection during his period of leave. But as Clarke's metropolitan Walton Empey pointed out, 'far from being quiet, he sought every opportunity to propagate his views through the media'. Furlong's stated position was that he believed in God but no longer in Jesus, whom he saw as a 'mistaken and misguided "end-time" prophet'. He found the incarnation implausible, the atonement doctrines incredible, and the divinity and resurrection of Christ untenable. Professor Andrew Mayes contended nonetheless that Furlong might still be accommodated within the Church of Ireland as a person 'of deep faith ... yet open to ever new understanding'. In contrast, Archbishop Empey did not see how it was possible for Furlong to minister in a Christian community, given that Christ was 'the centre and heartbeat of the Church of Ireland'. Empey held that English liberal theologians, and notably Bishops John Robinson and David Jenkins, 'could always subscribe to the belief that Jesus is Lord', but that 'the dean cannot and does not subscribe to this central tenet of the faith'. The episode provoked a lively correspondence in the secular and religious press, and prompted some to pursue their own agenda. Reform Ireland, with its penchant for *odium theologicum*, blamed the Theological College (where Furlong had spent one term) for teaching heresy, a charge which led Dean John Paterson publicly to challenge its chairman to name the guilty staff. At the end of his period of leave, Furlong was invited by his bishop to resign his offices as these were 'untenable in light of the doctrinal views held by him'. The dean declined this invitation and Bishop Clarke referred the case to the court of the General Synod.[170]

At the turn of the century, the Church of Ireland was variously involved with other Protestant churches. Through *The Reuilly Common Statement*, she and her sister Anglican churches in Great Britain joined with the Lutheran and Reformed Churches in France in 2000 in acknowledging one another's churches as catholic, apostolic, and equipped with God-given ministries; and in making a commitment both to share in worship and to work together towards a fuller communion as churches. Again, the diocese of Connor and the Swedish diocese of Linköping, under their respective bishops James Moore and Martin Lind, formed the first inter-diocesan partnership in the Porvoo communion. This was not an ecumenical project but a partnership between two dioceses, the one Anglican and the other Lutheran, in full communion with each other. From its inception on 23 October 1997 until 2001, the relationship was developed both at diocesan level and in 12 inter-parish links. Youth exchange programmes and exchanges of clergy, teachers and groups of parishioners made for a lively start to the partnership. It was assessed in 2001 by an inter-diocesan group and extended for another two years.[171] Meanwhile, formal relations with the Methodist Church were entrusted to a joint Methodist-Church of Ireland theological working party. Its early reports appeared to be influenced by an ecclesiolatry which was divorced from both history and theology, and attracted trenchant criticism on that account.

Formal relations with the Roman Catholic Church at the same period were influenced by two documents issued by that Church. The first, *One Bread One Body*, was produced by the Catholic Bishops' Conferences of the four home countries in 1998. The Church of Ireland's response dismissed the document's reference to her as a 'Christian community' rather than as a church. It also recognised the Roman Catholic Church 'as an authentic part of the church universal', and so the readiness of her own members to receive Holy Communion in the Roman Catholic Church. And, on the basis that there was agreement at the level of faith if not at the level of theology, the response reiterated that 'Anglicans invite Roman Catholics to receive Holy Communion'. The second document, *Dominus Iesus*, was issued in 2000 by the Congregation for the Doctrine of the Faith. Here the Church of Ireland's response wondered where she stood on a 'scale of ecclesial correctness' which denied the term 'church' to some communions and ascribed it to others. It also deplored an ecclesiology which was 'based entirely on issues of holy orders and the eucharistic theology of one tradition'. The response reached the sober conclusion that the two documents made it difficult for the Church of Ireland to maintain 'the momentum of ecumenical progress'. On 5th December 2000, Archbishop Eames confessed that he had seldom come to an Irish Inter-Church Meeting 'with a heavier heart, or a more troubled mind'. He pronounced the ecclesiology of the Roman Catholic Church to be flawed, and placed the situation in perspective:

> *Dominus Iesus*, like *One Bread One Body*, seems to us to be quite out of touch with attitudes in general. Many Roman Catholics have spoken to us of their embarrassment by these documents. These texts appear to us to be out of touch with the *sensus fidelium* and they clearly are out of touch with our times. Some people have now sadly questioned – and even worse, doubted – the point of the Week of Prayer for Christian Unity. That is nothing less than a tragedy.[172]

For all the time and resources invested in it over several decades, then, ecumenism at official level had achieved very little. Arguably the focus had been too narrow, and the price too high. The heavy engagement of clergy in central ecumenical activity was a new form of absenteeism. Ecumenism also had its blind spots. A living unity of Christians had been realized in the Christian Renewal Centre in Rostrevor under the leadership of Cecil Kerr, and elsewhere in Ireland through the Centre's outreach ministries. Ken Newell, minister of Fitzroy Presbyterian Church, wrote that the Kerrs had 'spoken to more Christians in Ireland than anyone else I know, and have not only been ambassadors for Christ but also for the Church of Ireland'.[173] Yet Cecil Kerr, a member of the General Synod, who had practised daily the ecumenism about which others theorized, retired in 2000 without having been honoured with a canonry by the church. That Trevor Williams, the leader of the Corrymeela community, should have deservedly been made a canon of the National Cathedral early in 2002, underlined the injustice of the oversight in Cecil Kerr's case.

Ecumenism was at its most authentic, not when engrossed centrally with formulae, but where it was expressed locally in the desire of Christian people to worship together, and to work in co-operation. In Lurgan from 1993, PAKT (Parents and Kids Together) was the joint initiative of the parish of Shankill and its neighbouring Roman Catholic parish, in breaking down barriers, building sustainable friendships, and exploring diversity. Bishop Jackson drew the attention of readers of *The Furrow* to 'the ready way in which ecumenism has become so important and instinctive to many of our people and clergy'. He instanced the twinning of the Church of Ireland and Roman Catholic cathedrals in Belfast in 1999 as 'a pledge of practical ecumenism' on the eve of the third millennium; and the generosity of the Roman Catholic dioceses of Cork and Ross under Bishop John Buckley in raising, during the Week of Prayer for Christian Unity in 2000, £67,021 for *Beyond 2000* – a project of community involvement, restoration, and development based in St Fin Barre's Cathedral. Again, in reference to the unique Week of Prayer for Repentance held by Roman Catholic and Protestant churches in Belfast early in 2002, David Jardine SSF expressed his hope that 'this communal act of humility, repentance and prayer will help to change the atmosphere of our city', polluted as it was by the prejudice, bigotry and hatred which had survived a reduced level of violence. Archbishop Eames claimed in July 2001 that relationships between Churches were much stronger and led to co-operation and a 'standing together' in ways which 'would have been impossible even a short time ago'. And not only as between churches. Eames commended the Apprentice Boys of Derry 'who have sought to understand the fears of their fellow citizens in Derry and who have involved children of all traditions in explaining and understanding their story and organization'.[174]

The church's situation in the southern state was paradoxical. In a society undergoing rapid and profound change, the Church of Ireland was perceived to exert an influence of which she seemed scarcely aware, and to face opportunities which she failed to grasp. In their response to residual sectarianism post-Vatican II, church people had become accustomed to avow their experiences in private while maintaining a public silence. That stance was discarded by a new genre of leaders. Harold Miller, after moving from Cork to Belfast in 1997, warned against the tendency to 'northernize sectarianism'; and Michael Jackson, who settled in Cork on his return from Oxford in 1997,observed that 'polite sectarianism is still around, alive and smiling through clenched teeth'. The church welcomed those who rose above it, as with President Mary McAleese when she received Holy Communion in Christ Church Cathedral in 1997. That much publicized event, as Bishop Jackson discerned, 'clarified the ecumenical reality of eucharistic hospitality in and by the Church of Ireland'; but the church might have made more of those cradle Catholics who, at her altars in Dublin, regularly shared their President's conviction and practice.[175] Again, at a time of great crisis in the Roman Catholic Church, induced both by a succession of child sex abuse scandals and an alarming decline in vocations, the Church of Ireland failed to take a proactive stance on the distinctive characteristics of Anglican priesthood. Even the acceptance into her ministry of former Roman Catholic priests, a quiet and unobtrusive fact of the late 1990s, was not fully appraised in its profound significance. Priests who took this step were able to marry; more than that, were able to continue to fulfil their priestly vocation in a branch of the church catholic where women also were priests. As to public ethics, the Church of Ireland had consistently contended that complex social issues should be dealt with by legislation and not by amending the Constitution. An amendment proposed early in 2002 sought to rule out the threat of suicide as a ground for abortion. Introduced by the Ahern government and supported by the Roman Catholic hierarchy, it was narrowly defeated in a referendum. Had it been carried, the distinguished Maynooth historian Oliver Rafferty conceded, it would have allowed those 'who adhere to Catholic teaching to declare, perhaps a bit smugly, that we do not have abortion in Ireland. That particular issue we export.' Protestant bishops decried more than smugness. John Neill deplored the 'serious hypocrisy' which informed the amendment, and Michael Mayes denounced its 'disastrous moral ambiguity' and the denial of help within Ireland to women who needed it. The new Ireland was listening, if not its politicians. Bishop Richard Clarke complained that, although a deputation had made the Church of Ireland's position on abortion clear to the All-Party Committee on the Constitution, 'not for the first time, our views have been set aside'. Patsy McGarry of the *Irish Times* pointed out, however, that 'although Protestant opinion had been ignored by the politicians, clearly it has not been ignored by the people, particularly in urban Ireland'. The episode highlighted the changing character of southern society. Fintan O'Toole concluded:

The right to hold and express an individual view is increasingly accepted. The Catholic culture of consensus is giving way to a Protestant culture of individual belief.[176]

Oliver Rafferty went so far as to claim that what the Roman Catholic Church was saying no longer 'resonated with the hearts and minds of our people', and to urge that in their post-referendum analysis the Catholic bishops must 'reflect on how the message of the gospel can be made accessible to the people'. That same emphasis had long exercised the mind of Eoghan Harris in relation to the Church of Ireland. His core criticism was that, when many Roman Catholics were at their most responsive, 'and would welcome a progressive evangelical Protestantism', she was 'taking refuge in an empty ecumenism that will end in assimilation'. He took the view that at a time when many young Roman Catholics were searching for 'the pure and simple faith of their fathers', many Protestant clergy were inhibited from preaching the gospel by their 'fear of proselytism'. Harris sought both to recall to the Church of Ireland her heroic efforts to evangelize Ireland in the 19th century, and to urge her to celebrate and renew that mission.[177]

By the spring of 2001, Robin Eames had been a bishop for 26 years, 15 of them as Primate of All Ireland. Beyond his immediate responsibilities as diocesan bishop, metropolitan, and Primate, he continued energetically to sustain his other roles of national and international importance. He had enjoyed both the trust of, and delegated authority from, two very different Archbishops of Canterbury in Robert Runcie and George Carey. By 2001, he was the senior Primate of the Anglican Communion. He had chaired the inter-Anglican theological commission which devised – in the Virginia Report – the agenda for the 1998 Lambeth Conference. David Ford, who attended as a theologian, noted:

It was striking that, in the debate on human sexuality (the most sensitive in the Conference) the vital role of chairing the plenary session was taken by the Primate of the Church of Ireland, just as he had chaired the Commission which dealt effectively with the issue of women priests and bishops that had threatened to explode the Anglican Communion at the previous Lambeth Conference.[178]

Eames's influence and understanding of conflict situations were attested when in July 2001 he was invited by Archbishop Carey to accompany him on a delicate visit to the Middle East at a time of renewed conflict and heightened tension. Eames remained also, inescapably, a spokesman for the Protestant community in Northern Ireland, and an interpreter of the province's agonies to audiences beyond its shores. Ken Newell wrote that many Presbyterians appreciated 'the clear thinking and constructive leadership' given by the Primate. In 2001, Eames delivered the annual Joseph Winter Lecture in Wakefield. Sensible of the 'steady rejection of interest' in Northern Ireland on the part of those outside, 'as apparent solutions are denied and suffering continues', he yet sought to present a fraught and fragile situation in a sympathetic light: 'Hurt runs deep – very deep. Divisions of the mind equal divisions in the loyalties of whole geographical areas.' He observed that the suffering of two communities, 'both prisoners of their past', had been immense, so that the inheritance of 30 years of violence would 'cloud issues and overshadow lives for generations'. He added that, although the majority of people in their yearning for peace had supported the *Good Friday* or *Belfast Agreement*, 'the cost of realizing that peace is a reality which has produced its own divisive atmosphere'. Among the *Agreement's* supporters there were doubts and questions, while it was opposed by those 'who, for various reasons, doubt its efficacy or integrity'. For that reason, pressures on the Church had become greater.

> How do you express genuine local fears, how do you represent those emotions as a church without allowing immediacy or local feelings to supersede the broader Christian voice?[179]

If the dilemma thus posed had recurred often in the three centuries since the Williamite Revolution, for Eames himself it was most immediately embodied in the annual event of *Drumcree* in his diocese.

That event continued to cause great anguish within the Church of Ireland. The service in Drumcree parish church, held each July to commemorate the sacrifice at the Somme in 1916 (but dating back to 1807), was attended by the Orange lodges from Portadown. But not since 1997, as determined by the new Parades Commission, had the lodges been permitted to return to the town by their traditional route along the Garvaghy Road. Their officers refused to talk with either the Commission or the Residents' Coalition, but publicly protested their right to march after the service. In both 1998 and 2000, Portadown District appealed for support province-wide, and violence erupted both during the stand-off at Drumcree and in many loyalist areas amid the tensions attending active demonstration of support. The cost of the elaborate security operation mounted each year was astronomical, the social costs incalculable. The pain and anger felt throughout the church was considerable, but constitutionally the authorities could not take control. The autonomy of the rector and select vestry of Drumcree parish was absolute. A delegation from the Standing Committee met with both Orange leaders and residents, placed on record the representations made to it, and noted the complexity of the problem. Archbishop Eames and the senior clergy of Armagh diocese wrote in July 1998 to Portadown District, welcoming its attendance at public worship, and acknowledging its right both to parade and to protest; but pointing out that unrest and disruption after worship degraded the spiritual and sacred nature of that worship. In 1999, after the widespread violence of the previous year, the Archbishop sought written pledges from the District officers that they would refrain from all action which diminished the sanctity of worship, obey the law of the land, and avoid using church property in any civil protest after the service. The General Synod supported this action, and resolved that the rector and select vestry be requested to withdraw their customary invitation to the lodges should the pledges not be given. Neither the District officers nor the parish replied to their respective communications, and the annual service in Drumcree church took place as usual.[180] The rector John Pickering was, however, able to influence the lodges to disperse after the service, and in 1999 the province was spared violence. In 2000, by contrast, a protest was staged at Drumcree in the week before the church service; widespread violence ensued before and after it. In 2001, *Drumcree Seven* passed off peacefully.

A common thread in the analysis of the *Drumcree* imbroglio was that it was totemic, that is a cameo or symbol of Northern Ireland at large, with its tensions and seemingly intractable conflicts. *The Times* observed in 1998 that 'Orangemen are stubborn, frightened and politically naïve', and that Sinn Féin's Gerry Adams had admitted that 'the manufactured confrontation' which sprang from the disruption of their marches was a gain for his movement.

It allows republicans to pose as defenders of victimised Catholics as well as underlining the Sinn Féin thesis that Northern Ireland is ungovernable under the Crown. It is in the context of such cynical subversion that the whole question of traditional marching routes must be viewed. The decision ... by the Parades Commission to reroute the Drumcree parade ... was, then, a concession to republicanism. It was the prospect of republican-inspired violence that made this march contentious in the first place. The descent into disorder by frustrated supporters of the Orangemen in past years has been unforgivable. But loyalist agitators were only responding to a situation where they saw violence and the threat of violence rewarded. In that respect Drumcree is a metaphor for all Ulster.

Conversely, to solve *Drumcree* would bring wider benefits. Archbishop Eames, who worked tirelessly to resolve the impasse, and whose proposal that a community forum be held in Portadown was widely accepted by 2001 as the way forward, was convinced that 'to find a solution locally would be a giant step towards solving larger issues'. The *Gazette* accepted that negotiations, if entered into in the right spirit, could have a healing effect, but warned that the core distemper of mutual fear and distrust which afflicted *Drumcree* also affected the ghettos: 'without ghettos, parades would not be a problem. When parades cease to be a problem, there will be no problem.'

Archbishop Eames observed that 'the Church of Ireland has learned much about itself as it has struggled with the implications and perceptions of Drumcree'. One lesson was that unity had been severely strained. The anger and embarrassment of southern church members were rekindled each July. But it was impossible to understand *Drumcree* without understanding Northern Ireland. The northern membership was divided also. When in 2000 the church group Catalyst charged the Primate with not condemning violence in specific terms, the criticism was so demonstrably inaccurate that a coded meaning was apparent. Northern church members divided into two camps: those who had empathy with the marching culture and those who had not. Catalyst was of the latter. Eames himself had of necessity a relentless engagement with *Drumcree*. His regular public statements disclosed his mind over the years. He kept the General Synod fully briefed by devoting part of his presidential address each year to the subject. On the ground, he encouraged both parties to find a solution. His denunciations of disruption and violence were uttered with prophetic fearlessness. In 2000, he criticised the Portadown leadership for its failure to defuse the situation at Drumcree, its instruction to spread protest throughout the province, its responsibility for the subversion of young people, and its escalating a confrontation with the security forces which issued in vilification and physical attack. 'The events at Drumcree ignore some very basic biblical teaching which the Orange Order claims to uphold and support.' In 2001, the Archbishop's pastoral letter was read to the Orangemen attending morning service in Drumcree church:

> I ask you in the name of the God you are worshipping to make your protest in a dignified and lawful manner, to respect the things of God, and to do nothing nor permit anything to happen which will allow those with evil intent to make use of your protest … I am deeply aware of the feelings of those who differ from you. They, too, have their fears and uncertainties. They, too, have their rights. They, too, are children of the same God. Somehow under God we have got to find a new way of trusting and respecting each other.

The Orangemen made a formal protest and then dispersed. The province was spared the mayhem of the previous year. The Primate believed that the seeds of an agreement existed, and that a solution was closer than was realized. It must be found, he wrote, 'not just for the good of Portadown, but for the good of two whole communities in Northern Ireland which deserve so much more than they presently endure'. And in a speech in the House of Lords early in 2002, Eames reminded government of its responsibility to effect such a solution.[181]

The Primate's was not the only prophetic voice, *Drumcree* not the only issue to warrant such a voice. In the 'personal *apologia*' which he published in 2000, *And is it true?*, Bishop Richard Clarke directed his prophetic fire, as so often in his sermons, upon 'the obvious foibles or repulsiveness' of the institutional church. Bishop Colton directed his at southern society for its rejection of the Nice Treaty out of, as he judged it, materialism and narrow self-interest. Dr Robert MacCarthy, Dean of St Patrick's from 1999, fired in all directions, possessed as he was of an intrepid and outspoken spirit not unworthy of Swift himself. Dr Houston McKelvey's election as Dean of Belfast in 2001 ensured that a trenchant and prophetic influence would be exerted at the heart of the northern capital also. The laity could be prophets also. At the time the Island of Ireland Memorial at Messines Ridge in Belgium was dedicated in 1998, David Robertson wrote:

> The Irish soldiers, sailors and airmen who fought and died in two World Wars have been airbrushed out of our history books as if they had never existed. They are Ireland's forgotten men, swept aside by an exclusive view of Irish history.

Having established that almost 30 per cent of former pupils at Wilson's Hospital in Multyfarnham county Westmeath had enlisted for war service, Robertson therefore told in his *Deeds not Words* 'the story of 200 young men from one small Church of Ireland community' who had served their country.[182] Archdeacon Gordon Linney kept up his perceptive criticism of public trends in contemporary Dublin. He discerned in 2000 the danger of losing the openness gained through the Forum for Peace and Reconciliation from 1994 – in particular a broader and more tolerant understanding of Irishness – and replacing it 'with elements of a bitter and resentful northern nationalism'. For him the danger consisted also in a tendency to rewrite recent Irish history so as 'to portray the perpetrators of violence as heroes and victims'.

As to the impasse on the decommissioning of republican arms, Linney commented: 'It is an issue not because people want victory, but because they have suffered too much and want to be safe.' By the summer of 2001, this core issue had precipitated the resignation of Northern Ireland's first minister David Trimble, and pitched the peace process into crisis. The British and Irish governments offered the political parties in August 2001 a non-negotiable package which avowedly covered the four outstanding issues of policing, normalisation, the stability of the devolved institutions, and decommissioning. *The Irish Times* commented bluntly, 'it does nothing of the sort'; for without action on decommissioning, 'democratic authority has been compromised as never before'.[183] The paper warned the two governments not to 'lend legitimacy to the armed conspiracy that remains in the shadows'. The IRA did subsequently disclose to the decommissioning body a method by which its arsenal might verifiably be put beyond use, should it ever decide to take this action, but even that hypothetical offer was withdrawn within days upon a pretext. Then, late in 2001, the IRA carried out a limited measure of decommissioning, enough to unblock the political way forward, but insufficient to allay Protestant fears and the tensions to which they gave rise.

In reference to the contentious issue of policing, *The Irish Times* warned that 'Sinn Féin and its alter ego the Provisional IRA should not be allowed to dictate the direction of democratic politics in Northern Ireland.' In clear prophetic tones, the *Church of Ireland Gazette* concluded in effect that the warning had come too late. Although IRA guns might be silent, 'they continue to wield a pernicious influence on state policy', notably in extorting concessions from the governments. This process, culminating in the August package, had been 'feeding the evil frenzy' of loyalist bigotry on the streets and 'driving the riots' – the worst in Belfast since 1981, particularly in Ardoyne (where in September 2001 ugly passions erupted in abuse and threats to young girls on their way to Holy Cross primary school). As to policing, it was the influence of illegal arms 'on the policies of civil government' that had delivered a revised plan which leaned heavily to the nationalist interest, 'largely at the instance of Dublin'. The *Gazette* warned that subversion in the northern state today would threaten the southern state tomorrow. Republican objectives were to enter a coalition government, gain control of Dáil Éireann, and ultimately destroy democracy. The newspaper therefore called on church members in the Republic, lulled by their obsession with *Drumcree*, to become alert to the dangers in their own state.[184] Such realism was timely. Organized (like Sinn Féin) on an all-Ireland basis, the Church of Ireland had a duty to speak to the times. With indications that the first quarter of the 21st century might bring political change in Ireland as profound as, and more permanent than, the same period in the 20th century, that role would require sustained prophetic courage and insight in the difficult years ahead.

At the turn of the century, then, the Church of Ireland faced critical choices. The pressure of events, and of the philosophical standpoints of those involved in them, forced her to re-evaluate essentials. But if she had the wisdom to perceive it, the church might be liberated by her history, rather than imprisoned by it. Though the tension between North and South was a phenomenon of the late 20th century, that between evangelical and political Protestantism had a long pedigree. 'Religion that despises the Word destroys Salvation': Archbishop King's warning seemed as apposite to the modern Church of Ireland as to that of his own day. But in determining what sectarianism connoted, or in what patriotism consisted, the church was at risk of repudiating both her historical identity and her confessional integrity: ultimately of questioning her very *raison d'etre*. Internally, calls to impose unprecedented tests of membership threatened her Anglican comprehensiveness. There was real danger that the church in Northern Ireland would become what she had long since become in the Republic – primarily a middle class institution. If she was to preserve her formal unity, both as between North and South and within Northern Ireland, she had to explore the meaning of unity in diversity, and come to terms with pluralism, tolerance and reality. The Church of Ireland's history over the past three centuries encouraged the thought that she had survived earlier crises – in 1689-91, in the last decades of the 18th century, in the 1830s and the years 1869-78, and again after partition. She had emerged from each of these intact, if not unscathed, and the stronger for the experience. She might yet discover that she had the capacity, the will, and above all, the leadership, to survive in the 21st century the critical problems which had developed from the late 1990s.

| Bishop | Diocese and Date | Elected by | To succeed |
| --- | --- | --- | --- |
| 1 Day M.F. | Cashel 1872 | Synods | Daly R. *deceased* |
| 2 Darley J.R. | Kilmore 1874 | Synods | Carson T. *deceased* |
| 3 Gregg R.S. | Ossory 1875 | Bishops | O'Brien J.T. *deceased* |
| 4 Plunket Lord | Meath 1876 | Synod | Butcher S. *deceased* |
| 5 Gregg R.S. | Cork 1878 | Synods | Gregg J. *deceased* |
| 6 Walsh W.P. | Ossory 1878 | Synods | Gregg R.S. *translated to Cork* |
| 7 Chester W.B. | Killaloe 1884 | Synods | Fitzgerald W. *deceased* |
| 8 Shone Samuel | Kilmore 1884 | Synods | Darley J.R. *deceased* |
| 9 Plunket Lord | Dublin 1884 | Synods | Trench R.C. *resigned* |
| 10 Reichel C.P. | Meath 1885 | Bishops | Plunket Lord *translated to Dublin* |
| 11 Reeves William | Down 1886 | Synods of Armagh and Clogher, *ad interim* | Knox R.B. *translated to PRIMACY* |
| 12 Knox R.B. | PRIMACY 1886 | Bishops | Beresford M.G. *deceased* |
| 13 Stack C.M. | Clogher 1886 | Synod | *On separation of Clogher from Armagh* |
| 14 O'Sullivan James | Tuam 1890 | Bishops | Bernard Hon. C.B. *deceased* |
| 15 Welland T.J. | Down 1892 | Synod | Reeves W. *deceased* |
| 16 Wynne F.R. | Killaloe 1893 | Bishops | Chester W.B. *deceased* |
| 17 Meade W.E. | Cork 1893 | Synod of Armagh, *ad interim* | Gregg R.S. *translated to PRIMACY* |
| 18 Gregg R.S. | PRIMACY 1893 | Bishops | Knox R.B. *deceased* |
| 19 Peacocke J.F. | Meath 1894 | Bishops | Reichel C.P. *deceased* |
| 20 Chadwick G.A. | Derry 1896 | Synod of Armagh, *ad interim* | Alexander W. *translated to PRIMACY* |

| | | | | |
|---|---|---|---|---|
| 21 | Alexander William | PRIMACY 1896 | Bishops | Gregg R.S. *deceased* |
| 22 | Archdale Mervyn | Killaloe 1897 | Synods | Wynne F.R. *deceased* |
| 23 | Peacocke J.F. | Dublin 1897 | Bishops | Plunket Lord *deceased* |
| 24 | Elliott A.G. | Kilmore 1897 | Synods | Shone S. *resigned* |
| 25 | Keene J.B. | Meath 1897 | Bishops | Peacocke J.F. *translated to Dublin* |
| 26 | Crozier J.B. | Ossory 1897 | Bishops | Walsh W.P. *resigned* |
| 27 | Bunbury Thomas | Limerick 1899 | Bishops | Graves C. *deceased* |
| 28 | O'Hara H.S. | Cashel 1900 | Bishops | Day M.F. *resigned* |
| 29 | D'Arcy C.F. | Clogher 1903 | Bishops | Stack C.M. *resigned* |
| 30 | Orpen R.d'A. | Limerick 1907 | Synods | Bunbury T. *deceased* |
| 31 | Crozier J.B. | Down 1907 | Synod | Welland T. *deceased* |
| 32 | D'Arcy C.F. | Ossory 1907 | Bishops | Crozier J.B. *translated to Down* |
| 33 | Day Maurice | Clogher 1907 | Bishops | D'Arcy C.F. *translated to Ossory* |
| 34 | Crozier J.B. | PRIMACY 1911 | Bishops | Alexander W. *resigned* |
| 35 | D'Arcy C.F. | Down 1911 | Synod | Crozier J.B. *translated to PRIMACY* |
| 36 | Bernard J.H. | Ossory 1911 | Bishops | D'Arcy C.F. *translated to Down* |
| 37 | Dowse C.B. | Killaloe 1912 (May) | Bishops | Archdale M. *resigned* |
| 38 | Dowse C.B. | Cork 1912 (Nov) | Synod | Meade W.E. *deceased* |
| 39 | Berry T.S. | Killaloe 1913 | Bishops | Dowse C.B. *translated to Cork* |
| 40 | Plunket B.J. | Tuam 1913 | Synods | O'Sullivan J. *resigned* |
| 41 | Bernard J.H. | Dublin 1915 | Bishops | Peacocke J.F. *resigned* |
| 42 | Moore W.R. | Kilmore 1915 | Synods | Elliott A.G. *deceased* |
| 43 | Gregg J.A.F. | Ossory 1915 | Synods | Bernard J.H. *translated to Dublin* |

| | Bishop | Diocese and Date | Elected by | To succeed |
|---|---|---|---|---|
| 44 | Peacocke J.I. | Derry 1916 | Bishops | Chadwick G.A. *resigned* |
| 45 | Miller Robert | Cashel 1919 | Bishops | O'Hara H.S. *resigned* |
| 46 | D'Arcy C.F. | Dublin 1919 | Bishops | Bernard J.H. *resigned* |
| 47 | Plunket B.J. | Meath 1919 | Synod | Keene J.B. *deceased* |
| 48 | Grierson C.T.P. | Down 1919 | Synods | D'Arcy C.F. *translated to Dublin* |
| 49 | Ross A.E. | Tuam 1920 | Synods | Plunket B.J. *translated to Meath* |
| 50 | Day J.G.F. | Ossory 1920 | Bishops, by resolution of Armagh Synod | Gregg J.A.F. *translated to Dublin* |
| 51 | D'Arcy C.F. | PRIMACY 1920 | Bishops | Crozier J.B. *deceased* |
| 52 | Gregg J.A.F. | Dublin 1920 | Bishops | D'Arcy C.F. *translated to PRIMACY* |
| 53 | White H.V. | Limerick 1921 | Bishops | Orpen R.d'A. *resigned* |
| 54 | MacManaway James | Clogher 1923 | Synod | Day M. *deceased* |
| 55 | Orr John | Tuam 1923 | Bishops | Ross A.E. *deceased* |
| 56 | Patton H.E. | Killaloe 1924 | Synod | Berry T.S. *resigned* |
| 57 | Collins T.G.G. | Meath 1926 | Synod | Plunket B.J. *resigned* |
| 58 | Orr John | Meath 1927 | Synod | Collins T.G.G. *deceased* |
| 59 | Harden J.M. | Tuam 1927 | Bishops | Orr J. *translated to Meath* |
| 60 | Barton A.W. | Kilmore 1930 | Synod | Moore W.R. *deceased* |
| 61 | McNeice J.F. | Cashel 1931 | Synod | Miller R. *deceased* |
| 62 | Holmes W.H. | Tuam 1931 | Bishops | Harden J.M. *deceased* |
| 63 | Flewett W.E. | Cork 1933 | Synod | Dowse C.B. *resigned* |
| 64 | Irwin C.K. | Limerick 1933 | Bishops | White H.V. *resigned* |
| 65 | McNeice J.F. | Down 1934 | Synod | Grierson C.T.P. *resigned* |

| No. | Name | See & Year | Elected by | Reason |
|---|---|---|---|---|
| 66 | Harvey T.A. | Cashel 1935 | Synod | McNeice J.F. *translated to Down* |
| 67 | Tichborne Ford | Ossory 1938 | Synod of Armagh, *ad interim* | Day J.G.F. *translated to PRIMACY* |
| 68 | Day J.G.F. | PRIMACY 1938 | Bishops | D'Arcy C.F. *deceased* |
| 69 | Holmes W.H. | Meath 1938 | Synod | Orr J. *deceased* |
| 70 | Hearn R.T. | Cork 1938 | Bishops | Flewett W.E. *deceased* |
| 71 | Crozier J.W. | Tuam 1938 | Synod | Holmes W.H. *translated to Meath* |
| 72 | Hughes A.E. | Kilmore 1938 | Bishops | Barton A.W. *translated to Dublin* |
| 73 | Gregg J.A.F. | PRIMACY 1938 | Bishops | Day J.G.F. *deceased* |
| 74 | Barton A.W. | Dublin 1939 | Synod | Gregg J.A.F. *translated to PRIMACY* |
| 75 | Phair J.P. | Ossory 1940 | Synod | Tichborne F. *deceased* |
| 76 | Irwin C.K. | Down 1942 | Bishops | McNeice J.F. *deceased* |
| 77 | Hodges E.C. | Limerick 1942 | Bishops | Irwin C.K. *translated to Down* |
| 78 | Boyd R.M. | Killaloe 1943 | Synod | Patton H.E. *deceased* |
| 79 | Tyner Richard | Clogher 1943 | Synod | Macmanaway J. *resigned* |
| 80 | Irwin C.K. | Connor 1945 | Own option | *On separation of Connor from Down and Dromore* |
| 81 | Kerr W.S. | Down 1944 | Synod | Peacocke J.I. *resigned* |
| 82 | Boyd R.M. | Derry 1945 | Bishops | Boyd R.M. *translated to Derry* |
| 83 | Webster Hedley | Killaloe 1945 | Bishops | Holmes W.H. *resigned* |
| 84 | McCann James | Meath 1945 | Synod | Hughes A.E. *resigned* |
| 85 | Mitchell F.J. | Kilmore 1950 | Synod | Hearn R.T. *deceased* |
| 86 | Simms G.O. | Cork 1952 | Synod | Webster H. *resigned* |
| 87 | Perdue R.G. | Killaloe 1953 | Synod | Kerr W.S. *resigned* |
| 88 | Mitchell F.J. | Down 1955 | Bishops | Mitchell F.J. *translated to Down* |
| 89 | Tyndall C.J. | Kilmore 1955 | Synod |  |

| Bishop | Diocese and Date | Elected by | To succeed |
|---|---|---|---|
| 90 Elliott R.C.H.G. | Connor 1956 | Synod | Irwin C.K. *resigned* |
| 91 Simms G.O. | Dublin 1956 | Synod | Barton A.W. *resigned* |
| 92 Perdue R.G. | Cork 1957 | Synod | Simms G.O. *translated to Dublin* |
| 93 Stanistreet H.A. | Killaloe 1957 | Synod | Perdue R.G. *translated to Cork* |
| 94 Butler A.H. | Tuam 1958 | Synod | Crozier J.W. *resigned* |
| 95 Buchanan A.A. | Clogher 1958 | Bishops | Tyner R. *deceased* |
| 96 De Pauley W.C. | Cashel 1958 | Bishops | Harvey T.A. *resigned* |
| 97 Tyndall C.J. | Derry 1958 | Bishops | Boyd R.M. *deceased* |
| 98 Moore E.F.B. | Kilmore 1958 | Synod | Tyndall C.J. *translated to Derry* |
| 99 McCann James | PRIMACY 1959 | Bishops | Gregg J.A.F. *resigned* |
| 100 Pike R.B. | Meath 1959 | Bishops | McCann J. *translated to PRIMACY* |
| 101 Jackson R.W. | Limerick 1960 | Electoral College | Hodges E.G. *resigned* |
| 102 McAdoo H.R. | Ossory 1962 | Electoral College | Phair J.P. *resigned* |
| 103 Armstrong J.W. | Cashel 1968 | Electoral College | De Pauley W.C. *deceased* |
| 104 Simms G.O. | PRIMACY 1969 | House of Bishops | McCann J. *retired* |
| 105 Buchanan A.A. | Dublin 1969 | Electoral College | Simms G.O. *translated to* PRIMACY |
| 106 Butler A.H. | Connor 1969 | Electoral College | Elliott R.C.H.G. *retired* |
| 107 Peacocke C.I. | Derry 1969 | Electoral College | Tyndall C.J. *retired* |
| 108 Quin G.A. | Down 1969 | Electoral College | Mitchell F.J. *retired* |
| 109 Duggan J.C. | Tuam 1969 | Electoral College | Butler A.H. *translated to Connor* |
| 110 Hanson R.P.C. | Clogher 1969 | House of Bishops | Buchanan A.A. *translated to Dublin* |

| 111 | Caird D.A.R. | Limerick 1970 | Electoral College | Jackson R.W. *retired* |
|---|---|---|---|---|
| 112 | Owen Edwin | Killaloe 1971 | Electoral College | Stanistreet H.A. *retired* |
| 113 | Heavener R.W. | Clogher 1973 | Electoral College | Hanson R.P.C. *resigned* |
| 114 | Eames R.H.A. | Derry 1975 | Electoral College | Peacocke C.I. *retired* |
| 115 | Caird D.A.R. | Meath 1976 | Electoral College | Pike R.B. *deceased* |

*Limerick and Killaloe united 1977 under Bishop Edwin Owen*
*Cashel and Ossory united 1977 under Bishop J.W. Armstrong*

| 116 | McAdoo H.R. | Dublin 1977 | Electoral College | Buchanan A.A. *retired* |
|---|---|---|---|---|
| 117 | Poyntz S.G. | Cork 1978 | House of Bishops | Perdue R.G. *retired* |
| 118 | Armstrong J.W. | PRIMACY 1980 | House of Bishops | Simms G.O. *retired* |
| 119 | Willoughby N.V. | Cashel 1980 | Electoral College | Armstrong J.W. *translated to PRIMACY* |

| 120 | Eames R.H.A. | Down 1980 | Electoral College | Quin G.A. *retired* |
|---|---|---|---|---|
| 121 | McMullan Gordon | Clogher 1980 | Electoral College | Heavener R.W. *retired* |
| 122 | Mehaffey James | Derry 1980 | Electoral College | Eames R.H.A. *translated to Down* |
| 123 | Empey W.N.F. | Limerick 1981 | Electoral College | Owen E. *retired* |
| 124 | Wilson W.G. | Kilmore 1981 | Electoral College | Moore E.F.B. *retired* |
| 125 | McCappin W.J. | Connor 1981 | House of Bishops | Butler A.H. *retired* |
| 126 | Caird D.A.R. | Dublin 1985 | Electoral College | McAdoo H.R. *retired* |
| 127 | Empey W.N.F. | Meath 1985 | Electoral College | Caird D.A.R. *translated to Dublin* |
| 128 | Darling E.F. | Limerick 1985 | Electoral College | Empey W.N.F. *translated to Meath* |
| 129 | Neill J.R.W. | Tuam 1986 | Electoral College | Duggan J.C. *retired* |
| 130 | Eames R.H.A. | PRIMACY 1986 | House of Bishops | Armstrong J.W. *retired* |
| 131 | McMullan Gordon | Down 1986 | Electoral College | Eames R.H.A. *translated to PRIMACY* |

| Bishop | Diocese and Date | Elected by | To succeed |
|---|---|---|---|
| 132 Hannon B.D.A. | Clogher 1986 | Electoral College | McMullan G. *translated to Down* |
| 133 Poyntz S.G. | Connor 1987 | House of Bishops | McCappin W.J. *retired* |
| 134 Warke R.A. | Cork 1987 | Electoral College | Poyntz S.G. *translated to Connor* |
| 135 Mayes M.H.G | Kilmore 1993 | Electoral College | Wilson W.G. *retired* |
| 136 Moore J.E. | Connor 1995 | Electoral College | Poyntz S.G. *retired* |
| 137 Empey W.N.F. | Dublin 1996 | Electoral College | Caird D.A.R. *retired* |
| 138 Clarke R.L. | Meath 1996 | Electoral College | Empey W.N.F. *translated to Dublin* |
| 139 Miller H.C. | Down 1997 | House of Bishops | McMullan G. *retired* |
| 140 Neill J.R.W. | Cashel 1997 | Electoral College | Willoughby N.V. *retired* |
| 141 Henderson R.C.A. | Tuam 1997 | Electoral College | Neill J.R.W. *translated to Cashel* |
| 142 Colton W.P. | Cork 1999 | Electoral College | Warke R.A. *retired* |
| 143 Mayes M.H.G. | Limerick 2000 | Electoral College | Darling E.F. *retired* |
| 144 Clarke K.H. | Kilmore 2000 | Electoral College | Mayes M.H.G. *translated to Limerick* |
| 145 Jackson M.G.St A. | Clogher 2001 | House of Bishops | Hannon B.D.A. *retired* |
| 146 Harper A.E.T. | Connor 2001 | Electoral College | Moore J.E. *retired* |
| 147 Good  K.R. | Derry 2002 | House of Bishops | Mehaffey J. *retired* |

1. *Church of Ireland Gazette,* 31 May 1966: hereafter *Gazette.*

2. Eleanor Alexander (ed.), *Primate Alexander* (London 1913), p. 142: hereafter identified by title only.

3. Jacqueline Hill, review of R. E. Burns, *Irish Parliamentary Politics in the 18th Century,* in *Irish Historical Studies,* xxviii, No.112 (Nov 1993) p. 453: hereafter *IHS.*

4. Alan Ford and Kenneth Milne (eds), 'The Church of Ireland: a Critical Bibliography 1536-1992' in ibid, p. 377.

5. Alan Ford, James McGuire and Kenneth Milne (eds), *As by Law Established: the Church of Ireland since the Reformation* (Lilliput, Dublin 1995).

6. *Gazette,* 28 April 1995. The Ven T. V. Stoney was Archdeacon of Dalriada,1985-92.

7. In *IHS,* No. 112, p. 370.

8. *The Church of Ireland: Ecclesiastical Reform and Revolution, 1800-85* (New Haven and London 1971), p. xi.

9. *The Church of Ireland in the Age of Catholic Emancipation* (New York and London 1982), p. 1.

10. *The Protestant Crusade in Ireland, 1800-70* (Dublin 1978), p. 45.

11. *Gazette,* 16 April 1993; Empey was then Bishop of Meath.

12. F. R. Bolton, *The Caroline Tradition of the Church of Ireland, with particular reference to Bishop Jeremy Taylor* (London 1958), pp. 6, 34n., 62-3; Philip Carrington, *The Anglican Church in Canada* (Toronto 1963), p. 47.

13. W. E. Vaughan and A. J. Fitzpatrick (eds), *Irish Historical Statistics: Population 1821-1971* (Dublin 1978), p. xiii, n.2; J. L. McCracken, 'The social structure and social life, 1714-60' in T. W. Moody and W. E.Vaughan (eds), *A New History of Ireland,* IV (Oxford 1986), pp. 34-7; J. C. Beckett, *The Anglo-Irish Tradition* (London 1976), pp. 64-65.

14. A. Browne, *The Ecclesiastical Law of Ireland,* 2nd edn (Dublin 1803), p. 20. Browne was professor of civil law in Dublin University.

15. E. D. Atkinson, *Dromore: An Ulster Diocese* (Dundalk 1925), pp. 124, 196, 251.

16. Though the Barchester novels portray the Church of England, the situation depicted here also obtained in Ireland, where Trollope worked for some years as post-office surveyor.

17. Public Record Office of Northern Ireland (PRONI): Roden Papers – copy of Roden's letter of 13 Sept 1824, quoting Thackeray's letter.

18. Richard Mant, *History of the Church of Ireland,* 2 vols. (London 1840), II 575. Hereafter Mant, as all references are to Vol. II: *From the Revolution to the Union of the Churches of England and Ireland, January 1 1801.*

19. S. Burdy, *The Life of Philip Skelton* (Oxford 1914: repr from 1792 edn), pp. 175-6.

20. J. B. Leslie, *Ferns Clergy and Parishes* (Dublin 1936), pp. 53-4.

21. *Clogher Clergy and Parishes* (Enniskillen 1933), p. 272.

22. J. Baird Ewens, *The Three Hermits: Short Studies in Christian Antiquity, Methodism and Tractarianism* (London 1956), p. 19.

23. *Primate Alexander,* p. 33.

24. Mant, p. 553.

25. J. C. Beckett, 'The Government of the Church of Ireland under William III and Anne' in *Confrontations: Studies in Irish History* (London 1972), p. 91.

26. Mant, pp. 426, 573-4, 542. The Derry 'allowance' was double the £20 minimum prescribed by statute in 1720.

27. J. C. Erck, *The Ecclesiastical Register* (Dublin 1820), p. xlvi.

## NOTES TO PART TWO

1. Mant, p. 95.
2. W. A. Phillips, (ed), *History of the Church of Ireland from the Earliest times to the Present Day* (London 1933), III 174.
3. C. A. Webster, *Diocese of Cork* (Cork 1920), pp. 270-1.
4. *Book of Common Prayer*: 'The Preface prefixed at the Revision of 1662' (APCK, Dublin 1960) pp. ix-xi; J. T. Ball, *The Reformed Church of Ireland 1537-1889*, 2nd edn (London 1890), pp. 154-67.
5. In Phillips, *Church of Ireland*, III 170-4, where a useful biography of James Bonnell is also given.
6. Thomas Carte, *An History of the Life of James Duke of Ormonde*, 3 vols. (London 1736), II, App. 127-32.
7. *Poems on most of the Festivals of the Church* (London 1681).
8. H. Vere White, *Children of St Columba: A Sketch of the History, at Home and Abroad, of the Irish Auxiliary of the Society for the Propagation of the Gospel* (Dublin 1914), p.11; Mant, p. 409.
9. ibid., p. 9. Mant, Leslie, and *DNB* are the sources here in general.
10. C. S. King (ed), *A Great Archbishop of Dublin, William King DD, 1650-1729* (London 1906), pp. 291-2. Hereafter, King.
11. King, p. 23n.
12. *Clergy of Connor from Patrician times to the present day*, (Belfast 1993), pp. 32, 643; Mant, pp. 41-2.
13. Beckett, *Confrontations*, p. 90.
14. King, p. 71n.; Mant, p. 44.
15. ibid., pp. 10, 101; King, p. 76n. During the 13 years of William III's reign, 20 bishops died; nine during Anne's 12-year reign.
16. Mant, pp. 24, 90.
17. ibid., pp. 284-5, 314-5, 366, 445. Archbishop Cairncross's 'descent' to Raphoe is over looked whenever that of St Clair Donaldson from the archbishopric of Brisbane to the bishopric of Salisbury in 1921 is claimed as the first in Anglican history. I am indebted to the late Mr H. A. Boyd for this observation.
18. Beckett, *Confrontations*, pp. 89-90, 92-3.
19. T. Olden, *The Church of Ireland* (London 1892), p. 372.
20. Beckett, *Confrontations*, pp. 92, 106.
21. Webster, *Cork*, pp. 281-94; 297-302; 307-17, is the source for this section..
22. Christ Church was the dedication of the parish church of Holy Trinity.
23. G. W. O. Addleshaw and F. Etchells, *The Architectural Setting of Anglican Worship* (London 1948), pp. 52-4, 58, 61, 78; Bolton, *Caroline Tradition*, pp. 208, 217, 235-6.
24. ibid., pp. 144, 155, 171-3, 175, 177-8, 180, 249n.
25. *Gazette*, 14 March 1997; Bolton, *Caroline Tradition*, pp. 153, 160, 191n., 195, 198, 249.
26. ibid., pp. 48, 149; Mant, pp. 260-1; G.J. Cuming, *A History of Anglican Liturgy* (London 1969), pp. 169-70.
27. J. B. Leslie, *Ossory Clergy and Parishes* (Enniskillen 1933), pp. 22-3; Mant, pp. 117-19.
28. 'Irish Times Notes', reprinted in *Gazette*, 29 July 1994; Bolton, *Caroline Tradition*, p. 48; G. M. D. Woodworth, *Cashel's Museum of Printing and Early Books* (Cashel 1994); *Gazette*, 7 July 1995.
29. S. Smiles, *The Huguenots: their Settlements, Churches and Industries in England and Ireland* (London 1867), is a principal source for this section.
30. Vivien Hick, 'The Palatine Settlement in Ireland: the Early Years' in *Eighteenth Century Ireland*, 4 (1989), pp. 119-20, 124, 128.
31. Mary Daly, review of C. E. J. Caldicott *et al* (eds), *The Huguenots and Ireland. Anatomy of an Emigration* (Dublin 1987) in ibid., 3 (1988), pp. 162-3; Mant, pp. 642-4.
32. Smiles, *Huguenots*, p. 315.
33. Bolton, *Caroline Tradition*, pp. 75-6, 76n.

34. Phillips, *Church of Ireland*, III 172, noticed this movement briefly, but detailed analysis is more recent. It includes T.C. Barnard, 'Reforming Irish Manners: the Religious Societies in Dublin during the 1890s' in *The Historical Journal*, 35 (1992), pp.805-38; and two chapters in Ford, McGuire and Milne, *As by Law Established*: S. J. Connolly, 'Reformers and highflyers: the post-Revolution Church', pp. 152-65; and David Hayton, 'Did Protestantism fail in early eighteenth century Ireland? Charity Schools and the enterprise of religious and social reformation, c.1690-1730', pp. 166-86.

35. Bolton, *Caroline Tradition*, pp. 182, 192.

36. Through his copious letters, King is his own biographer. Those published by Mant and/or Sir Charles King are the principal source for this section.

37. King, pp. 171n, 278, 294-5. The seven were Synge (Raphoe), Forster (Killaloe), Goodwin (Kilmore), Lambert (Dromore), Theophilus Bolton (Clonfert), Maule (Cloyne), and Howard (Killala). Details follow in the text.

38. King, pp. 248-51.

39. ibid., pp. 72, 195n., 239. The two Boltons were confused by Mant, p. 389, where Theophilus, rather than John, is given as Dean of Derry (and chaplain to Lord Berkeley). Constantia Maxwell, *Country and Town in Ireland under the Georges* (Dundalk 1949), p. 319, retailed this mistake. For John Bolton, see J. B. Leslie, *Derry Clergy and Parishes* (Enniskillen 1939), pp. 36-7.

40. Mant, pp. 453-5.

41. King, pp. 265-6.

42. Beckett, *Confrontations*, p. 90; Mant, pp. 206, 375-9.

43. ibid., pp. 156, 365, 553.

44. ibid., pp. 154-6; King, p. 249n.

45. ibid., pp. 195, 320; J. C. Beckett, 'Swift: the priest in politics' in *Confrontations*, p. 111.

46. Patrick Fagan, 'The Population of Dublin ... with particular reference to the proportions of Protestants and Catholics' in *Eighteenth Century Ireland*, 6 (1991), p. 149.

47. Mant, pp. 204, 206-7, 347-9, 492; Fagan, 'Population of Dublin', pp. 125, 150; King, p. 210.

48. Mant, pp. 205, 348, 350.

49. *Gazette*, 1 July 1994.

50. King, p. 214. Hayton, 'Did protestantism fail?', tabulates evidence which allows this claim to be tested.

51. Mant, pp. 205, 351-3.

52. ibid., pp. 347-50.

53. ibid., pp. 152-4.

54. King, p. 281; Mant, pp. 203, 209-10.

55. King, p. 210; Mant, pp. 168-73.

56. *Primate Alexander*, p. 7.

57. R. F. G. Holmes, *Our Irish Presbyterian Heritage* (Belfast 1985), p. 17.

58. Andrew Carpenter, 'William King and the threats to the Church of Ireland during the reign of James II' in *IHS*, xviii, No. 69 (March 1972), pp. 27-8.

59. ibid., pp. 26-7.

60. Beckett, *Confrontations*, p. 89.

61. A. W. G. Brown, *The Great Mr Boyse* (Belfast 1988).

62. Beckett, *Confrontations*, p. 96; Holmes, *Presbyterian Heritage*, p. 17.

63. G. P. Moriarty, *Dean Swift and his Writings* (London 1893), pp. 314-16.

64. p. 122.

65. This tradition is traced in T. C. Barnard, 'The uses of 23 October 1641 and the Irish Protestant celebrations' in *English Historical Review*, 106 (1991), pp. 889-920.

66. S. J. Connolly, 'The Penal Laws' in W. A. Maguire (ed), *Kings in Conflict* (Belfast 1990), pp. 156, 169-72.

67. Holmes, *Presbyterian Heritage*, p. 59.

68. Mant, pp. 140, 212-13, 487, 476.

69. ibid., pp. 123, 720-2.
70. ibid, pp. 511-13.
71. *DNB* has entries for both men, and a complete list of Dean Richardson's publications.
72. Mant, pp. 165-8, 218-9; King, p. 295.
73. Mant, pp. 164-5, 178, 217-18, 220-4.
74. King, pp. 291-6; Mant, pp. 226-30, 520.
75. Olden, *Church of Ireland,* p. 36; King, pp. 289, 292; Mant, pp. 21, 228.
76. ibid., p. 234.

## NOTES TO PART THREE

1. S. Madden, *Memoir of Rev Peter Roe* (Dublin 1842), p. 64.
2. Mant, pp. 779-80; *Primate Alexander*, pp. 108-09.
3. H. Seddall, *Edward Nangle: the Apostle of Achill* (London and Dublin 1884), p. xxvii; *Christian Examiner*, 1841, pp. 34, 88-9.
4. 'An Account of the number of Parishes in Ireland … in 1791' was received by the British House of Commons in 1805. Its main findings were given in the *Christian Observer*, 1806, pp. 516-17. Mant, pp. 776-7, and Phillips, *Church of Ireland,* III 278-9, have fuller details without disclosing their source.
5. A. A. Luce and T. E. Jessop (eds), *The Works of George Berkeley* (1953), VII 211.
6. *A Sermon Preached before the Association for Discountenancing Vice etc* (Dublin 1796), pp. 32-47.
7. G. R. Cragg, *The Church and the Age of Reason* (Harmondsworth 1960), p. 129; A. K. Palmer, *Notes on the Parish of Geashill and Killeagh* (Naas 1964), intro. by R. W. Jackson; Ian Green, '"The necessary knowledge of the principles of religion": catechisms and catechizing in Ireland, c.1560-1800' in Ford, McGuire and Milne, *As by Law Established,* pp. 84-5.
8. Moriarty, *Swift and His Writings*, pp. 205, 218, 266-7.
9. W. H. Crawford and B. Trainor (eds), *Aspects of Irish Social History* 1750-1800 (Belfast 1969), pp. 2, 81. This section is informed by other documents in this valuable collection.
10. Moriarty, *Swift and His Writings*, pp. 314-16; Mant, p. 542.
11. ibid., pp. 427-8.
12. ibid., pp. 420-3, 490.
13. ibid., p. 564 ; J. T. Ball, *The Reformed Church of Ireland,* 1537-1886 (London and Dublin 1886), p. 181; Bowen, *Protestant Crusade*, pp. 40-1; H. A. Boyd, article on Glynn (Magheramorne) parish in *Northern Constitution,* 31 Dec 1942.
14. George Whitefield's *Journals,* New edn (London 1960), p. 184n; Mant, pp. 492, 597, 602-04.
15. Akenson, *Church of Ireland,* pp. 75-9; Bowen, *Protestant Crusade*, p. 41.
16. In *Evangelicals in the Church of England*, 1734-1984 (Edinburgh 1988), p. 7. Cragg, *Age of Reason*, is a principal source for this section
17. Moriarty, *Swift and His Writings*, p. 56. Witherow was professor of church history at Magee University College, 1865-90.
18. Cragg, *Age of Reason*, pp. 165, 171-2 ; Ball, *Reformed Church of Ireland*, p. 1; N. Aston, 'Horne and Heterodoxy : the Defence of Anglican Beliefs in the Late Enlightenment' in *English Historical Review*, 108 (1993), pp. 902, 918-19. Secker was Archbishop of Canterbury 1758-68.
19. [A. C. H. Seymour], *The Life and Times of Selina, Countess of Huntingdon* (London 1844), II 196n., 199; J.and F. Wills, *The Irish Nation: Its History and Biography* (London and Edinburgh 1875), IV 370-2. Phillips, *Church of Ireland*, III 272, names Kirwan wrongly as William Burke.
20. cp. Cragg, p. 281: 'In hymnody the Age of Reason stands pre-eminent'; A. S. Wood, *The Inextinguishable Blaze: Spiritual Renewal and Advance in the Eighteenth Century* (London 1960).

21. ibid., p. 160: the source is not indicated.
22. Whitefield's *Journals*, pp. 182-3; *Countess of Huntingdon*, pp. 159, 196.
23. For the lifestyle of a typical prelate of this kind, see Marie-Louise Legg (ed), *The Synge Letters* (Lilliput, Dublin 1996).
24. Mant, pp. 314, 561, 585-8, 623-5, 662-3, 681-3; Cragg, *Age of Reason*, p. 119.
25. Maxwell, *Country and Town*, p. 332 ; Mant, pp. 613-18, 688-95: Webster, *Cork*, p. 320, lists Clayton's works, and Phillips, *Church of Ireland*, III 231, discusses his beliefs.
26. Mant, pp. 684-6, 708-10, 742-5, 756-8; Ball, *Reformed Church of Ireland*, pp. 206-10; Wills, *Irish Nation*, IV 376-9, 431-2.
27. Webster, *Cork*, pp. 133-7, 150-2, 161, 319-30, 337-8; Mant, pp. 574, 651.
28. C. H. Crookshank, *History of Methodism in Ireland* (Belfast and London 1885) I 145, 459; Smiles, *Huguenots*, p. 365 ; *Clergy of Connor*, pp. 312-3; Palmer, *Parish of Geashill.*
29. PRONI, Johnston of Kilmore MSS; Leslie, *Ossory*, p. 348.
30. Bolton, *Caroline Tradition*, pp. 50, 118-19, 182; Phillips, *Church of Ireland*, III 392.
31. Carrington, *Anglican Church in Canada*, pp. 43-53, 62; Vere White, *Children of St Columba*, pp. 28-35.
32. *Australian Dictionary of Biography* (*ADB*) is unreliable for Fulton's early years. Marjorie Quarton, author of *Renegade* (London 1991), a novel based on Fulton's experience, has kindly shared with me her research on his Irish background.
33. *The Buildings of Ireland: North West Ulster* (Harmondsworth 1979), pp. 36, 39, 45-6.
34. *Gazette*, 23 Oct. 1992; *Church Review* (Dublin and Glendalough), Jan 1995; *Belfast Cathedral Magazine*, Sept 1935.
35. P. Fagan, 'Population of Dublin', pp. 145-9; H. A. Wheeler and M. J. Craig, *The Dublin City Churches of the Church of Ireland* (Dublin 1948), pp. 16-18, 39, 45; Addleshaw and Etchells, *Architectural Setting*, pp. 59, 76, 184-7, 191-2, 197-200.
36. F. L. Harrison, 'Music, Poetry and Polity in the age of Swift' in *Eighteenth Century Ireland*, 1 (1986), p. 39.
37. Maxwell, *Country and Town*, p. 335; Bolton, *Caroline Tradition*, pp. 195, 209, 215; Addleshaw and Etchells, pp. 76n., 78-80, 155-6, 157n., 159n.
38. J. C. Beckett, *The Making of Modern Ireland*, 1603-1923 (London 1966), pp. 175-6; Maxwell, *Country and Town*, pp. 201-02, 330, 334; *Belfast Cathedral Magazine*, Sept 1935. C. Woodham-Smith, *The Great Hunger* (London 1962), p. 38; Webster, *Cork*, pp. 333-5.
39. E. Malcolm, *Swift's Hospital* (Gill and Macmillan, Dublin 1989); *Countess of Huntingdon*, p. 198; J. Walker, *Substance of a Charity Sermon Preached in the Parish Church of St John's Dublin* (Dublin 1796), p. 48.
40. Wheeler and Craig, *Dublin Churches*, pp. 28-9, 33; *DNB*; M. Guinness, *The Guinness Legend* (London 1989), c.3: 'The Life and Times of Arthur the Second'; *Gazette*, 30 March 1984.
41. *Christian Examiner*, 1867, pp. 312-14; Bolton, *Caroline Tradition*, p. 161.
42. Mant, p. 589; Crookshank, *Methodism*, I 130; A. S. Wood, *The Burning Heart: John Wesley, Evangelist* (Exeter 1967), p. 148.
43. ibid., pp. 123, 130, 133-5; Mant, pp. 589-94, 696; Crookshank, *Methodism*, I 8, 10, 38, 113-14, 123, 160, 273, 400, 439.
44. Vivien Hick, 'The Palatine Settlement', p. 129; *idem*, 'John Wesley and the Irish Rhinelanders' in *Eighteenth Century Ireland*, 5 (1990), pp. 92, 95-6, 98.
45. Mant, pp. 589-90, 695-7; Wood, *Burning Heart*, pp. 202-05; Crookshank, *Methodism*, I 69, 80-2, 128, 320, 324, 328, 350-1, 375.
46. Wood, *Burning Heart*, p. 189.
47. *Evangelical Protestantism in Ulster Society 1740-1890* (London and New York 1992), p. 189.
48. H. D. Rack, *Reasonable Enthusiast: John Wesley and the Rise of Methodism* (London 1988), p. 33; John Wolffe, *The Protestant Crusade in Great Britain 1829-60* (Oxford 1991), p. 9.
49. Mant, pp. 735-7, 754-5.

50. Journal of Rev Adam Averell 1792-1807, pp. 226-8, 241.
51. Quoted in Hans Hamillton, *Two Act Sermons, Preached Before the University, in the Chapel of Trinity College*, Dublin (London 1818), pp. 51-2 n.
52. *Twenty One Sermons* (Dublin 1838): Sermon I.
53. Webster, *Cork*, p. 327; J. D. Sirr, *A Memoir of Power Le Poer Trench, Last Archbishop of Tuam* (Dublin and London 1845), pp. 3, 8-9, 11-12, 19.
54. Mant, pp. 737-8; Sirr, *Power Trench*, pp. 27-8.
55. Averell's Journal, p. 152; Sirr, *Power Trench*, pp. 309-10; M. C. Motherwell, *A Memoir of Albert Blest* (Dublin 1843), pp. 9-10; W. C. Plunket, *A Short Visit to the Connemara Missions* (Dublin 1863), p. 44; Mant, p. 572; Madden, *Peter Roe*, pp. 83-4.
56. H. A. Boyd, 'Glynn'; *Clergy of Connor*, pp. 456-7; Crawford and Trainor, *Social History*, pp. 112-13.
57. Quoted in C. Knox, *Two Sermons on Schism* (Dublin 1816), p. 48.
58. Phillips, *Church of Ireland*, III 291; Bowen, *Protestant Crusade*, p. 45; RCB Library : Beresford Correspondence Vol. VI, No.238: 'Memoir of First Fruits Commissioners'.
59. E. Brynn, 'A Church of Ireland Diocese in the Age of Catholic Emancipation' in *Historical Magazine of the Protestant Episcopal Church*, XL (1971), pp. 187-90; Leslie, *Clogher*, pp. 37, 47, 56, 76; G. H. Sumner, *Life of Charles Richard Sumner D.D., Bishop of Winchester* (London 1876), pp. 48-52.
60. CMS Archives: 'Report of the Visit to Ireland of Revs J. Pratt, D. Wilson, and W. Jowett, June 1814', pp. 38-9; *Christian Examiner*, 1825, pp. 341-4.
61. Sirr, *Power Trench*, pp. 25-39, 44-55, 61-3.
62. This analysis is sourced in Coote's *Statistical Survey of the County of Armagh* (Dublin 1804), pp. 10-17, and J. B. Leslie, *Armagh Clergy and Parishes* (Dundalk 1911).
63. J. A. Russell, *Remains of Rev Charles Wolfe, A.B., with a brief Memoir of His Life*, 4th edn (London 1829), pp. 153, 192; Leslie, *Armagh*; *Countess of Huntingdon*, pp. 221-3.
64. CMS Archives: Daniel Wilson's 'Notes of a Journey to Armagh', and his letter to Pratt from Armagh, June 1814.
65. Kenneth Milne, *APCK: the Early Decades*, (repr. from *Search*), pp. 2-7; *Christian Examiner*, 1825, p. 71,1826, p. 405; James Morgan, *Recollections of My Life and Times* (Belfast 1874), pp. 18-19; PRONI: Roden Papers; J. R. R. Adams, *The Printed Word and the Common Man: Popular Culture in Ulster, 1700-1900* (Belfast 1987).
66. Early numbers of the *Christian Examiner*, where the Commission's Reports are extensively quoted; Milne, *APCK*, pp. 7-8; Bowen, *Protestant Crusade*, pp. x-xi; CMS Archives: 'Visit to Ireland', pp. 45-6.
67. C. Hole, *The Early History of the Church Missionary Society* (London 1896), pp. 481-504; W. Carus (ed), *Memoirs of the Life of the Rev Charles Simeon*, 3rd edn (London 1848), p. 393.
68. H. J. Garland, *Henry Francis Lyte* (Manchester n.d.), pp. 22-3, quoting Lyte's diary; T. Lefroy (ed), *Memoir of Chief Justice Lefroy* (Dublin 1871), p. ii; *Countess of Huntingdon*, pp. 155n., 179-81, 185, 200.
69. Sirr, *Power Trench*, pp. 57-61, 63-9, 78-9, 88.
70. P. Roe, *Thoughts on the Death of George Hamilton* (Dublin 1830); *Christian Observer*, V (1806), pp. 66-7, had an obituary of the bishop.
71. Crookshank, *Methodism*, I 281, 301-03. The case was documented in Smyth's *An Account of the Trial of Edward Smyth* (Dublin 1777).
72. Hick, 'Irish Rhinelanders', pp. 98-9; Averell's Journal, p. 197; *Countess of Huntingdon*, p. 192n.
73. Sirr, *Power Trench*, pp. 81, 83; Motherwell, *Albert Blest*, pp. 114-15; [Mrs] H. Madden, *Memoir of the late Right Rev Robert Daly* (London 1875).
74. J. F. Berry, *The Story of St Nicholas' Collegiate Church, Galway* (Galway 1912), pp. 74-5; Maturin's letter in CMS Archives; J. B. Leslie, *Raphoe Clergy and Parishes* (Enniskillen 1940), pp. 22, 35, 51, 56.
75. Averell's Journal, pp. 155, 195, 224, 291; J. B. Leslie, *Ardfert and Aghadoe Clergy and Parishes* (Dublin 1940), p. 67; Motherwell, *Albert Blest*, p. 64.

76. CMS Archives: letters of George Carr (18 April 1804) and Peter Roe (16 May 1804).
77. Madden, *Peter Roe*, pp. 61-2, 77; P. Roe, *A Sermon ... on the Death of the Rev Edward Pidgeon* (Dublin 1808), p. 30.
78. Madden, *Peter Roe*, pp. 82, 87, 100, 106-07, 132-3, 307.
79. CMS Archives: letters of George Carr (18 Feb 1805) and Robert Shaw (27 Jan 1814).
80. Madden, *Peter Roe*, pp. 37-8, 52-7, 105-07, 130-1, 135, 153, 156-9, 166, 337, 530.
81. *Evangelicalism in Ulster Society*, p.14.
82. ibid., pp. 47-50; A. R. Acheson, 'Evangelicals in the Church of Ireland 1784-1859', Ph.D thesis, Queen's University Belfast 1967, pp. 94-7, 148-52 , and Appendix A for the status and significance of Bethesda chapel.
83. The separatists were numerically insignificant. Walker had 130 members in his congregation in Strafford Street, Dublin and some 10 small congregations elsewhere: Wills, *Irish Nation*, IV 454.
84. J. T. O'Brien, *A Charge to the Clergy of the United Dioceses of Ossory, Ferns and Leighlin* (Dublin 1866), pp. 17, 21-3; J. B. B Clarke (ed), *An Account of the Infancy, Religious and Literary Life of Adam Clarke* (London 1833); Garland, *Lyte*, p. 23; B. W. Mathias, *An Inquiry into the Antiquity and Orthodoxy of the Doctrines of the Reformation which treat of the Ruin and Recovery of Mankind* (Dublin 1814).
85. *A Sermon Preached at the Funeral of the Rev W. D. Hoare, in the Cathedral Church of Limerick* (Cork 1823), pp. 13-14.
86. Beckett, *Anglo-Irish Tradition*, pp. 104-07; Milne, *APCK*, p. 2. RCB Library, Beresford Correspondence, Vol. VI, Nos. 258-60; Carus, *Simeon*, p. 394.
87. Sirr, *Power Trench*, pp. 461-5, gives the text of Trench's speech.

### NOTES TO PART FOUR

1. W. P. Walsh (ed), *Remains of the Venerable Henry Irwin* (Dublin 1858), p. 150.
2. Wills, *Irish Nation*, IV 409.
3. C. Póirtéir (ed), *The Great Irish Famine* (RTE/Mercier, Dublin 1995).
4. D. H. Akenson, *The Irish Education Experiment: The National System of Education in the Nineteenth Century* (London 1970), p. 91; Bowen, *Protestant Crusade*, pp. 63-4; Guinness, *Guinness Legend, p. 38*; P. Lynch and J. Vaizey, *Guinness's Brewery in the Irish Economy 1759-1876* (Cambridge 1960), pp. 105-06; Beckett, *Modern Ireland*, p. 304.
5. John Keble's famous Assize Sermon at Oxford on 'National Apostasy' was occasioned by the Whig reforms of the Irish Church.
6. Sirr, *Power Trench*, p. 458; D. J. Hickey and J. E. Doherty, *A Dictionary of Irish History since 1800* (Dublin 1980), art. 'Tithe War'; Charlotte Elizabeth [Phelan], *Personal Recollections* (London 1841), pp. 136-9, 352-5; Leslie, *Ossory*, p. 314.
7. RCB Library: Beresford Correspondence, Vol. VI, Nos. 124 (3 Nov. 1834) and 99 (11 Nov 1834); Akenson, *Church of Ireland*, p.193.
8. D. H. Akenson, *A Protestant in Purgatory: Richard Whately, Archbishop of Dublin* (Hamden, Connecticut 1981), pp. 179-86.
9. Idem, *Church of Ireland*, pp. 168-79.
10. RCB Library: Beresford Correspondence, Vol. VI, Nos. 18 (30 Sept 1832), 59 (1 Feb 1830), and 240 (undated).
11. ibid., Nos. 18, 60 (9 Dec 1831), 65 (10 Nov 1832), and 141 (16 March 1833).
12. In W. J. Shiels and D. Woods (eds), *The Churches, Ireland and the Irish* (Oxford 1989), p. 246.
13. 1825, p. 14; 1840, pp. 125-6. In subsequent notes the *Christian Examiner* is abbreviated as *CE*.
14. S. Piggin, *The Making of Modern Missionaries 1795-1858* (Abingdon 1986), pp. 203-04; T. Woodward (ed), *Sermons Doctrinal and Practical by the Rev. William Archer Butler, with a Memoir of the Author's Life,* 3rd edn (Cambridge 1855), pp. xv, xvii; Sirr, *Power Trench*, p. 259.
15. *Recollections of the Irish Church* (London 1877), pp. 36, 45.

16. Akenson, *Church of Ireland*, pp. 119, 121; J. H. Gebbie (ed), *In his Hand* (Newtownabbey, c.1970); *CE*, 1825, p. 339; Leslie, *Armagh*, pp. 266-7, 401.

17. J. T. Waller, *A Short History of the Origin of Trinity Church and St. Michael's Church in the City of Limerick* (Limerick 1954), pp. 1-8.

18. W. Urwick, *Biographic Sketches of J. D. La Touche* (Dublin 1868), pp. 220-1: *CE*, 1825, p. 71; 1826, p. 152; 1828, p. 460.

19. W. B. Stanford and R. B. McDowell, *Mahaffy:a biography of an Anglo-Irishman* (London 1971), p. 5; Brooke, *Recollections*, p. 96; Anon, *St James' Crinken 1840-1990* [n.d.], pp. 5-9; R. S. Gregg, *Memorials of the Life of John Gregg* (Dublin 1879), pp. 48-52.

20. RCB Library: A. Dawson, 'The Annals of Christ Church, Belfast, from its foundation in 1831' (typescript 1858); T. Drew, *The Church in Belfast* (Belfast 1838); *Account of the Proceedings of the Down and Connor Clergy Aid Society* (Belfast 1838), p. 8; *Great Meeting of the Diocese of Down and Connor for Church Extension* (Belfast 1838), p. 42; Wills, *Irish Nation*, IV 536-8.

21. This section is derived from F. R. Bolton, 'Richard Mant (1776-1848) Compared with other Pre-Tractarian Irish Churchmen': a paper read at the Summer School of Theology in St Deiniol's Library, June 1948, and published in *Church of Ireland Gazette*, 28 Jan, 4 & 11 Feb 1949.

22. Addleshaw & Etchells, *Anglican Worship*, p. 210.

23. 'A Transatlantic Community of Saints: the Great Awakening and the First Evangelical Network, 1735-55' in *American Historical Review*, 91 (1986), p. 831.

24. *Primate Alexander*, pp. 29-30; *CE*, 1840, pp. 122-3; Wills, *Irish Nation* IV 411, 416-7.

25. PRONI: Johnston MSS, letter dated 11 July 1822.

26. Sirr, *Power Trench*, pp. 126-7, 130, 179, 195, 201-05, 210, 239, 245-6, 254, 378-9, 425, 773-4.

27. ibid., pp. 616-19; *CE*, 1835, pp. 609-12, 642-5; Dawson, 'Annals', where a useful summary is given.

28. Some 14 of 35 pages in Vol. III,Chap.VIII, 'Church Life in the Nineteenth Century'.

29. Sirr, *Power Trench*, pp. 556-7, has the text of the resolutions.

30. PRONI: Roden Papers – Winning's letter is dated 4 April 1827; Roden received a 'True Copy' of Johnston's letter of 8 March from the Irish Society.

31. Madden, *Bishop Daly*, pp. 94-5; Phillips, *Church of Ireland*, III 337-8.

32. PRONI: Johnston MSS, letter dated 17 Jan 1825.

33. H. Cotton, *Rhemes and Douay. An Attempt to Show what has been Done by Roman Catholics for the Diffusion of the Holy Scriptures* (Oxford 1855), pp. 119-22.

34. Sirr, *Power Trench*, p. 469; Phillips, *Church of Ireland*, III 338-40; N. D.Emerson, *A Short History of the [College Theological] Society* (Dublin 1930).

35. 'A Study of the Principles and Outlook of a Nineteenth Century Evangelical Leader', B. Litt. thesis, TCD, n.d., where (p. 203) the text of Leo XII's Encyclical is given.

36. Brooke, *Recollections*, pp. 146-7: Plunket was Dean of Tuam; *CE*, 1829, pp. 286-8, 1831, p. 77, 1861, p. 313, 1867, pp. 87-8; Sirr, *Power Trench*, pp. 564-5, 633, 637-8, 641-6; R. Braithwaite (ed), *The Life and Letters of Rev William Pennefather*, 2nd edn (London n.d.), pp. 86-9; PRONI, *Roden Papers*; Wills, *Irish Nation*, IV 422.

37. C. R. Maturin, *Five Sermons on the Errors of the Church of Rome* (Dublin 1824): Sermon IV 121.

38. Gregg, *John Gregg*, pp. 56-7; *Primate Alexander*, p. 18; RCB Library: Beresford Correspondence, Vol. VI, No. 139; Desmond Bowen, *Souperism: Myth or Reality?* (Cork 1970), p. 130.

39. *CE*, 1831, pp. 158, 239, 480.

40. R. Traill, 'Diary 1832 -1838', pp. 2-4, 9, 25, 28. The diary was privately printed, with preface by Traill's great-great-grandson, 'RSH' [R(obert) Synge Harbord]. I am grateful to the Revd Warren Nelson for sight of a copy of it.

41. PRONI, *Roden Papers*; RCB Library, *Beresford Correspondence* Vol. VI, No. 85.

42. Sirr, *Power Trench*, Chap. IV, 'Famine of 1822', Chap. X, 'Connaught Penury', and pp. 192, 198.

43. Akenson, *Church of Ireland*, p. 210, tabulates the church population of 1834 and 1861.
44. ibid., pp. 195, 198-201; Rowan, *North West Ulster*, p. 56.
45. Dawson, 'Annals', lists the churches in 1858; *Clergy of Connor* has brief details for those subsequently built in north and west Belfast.
46. Addleshaw and Etchells, *Anglican Worship*, pp. 203-10; Cuming, *Anglican Liturgy*, pp. 193-4.
47. D. M. McFarlan, *Lift thy Banner: Church of Ireland Scenes 1870-1900* (Dundalk 1990), pp. 35-8. Copies of hymnals referred to are in RCB Library.
48. Bowen, *Souperism*, p. 230; Ball, *Reformed Church of Ireland*, 2nd edn, p. 274; T. de V. White, *The Parents of Oscar Wilde*, (London 1967), p. 27.
49. 'Early Irish Ecclesiastical Studies' in M. Hurley (ed.), *Irish Anglicanism 1869-1969* (Dublin 1970), pp. 43, 47.
50. Olden, *Church of Ireland*, p. 395; David Mitchell, *A 'Peculiar' Place: The Adelaide Hospital, Dublin 1839-1989* (Dublin n.d.), pp. 32, 41, 46: *CE*, 1853, p. 235; 1857, p. 235; 1858, p. 34; 1860, p. 207; 1861, p 27; Kenneth Milne, *Protestant Aid: a History of the Association for the Relief of Distressed Protestants* (Dublin 1989), p. 4; RCB Library, Fleet Market account book, P. 30.7. 4: DPA Minute Book, 1847-1868, MS 129.1.1.
51. *The Times*, 25 March 1870; *Newry Telegraph*, 28 March 1870; *Guinness Legend, p. 42*; Lynch and Vaizey, *Guinness's Brewery*, p. 245.
52. *CE*, 1854, p. 408; RCB Library: *Beresford Correspondence*, Vol. VI, Nos. 242-5, 248; Akenson, *Church of Ireland*, pp. 204-05.
53. Stanford and McDowell, *Mahaffy*, pp. 12-13; Donal McCartney, *W. E. H. Lecky: Historian and Politician 1838-1903* (Lilliput, Dublin 1994), p. 12.
54. See my entries on these five bishops (and prominent Irish clergy and laity) in *The Blackwell Dictionary of Evangelical Biography 1730-1860*, 2 vols, (Oxford 1995).
55. *History of the Church Missionary Society* (London 1899), I 374.
56. Leslie, *Clogher*, p. 21; Stanford and McDowell, *Mahaffy*, p.138 and n.22; *ADB* entries for Justices Foster and Stawell.
57. *History of England* (London 1878), II 611.
58. As Magee's tense indicates, he was unable to accept the initial invitation, but did preach the CMS Sermon several years later.
59. Irwin had been his father (Henry Irwin's) assistant in Sandford Chapel. He became Precentor of Armagh, and is commemorated in the Cathedral.
60. *Three Sermons on Confirmation and the Lord's Supper* (Dublin 1857), p. 12.
61. Boyd Hilton, 'Whiggery, Religion and Social Reform: the case of Lord Morpeth' in *Historical Journal*, 37 (1994), pp. 844, 853-4.
62. Akenson, *Whately*, p. 154; Stanford and McDowell, *Mahaffy*, p. 13; PRONI: Crawford MSS. Mandeville published *Things Hoped For: the Doctrine of the Second Advent*, and other works.
63. Lee's work, which issued five editions, was noticed in *CE*, 1854, pp. 507-08, 522-3.
64. Akenson, *Whately*, pp. 154, 195: *CE*, 1838, pp. 383, 566-9, 624-7; 1840, p. 160; 1854, p. 337; 1846, p. 66.
65. *Short Studies on Great Subjects*, New edn (London 1891), IV 296-301.
66. *Life of Frederick Richards Wynne* (London 1897), pp. 7-8, 14, 22; R. B. McDowell, *Church of Ireland 1869-1969* (London & Boston 1975), p. 75.
67. P. B. Nockles, *The Oxford Movement in Context: Anglican High Churchmanship, 1760-1857* (Cambridge 1994), pp. 307-08.
68. idem., 'The Church of Ireland and the Oxford Movement', pp. 33, 59-60, 62, 78-80. I am grateful to Dr Jennifer Moreton for drawing my attention to this first draft, which later appeared in the *Historical Journal*.
69. *CE*, 1840, pp. 52, 285; Phillips, *Church of Ireland*, III 312-13; Acheson, 'Evangelicals', pp. 206-17, explores the relationship in some detail.
70. *Journal of the General Synod*, 1905, pp. lxvii-viii. The bishop alluded to was John Gregg.
71. Cited in the *Gazette's* centenary edition, 28 Jan 1955.

72. Brooke, *Recollections*, pp. 46-7, 108; *Clergy of Connor*, p. 469; Waller, *Trinity Church*, p. 8; *CE*, 1860, p. 186; Walsh, *Henry Irwin*, p. 241.

73. *Unforgotten* (APCK 1951), pp. 201, 208.

74. Stanford and McDowell, *Mahaffy*, pp. 13-14; Gregg, *John Gregg*, pp. 71-2, 75-6; McCartney, *Lecky*, p. 11.

75. *CE*, 1845, p. 460, 1860, p. 238; PRONI, Roden Papers: letters from Roden from Europe, 16 April 1844 and during Oct-Nov 1852.

76. White, *Children of St Columba*, pp. 63-6.

77. S. Judd and K. Cable, *Sydney Anglicans* (Sydney 1987), pp. 75, 80; D. Hilliard, *Godliness and Good Order : A History of the Anglican Church in South Australia* (Netley, SA, 1986), pp. 5, 8. I am indebted to Dr Brian Dickey of Adelaide for the Perry quotation.

78. F. E. Bland, *How the Church Missionary Society came to Ireland* (Dublin 1935), Appendix II ; Brooke, *Recollections*, p. 49.

79. Patrick Comerford, 'Church of Ireland Missionaries in Southern Africa', a paper read to the Church of Ireland Historical Society on 9 Nov 1996.

80. White, *Children of St Columba*, pp. 37-8; Sirr, *Power Trench*, p. 773; Carrington, *Anglican Church in Canada*, pp. 118, 129, 131, 135, 143.

81. Patrick Hickey, 'Famine, mortality and emigration: a profile of six parishes in the Poor Law Union of Skibbereen, 1846-7' in P. O'Flanagan and C. G. Buttimer (eds), *Cork: History and Society* (Dublin 1993), p. 912. Cullen is quoted by Hickey, Carleton and *Freeman's Journal* in Bowen, *Souperism*, pp. 13, 231.

82. Carrington, *Anglican Church in Canada*, p. 104; Woodward, *Sermons by William Archer Butler*, pp. xxviii-xxix.

83. *Souperism*, pp. 12, 191.

84. H. A. Boyd, *A History of the Church of Ireland in Dunluce Parish* (Coleraine 1937), n.p; *Clergy of Connor*, p. 583.

85. Braithwaite, *Life and Letters*, pp. 194-5, 209-10. There is something unexplained here, as William's brother, Richard Pennefather, was under secretary of state in Dublin.

86. *CE*, 1862, p. 39; Hickey, 'Profile of six parishes', pp. 874, 879-80, 883-7.

87. Patsy Adam-Smith, *Heart of Exile* (Nelson, Australia, 1986), pp. 68-9, 212-13.

88. Bowen, *Souperism*, pp. 187-8, 198-202, 211-12, 221-2.

89. Dawson, 'Annals'; Hickey, 'Profile of six parishes', pp. 888, 912; D. H. Greene and E. M. Stephens, *J. M. Synge* (New York 1961), p. 15.

90. 'Themes': final working text dated 20 August 1985.

91. *Souperism*, p. 233.

92. *Christian Examiner* (April-Dec 1859); Acheson, 'Evangelicals', Chap. X: 'Eighteen Fifty Nine'.

93. J. Weir, *The Ulster Awakening: its Origin, Progress and Fruit* (London 1860), p. 205; *Religious Revivals in the North of Ireland, as described … by the Lord Bishop of Down etc., the Rev.C. Seaver … and the Rev. Dr. McCosh* (Dublin 1859), pp. 7-8, 34-5; J. W. Massie, *Revivals in Ireland, Facts, Documents and Correspondence* (London 1859), p. 41.

94. *CE*, 1835, pp. 614, 875-888; 1859, p. 102.

95. Weir, *Ulster Awakening*, pp. 115, 132, 153-4.

96. Nelson published *Year of Delusion* over against the Moderator, Dr William Gibson's *Year of Grace*. E. A. Stopford, *The Work and the Counterwork* (Dublin 1859) corroborates Nelson, but is distinguished by greater balance and objectivity.

97. M. Hennell, *Sons of the Prophets* (SPCK 1979), pp. 87-9; Hylson-Smith, *Evangelicals*, pp. 188-90: both quote Stock, *My Recollections* (1909), p. 83.

98. Ford, McGuire and Milne, *As by Law Established*, p. 25.

99. Introduction to Seddall, *Edward Nangle*, pp. xx-xxi.

100. Preface to Vol. I. Bowen, *Protestant Crusade*, ignores this journal and the controversial scholarship of its founders in general.

101. *The Infallibility of the Church* (London 1888), pp. 1-2, 6.

102. Bowen, *Protestant Crusade*, p. 218: *CE*, 1851, p. 35; 1853, pp. 3, 95; 1854. p. 476; 1863, p. 64.

103. ibid., 1854, p. 355. The myth of neglect was sustained in G. R. Balleine, *History of the Evangelical Party in the Church of England* (London 1908), pp. 207-08.

104. Seddall, *Edward Nangle*, pp. xxviii-xxx.

105. *Gazette*, 10 March 1995.

106. Seddall, *Edward Nangle*, pp. xix, xxv; Salmon, *Infallibility*, p. 2; Bowen, *Souperism*, p. 164.

107. *CE*, 1851, p. 101; 1853, pp. 3, 48.

108. Akenson, *Whately*, pp. 137-8, 170-1, 187, 194-204, 208-09, 213.

## NOTES TO PART FIVE

1. *Journal of the General Synod* [hereafter *JGS*], 1912, p. lxii, 1942, pp. lxxvi-vii; *Gazette*, 14 May 1993.

2. The text of the relevant section of the Act is given in *Journal of the General Convention* of *the Church of Ireland: First Session 1870*. (Dublin 1870), p.v [Hereafter *JGC* I].

3. This account is derived from the outline of events in *JGC* I, pp. vi-ix, 3.

4. ibid., pp. ix-x, 2, 177; *Journal of the General Convention: Second Session 1870* (Dublin 1871), pp. 1,55. [Hereafter *JGC* II].

5. The text of the Constitution is given in *JGC* I, pp.185-207, and II, pp. 61-8.

6. ibid., II, pp. 1, 77-80. The text of the Draft Charter drawn up by the Convention is given in I, pp. 208-13, and of the Charter of Incorporation, which showed only minor changes, in II, pp. 69-76.

7. Ball, *Reformed Church of Ireland*, 2nd edn, p. 301. (Ball gave the date of the Charter wrongly as 19 October, p. 299.)

8. *JGC* I, p. 3; II, pp. 10-11, 38.

9. This analysis is derived from the 'List of Delegates from Each Diocese' in *JGC* I, pp. xv-xxi.

10. ibid.

11. ibid., p. 2.

12. ibid., pp. x, 3, Appendix p. 57.

13. ibid., pp. 9, 17, 37-8, 176-7; II, pp. 14, 39-41, 48-9, 51-2, 56.

14. Ball, *Reformed Church of Ireland*, 2nd edn, pp. 306-10; W. R. Moore, 'The Financial System of the Church of Ireland since Disestablishment' in H. E. Patton, *Fifty Years of Disestablishment* (APCK, Dublin 1922), Appendix A, pp. 315-17. Bishop Moore had given his analysis in an address to his diocesan synod in Kilmore in 1916.

15. *JGC* I, Appendix pp. 56-63.

16. Hugh Shearman, *How the Church of Ireland was Disestablished* (Dublin 1970), p. 39; Ball, *Reformed Church of Ireland*, Appendix p. 356; *JGS*, 1895, pp. xlvii, xlix; Moore, 'Financial System', p. 320.

17. Shearman, *How Disestablished*, p. 41; Moore, 'Financial System', p. 317; Ball, *Reformed Church of Ireland*, p. 356.

18. *JGS*, 1897, p. xlvii. Alexander's figure compares with Shearman's 2280 annuitants, *How Disestablished*, p. 40.

19. *JGS*, 1926, p. lviii. The two clergy were Canon Bookey, 'a notable scholar' in Armagh diocese, and Canon Armstrong, rector of Castlerock (Derry) for 58 years.

20. Ball, *Reformed Church of Ireland*, p. 356; Moore, 'Financial System', p. 318; Carrington, *Anglican Church in Canada*, p. 117.

21. *JGS*, 1926, p. lviii; G. Daly, 'Church Renewal: 1869-1877' in Hurley, *Irish Anglicanism*, p. 25.

22. *JGS*, 1914, p. xlviii, 1915, p. xlviii.

23. *JGC* I, p. 185; F. C. Jameson, 'The Church of Ireland' in C. O. Buchanan (ed), *Modern Anglican Liturgies* (London 1968), p. 174.

24. Quoted Daly, 'Church Renewal', p. 30.

25. Patton, *Fifty Years*, pp. 34, 63.

26. ibid., pp. 40-1, 64.

27. Daly, 'Church Renewal', pp. 36-7.

28. Ball, *Reformed Church of Ireland*, gives the changes in full as Note RR, pp. 359-64.

29. Daly, 'Church Renewal', p. 37; F. D. How, *William Conyngham Plunket, Fourth Baron Plunket and Sixty First Archbishop of Dublin* (London 1900), p. 110; Patton, *Fifty Years*, p. 57.

30. S. Neill, *Anglicanism*, (Harmondsworth 1958), p. 296; *JGC* I, p. 30; W. G. Wilson, The *Church of Ireland: why Conservative?* (APCK, Dublin 1970), pp. 16-18.

31. See Chap. Two above, p. 39; *JGS*, 1941, p. lxxiii. The 1973 report of the Select Committee on the Canons surveyed the status of 19th century canon law: *General Synod 1973: Reports*, pp. 246-51.

32. Patton, *Fifty Years*, pp. 106-7; Daly, 'Church Renewal', p. 38.

33. BCP, Preamble and Declaration, 1870; F. R. Wynne, *Spent in the Service: A Memoir of the Very Rev. Achilles Daunt DD, Dean of Cork*, 3rd edn (London 1880), pp. 225, 379-91.

34. This analysis is based on 'Episcopal Elections in the Church of Ireland 1872-1963' in *Church of Ireland Directory 1964*, pp. 100-01.

35. Patton, *Fifty Years*, p. 76; *Primate Alexander*, p. 306.

36. Narcissus Marsh (1703), Hoadly (1742), and Lord John George Beresford (1822).

37. R. H. Murray, *Archbishop Bernard: Professor, Prelate and Provost* (London 1931), pp. 216, 330.

38. Technically the bishops elected Day, but 'by resolution of the Armagh Synod'.

39. Letter of 22 Jan 1939 to Mr H. A. Boyd, in which Lord Belmore gave 'my version of the "King's refusal" story' of the previous November. On the decisive day he had lunched at the University Club with Bishop Peacocke, his brother Archdeacon Peacocke of Kildare, and Mr J. R. Scott of Derry. George Seaver, *John Allen Fitzgerald Gregg Archbishop* (Dublin 1963), p. 222.

40. *JGS*, 1883, pp. lxxvi-vii; *JGC* I, pp. 201-02.

41. McFarlan, *Lift thy Banner*, pp. 104-05.

42. *Church Hymnal*, Music edn 1960, Preface; Patton, *Fifty Years* pp. 149-50.

43. BCP, Preface of 1926; Cuming, *Anglican Liturgy*, pp. 240-1; *JGS*, 1914, p. li.

44. McFarlan, *Lift thy Banner*, pp. 17-19; J. V. Luce, 'The Church of Ireland and Trinity College Dublin, 1592-1992' in *Search*, xv, No. 1 (spring 1992), p. 13; Patton, *Fifty Years* pp. 233-8; *JGS*, 1913, p. xlix, 1914, p. li.

45. *Lift thy Banner*, pp. 27, 30-5, 48-9, 58-9, 60-6.

46. Patton, *Fifty Years*, pp. 65-6, 71-2, 174-80, 210; C. F. D'Arcy, *The Adventures of a Bishop. A Phase of Irish Life: A Personal and Historical Narrative* (London 1934), pp. 124, 258-9; *Irish Times*, 21 Sept 1996.

47. *Primate Alexander*, p. 291; McDowell, *Church of Ireland*, p. 76; D'Arcy, *Adventures of a Bishop*, pp. 177-8; *JGS*, 1920, pp. lvii-iii.

48. *Clergy of Connor*, pp. 122, 212, 240; *JGS*, 1922, p. xcv, 1930, p. lxxvi, 1938, pp. 27-9.

49. ibid., 1914, pp. lii-iii; McFarlan, *Lift thy Banner*, pp. 94-9.

50. *JGC* I, pp. 80, 85-6; *JGS*, 1914, pp. liii, lxcxxv-vi, 1920, pp. lxiii-vi, xcii; Patton, *Fifty Years*, pp. 288-92.

51. *JGS*, 1920, pp. lvii-iii; 1920 (Special), pp. v, 3,14-16,39; 1921, pp. liv, lxvii-ix, lxxxvi; McDowell, *Church of Ireland*, pp. 125-9.

52. Stanford and McDowell, *Mahaffy*, pp. 127, 133-4; *JGS*, 1902, p. xlvii; Patton, *Fifty Years*, p. 198; M. Maguire, 'The Church of Ireland and the problem of the Protestant working-class of Dublin, 1870s-1930s', in Ford, McGuire and Milne, *As by Law Established*, pp. 198-201.

53. *JGS*, 1914, p. liii; J. Hodgins, *Sister Island: A History of CMS in Ireland, 1814-1994* (Dunmurry 1994), pp. 83-4, 86; McFarlan, *Lift thy Banner*, pp. 72-4; White, *Children of St Columba*, pp. 48-50.

54. Hodgins, *Sister Island*, pp. 61, 86; *JGS*, 1898, p. lvii, 1900, p. xlviii, 1914, pp. 290-6, 1915, p. 284; *Irish Ecclesiastical Gazette*, 1 Feb 1879; McDowell, *Church of Ireland*, p. 85.

55. Carrington, *Anglican Church in Canada*, pp. 74, 164, 178, 185, 197, 210, 218, 229-30, 233; McFarlan, *Lift thy Banner*, pp. 74-5.

56. White, *Children of St Columba*, pp. 46-7, 54-7, 66-71; Comerford, 'Missionaries in Southern Africa'.

57. Thomas McDonald, 'The Church Overseas' in Hurley, *Irish Anglicanism*, pp. 98-100.
58. *JGS*, 1938, pp. lxxiv-vi, 262-90.
59. ibid, 1897, pp. liii-iv, 1912, p. liii, 1938, p. 189.
60. ibid, 1886, pp. liii-vii, lxii-iv, lxvii.
61. ibid, 1893, pp. xlviii, 259-62.
62. 1957 edn (APCK, Dublin), pp. 9, 12-13.
63. *JGS*, 1900, p. xlvii, 1912, pp. lviii, lxi-ii.
64. *Ireland's English Question* (London 1971), p. 245.
65. *JGS*, 1912, pp. xlix, lii, 444.
66. D'Arcy, *Adventures of a Bishop*, pp. 186-94; Anne de Courcy, *Circe: The Life of Edith, Marchioness of Londonderry* (London 1992), p. 97. The best account of these events is A. T. Q. Stewart, *The Ulster Crisis* (London 1967).
67. *JGS*, 1915, p. xlvii; D'Arcy, *Adventures of a Bishop*, p. 197; Murray, *Archbishop Bernard*, p. 76; McDowell, *Church of Ireland*, p. 106.
68. Patton, *Fifty Years*, pp. 271-3.
69. *Irish Church Directory 1956*, pp. 69, 99.
70. Patton, *Fifty Years*, pp. 272, 281-2; Murray, *Archbishop Bernard* p. 315.
71. *JGS*, 1921, pp. viii-ix, liii.
72. Seaver, *Gregg*, pp. 120-1; *JGS*, 1922, pp. liv, ciii.
73. Maguire, 'Protestant working-class of Dublin', pp. 194, 202; T. Keane, 'Demographic Trends' in Hurley, *Irish Anglicanism*, pp. 168-9.
74. *JGS*, 1939, pp. lxxvii-xxx, 1946, p. lxxxiv. Inexplicably, Gregg overstated by some 50,000 the Church's population in Eire.
75. cf. *General Synod 1994: Reports*, pp. 272 - 3.
76. Lesley Whiteside, *George Otto Simms: a Biography* (Gerrards Cross 1990), pp. 47-50, 53-55, 76.
77. *Administration 1967* (Dublin 1967), pp. 7-8; Whiteside, *Simms*, pp. 112-17, discusses this report fully. See above, p. 219, for the 1919-20 report.
78. Victor Griffin, *Mark of Protest*, (Gill and Macmillan, Dublin 1993), p. 83.
79. In conversation in my home on 31 Jan 1972.
80. In 'Recent Liturgical Reform' in Hurley, *Irish Anglicanism*, p. 191.
81. *JGS*, 1946, p. lxxxii.
82. Quoted in conversation with Bishop Quin on 25 April 1974.
83. Seaver, *Gregg*, pp. 251-2.
84. ibid., pp. 312-13.
85. *JGS*, 1941, p. lxxix.
86. *Gazette*, 13 May 1949, 5 June 1953; *Irish Times*, 7 Feb 1952.
87. Whiteside, *Simms*, pp. 36, 50-2: *Gazette*, 18 & 25 June 1937.
88. Seaver, *Gregg*, pp. 317-9, 334.
89. Griffin, *Mark of Protest*, pp. 91-3, 96-103.
90. Vaughan and Fitzpatrick (eds), *Irish Historical Statistics* , pp. 4, 49-50.
91. *Administration 1967*, pp. 12, 104, 107, 109-10, 113-14, 123.
92. Whiteside, *Simms*, pp. 82-3.
93. 'General Synod, 1971: List of Representatives', pp. 3-8.
94. Whiteside, *Simms*, pp. 57-8.
95. *Church of Ireland Directory 2002*, pp. 229-32.
96. *General Synod 1973: Reports*, pp. 254-8. The committee was influenced also by the English Canons of 1969.
97. The resolution was moved by two Northerners, Canon (later Bishop) W. G. Wilson and myself. It was tactically necessary, but intrinsically unjust.
98. Music edn 1960, Preface.
99. Jameson, 'Church of Ireland', pp. 179-88, gives the text.
100. *Search,* i, No. 1 (spring 1978), p. 2.
101. Whiteside, *Simms*, pp. 124, 149-50, 167.

102. At the annual dinner that evening of the TCD Association of Northern Ireland, of which Simms was then President.
103. Luce, 'Church of Ireland and Trinity', p. 17.
104. F. Jeffery, 'Anglican-Methodist relations' in Hurley, *Irish Anglicanism*, p. 91.
105. Notes made at the Inter-Church Conference, 1974.
106. *Gazette*, 20 Sept 1996: Luce, 'Church of Ireland and Trinity', pp. 14-17.
107. *An Australian Prayer Book* (Sydney 1978), pp. 498-636; *The Alternative Service Book* (London 1980), Preface, pp. 211-1093.
108. Edna Burrows and Patricia Mayes, *Specially Concerned: The Mothers' Union in Ireland 1887-1987* (Dublin 1987), p. 31; *General Synod 1973: Reports*, p. 163, *1981*, p. 167, *1995*, p. 244, *2000*, p. 212. Incomes in sterling and punts have been aggregated at par.
109. *Gazette*, 21 March 1997; *General Synod 1995: Reports*, pp. 243-4, *2001*, p. 269; Hodgins, *Sister Island*, pp. xvii-xx, lists the CMSI partners.
110. *Primate Alexander*, p. 142.
111. *Gazette*, 27 Sept 1996; *General Synod 1995: Reports*, pp. 174-5, gives the text of the Porvoo Declaration and a list of the participating churches.
112. I am grateful to Dr Godfrey Brown for this recollection.
113. The Bradford Interview: *Ulster News Letter*, 15 June 1992.
114. *Gazette*, 27 May 1994.
115. The Bradford Interview: *Ulster News Letter*, 15 June 1992.
116. *General Synod 1994: Reports*, pp. 98-109; 'Agenda Paper of the General Synod, 1996', pp. 7-8; *Church Review*, Nov 1995, p. 19.
117. Canon Edgar Turner alone served on both committees from 1973 to 1996.
118. *General Synod 1980: Reports*, pp. 217-20, 226.
119. ibid., 1993, p. 239; *Gazette*, 17 May 1996.
120. *General Synod 1994: Reports*, p. 131; *Gazette*, 28 June 1996.
121. *Church Hymnal: Fifth Edition* (Oxford 2000), pp. vii-xii: *General Synod 1995: Reports*, pp. 259-62, 289-90, *2001*, p. 142.
122. *General Synod 1994: Reports*, p. 267.
123. The theological rationale was set out by Harold Miller and John Paterson in 'Liturgical Space' in *Search*, xviii, No.1 (spring 1995), pp. 24-34.
124. *General Synod 1994: Reports*, p. 229; *Church Review*, Nov 1995, p. 20; 'Connor Times', No. 10 (Advent 1996).
125. *Gazette*, 21 March 1997; R. Warke, 'Youth work in the Church of Ireland: signs of hope' in *Search*, xvii, No.1 (spring 1994), pp. 49-51.
126. Peter Rhys Thomas, 'Cork church restored and re-dedicated' in *Gazette*, 14 Feb 1997.
127. *General Synod 1994: Reports*, pp. 135-6; *1995*, pp. 146, 153-5; *1999*, p. 128; *2000*, p. 168; *2001*, pp. 167-8, 170-2.
128. In his 1994 presidential address: *Gazette*, 17 May 1994.
129. *Church Review*, Nov 1995, p. 20, Dec 1995, p. 22; Cecil Kerr's article in *Gazette*, 2 Aug 1996.
130. Bishop Brian Hannon's article in *Gazette*, 25 July 1996; ibid 21 Feb 1997; 'Connor Times', No. 10 (Advent 1996).
131. *Gazette*, 28 June 1996.
132. 'Draft Report of the General Synod Commission on Episcopal Ministry and Diocesan Boundaries, submitted for comment to the Standing Committee of General Synod, September 1996', p. 10.
133. H. T. Morrison, 'The central administration of the Church' in *Search* i, No. 1 (spring 1978), p. 36.
134. The committee was served with unfailing courtesy and efficiency by David Meredith, assistant secretary General Synod.
135. Vaughan and Fitzpatrick, *Statistics*, pp. 4, 49-50; J. L. B. Deane and R. E. Turner, 'The 1991 census and the Church of Ireland' in *Search*, xix, No. 1 (spring 1996), pp. 26-8, 41-2.
136. *Irish Times,* 19 April 1994; *Gazette*, 6 May 1994.
137. Deane and Turner, '1991 Census', pp. 26, 40.

138. The Bradford Interview: *Ulster Newsletter.* 15 June 1992; *Gazette,* 27 May 1994.
139. 'Draft report', pp. 5,12,14-19.
140. *Irish Times,* 28 Sept 1996.
141. In March 2002, the House of Bishops elected Archdeacon Kenneth Good, an Evangelical, as Bishop of Derry and Raphoe.
142. *Gazette,* 27 May 1994.
143. Gazette, 11 & 18 Oct, *News Letter,* 28 Oct, *Irish Times,* 23 Oct 1996.
144. *Protestants in a Catholic State: Ireland's Privileged Minority* (Kingston and Montreal 1983), pp. 203, 209.
145. 'The Church of Ireland Submission to the Forum for Peace and Reconciliation', May 1995, *Gazette Supplement,* pp. V, VIII; *Church Review,* Nov 1995, p. 17.
146. *Irish Times,* 12 May 1993.
147. *Privileged Minority,* pp. 203, 207-08.
148. *Gazette,* 30 Aug 1996.
149. ibid., 14 March, 23 May 1997.
150. 'Cromlyn's' summary in *Gazette,* 10 Jan 1997.
151. *Irish Times,* 12 May 1993; Personal Statement by the Primate to Standing Committee, Nov 1993, in *General Synod 1994: Reports,* pp. 133-4; *Year Book of the Diocese of Sydney 1989* (Sydney 1989), p. 264.
152. *Mark of Protest,* pp. 100,111.
153. 'Religion and Politics': The New University of Ulster Tenth Annual Convocation Lecture, 9 May 1983.
154. *Gazette,* 3 Jan 1997, where the text of Dr Mansergh's lecture is given; *Opposing Violence/Building Bridges* (Belfast 1996), pp. 186-7.
155. 'Submission to the Forum', p. VI; *The Times,* 10 July 1996; *News Letter,* 14 Oct 1996.
156. *Sunday Independent,* 27 April 1997.
157. Robin Eames, *Chains to be Broken: A Personal Reflection on Northern Ireland and its People* (London 1992) p. 29; Personal Statement by the Primate, *General Synod 1994: Reports,* pp. 133-4.
158. D. Bowen, *History and the Shaping of Irish Protestantism* (New York 1995), pp. 440-3, documents this interaction.
159. The Bradford Interview, *Ulster News Letter,* 15 June 1992; *Chains to be Broken,* pp. 173-4. The meeting with the late Brian Lenihan, then Minister for Foreign Affairs, took place in Church of Ireland House on 15 April 1980.
160. Bowen, *History and Irish Protestantism,* p. 449; *Chains to be Broken,* pp. 52-60; *Irish Times,* 18 May 1990, 12 May 1993.
161. E. Mallie and D. McKittrick, *The Fight for Peace: the Secret Story behind the Irish Peace Process* (London 1996), pp. 222-3, 268; idem, *Endgame in Ireland* (London 2001), pp. 138-9, 178-9; Personal Statement by the Primate, Nov 1993.
162. *Gazette,* 26 July, *The Times,* 10 July 1996.
163. *The Daily Telegraph,* 8 July, *Gazette* 23 May 1997.
164. *The Daily Telegraph,* 29 April, *Gazette,* 11 Oct 1996.
165. *Irish Times,* 23 Oct 1996; *Gazette,* 26 July, 11 Oct, 1 & 8 Nov1996.
166. *Gazette,* 20 April 2001; *The Furrow,* Jan 2001; personal letter and private paper 'Cathedrals – Some Thoughts', 27 Sept 2001.
167. 'Diocese of Connor: Report of the Diocesan Council 2000-2001', p.29; *Resourcing Bishops* (Church House Publishing 2001), pp.120-1.
168. *General Synod 1999: Reports,* pp.203-13; *2000,* pp.155-9; *2001,* pp.211-14.
169. Ibid, 1999, pp.337-8; *2000,* pp.267-71; 'Connor Council Report 2001', p.13.
170. *Sunday Times,* 23 Dec 2000; *Irish Times,* 29 Dec 2001, 9 Jan & 16 March 2002; *Gazette,* 25 Jan & 1 March 2002. The Court of the General Synod adjourned its sitting until 10 May 2002 on the application of the defendant's counsel. It did not resume because Dean Furlong resigned his offices.
171. *General Synod 2000: Reports,* pp.126, 129-31; 'Connor Council Report 2001', pp. 16-22.

172. *General Synod 2000*: Reports, pp.224-7; *2001*, pp.137, 185-93.
173. S.R. White (ed), *A Time to Build: Essays for Tomorrow's Church,* (APCK 1999), pp.158-9.
174. PAKT Lurgan, 'Annual Report 2000'; *The Furrow,* Jan 2001; *Gazette,* 28 July 2000, 8 Feb 2002; *Irish Times,* 10 July 2001.
175. Bishop Miller's speech at General Synod 1998; *Gazette,* 15 Feb 2002; *The Furrow,* Jan 2001.
176. *Irish Times,* 27 Feb, 8 & 9 March 2002; *Gazette,* 1 March 2002.
177. *Irish Times,* 9 March 2002; *Sunday Times,* 1 Oct 2000.
178. S.R. White (ed), *A Time to Build,* p.8.
179. Ibid, p.159; *Gazette,* 3 Aug 2001.
180. *General Synod 1999: Reports,* pp. 112-13, 122, 145-60; *2000,* p.120.
181. *The Times,* 2 & 13 July 1998; *Irish News,* 10 July 2001; *Irish Times,* 10 July 2001; *Gazette,* 28 July 2000, 13 July 2001, 22 Feb 2002. The church's links with orangeism have been examined in Earl Storey's *Traditional Roots: Towards an appropriate relationship between the Church of Ireland and the Orange Order* (The Columba Press 2002).
182. Richard Clarke, *And is it True? Truth God and No-Man's Land* (Dublin 2000) p.10; David Robertson, *Deeds Not Words* (Longford 1998), inside cover & p.xi.
183. *Gazette,* 10 Nov 2000; *Irish Times,* 2 Aug 2001.
184. Ibid, 18 Aug 2001; *Gazette,* 3, 10 & 31 Aug 2001.

# Bibliography

### I. PRIMARY SOURCES

*a. Unpublished*

Belmore, Lord: letter to H.A. Boyd dated 22 Jan 1939
CMS Archives:
    Letters from Irish clergy to CMS Secretary 1800 - 20
    'Report of the Visit to Ireland of Revs J.Pratt, D.Wilson and W.Jowett, June 1814'
    Wilson, D. 'Notes of a Journey to Armagh': letter to J.Pratt from Armagh, June 1814
Comerford, P. 'Church of Ireland Missionaries to Southern Africa', Nov 1996
'Draft Report of the General Synod Commission on Episcopal Ministry and Diocesan
    Boundaries, submitted for comment to the Standing Committee of General Synod,
    September 1996'
Journal of Rev Adam Averell 1792 - 1807 (Wesley Historical Society Ireland)
PRONI
    Crawford Mss
    Johnston of Kilmore Mss
    Roden Papers
RCB Library
    Beresford Correspondence, Vol VI
    Dawson, A. 'The Annals of Christ Church, Belfast, from its foundation in 1831' (1858)
    DPA Minute Book, 1847 - 1868
    Fleet Market account book
Traill, R. 'Diary 1832 -1838'

*b. Printed*

*Administration 1967* (Dublin 1967)
'Agenda paper of the General Synod 1996'
Anon., *An Account of the Trial of Edward Smyth* (Dublin 1777)
Brooke, R.S. *Recollections of the Irish Church* (London 1877)
Browne, A. *The Ecclesiastical Law of Ireland*, 2nd edn (Dublin 1803)
*Church Hymnal: Fifth Edition* (Oxford 2000)
*Church of Ireland Directory*
'The Church of Ireland Submission to the Forum for Peace and Reconciliation', May 1995
'Connor Times'
Clarke, R. *And is it True? Truth, God and No-man's Land* (Dublin 2000)
Coote, C. *Statistical Survey of the County of Armagh* (Dublin 1804)
'Diocese of Connor: Report of the Diocesan Council 2000-2001'
Drew, T. *The Church in Belfast* (Belfast 1838)
Erck, J.C. *The Ecclesiastical Register* (Dublin 1820)
'General Synod, 1971: List of Representatives'; idem, 2001
*General Synod: Reports*
*Great Meeting of the Diocese of Down and Connor for Church Extension* (Belfast 1838)
Gregg, J.A.F. *The Primitive Faith and Roman Catholic Developments* (Cork 1909)
Hamilton, H. *Two Act Sermons* (London 1818)
Jebb, J. *A Sermon Preached at the Funeral of the Rev W.D. Hoare, in the Cathedral Church of
    Limerick* (Cork 1823)
*Journal of the General Convention of the Church of Ireland: First Session 1870* (Dublin 1870);
    *Second Session 1870* (Dublin 1871)
*Journal of the General Synod : 1871-1996*
Knox, C. *Two Sermons on Schism* (Dublin 1816)
Krause, W.H. *Three Sermons on Confirmation and the Lord's Supper* (Dublin 1857)
McMullan, G. *Opposing Violence / Building Bridges* (Belfast 1996)

Magee, W. *A Sermon Preached before the Association for Discountenancing Vice [etc]* (Dublin 1796)

Massie, J.W. *Revivals in Ireland, Facts, Documents and Correspondence* (London 1859)

Mathias, B.W. *An Inquiry into the Antiquity and Orthodoxy of the Doctrines of the Reformation which treat of the Ruin and Recovery of Mankind* (Dublin 1813)

— *Twenty One Sermons* (Dublin 1838)

— *Vindiciae Laicae* (Dublin 1827)

Maturin, C.R. *Five Sermons on the Errors of the Church of Rome* (Dublin 1824)

O'Brien, C.C. 'Religion and Politics': The New University of Ulster Tenth Annual Convocation Lecture, 9 May 1983

O'Brien, J.T. *A Charge to the Clergy of the United Dioceses of Ossory, Ferns and Leighlin* (Dublin 1866)

— *Ten Sermons upon the Nature and Effects of Faith* (London 1833)

PAKT Lurgan, 'Annual Report 2000'

Plunket, W.C. *A Short Visit to the Connemara Missions* (Dublin 1863)

*Proceedings of the Down and Connor Clergy Aid Society* (Belfast 1838)

*Religious Revivals in the North of Ireland, as described ... by the Lord Bishop of Down etc., the Rev. C. Seaver ... and the Rev. Dr. McCosh* (Dublin 1859)

*Resourcing Bishops* (Church House Publishing 2001)

Roe, P. *A Sermon ... on the Death of the Rev. Edward Pidgeon* (Dublin 1808)

— *Thoughts on the Death of George Hamilton* (Dublin 1830)

Salmon, G. *The Infallibility of the Church* (London 1888)

Stopford, E.A. *The Work and the Counterwork* (Dublin 1859)

Walker, J. *Substance of a Charity Sermon Preached in the Parish Church of St John's Dublin* (Dublin 1796)

Weir, J. *The Ulster Awakening: its Origin, Progress and Fruit* (London 1860)

Whitefield, G. *Journals,* New edn (London 1960)

Woodward, T. (ed) *Sermons Doctrinal and Practical by the Rev. William Archer Butler, with a Memoir of the Author's Life,* 3rd edn (Cambridge 1855)

*Year Book of the Diocese of Sydney 1989* (Sydney 1989)

*c. Periodicals and newspapers*
*Belfast Cathedral Magazine*
*Christian Examiner*
*Christian Observer*
*Church Review* (Dublin and Glendalough)
*The Daily Telegraph*
*The Furrow*
*Irish Ecclesiastical Gazette / Church of Ireland Gazette*
*Irish News*
*The Irish Times*
*Newry Telegraph*
*Northern Constitution*
*Search*
*Sunday Independent*
*The Sunday Times*
*The Times*
*Ulster* (formerly *Belfast*) *Newsletter*

## 2. SECONDARY SOURCES

*a. Books on the Church of Ireland*
Akenson, D.H. *The Church of Ireland: Ecclesiastical Reform and Revolution, 1800-85* (New Haven and London 1971)

Atkinson, E.D. *Dromore: An Ulster Diocese* (Dundalk 1925)

Ball, J.T. *The Reformed Church of Ireland, 1537-1886* (London and Dublin 1886); 2nd edn (London 1890)

Berry, J.F. *The Story of St Nicholas' Collegiate Church, Galway* (Galway 1912)

Bland, F.E. *How the Church Missionary Society came to Ireland* (Dublin 1935)

Bolton, F.R. *The Caroline Tradition of the Church of Ireland, with particular reference to Bishop Jeremy Taylor* (London 1958)

Bowen, D. *Souperism: Myth or Reality?* (Cork 1970)

— *The Protestant Crusade in Ireland, 1800-70* (Dublin 1978)

Boyd, H.A. *A History of the Church of Ireland in Dunluce Parish* (Coleraine 1937)

Brynn, E. *The Church of Ireland in the Age of Catholic Emancipation* (New York and London 1982)

Burrows, E. and Mayes, P. *Specially Concerned: The Mothers' Union in Ireland, 1887-1987* (Dublin 1987)

Emerson, N.D. *The Church of Ireland and the 1859 Revival* (Belfast 1959)

Ford A., McGuire, J. and Milne, K. (eds) *As by Law Established: the Church of Ireland since the Reformation* (Dublin 1995)

Ford, A. and Milne, K. (eds) *The Church of Ireland: A Critical Bibliography 1536-1992* (Antrim 1994)

Gebbie, J.H. (ed) *In His Hand* (Newtownabbey c. 1970)

Hodgins, J. *Sister Island: A History of CMS in Ireland, 1814-1994* (Dunmurry 1994)

Hurley, M. (ed) *Irish Anglicanism 1869-1969* (Dublin 1970)

Leslie, J.B. *Ardfert and Aghadoe Clergy and Parishes* (Dublin 1940)

— *Armagh Clergy and Parishes* (Dundalk 1911)

— *Clogher Clergy and Parishes* (Enniskillen 1929)

— *Derry Clergy and Parishes* (Enniskillen 1937)

— *Ferns Clergy and Parishes* (Dublin 1936)

— *Ossory Clergy and Parishes* (Enniskillen 1933)

— *Raphoe Clergy and Parishes* (Enniskillen 1940)

McDowell R.B. *The Church of Ireland, 1869-1969* (London and Boston 1975)

McFarlan, D. *Lift thy Banner: Church of Ireland Scenes 1870-1900* (Dundalk 1990)

Mant, R. *History of the Church of Ireland, from the Revolution to the Union of the Churches of England and Ireland, January, 1801*, 2 vols (London 1840)

Milne, K. *APCK: the Early Decades* (Dublin 1992)

– *Christchurch Cathedral, Dublin: A History* (Dublin 2000)

Olden, T. *The Church of Ireland* (London 1892)

Palmer, A.K. *Notes on the Parish of Geashill and Killeagh* (Naas 1964)

Patton, H.E. *Fifty Years of Disestablishment* (Dublin 1922)

Phillips, W.A. (ed) *History of the Church of Ireland* 3 vols (Oxford 1933-4)

Shearman, H. *How the Church of Ireland was Disestablished* (Dublin 1970)

Vere White, H. *Children of St Columba: A Sketch of the History, at Home and Abroad, of the Irish Auxiliary of the Society for the Propagation of the Gospel* (Dublin 1914)

Waller, J.T. *A Short History of the Origin of Trinity Church and St Michael's Church in the City of Limerick* (Limerick 1954)

Webster, C.A. *The Chalice in the Church* New edn (London and Oxford 1924)

— *The Diocese of Cork* (Cork 1920)

Wheeler, H.A. and Craig, M.J. *The Dublin City Churches of the Church of Ireland* (Dublin 1948)

White, S.R. (ed) *A Time to Build: Essays for Tomorrow's Church* (APCK 1999)

Wilson, W.G. *The Church of Ireland: Why Conservative?* (Dublin 1970)

Woodworth, G.M.D. *Cashel's Museum of Printing and Early Books* (Cashel 1994)

*b. Books on Irish history*

Adams, J.R.R. *The Printed Word and the Common Man: Popular Culture in Ulster, 1700-1900* (Belfast 1987)

Akenson, D.H. *The Irish Education Experiment: The National System of Education in the Nineteenth Century* (London 1970)

Beckett, J.C. *The Anglo-Irish Tradition* (London 1976)

— *Confrontations: Studies in Irish History* (London 1972)

— *The Making of Modern Ireland, 1603-1923* (London 1966)

Bowen, D. *History and the Shaping of Irish Protestantism* (New York 1995)

Bowen, K. *Protestants in a Catholic State: Ireland's Privileged Minority* (Kingston and Montreal 1983)

Charlotte Elizabeth [Phelan] *Personal Recollections* (London 1841)

Crawford, W.H. and Trainor, B. (eds) *Aspects of Irish Social History 1750-1800* (Belfast 1969)

Eames, R.H.A. *Chains to be Broken: A Personal Reflection on Northern Ireland and its People* (London 1992)

Froude, J.A. *Short Studies on Great Subjects,* New edn (London 1891)

Hempton, D. and Hill, M. *Evangelical Protestantism in Ulster Society 1740-1890* (London and New York 1992)

Legg, M.-L (ed) *The Synge Letters* (Dublin 1996)

Lynch, P. and Vaizey, J. *Guinness's Brewery in the Irish Economy, 1759-1876* (Cambridge 1960)

Maguire, W.A. (ed) *Kings in Conflict* (Belfast 1990)

Malcolm, E. *Swift's Hospital* (Dublin 1989)

Mallie E. and McKittrick D. *The Fight for Peace: the Secret Story behind the Irish Peace Process* (London 1996)

– *Endgame in Ireland* (London 2001)

Maxwell, C. *Country and Town in Ireland under the Georges* (Dundalk 1949)

Mitchell, D. *A 'Peculiar' Place: The Adelaide Hospital, Dublin 1839-1989* (Dublin n.d.)

Moody, T.W. and Vaughan, W.E. (eds) *A New History of Ireland, IV* (Oxford 1986)

O'Farrell, P. *Ireland's English Question* (London 1971)

O'Flanagan, P. and Buttimer C. G. (eds) *Cork: History and Society* (Dublin 1993)

Póirtéir, C. (ed) *The Great Irish Famine* (Dublin 1995)

Robertson, D.S. *Deeds not Words* (Longford 1998)

Rowan, A. *The Buildings of Ireland: North West Ulster* (Harmondsworth 1979)

Smiles, S. *The Huguenots: their Settlements, Churches and Industries in England and Ireland* (London 1867)

Vaughan W.E. and Fitzpatrick, A.J. (eds) *Irish Historical Statistics: Population 1821-1971* (Dublin 1978)

Woodham-Smith, C. *The Great Hunger* (London 1962)

*c. Books on Church history*

Addleshaw, G.W.O. and Etchells, F. *The Architectural Setting of Anglican Worship* (London 1948)

Buchanan, C.O. (ed) *Modern Anglican Liturgies* (London 1968)

Carrington, P. *The Anglican Church in Canada* (Toronto 1963)

Cotton, H. *Rhemes and Douay. An Attempt to Show what has been Done by Roman Catholics for the Diffusion of the Holy Scriptures* (Oxford 1855)

Cragg, G.R. *The Church in the Age of Reason* (Harmondsworth 1960)

Crookshank, C.H. *History of Methodism in Ireland* 3 vols (London 1855 - 8)

Cuming, G.J. *A History of Anglican Liturgy* (London 1969)

Ewens, J.B. *The Three Hermits; Short Studies in Christian Antiquity, Methodism and Tractarianism* (London 1956)

Hennell, M. *Sons of the Prophets* (London 1979)

Hilliard, D. *Godliness and Good Order: A History of the Anglican Church in South Australia* (Netley, SA 1986)

Hole, C. *The Early History of the Church Missionary Society* (London 1896)

Holmes, R.F.G. *Our Irish Presbyterian Heritage* (Belfast 1985)

Hylson-Smith, K. *Evangelicals in the Church of England, 1734-1984* (Edinburgh 1988)

Judd, S. and Cable, K. *Sydney Anglicans* (Sydney 1987)

Neill, S. *Anglicanism* (Harmondsworth 1958)

Nockles, P.B. *The Oxford Movement in Context: Anglican High Churchmanship, 1760-1857* (Cambridge 1994)

Piggin, S. *The Making of Modern Missionaries 1795-1858* (Abingdon 1986)

Shiels, W.J. and Woods, D. (eds) *The Churches, Ireland and the Irish* (Oxford 1989)

Stock, E. *History of the Church Missionary Society* (London 1899)

Wolffe, J. *The Protestant Crusade in Great Britain, 1829-60* (Oxford 1991)

Wood, A.S. *The Inextinguishable Blaze: Spiritual Renewal and Advance in the Eighteenth Century* (London 1960)

Yates, N. *Anglican Ritualism in Victorian Britain, 1830-1910* (Oxford 1999)

*d. Biographies*

Adam-Smith, P. *Heart of Exile* (Nelson, Australia 1986)

Akenson, D.H. *A Protestant in Purgatory: Richard Whately, Archbishop of Dublin* (Hamden, Connecticut 1981)

Alexander, E. (ed) *Primate Alexander: a Memoir* (London 1913)

*Australian Dictionary of Biography*

*The Blackwell Dictionary of Evangelical Biography 1730-1860* 2 vols (Oxford 1995)

Braithwaite, R. (ed) *The Life and Letters of Rev Willam Pennefather* 2nd edn (London n.d.)

Brown, A.W.G. *The Great Mr Boyse* (Belfast 1988)

Burdy, S. *The Life of Philip Skelton* (Oxford 1914: repr from 1792 edn)

Carte, T. *An History of the Life of James Duke of Ormonde* 3 vols (London 1736)

Carus, W. (ed ) *Memoirs of the Life of the Rev Charles Simeon* 3rd edn (London 1848)

Clarke, J.B.B. (ed) *An Account of the Infancy, Religious and Literary Life of Adam Clarke* (London 1833)

*Clergy of Connor from Patrician Times to the Present Day* (Belfast 1993)

D'Arcy, C. F. *The Adventures of a Bishop, A Phase of Irish Life: A Personal and Historical Narrative* (London 1934)

Drury, T.W.E. *Unforgotten* (Dublin 1951)

*Dictionary of National Biography*

Garland, H.J. *Henry Francis Lyte* (Manchester n.d.)

Greene, D.H. and Stephens, E.M. *J.M. Synge* (New York 1961)

Gregg, R.S. *Memorials of the Life of John Gregg* (Dublin 1879)

Griffin, V. *Mark of Protest* (Dublin 1993)

Guinness, M. *The Guinness Legend* (London 1989)

Hannay, J.O. *Life of Frederick Richards Wynne* (London 1897)

How, F.D. *William Conyngham Plunket, Fourth Baron Plunket and Sixty First Archbishop of Dublin* (London 1900)

King, C.S. (ed) *A Great Archbishop of Dublin, William King DD, 1650-1729* (London 1906)

Lefroy, T. (ed) *Memoir of Chief Justice Lefroy* (Dublin 1871)

McAdoo, H.R. *Jeremy Taylor: Anglican Theologian* (Omagh 1997)

McCartney, D. *W.E.H. Lecky: Historian and Politician 1838-1903* (Dublin 1994)

Madden, H. *Memoir of the Right Rev Robert Daly* (London 1875)

Madden, S. *Memoir of Rev Peter Roe* (Dublin 1842)

Morgan, J. *Recollections of My Life and Times* (Belfast 1874)

Moriarty, G.P. *Dean Swift and his Writings* (London 1893)

Motherwell, M.C. *A Memoir of Albert Blest* (Dublin 1843)

Murray, R.H. *Archbishop Bernard: Professor, Prelate and Provost* (London 1931)

O'Regan, P. *Archbishop William King of Dublin (1650-1729) and the Constitution in Church and State* (Dublin 2000)

Rack, H.D. *Reasonable Enthusiast: John Wesley and the Rise of Methodism* (London 1988)

Russell, J.A. *Remains of Rev Charles Wolfe, A.B., with a brief Memoir of His Life* 4th edn (London 1829)

Seaver, G. *John Allen Fitzgerald Gregg: Archbishop* (London and Dublin 1963)

Seddall. H. *Edward Nangle: the Apostle of Achill* (London and Dublin 1884)

Seymour, A.C.H. *The Life and Times of Selina, Countess of Huntingdon* (London 1844)

Sirr, J.D'A. *A Memoir of Power Le Poer Trench, Last Archbishop of Tuam* (Dublin and London 1845)

Stanford, W.B. and McDowell, R.B. *Mahaffy: a Biography of an Anglo-Irishman* (London 1971)

Sumner, G.H. *Life of Charles Richard Sumner, D.D., Bishop of Winchester* (London 1876)

Urwick, W. *Biographic Sketches of J.D. La Touche* (Dublin 1868)

Walsh, W.P. (ed) *Remains of the Venerable Henry Irwin* (Dublin 1858)

White, T. de V. *The Parents of Oscar Wilde* (London 1967)

Whiteside, L. *George Otto Simms: a Biography* (Gerrards Cross 1990)

Wills, J. and F. *The Irish Nation: Its History and Biography IV* (London and Edinburgh 1875)

Wood, A.S. *The Burning Heart: John Wesley, Evangelist* (Exeter 1967)

Wynne, F.R. *Spent in the Service: A Memoir of the Very Rev Achilles Daunt DD, Dean of Cork* 3rd edn (London 1880)


*e. Articles in journals*

Acheson, A.R. 'An Eirenic High Churchman: Bishop John Jebb (1775-1833)', *Search* 23, 1 (spring 2000)

Aston, N. 'Horne and heterodoxy: the defence of Anglican beliefs in the late Enlightenment', *English Historical Review* 108 (1993)

Barnard, T.C. 'Reforming Irish manners: the religious societies in Dublin during the 1890s', *Historical Journal* 35 (1992)

— 'The uses of 23 October 1641 and the Irish Protestant celebrations', *English Historical Review* 106 (1991)

Barrett, P.F. 'Alexander Knox: Lay Theologian of the Church of Ireland', *Search* 23, 1 (spring 2000)

Bolton, F.R. ' Richard Mant (1776-1848) compared with other pre-Tractarian Irish churchmen', *Church of Ireland Gazette* 28 Jan, 4 and 11 Feb 1949

Brynn, E. 'A Church of Ireland diocese in the age of Catholic Emancipation', *Historical Magazine of the Protestant Episcopal Church,* 40 (1971)

Carpenter, A. 'William King and the threats to the Church of Ireland during the reign of James II', *IHS* 18, 69 (March 1972)

Deane, J.L.B. and Turner, R.E. 'The 1991 census and the Church of Ireland', *Search* 19,1 (spring 1996)

Fagan, P. 'The population of Dublin in the eighteenth century with particular reference to the proportions of Protestants and Catholics', *Eighteenth Century Ireland* 6 (1991)

Harrison, F.L. 'Music, poetry and polity in the age of Swift', *idem* 1 (1986)

Hick, V. 'The Palatine settlement in Ireland: the early years', *idem* 4 (1989)

— 'John Wesley and the Irish Rhinelanders', *idem* 5 (1990)

Hilton, B. 'Whiggery, religion and social reform: the case of Lord Morpeth', *Historical Journal* 37 (1994)

Luce, J.V. 'The Church of Ireland and Trinity College Dublin, 1592-1992', *Search* 15, 1 (spring 1992)

Miller, H. and Paterson, J. 'Liturgical space', *idem* 18,1 (spring 1995)

Morrison, H.T. 'The central administration of the Church', *idem* 1,1 (spring 1978)

O'Brien, S. 'A transatlantic community of saints: the Great Awakening and the first Evangelical network, 1735-55', *American Historical Review* 91 (1986)

Warke, R. 'Youth work in the Church of Ireland: signs of hope', *Search* 17, 1 (spring 1994)

# Index